PHILOSOPHERS

of the

RENAISSANCE

Edited by Paul Richard Blum

TRANSLATED BY BRIAN MCNEIL

The Catholic University of America Press
Washington, D.C.

KH

First published as *Philosophen der Renaissance* by WBG
(Wissenschafliche Buchgesellschaft), Darmstadt. © 1999 WBG.

The production of this book was made possible through generous support
from the Center for the Humanities and the Dean of the College of Arts and
Sciences of Loyola College in Maryland and the Foundation for Intellectual
History (London, UK).

Library of Congress Cataloging-in-Publication Data
Philosophen der Renaissance. English.
Philosophers of the Renaissance / edited by Paul Richard Blum ;
translated by Brian McNeil.
p. cm.
Includes bibliographical references and index.
ISBN 978-0-8132-1726-0 (pbk. : alk. paper)   1. Philosophy, Renaissance.
2. Philosophers, Medieval.   I. Blum, Paul Richard.   II. Title.
B775.P4513 2010

190.9′031—dc22   2009045342

3/23/11

PHILOSOPHERS
of the
RENAISSANCE

CONTENTS

PHILOSOPHERS
of the
RENAISSANCE

Introduction

PHILOSOPHY IN THE RENAISSANCE

Paul Richard Blum

Any volume of portraits of Renaissance philosophers invites comparison with Paul Oskar Kristeller's book *Eight Philosophers of the Renaissance,* which was published in 1964. The genre and the genesis of the present book are different (Kristeller's text was originally delivered as lectures), but its intention is in fact the same: to give readers a comprehensible introduction to the philosophy of the Renaissance by presenting in chronological order a series of writers, including writers who worked outside Italy. Specialists present "their" author in the appropriate style. The present introduction seeks to weave these monographs together to illustrate the picture of Renaissance philosophy that the reader will encounter in the course of this book. One can read it systematically from cover to cover, or else move from one chapter to another guided by the internal cross-references or the index. In either case, the reader will see both a great unity and a number of threads that run through the whole book, namely, methodology, universal principles, language, and praxis.

METHODOLOGY

Although Ramon Lull lived at a much earlier period, every reader who is aware of his influence on the following centuries and of his novelty vis-à-vis the Scholastic Middle Ages will look for him in a book about the Renaissance. He already unites some of these threads and is well known—depending on which of his interests one wishes to emphasize—as a logician, as a universal scholar, or as a missionary. His logic is based on an idea of the unity of the world, in which the human person occupies a prominent place. This means, on the one hand, that the human person is assured of his knowledge of the principles that govern the world, thanks to his participation in that which he has come to know; on the other hand, however, he has been given the ability to take an attitude of distance from the world, and this attitude allows him to investigate it. Subsequently, this motif recurs in almost all the philosophers of the Renaissance and even later: in the voluminous literature about the position of the human being in the world and in relation to God, in the theories of the world-soul (e.g., in Marsilio Ficino or Giordano Bruno), or in the attempts to define the universal principles of nature (e.g., in Bernardino Telesio or Francesco Patrizi). It occurs in another form in the writings about magic (represented in this book by Agrippa von Nettesheim), and finally in the numerous treatises about the philosophy of love (e.g., Ficino).

The basic problem is that knowledge always entails a difference between the object and the one who knows. At best, this can be reduced to a minimum, but it can never be removed completely. The strategies offering a solution are thus either to ensure the truth of that which is known or to abolish the difference. A methodology is required, if the truth is to be ensured; if the distance is to be negated, one must identify a universal principle. If it is correct to say that the epistemological value of an affirmation depends on whether its content is "objectively" correct and "subjectively" acceptable, and on whether good reasons can be adduced in its favor, it follows that the methodology must primarily be concerned with the reasons which (hopefully) will yield the objective facts.

One tool employed by Lull here is the analysis of the grammatical forms of the verbs that are de facto used, in order to establish the link between facts and to create the possibility of new affirmations in the future. Lorenzo Valla too finds his orientation in the grammar and the formation of words in language, in order to demonstrate almost empirically how people think and what affirmations—about things in nature, just as much as about matters of morality—can be called scientific. For theorist

of art Leon Battista Alberti, the assurance of truth lies in the evidence of
the productive contribution made to perception by the act of seeing and
in the practical application of numerical relationships in finding orientation in the world. Peter Ramus and Jacopo Zabarella, who represent in this
book the theorists of methodology in the narrower sense of the term, mod-
ernized traditional Aristotelian logic by drawing a clear distinction between the ontological and the quasi-subjective claims of scientific argumentation. It is no longer important whether something is a substance or
an accident, a genus, a species, or a category, or the like; what matters is
whether we arrive at successful results by means of justified affirmations.
If classifications of the type proposed by Ramus make the world comprehensible, this suffices in the long term for affirmations that contain knowledge (Schmidt-Biggemann 1983). With his reduction of all classifications
to the *res extensa* and the *res cogitans* (matter and mind), René Descartes
(1596–1650) sought to make good the inadequacy of this seemingly only
pragmatic structure of affirmations: if everything that exists is either matter (extended) or spirit (thinking), we have not only a methodologically
obligatory and universally acceptable starting point for research, but also a
substantially correct, that is, ontologically certain, guarantee of all further
investigation.

UNIVERSAL PRINCIPLES:
THE MANY AS THE ONE

The other strategy for tackling the problem of knowledge is the aboli-
tion of distance. This, however, succeeds only through the demonstration
of a universal principle that binds the knowledge into the totality of being
in such a way that the distance between the object of knowledge and the
one who knows can be portrayed as a difference in the mode of being—
but a difference that is dissolved in the metaphysical unity of the principle
itself. In Campanella, this leads to the proposition: "That which knows is
the being of that which is known" *(cognoscens est esse cogniti),* which recalls
the formulation by George Berkeley (1685–1753), "To be is to be known"
(esse est percipi). It is here that a door of opportunity is opened for the freedom that shows itself in the human person's ability to make intellectual
and linguistic differentiations of this kind, which per se are no distinctions

at all. The paradoxical outcome is the contemplation of human thinking from within, that is, the justification of the subjectivity and autonomy of thinking; this was to have momentous consequences for the future.

Here too Lull had already shown the way. In the tradition of negative theology, God could be thought of only as the sum of all possible predicates—something that was a contradiction in earthly terms—and the world was the finite unfolding of precisely these qualities of God. It became a system of signs in which the infinite God "expressed himself." This is not to be understood in the sense of the Enlightenment physicotheology; nor of the so-called natural theology that inferred the existence of God from the ordering of the world and then gave God the responsibility for the regularity of the natural laws and for morality; nor in the sense of the well-meaning justification offered for religion within a rationalistic and empiricist explanation of the world. Rather, the primary question for the Renaissance thinkers was precisely the knowability of the finite world. What guaranteed the correctness of this knowledge? For Nicholas of Cusa, as for others who pursued the idea of universality, the world was God's language, and the signs he employed were those that were valid for the human person. We see in Vives how this idea can oscillate between confidence in God and skepticism.

Lull had already been able to appeal to Arabic and Platonic sources. But the penetration of the Latin culture of Europe by the writings of Plato and of ancient Platonism, as a result of the emigration of Byzantine scholars, was an epochal event. Already Petrarch (1304–1374) had seen in a Plato a philosophical alternative to the Aristotelianism of late Scholasticism, but more for historical, aesthetic, and moral-philosophical considerations than for reasons of cosmology and epistemology. As the debate among the fifteenth-century Greeks about the compatibility of Plato and Aristotle shows, this was initially "only" a question of the applicability of Aristotelian or Platonic thought to Christian theology. If, however, theology is only one special instance of philosophy, when it deals with the highest principle—or putting it the other way round, if philosophy's noblest task is to make the truth of revelation rationally comprehensible (a point on which all the Renaissance thinkers, even alleged heretics like Pomponazzi and Bruno, agreed with the mediaeval theologians)—then the object under examination in these debates was not only the success of the competing approaches. Rather, the competition between wisdoms from distant times and regions[1] gave the epoch syncretistic traits. The Neoplatonic interpretation of Plato, which found its most important support in his *Parmenides* and *Timaeus*, received considerable impetus from the gradual discovery of Plotinus, Proclus, and above all the so-called Hermetic writings, texts that Ficino made accessible to the Latin world. The proposed solutions varied on individual points, but all agreed in assuming the presence in time and in the finite world of the Eternal and the Infinite, to which the knowing human soul must draw near. Even the debate over the immortality of the soul was a debate over the methodological versus the cosmological approach to knowledge. The immortality debate, which is represented in this volume by the proponents of Platonism (Ficino) and of secular Aristotelianism (Pomponazzi), gained momentum during the Renaissance and lead to the early modern contention between rationalism and empiricism. This is why epistemology in the Renaissance always tended to be cosmology as well; and indeed, it tended to be ethics, because the process of knowledge, understood in this way, contained a volitional element, an intentional opening up of oneself or a drawing near to the Infinite. Benedict Spinoza (1632–1677) inherited from the Renaissance the ethical significance of a theologically motivated epistemology. He calls his rational doctrine of God or metaphysics *Ethics,* because he portrays the knowledge of God as the purification from the passions.

This indicates the possible outcomes of these philosophical strategies, namely, natural philosophy, philosophy of science, and religious reform. The cosmological aspect of the problem of creation led to an intensive search to identify the principle (or at any rate, as few principles as possible) by which everything that takes place is governed. For the sake of finitude, this principle may not be directly God himself (the accusation of pantheism was occasionally leveled, e.g., against Nicholas of Cusa; but this became fashionable only in the eighteenth century). This is why Telesio and Campanella propose qualities such as warmth and cold. Agrippa and Bruno, under the influence of Ficino, speak of the world-soul, monads, and Pythagorean numerical structures, while light and spirit or other forms of soul are the candidates in Ficino, Pico, Patrizi, and others. The physicians

1. See, e.g., Stausberg 1998, on Zoroaster.

Girolamo Fracastoro (1476–1553) and Girolamo Cardano (1501–1576) give the principle names such as "sympathy"[2] and "subtlety,"[3] thereby designating precisely that which these examples (despite all their differences) represent, namely, nothing other than the search for the principle that enables us to make epistemologically substantial affirmations about the world, on the presupposition that knowledge is to be based not merely on an inter-subjective consensus and a coherence immanent to the system itself, but on the very truth of that which is known. This leads to a question which had not in the least been obvious up to that point: What is nature?

Telesio and Bruno, Campanella and Cardano have recourse to Pre-Socratic and Epicurean sources in their search for "nature's own proper principles." Since the theorists of astrology and the practitioners of magic (like Campanella and Cardano) were obliged to demonstrate the technical functioning of the active principles, they had recourse to what would later be called induction, namely, the demonstration of the principles in individual instances (cf. Zabarella). Later, Francis Bacon (1561–1626) declared this to be his research project. It was, however, also possible to deny the competence of a spiritual universal principle for knowledge. This is what Pomponazzi did. He was aware of the problems of an Averroist view (discussed by Zabarella and others), according to which all human persons have an intellect that guarantees knowledge. He proposed an almost materialistic doctrine of the soul and of perception; in Pomponazzi, however, the principle is materialistic but does not cease to work universally.

From then on the question of God became less urgent, although not obsolete. This in turn affected the competence of the institutionalized theology, of the church, and of religion. Many Reformers, above all Martin Luther (1483–1546), saw the philosophy of the Renaissance as a threat to belief in a revelation and redemption that are not at the disposal of human beings. Melanchthon drew on the Aristotelian philosophy of science and the Platonizing doctrine of the spirit for an improved philosophy of science that was compatible with Christianity, and the school philosophers of

2. Hieronymus Fracastorius, *De sympathia et antipathia rerum,* in Idem, *Opera omnia* (Venice, 1555), 79–104. Cf. Spencer Pearce, "Nature and Supernature in the Dialogues of Girolamo Fracastoro," *Sixteenth-Century Journal* 27 (1996): 111–132.

3. *De subtilitate* (1550), in Hieronymus Cardanus, *Opera omnia* (Lyons, 1663; reprint Stuttgart–Bad Cannstatt, 1966); cf. Eckhard Kessler, ed., *Girolamo Cardano: Philosoph, Naturforscher, Arzt* (Wiesbaden, 1994).

the late Renaissance, especially the Jesuits, employed the instruments of an Aristotelianism that was based on new editions and interpretations in order to accomplish an academic safeguarding of dogmatic theology that would protect the essentials of Catholic theology (the Incarnation, the Eucharist, etc.) against atomistic and empiricist theories of nature.[4] Nevertheless, we are not absolutely obliged to see the Reformation as a defensive reaction against Renaissance thought. Rather, the Reformation itself was one fruit of this thought, since the reform of spiritual life had been a central point in the program since the early humanists, thanks to their intensive study of the question of God. It was possible to guarantee knowledge only on the basis of a kind of parallel between God's revelation and utterance and the human person's access to the world. This is why the idea of the human person as God's image was both a fundamental cosmological principle and a task for speculation.[5] In some authors (Nicholas of Cusa, Pico, and Ficino, as well as Montaigne), this speculation had a mystical, or at least a religious, character.[6]

THE PRAXIS OF LANGUAGE

The fact that reading the world as God's sign had such consequences presupposed a shift of perspective. Let us prescind from every risky interpretation of "the" Middle Ages and simply describe this shift as it affected Renaissance humanism, which is usually considered to begin with Petrarch. He insisted that all activities be seen in their relationship to the human person, whose being must be defined as political, linguistic, and historical. An optimization here on earth (education) and after death (the salvation of the soul) is in store for the human person. In his programmatic and polemical treatises, letters, and Italian poems he spoke of the reflexive character of the world and of the sciences that cultivate this world in view of these goals.[7] The outcome is a paradoxical closeness and foreignness, which constitute the specifically human perspective. Language proves to be the instrument par excellence that both bridges and creates the dis-

4. Cf. Leinsle 1985; Blum 1998; Celenza 2004.
5. Cf. Blum 2004, ch. 8.
6. Trinkaus 1970; O'Malley 1993.
7. Cf., e.g., Petrarch, *De sui ipsius et multorum ignorantia*, in Francesco Petrarca, *Invec-*

tance. In languages, the classical authors are both foreign and accessible to us; communication reaches the other and at the same time gives him his own autonomy. This finds expression in the fictional letters to personages of classical antiquity. From that time onward, a philological program of education, the *studia humanitatis*, which distances itself clearly from the medieval schools, is propagated first in the fourteenth-century Florentine republic and then spreads to the whole of Italy and of Europe. This is commonly known as "humanism."[8] The humanistic cultivation of linguistic style had its origin in the late medieval chancelleries, but its spread to every area of culture made it a political issue, as we see in the essays on Valla, Alberti, and Machiavelli in the present book. They were heirs to the politician-humanists of Florence, whose earliest representative was Petrarca's pupil Coluccio Salutati (1331–1406). Salutati moved the human praxis of the sciences into the foreground, so that he ascribed a higher scientific quality to political jurisprudence than to a discipline such as medicine, which is oriented to "mere nature."[9] This explains the priority the humanists gave to ethics (Kristeller).

On the other hand, the new perspective made the human person's potential for autonomous action very problematic, if at the same time the Christian interpretation of the ordering of the world by Providence is allowed to stand. Salutati therefore distinguishes this Providence from the pagan, deterministic concept of fate *(fatum)* and affirms the compatibility of the divine plan and individual freedom.[10] The alternative: "Either Providence (as the unity of knowledge and intentional action in God) determines the acts of the human person too, or else the human person is free to perform acts that are not predetermined" leads to a logical stalemate, if the human person's character as image of God consists precisely in the capacity for autonomous action. In the theistic context, this becomes a paradox of anthropology—as we see in Lorenzo Valla, in the speculation

---

tives, ed. and trans. David Marsh (Cambridge, Mass.: Harvard University Press, 2003). Cf. Eckhard Kessler, *Petrarca und die Geschichte. Geschichtsschreibung, Rhetorik, Philosophie im Übergang vom Mittelalter zur Neuzeit* (Munich, 2004). Cf. Kircher 2006.

8. Rummel 1995; Witt 2003. See the collection of sources in Garin 1964–1967; Kallendorf 2002.

9. Coluccio Salutati, *Vom Vorrang der Jurisprudenz oder der Medizin, De nobilitate legum et medicinae*, Latin-German, trans. Peter Michael Schenkel (Munich, 1990).

10. Coluccio Salutati, *De fato et fortuna*, ed. Concetta Bianca (Florence, 1985).

about "the dignity of the human person" (Pico), and later in Erasmus of Rotterdam (1469–1536) and Suárez—and remains so to the present day. One attempt at resolving this paradox drew on an Augustinian concept of grace, because when the freedom of the human person is called into question, this also raises doubts about his capacity for sin or for "good works." The Jesuit Luis de Molina (1535–1600) played an influential but controversial role here; his solution, positing a "middle knowledge" of God (whereby God refrains from intervening in the alternative actions of the human person, which he knows beforehand), is relevant to the modern debates.[11] It was precisely this problem that differentiated the Christian confessions that came into being in the sixteenth century. From Petrarch onward, the attempts of the Renaissance thinkers to salvage both the world and the salvation of souls appealed to Augustine, whose thinking enjoyed great popularity in the Jansenism of the seventeenth century, alongside the rationalism of a thinker like Descartes. Where, however, the Christian framework disappears (as may be the case already in Pomponazzi and Bruno), freedom is left as an inadequate ontological determination of the human person, which in terms of substance is scarcely different from the emptiness and care of the *condition humaine* in the existential philosophy of the modern period.

Most of the theories of the Renaissance contain strong narrative, "literary" elements that require translation into systematic problems. This applies particularly to the various theories about nature. Nevertheless, the literary character of the theories is at the same time a positive achievement, if it is true that the accessibility of knowledge is conditioned by language— as is most obviously the case with ethical and political questions.[12] The borders of the narration of philosophy are marked by utopias: in Campanella's "City of the Sun," the order of the world is painted on walls outside of which there is no world and within which there is no more history. For all these authors, knowledge and action can be portrayed only linguistically, that is, in substantially appropriate forms of speaking and writing such as

11. Ludovicus de Molina, *Liberi arbitrii cum gratiae donis, divina praescientiae, providentia, praedestinatione et reprobatione concodia,* ed. Johannes Rabeneck (Cuenca and Madrid, 1953), pars 4, qu. 14, art. 13, disp. 52, n. 9. Cf. Thomas P. Flint, *Divine Providence: The Molinist Account* (Ithaca, N.Y., and London, 1998).

12. Cf., e.g., Martha C. Nussbaum, *Love's Knowledge: Essays on Philosophy and Literature* (New York, 1990).

letters to friends who are far distant in time and place. This is why Valla makes the philological study of sources a political issue, and Machiavelli sees the Roman historians as witnesses equal in value to his own contemporaries. Finally, Patrizi draws a difference between the metaphysical and the narrative meanings of history, while Montaigne goes so far as to concentrate the philosopher's task on self-narration.

The editor has had the privilege of being the first to read the essays in the context of the book as a whole. Readers are welcome to derive further philosophical reflections from this volume.

PRACTICAL INFORMATION

The portraits are arranged chronologically, following the year of the author's death. Where no specific information about translations from the sources is given, these are the work of the authors or of the translator.

In all the articles, references to the sources employ abbreviations. Where these are not self-explanatory, they are explained in the bibliography. The bibliographies were expanded and revised for an English-language readership. In selecting the readings emphasis was laid on authoritative editions and English translations of primary works and on the most important research, with some preference for studies in English.

All the essays were revised for this English edition, with the exception of the essay on Vives, which was written anew for this volume. The chapters on Vives, Pomponazzi, and Ramus were written in English. The essay on Campanella was written in Italian. All the other essays have been translated from German.

Loyola College in Maryland,
Baltimore,
November 1, 2008
PAUL RICHARD BLUM

Note: For further reading see general works on Renaissance philosophy authored or edited by Backus; Blackwell; Blum; Brooke and Maclean; Burckhardt; Cassirer; Celenza; Copenhaver and Schmitt; Di Liscia; Ebbersmeyer; French; Garin; Hankins; Kessler and Ian Maclean; Kircher; Kraye; Kretzmann; Kristeller; Kusukawa and Maclean; Levi; Lohr; O'Malley; Popkin; Risse; Rummel; Schmidt-Biggemann; Schmitt; Spruit; Trinkaus; Verdon; Walker; and Wind.

For anthologies with Texts of Renaissance philosophy see Eugenio Garin, *Geschichte und Dokumente der abendländischen Pädagogik,* 3 vols. (Reinbek: Rowohlt, 1964–1967), texts in Latin and German; Craig W. Kallendorf, ed., *Humanist Educational Treatises* (Cambridge, Mass.: Cambridge University Press, 2002); Ernst Cassirer, Paul Oskar Kristeller, and John Herman Randall, eds., *The Renaissance Philosophy of Man: Selections in Translation* (Chicago: University of Chicago Press, 1948); and Jill Kraye, ed., *Cambridge Translations of Renaissance Philosophical Texts,* 2 vols.: vol. 1, *Moral Philosophy,* vol. 2, *Political Philosophy* (Cambridge: Cambridge University Press, 1997).

A bibliographical tool is *Bibliographie internationale de l'humanisme et de la Renaissance.*

The following Internet sites are helpful: Web4Ren Forum (W4RF), a message board organized by Heinrich C. Kuhn: http://www.phil-hum-ren.uni-muenchen.de/W4RF/YaBB.pl. "Iter," databases including bibliographies and Paul Oskar Kristeller's inventory of Renaissance manuscripts: *Iter Italicum:* http://www.itergateway.org (subscription required). "Scholasticon," online resources for the study of early modern Scholasticism (1500–1800), authors, sources, institutions, organized by Jacob Schmutz: http://www.scholasticon.fr.

1

RAMON LULL

(1232–1316)

*The Activity of God and the
Hominization of the World*

Charles Lohr

In the last years of the eleventh century and the first years of
the twelfth, there appeared in the western regions bordering on
Islam—in Catalonia and southern France, and in the kingdoms
of Toledo and Sicily—a new conception of knowledge and of reality which were the inception of a fundamentally new period in
Western intellectual history. The material basis for this was provided by the trade and commercial activities that flourished in the
Mediterranean area. The spirit that inspired this new conception
was the rare spirit of openness and tolerance, born of the contact
between the three great cultures of the Mediterranean world: Islam, Judaism, and Christianity.

In Toledo, Christians and Jews collaborated on the project of
making accessible to the Latin West the achievements of Greek
philosophy and science, which had been transmitted in Arabic.
Frederick II of Sicily visited Muslim philosophers in search of solutions to the problems generated by the confrontation between
pagan science and the Christian tradition. In the region around

Barcelona and the Catalan coast of southern France, Jewish scholars, who had been expelled from Islamic Spain by Almohade rulers, translated not only Arabic works into Hebrew, but also Hebrew and Arabic works into Latin; indeed, they even translated Latin works into Hebrew. In Salerno and Montpellier, medical scholars who wrote in Latin founded a new natural philosophy on the basis of the Arabic transmission of Galen.

Ramon Lull was one of the most remarkable personalities in this exchange between the three great Mediterranean cultures. Majorca, his native island, was not only a center of trade in the Mediterranean world, but also a place of encounter between Islam, Judaism, and Christianity. Lull was born in 1232, shortly after James the Conqueror had won the island back from the Saracens. He died in 1316 on a ship that was taking him home from North Africa, where he had preached the Christian faith. This *vir phantasticus,* who wore pilgrim's clothing and probably spoke better Arabic than Latin, labored indefatigably to win the powerful men of his age, in Europe, Africa, and the Near East, for the idea of concord among the people. Aware that he was moving on the border between the three great religions, this *arabicus christianus* attempted to use methods characteristic of the Arabic tradition in order to achieve an understanding between Muslims, Jews, and Christians.

On the basis of both Arabic and Latin models, Lull elaborated the idea of a new method, an *ars inveniendi veritatem,* which could serve his purposes. In the pursuit of these goals, he wrote an immense body of literature in the course of his long life. He wrote more than two hundred and fifty works, some of them very extensive. In keeping with his project, he composed his works not only in Latin and Catalan, but also in Arabic.

Lull's endeavors to bring Muslims, Jews, and Christians together were not confined to his activity as an author. He also fought for the establishment of a new educational institution that would be different from the clerical universities of Paris and Oxford—an institution in which a genuine dialogue between the three great cultures of the Mediterranean world would be possible. He submitted many petitions to popes and kings, appealing to them to found schools in which those languages and doctrines would be taught that were necessary for the dialogue with Saracens and Jews.

Lull was, and remained, a layman; in his thirties, however, he resolved to dedicate his life to a missionary apostolate. His initial intention was to go to Paris, in order to equip himself for this task by studying the Latin language and Scholastic theology; but Raymond of Peñafort, the general of the Dominican Order (who inspired Thomas Aquinas to write his *Summa contra gentiles*), advised him to return to his native island, where he could familiarize himself with the Arabic language and Muslim thought.

In Majorca, Lull not only learned Arabic, but also sketched the idea of a new discipline on the basis of both Arabic and Latin models—an *ars inveniendi veritatem* that could be of service to his missionary aims. Since this new *ars* was designed for all the peoples of the world, it ought not to be of a purely theological nature: it should be a universal discipline capable of application to all the individual disciplines of the epoch. This led Lull to change the name of his *ars inveniendi veritatem* to *ars generalis,* and to revise the treatise continually in the course of his life.

Behind this universal discipline lay the fundamental vision of a natural theology that intends to draw closer to the true God through a method of the contemplation of the names of God. Lull calls these concepts *dignitates* or *principia,* and lists nine of them in the final version of the *ars: bonitas, magnitudo, duratio; potentia, sapientia, voluntas; virtus, veritas, gloria.*

Lull's understanding of the names seems in fact to have been inspired by the writings of Arabic mystics. He wrote a *Liber de centum nominibus Dei* (Rome, 1289; ORL 19.79–120), in which he tells us that God has put more power into his names than into the animals, the plants, and the precious stones. Consequently, one can understand his method of contemplation aright only when the *dignitates* are regarded as proxies for active powers.

Lull's primary intention was to make those Christian doctrines comprehensible which had led to the breakdown of every missionary activity, namely, the doctrines of the divine Trinity and the Incarnation of the Messiah. His first step is to ask what we understand when we say that the powers of the divine names are active. He affirms that we cannot truly call something good if it does not produce anything good.

In this way, Lull introduced a completely new category into the history of metaphysics. His apologetic intentions led him to speak, not of principles of being, but above all of principles of activity. His thesis is that God is not only active in the creation *contingenter* and *ad extra* (in a contingent way and externally—as the Muslim and Jewish theologians likewise taught): God is also productive *necessarie* and *ad intra* (necessarily and internally) in the divine Persons.

He takes as his starting point the dynamism which his Islamic partners in dialogue accepted, that is, the dynamism in the process of knowledge (the intellect that knows, the object that is known, and the act of knowledge) and in love (the lover, the beloved, and love itself), and affirms that this obliges us to acknowledge the activity of all the divine perfections: the true *goodness* must bring forth something *good*, the true *greatness* must bring forth something *great*.

Since all activity presupposes a principle, an object, and a link between these two, Lull speaks of three *correlativa* of the activity of all the divine *dignitates*. The *proprietates* of the traditional Trinitarian theology correspond to the *correlativa*, but Lull gives them names that probably have their origin in Arabic verbal forms. In a sermon preached in Tunis, he expresses this as follows: *Actus bonitatis dico bonificativum, bonificabile, bonificare; actus etiam magnitudinis sunt magnificativum, magnificabile, magnificare, et sic de aliis omnibus divinis dignitatibus* ("The acts of goodness are that which makes good, that which can be made good, the making good; also the acts of greatness are that which magnifies, that which is magnifiable, and the act of magnifying; and so on with all divine dignities"; *Vita coaetanea* 26, ROL 8. 290).

He generalizes this idea to such an extent that he can use the concepts *-tivum, -bile,* and *-are* to designate the elements of all activity. He declares that these elements present the substantial and intrinsic principles of activity, and that they are valid for every reality. The *correlativa*, which are implicit in the activity of all objects, are an absolute ontological principle. Since they are an essential prerequisite of all activity, *actio* and *passio* are basically not accidents, as they are for Aristotle. For Lull, it is not only being, but also activity that belongs to the substance of things. The divine unity too is structured. As an active unity, the unity of God must be a mediated unity. If God is truly one, in the active sense of this term, he must be triune. In this way, Lull was able to recognize images of the triune Christian God in every aspect of the created world.

This is how Lull attempts to present the Christian Trinity; and in a similar way he seeks to make the doctrine of the Incarnation of Christ comprehensible to unbelievers with the help of the dynamic principles of his *ars*. Here, he appeals to the distinction (which he found in the doctrine of creation) between necessary activity *ad intra* and contingent activity *ad extra*. The divine activity *ad intra* is necessary; the creation of the world is contingent, and depends on the divine will. If, however, God, the first cause, has freely chosen the creation, he can achieve the concordance of both with his activity only "in the incarnation of God's Son through participation, i.e., through the union of creator and creature in the one person of Christ."[1]

When he goes on to apply his ideas to the creation of the world, Lull emphasizes not only the dynamic character of the causal activity of God, but also the dynamic character of the effect of this activity, which is the created world itself. He applies to created activity too the distinction between a necessary activity *ad intra* and a contingent activity *ad extra*.

In this context, Lull developed a new and fundamental understanding of the intentions of an activity. His understanding gave birth to a new logic in which the distinction between first and second intention was applied much more fundamentally than in the traditional logic of Latin Scholasticism. His *Logica nova,* completed in Genoa in 1303, seems to belong to the Arabic tradition. His understanding of the expression "according to the first/second intention" corresponds to the usage of the Muslim "Brethren of Purity" *(ikhwân as-ṣafâ'),* whose philosophical encyclopedia was widely read in the Islamic Spain of the thirteenth century. For example, in their presentation of the divine activity in the creation, these authors affirmed that the first intention of the Creator cannot lie outside his own self; it is only as a second intention that his activity is the cause of the world. The distinction is clearly formulated with regard to the question of divine providence: God's activity possesses its own goal in itself, and this goal corresponds to God's first intention. The instruments that are appropriated in order to attain this goal belong to God's second intention; they are accidental conditions, not substantial.

Like their Creator, the things of this world are active. Each thing strives necessarily and "in the first intention" toward its own perfection *ad intra*. As a creature, however, it cannot attain its goal without the activity *ad extra*. In order to realize its own self, the finite *-tivum* must go out to a *-bile*

---

1. "In Filii Dei incarnationem, per participationem, scilicet unionis creatoris et creaturae, in una persona Christi" (*Vita coaetanea* 27, ROL 8.291).

ad extra. In this way, the objects that are *per se* extrinsic become instruments that serve the goal of intrinsic perfection "in the second intention." The created things depend on each other. The only thing that matters is that the first intention comes before the second.

In this way, Lull was able to apply the distinction between the two intentions in order to explain the origin of accidents. One example of his theory is the properties *(proprietates)* of a subject: in terms of its nature—in the first intention—fire must necessarily *(necessarie)* burn in itself *(ad intra).* Whether it warms the water or the earth (in the second intention, *ad extra*), is contingent *(contingens).* In itself, the fire is active "in the proper manner" *(proprie)* and "substantially" *(substantialiter);* in the water or in the earth, it is active "in an appropriated manner" *(appropriate)* or "accidentally" *(accidentaliter).*

The gift of being to the world does not put an end to God's creative working. His activity is continued in the striving of things toward their perfection. When fire warms another body, or when the form of whiteness *(albedo)* whitens *(albificat)* one or another body in a contingent manner, these forms are present as perfections in these bodies. In Lull's terminology, they are present "in a contracted manner" *(contracte).* The *albedo* can attempt to intensify their "contracted" perfection by whitening an increasing number of individual bodies. The Creator has created the world in such a way that the individual species strive to intensify their perfection by means of numerical multiplication.

Taken as a whole, the world that God created is likewise active, and strives toward its own perfection. Lull understands the individuals, species, and genera that the human person encounters in the world as parts of a whole, as components of a unity that reflects the dynamic greatness of the Creator. His understanding of this totality—this universe—is presented most clearly in his epoch-making *Liber chaos* (Montpellier, ca. 1283: MOG 3.44ff.), a work he appended to the *Ars demonstrativa* (the second redaction of the *Ars magna*).

In this treatise, Lull breaks with the medieval idea of a cosmos constructed of successive stages. His interest focuses on the sublunary world of the four elements and the human person. The chaos treated in this book is not understood as a *receptaculum* (in the sense of Plato's *Timaeus*), nor as *materia informis* (in the sense of the Augustinian theology of creation).

Rather, Lull understands the chaos as the coexistence of all the potentialities that are created in one single act—possibilities that can become reality—and of all the definitions that categorize these potentialities.

The chaos contains the *semina causalia*—the *forma universalis* and the *materia universalis,* the *genera* and the *species,* the *substantiae* and the *accidentia*—in which all the individual objects are based. Everything under the sphere of the Moon proceeds from chaos. All the possibilities of the most varied individual developments *(transmutationes)* are already present in the chaos. Accordingly, these developments do not go beyond the essence of the chaos; rather, they are various articulations of something that is already present *in potentia.*

Lull combines a great many different themes from the philosophical tradition in his concept of chaos. On the first level of the chaos (which he divides into three *gradus*), we encounter the *rationes seminales* of the Stoics as the generic term both for the Platonic idea of the world-soul and for the Aristotelian *praedicabilia* and *praedicamenta.* On the second level, we find the first individuals of the separate species. The third level consists of the further multiplications of the first individuals.

However, these themes are subjected by Lull to a radical reinterpretation. The Platonic idea of the *anima mundi* is presented in connection with the Aristotelian teaching about *materia* and *forma,* but is understood in the sense of Lull's teaching about the *correlativa.* The chaos is determined by the four abstract essentialities of the elements fire, air, water, and earth: *igneitas, aereitas, aequeitas,* and *terreitas.*[2] Each essentiality acts upon its own proper *correlativa*: its proper form *(ignificativum),* its proper matter *(ignificabile),* and its proper act *(ignificare).*

It is impossible to think of the form and matter in the individual essentialities independently of each other. Rather, all the proper forms coalesce in one single universal form—a world-soul, which is the sum of all possible *-iva.* All the proper matters coalesce in one single universal matter—a world-body, which is the sum of all possible *-bilia.* The *unum ens, unum esse, unum suppositum,* which Lull calls "chaos," consists of the union of this form and this matter. From the universal form and matter, there proceed first the *genera* and the *species,* then the *substantiae* and the *accidentia,* and

2. These words minted by Lull would sound in English as fire-ness, air-ness, water-ness, and earth-ness.

finally the individual beings, which are composed of special forms and matters. Each special form and each special matter is based in the universal form and matter.

Lull presents the second level of chaos as the midpoint between the fundamental *semina causalia* (causal seeds) and the realization that the first individuals find in the numerical multiplication of the *species*. The concrete individual objects that have proceeded from the *semina causalia* do not, however, only strive to attain their extrinsic, numerical multiplication: they also seek their own inner perfection. By their very nature, all the concrete objects attempt to return to the real (but abstract) essentialities of which they are the articulations. Although the world is full of individual realities that are in a continuous process of coming into existence and that strive to attain their own perfection, these individual realities cannot achieve the full perfection of their own kind. The *species* remains the boundary toward which the perfection of the individual draws close: the *genus* forms the boundary of the *species*.

Lull is often accused of asserting an extreme realism. In fact, however, the problem of universals does not exist for him. He maintains that the *praedicabilia* and *praedicamenta* are real, since the abstract is always present a priori in the individual objects—as the boundary value for the striving of the concrete toward infinity. In his *Liber de natura* (Cyprus, 1301; ed. Palma, 1744), a treatise written in connection with the *Ars generalis ultima* (the final redaction of the *Ars*), Lull defines nature as the principle by means of which the *entia concreta* (e.g., the individual human being, *homo*) come ever closer to the *entia abstracta*—the essentiality of humanness (*humanitas*, 1.2).

The metaphysical distinction between necessary activity in the first intention *ad intra* and contingent activity in the second intention *ad extra* was fundamental for Lull's understanding of the human person, above all because it enabled him to undertake a profound analysis of the nature of human knowledge. He maintained the position that objects such as fire and whiteness possess their own necessary, intrinsic, and specific (*necessaria, propria, intrinseca*) *correlativa* of their activity, whereas their objects *ad extra* (the earth or the water, this or that body) are contingent, extrinsic, and appropriated by them (*contingentia, appropriata, extrinseca*).

In his important late work *De potentia, obiecto et actu* (Rome, 1296),

Lull draws conclusions about human knowledge from this idea. The knowable objects that the spirit encounters in the world are not necessary objects of knowledge. Even the instruments and tools that the spirit creates are objects that it has appropriated. The proper object of the spirit must be an inner reality. Just as the proper object of fire is not the earth or water, but rather the fire itself, inasmuch as it is fiery, so too the proper object of the spirit can only be the spirit itself, inasmuch as it is knowable.

In order to know its true self, the spirit must withdraw from the difference and the contingency that ensue upon sensory perception and rational knowledge. The spirit must turn inward. It must turn aside from its contingent activity *ad extra* and ascend to its own intrinsic dynamism.

This ascent finds its correspondence in Lull's method of contemplation. He develops his method not only by distinguishing nine different divine names (in the horizontal dimension, so to speak), but also by clearly specifying three vertical levels of the power of these names. The *Ars* was intended as an ascending method, to be undertaken in two steps.

Lull affirms that sensory perception is not an appropriate basis on which to attain the truth, since sensory perception remains on the positive stage, which is the level of transitory things. By attaining the rational knowledge of things, however, the reason can lift itself up to the comparative level. Lull holds that Aristotle's philosophy attained this level of discursive knowledge; but Averroes attained only the positive stage of sensory perception and imagination.

Nevertheless, the stage of rational knowledge is not yet the stage of true knowledge. It is only by means of a second ascent that the intellect reaches the level of the eternal truth. On this superlative level, the distinctions of the first level become obsolete. Since God is the best *(optimum)* on the superlative level, it is no longer possible to distinguish the greatest *(maximum)* from the most powerful *(potentissimum)*. On this superlative level of reality, the mystic discovers the highest Being, in whom all the divine names merge.

By reflecting in this manner, the human person discovers that he himself is something knowable. In order to explain the necessary process of human knowledge *ad intra,* Lull appeals to his theory of the *correlativa* of activity. The one who knows *(intelligens)* knows himself as a knowable object *(intelligibile)* in the act of knowledge *(intelligere).*

At the same time, however, the human person becomes aware of his finitude. Limits are placed on his knowledge not only by the fact that it must have recourse to images perceptible to the senses; in order to understand the things that the spirit encounters in the world—things that are in a continuous process of development and strive toward their own perfection—he must reduce these things to the static categories of the discursive understanding.

From the standpoint that we have thus reached, it is now possible to assess the novelty of Lull's *Logica nova*. The logic of this treatise, written in the period of the last redaction of the *Ars* (the *Ars generalis ultima*, 1305–1308), is new because it is conceived as a logic of pure knowledge, a logic that has the highest goal *(prima intentio)* of considering those things that are the specific *(propria)* object of the intellect. It is only at a secondary stage *(secunda intentio)* that the new logic must treat the ideas that the spirit has appropriated *(appropriata),* that is, the ideas that the intellect abstracts from the perceptible physical objects.

Since the *Logica nova* is conceived as a logic for the third level of knowledge—for the reason, regarded as distinct from the understanding—it is *eo ipso* a critique of the traditional logic and of the epistemology on which that was based. Lull regarded Aristotle's logic as inadequate, since it limited itself to the rational knowing of things perceptible to the senses.

In the twelfth century, some thinkers grasped the possibility of a logic of the knowledge of intellectual matters. Following Boethius, they drew a distinction between *intelligibilia,* that is, the objects on the second level of knowledge, and *intellectibilia,* the objects on the third level.

However, the clerical reception of Aristotle in the thirteenth century turned academic attention to the formulation of a logic of the second level of knowledge, that is, the rational knowledge of things perceptible to the senses. This excluded any attempt at analyzing the conditions that made this possible.

This is why Lull's prologue to the *Logica nova* speaks of the unstable character of the traditional logic, and why Lull proposes that it be reshaped on a new basis—that is, on the foundation of the third level of knowledge. Since this level concerns the grasping of intellectual matters, Lull speaks of the highest level of knowledge as a "natural" kind of knowledge *(naturalis modus intelligendi).*

Employing his distinction between necessary and contingent *correlativa* of activity, Lull regards intellectual objects as necessary, proper, and intrinsic *(necessaria, propria, intrinseca)* objects of knowledge, and criticizes the traditional logic as a logic that deals only with "pilgrim" *(peregrina)* knowledge, with the knowledge of contingent, appropriated, and extrinsic *(contingentia, appropriata, extrinseca)* objects—namely, the perceptible things that human beings encounter in this world.

The true nature of the human person—in the first intention—is intellectual, and is oriented to spiritual things. In the second intention, however, the human person must go forth to physical reality and appropriate perceptible things, in order to be able to return to his true self. Physical things—the *subiecta* that Lull lists in the *Ars: imaginativa, sensitiva, vegetativa,* and *elementativa*—are only instruments for the realization of reason in the world through the human person.

This is why the *Logica nova* locates the human person on the boundary between intellectual and physical reality. The *Logica nova* defines him enigmatically as *homificans animal* (human-making animal; 1.5), whose true function consists in the hominization of the realm of animals, plants, and elements, and through these, in the hominization of the entire world.

For Lull, the human person is a human person not only because he attempts to draw ever nearer to his abstract essentiality as *animal rationale,* but also because he strives for the perfect reshaping of his *genus.* The *individuum* strives upward to the *species,* the *species* to the *genus,* and the *genus* to the original cosmic unity that is made up of universal matter and universal form.

The human person is the link that holds together intellectual and physical reality, because the *-tivum* of his rational nature is capable of appropriating the various objects of which the universe consists.

Note: For further reading see the works by Llull in the References. For secondary sources see Bonner; Domínguez Reboiras; Hillgarth; Platzek; and Pring-Mill.

2

GEORGE GEMISTOS PLETHON

(CA. 1360–1454),

GEORGE OF TREBIZOND

(1396–1472), AND

CARDINAL BESSARION

(1403–1472)

*The Controversy between
Platonists and Aristotelians
in the Fifteenth Century*

Peter Schulz

Marsilio Ficino completed his translation of Plato's works for the Platonic Academy in Florence in 1477. This Latinization was preceded by a lengthy phase of reception of the Greek philosopher. Apart from the Latin translation of the *Timaeus*, which was already available in the Middle Ages, the following Platonic dialogues were known: *Phaedo, Gorgias, Crito,* the *Symposium,* and the *Apology,* as well as the Letters, which the poet Leonardo Bruni had translated at the beginning of the fifteenth century. However, these translations were very free and frequently distorted the meaning of the original text. Accordingly, Cardinal Bessarion could assert at the end of the 1450s that Plato's writings were not yet genuinely accessible to the Latins. This widespread lack of knowledge was an important contributory factor to the "ideological" character of the debate about the significance of Plato's oeuvre between 1439 and 1469.

The early phase of the reception of Plato has been studied in detail only in the course of the past two decades. At the center of interest stand inter alia the three authors whom we shall discuss in the present essay: Gemistos Plethon, George of Trebizond, and Cardinal Bessarion. Thanks to the positions that they took—in the form of an almost boundless admiration, a harsh critique, or a sober presentation of what Plato had said—the interest of the Latin humanists came to focus on Plato.

GEORGE GEMISTOS PLETHON

The reception of Plato in the fifteenth century received a decisively important impetus from the Greek George Gemistos (ca. 1360–1454), who founded an academy on the Platonic model in Mistra near Sparta. Under the guidance of Gemistos, who also called himself Plethon in imitation of his model,[1] the works of Plato were studied and interpreted with the help of Neoplatonic commentaries. Plethon's posthumously published *Treatise on the Laws* shows that the program of this academy included not only the dissemination of Plato's teaching, but also the formation of a philosophical community. In the surviving fragments of this work, Plethon sets out the regulations for the shared life of a philosophical community on the basis of a revived ancient religion. Although the title of his work evokes the tradition of Plato, it presents an independent teaching that is much more strongly influenced by Neoplatonism than by Plato himself. Zoroastrian elements are combined with Stoic ideas, and it was above all these aspects that led later critics such as George of Trebizond to rebut it fiercely. The protagonist in this early phase of the controversy between Platonists and Aristotelians was always accused of holding pagan views; this has been regarded as the real criterion at work in the criticism by his adversaries, such as George Scholarios and George of Trebizond.[2]

Plethon's influence on the reception of Plato in humanist circles began

---

1. On his life and work, cf. Woodhouse 1986 and Masai 1956. Cf. Monfasani 2005.
2. Bibliography in Hankins 1991, 197, nn. 74 and 75.

with his journey to the Union Council in Ferrara/Florence (1438–1439), where he accompanied Emperor John Palaeologus as his theological adviser. At the suggestion of his Latin hearers in Florence, to whom he gave an introduction to Plato's works, he wrote the *De differentiis Aristotelis et Platonis* (The Differences between Aristotle and Plato). The programmatic introduction declares that he wishes to imitate the Church Fathers by salvaging the honor of Plato and dethroning Aristotle, who was overvalued above all in the theology of the West. One indicator of the extent of the influence that Plethon was thought to have had on the early Platonic renaissance is the fact that Marsilio Ficino, in the foreword to his translation of Plotinus, mistakenly attributes to Plethon's influence the foundation of the Platonic Academy by Cosimo Medici.[3]

Plethon begins *De differentiis* with the observation that whereas the Greeks and the Romans valued Plato much more highly than Aristotle, people in the West now want to be cleverer than their ancestors. They follow the Arab Averroes, who regarded the Aristotelian teaching about nature as the perfection of all wisdom, but they do not notice that this man maintained foolish doctrines such as the mortality of the soul. *De differentiis* offers a detailed comparison of the two Greek philosophers which is guided by a central question: Whose writings are more appropriate for the presentation of theological matters? The core of his criticism is that Aristotle did not propose any plausible basis for fundamental axioms such as the understanding of creation. For example, Plethon writes in the first chapter that Aristotle teaches only that God is the final cause of movement, whereas Plato assumes a cause at least with regard to the question of how time came into being (Plethon refers here to *Timaeus* 36e). Plethon also criticizes Aristotle's definition of the human intellect. In the *Metaphysics* (12.3.1070 a 24–27) and *De anima* (4.408 b 19–20), we are told that the intellect is imperishable; but Aristotle abandons this doctrine in the *Nicomachaean Ethics* where precisely this theorem would be necessary as the most important principle for morally excellent conduct. Without this theorem, one cannot conceive of a reward for the human being after the end of his earthly life. Plethon also criticizes Aristotle's emphasis on the precedence of the first substance vis-à-vis the universal, and Aristotle's critique

3. On this, cf. Kristeller 1972, 105.

of Plato's doctrine of the ideas. Since he rejects the ideas, all that Aristotle is left with is the doctrine of perpetual motion—which of course is diametrically opposed to Christianity. According to Gemistos, Plato's work proves in almost every respect to be much more appropriate than Aristotle's for the presentation of central Christian doctrines.

George Scholarios was the first of the Byzantines to write polemically against Plethon in defense of the fundamental Aristotelian-Scholastic theological concepts, in 1443. He was especially concerned to show that Aristotle's writings speak of God not only as the unmoved mover, but also as the cause of the universe. Bessarion wrote to Plethon circa 1447 and requested a further explanation of two unclear passages in *De differentiis Aristotelis et Platonis*. Somewhat later, he himself attempted to take an intermediary position between Plethon's insistence on the primacy of the universal and Aristotle's doctrine of the primacy of the individual substance.[4] Other Byzantine scholars such as Theodore Gaza, the monk Isaiah, Michael Apostolios, and Andronicus Callistus took part in this controversy, which however remained confined to the circle of Byzantine émigrés.[5] In general, this first phase of the controversy about the value of Platonic thinking remained largely confined to the circle of Byzantine scholars, and their influence on the discussion among Latin scholars should not be overestimated.[6]

GEORGE OF TREBIZOND

This was to change in 1458 with the publication of the *Comparatio philosophorum Aristotelis et Platonis* by George of Trebizond (1396–1472), a Byzantine scholar who wrote in Latin and thereby had a wide influence on educated circles in Italy.[7] He had already lived for a long period in Italy, where he worked as a teacher and translator. In this and other writings,

---

4. In the brief text *Pros ta Plethonos pros Aristotele peri ousias* (1458), printed in Mohler 1942, 3.149–50. On this and on other short philosophical texts by Bessarion, see also Monfasani 1995, 137–260 (7).

5. On the first phase of this controversy, cf. Monfasani 1976, 201–12, and Garin 1955, 339–74.

6. On this, see also Hankins 1991, 1.193–216, and 2.436–40. Monfasani 1976, 201–29, lists other Latin works that refer directly to this controversy; some of these are still unpublished.

7. On George of Trebizond, see the relevant study by Monfasani 1976.

he not only wrote polemically against Plethon and his classical model; he also described in apocalyptic tones the Platonist conspiracy in which he believed Bessarion and his circle were engaged. George had earlier made a thorough study of Plato under Vittorino da Feltre, and had translated the *Parmenides* and the *Laws* into Latin[8] at the request of Pope Nicholas V, so it remains unclear what exactly motivated him to compose such tirades against the Platonists. His own explanation, at the beginning of the *Comparatio philosophorum Aristotelis et Platonis,* is unconvincing, namely, that he had realized when reading the *Gorgias* that Plato had slandered the great statesmen of Athens, Miltiades, Themistocles, and Pericles, as mere rhetoricians, although it was precisely these men that had brought Athens to its greatness. It is more likely that his polemical fulminations against Plato were based on the simple supposition that Roman Catholicism was based on the Aristotelian philosophy, while the "corrupt" Byzantine Church was based on Platonism. This would explain his assertion that the Platonic ontology *sensu stricto* is responsible for the heresy of the Greeks with regard to the *Filioque* formula.[9]

Similarly, the debate with Plethon in the *Comparatio* mostly remains on the level of a church-political squabble. It does not seek a sober and argumentative discussion with the representative of Platonic doctrines. For example, George begins his response to Plethon by describing how they met during the Council of Florence. During their conversation, Plethon revealed his hope that in some years, instead of Christ and Mohammed, a new pagan religion would come into existence.[10] George's personal attacks encompass all those who belong to the intellectual tradition of Plato. He gives pride of place to Bessarion and his humanist circle.[11]

CARDINAL BESSARION'S
IN CALUMNIATOREM PLATONIS

Bessarion replied to the "slanderer" of Plato in a refutation published in Rome in August 1469 under the title *In calumniatorem Platonis*.[12] The

---

8. On his translations into Latin, see especially Hankins 1991, 180–92.
9. G. Trapezuntius 1965, 2.16. 10. G. Trapezuntius 1965, 3.21.
11. On this, cf. Monfasani 1976, 160ff., and Garin 1973, 113–20.
12. On the textual history, see Mohler 1923, 1.358ff.

first Greek version of this work was written in 1459. It quickly won a widespread readership: only one year after its publication, a copy had made its way to Paris. This was not the only response to the Aristotelian George of Trebizond: other responses by authors such as Fernando Cordovano, Domizio Calderini, and Giorgio Benigno were to follow. But Bessarion's treatise made a particularly lasting impact on contemporaries.[13] The reactions of the Italian humanists to this work show that Bessarion's overall presentation of Platonic philosophy contributed to a more detailed knowledge of Plato's writings in the Latin hemisphere and to their wider reception. This is why *In calumniatorem Platonis* has sometimes been compared to the reception of Aristotle by Albert the Great and Thomas Aquinas, who pressed the Aristotelian texts into the service of the Christian faith and dogma. Bessarion translated other Greek authors into Latin, including the *Metaphysics* of Aristotle, which was published in Paris in 1515. At a later date, Becker included it in the Aristotle edition of the Berlin Academy, as the best of all existing translations.[14]

Bessarion, who was born in 1403 in Trebizond on the Black Sea and ordained to the priesthood in 1431, owed his profound knowledge of Plato to his five years of study under Plethon in Mistra. During his time at Plethon's academy, Bessarion had his first diplomatic successes when John, emperor of Constantinople, appointed him leader of the negotiations between Byzantium and Trebizond, in order to unite both states in a league against the renewed danger of a Turkish invasion. As archbishop of the Byzantine Church, Bessarion led the conciliar negotiations at the Union Council of Ferrara/Florence. After the council, he converted to the Roman Catholic Church and was created cardinal in 1439. Later, in 1463, he was appointed Latin patriarch of Constantinople. His extensive church-political activities are probably one reason why most subsequent portraits of the cardinal fail to take into account his literary activity or his influence on the history of ideas.

His theological writings, which contain recurrent discussions of the

13. Mohler 1923, 1.384–89. The lasting reception of this work is impressively attested in the letters from humanist friends of Bessarion which Mohler edits in the third volume of his monograph on Bessarion. On this, cf. also Neuhausen and Trapp 1979, 141–65.

14. On this, cf. Bernardinello 1968; Mioni 1960. Reprint in Aristoteles 1995. Nicholas of Cusa, who received a copy of the translation from Bessarion in 1453, was full of praise: *Istam translacionem fecit rev. d. card. Nicenus, que non posset esse meglior.*

dogmatic questions that were disputed between Byzantium and Rome, were addressed primarily to the narrow circle of professional theologians;[15] these are less significant in the present context than his writings about authors of classical antiquity. Bessarion won great fame among the Italian humanists especially for his knowledge of the Greek authors. Both Greeks and Latins were guests in his house, including men such as Lorenzo Valla, the Aristotelian Theodore Gaza (1400–1476), and for a time also George of Trebizond. He corresponded regularly with other leading humanists, such as Francesco Filelfo, Marsilio Ficino, Michael Apostolios, Andronicus Callistus, and Nicholas of Cusa.[16] His Roman residence became the meeting place of the "Friends of Greek Language and Literature,"[17] not least thanks to his extensive private library, which he had assembled over the years through purchases of manuscripts and copies. It contained not only works by Plato and Aristotle and numerous commentaries on their texts, but also Neoplatonic works by Plotinus, Iamblichus, and Proclus, as well as many patristic texts. The pope had charged Bessarion in 1446 with the supervision of the Basilian monasteries in Italy, and this had enabled him to collect texts. During his lifetime, his library with its 747 manuscripts (including 482 in Greek) was the largest collection of Greek manuscripts in the West.[18] Before his death, he bequeathed it to the Republic of Venice, where the collection became the basis of the later Library of Saint Mark's.

Because of its detailed exposition, his presentation of Plato's philosophy—originally written in Greek, and published shortly afterward in a Latin translation in four books—initiated a new reception of Plato. The first book offers a systematic presentation of Plato's teachings by means of a division into the categories of grammar, rhetoric, and logic. This is followed by a synthesis of Plato's statements on natural philosophy and theology, and then on mathematics, music, and astronomy. The *Cratylus* gives us a particular insight into Plato's contribution to grammar (1.4.1).[19] The dialogues *Phaedrus, Gorgias,* and the *Republic* show that despite his criticism of the rhetoricians, Plato himself made a considerable contribution to

15. On his early writings, see Stormon 1981.
16. On Bessarion and Nicholas of Cusa, see Lotti 1994, 8ff.
17. Mohler 1923, 5.
18. On this, cf. Bianca 1983 and Labowsky 1979.
19. The Greek and Latin versions were edited by Mohler 1927, Vol. 2. I cite from this edition, indicating the book, chapter, and section in Arabic numerals.

the development of this discipline (1.4.2–16). The same applies to logic. Although Plato did not present this systematically in a manner comparable to Aristotle, the twenty-four figures of the logical conclusion in the *Parmenides* show that he had a remarkable knowledge of logic (1.5.2–7). Plato also made a decisive contribution to the development of natural philosophy, of theology, and of mathematics, so that in these fields too George of Trebizond is completely incorrect to accuse Plato of philosophical dilettantism (1.9).

In the second book of *In calumniatorem Platonis,* Bessarion takes up the question of how far the philosophy of Plato and of Aristotle is suited to the presentation of Christian doctrines, and examines the differences between the two Greek thinkers. Bearing in mind the fact that neither of them could take account of central doctrines of Christianity, Bessarion investigates whether Plato and Aristotle taught anything incompatible with Christianity, or anything that contradicted its doctrines, on the questions of the existence of God (2.3), the doctrine of the Trinity (2.4.1–2), the creation of the world (2.5 and 6), the immortality of the soul (2.7), and predestination (2.8.3–6; 2.9.1–3). George of Trebizond had claimed that Aristotle held specific Christian views, and Bessarion affirms that these are indeed genuinely Christian teachings; but the fine differentiations this involves also lead Bessarion to ask whether Plato's philosophy too has close points of contact with Christian teachings. For example, the speculations in the *Parmenides* about "the One" agree with Pseudo-Dionyius's doctrine of "God's supersubstantial divinity." (As is well known, Pseudo-Dionysius was regarded as a pupil of Saint Paul, and his writings too were considered authoritative.)

The third book differs from the others in its diction and its structure, and has obviously been revised by other hands.[20] Here, Bessarion discusses in detail the description given by George of Trebizond of Plato's dubious character and habits. George appealed in support of these accusations not only to the account by Diogenes Laertius, but also to the affirmations about love (e.g., in the *Symposium*)—as if the positions taken by some of

20. There is no doubt that this part of the work too is by Bessarion, although the Greek humanist Theodore Gaza made a contribution to the composition of the third book in particular, and the theologian Giovanni Gatto was responsible for backing up the argument by quotations from Scholastic sources. On Gaza's collaboration, see Labowsky 1968.

the participants in the symposium were those of Plato himself. Another important piece of evidence for George's assessment of Plato as a philosopher of dubious worth is the *Republic* with its teachings about a communism of goods, the fellowship of women, and other regulations of the Platonic state. Because of a similar evaluation, Leonardo Bruni had earlier refused to translate this dialogue.

Bessarion appeals both to other ancient authors and to the Church Fathers when he rejects the accusations leveled at Plato's way of life. He also shows convincingly that if we are to understand Plato's writings correctly, we cannot equate the positions expressed in these texts with the personal views of their author (4.2.20–27). Bessarion's defense of the *Republic* is particularly detailed (4.3.1–12; 4.5–14). He attempts to justify specific regulations and organizations partly as time-conditioned, and partly through a comparison with the corrections that Plato himself makes in the *Laws* (e.g., on the fellowship of women). It may have been precisely this detailed exposition of the many ordinances envisaged by Plato in his project for a state that led Bessarion's contemporaries to evaluate this work so highly: *In calumniatorem Platonis* was in fact the first text to give them comprehensive information about Plato's work.

In support of his conviction about *Plato christianus,* Bessarion appeals not only to the tradition of the Greek fathers and to Augustine (2.1.2), but also to the Neoplatonists Plotinus and Porphyry. Although one cannot expect to find orthodox Christian doctrines in either Plato or Aristotle, Plato in particular came very close to the Christian doctrine of the Trinity in his divine triad of the One, the spirit, and the soul (2.3.5). In the controversy about which of the two Greek teachers is to be preferred, Bessarion attempts to demonstrate that they diverge at most in words, not in doctrine (2.9.16; cf. 1.17). This is not affected by the fact that Plato is the more important metaphysician and Aristotle has the greater advantage in physics (1.7.1–2; 1.6.2). With this interpretation, Bessarion positions himself squarely in the tradition of Neoplatonism, which regarded the corpus of Aristotelian works as a meaningful supplement in the discussion of those scientific problems which were not sufficiently treated in the Platonic dialogues.

The controversy ended with Bessarion's death in 1472. In the course of the scholarly debates, a large number of Platonic, Neoplatonic, and patristic texts were published. The controversy not only generated heated discussions of philosophical questions among the humanists, but also prompted serious academic investigations thanks to the comparison which was drawn between Plato and Aristotle. Developments after the cardinal's death, for example, in the form of Florentine Platonism under Marsilio Ficino, had, however, at most a marginal contact with this controversy, in which the Byzantine theologian had played such a central role.[21]

21. We find an echo of this controversy toward the end of the century in Pico della Mirandola's work *De ente et uno*. On this, see Kristeller 1970, 1–55.

Note: For further reading on Plethon see works by Plethon in the References; Lagarde; and *Oracles Chaldaïques*. On Bessarion, see works by Bessarion; Mohler; and Aristoteles latine (contains Bessarion's translation of Aristotle's *Metaphysics*. On George of Trebizond, see Georgius Trapezuntius; Monfasani 1984; Ruocco. For secondary sources see Anastos; Athanassiadi; Bernardinello; Bianca; Garin 1955 and 1973; Hankins 1994; Karamanolis; Kristeller 1972; Labowsky; Lotti; Masai; Mioni; Monfasani; Neuhausen and Trapp; Stausberg; Stormon; Tambrun; Webb; and Woodhouse.

3

LORENZO VALLA

(1406/7–1457)

Humanism as Philosophy

Paul Richard Blum

Lorenzo Valla (1406/7–1457) was born in Rome and studied under humanists such as Leonardo Bruni. As a young man, he worked in northern Italy, where his principal post was as professor of rhetoric in Pavia from 1429. After trying unsuccessfully to become papal secretary or to get support of some other kind from Popes Martin V and Eugene IV, he entered the service of Alfonso of Aragon, king of Sicily and Naples, who was embroiled in a political conflict with the pope, in 1433. In 1447, Nicholas V finally summoned Valla to Rome, where he taught rhetoric from 1455. He died in 1457. A large part of his oeuvre consists of philological investigations, which provoked polemical reactions. But he is a model humanist in the sense that these works are always undertaken in the context of wide-ranging philosophical and political questions.

As a writer, he was convinced that his polemics, unlike those of his adversaries, would remain valid even after his own death (*Epistole* 13, p. 208f.), not because of the polemic itself (as Erasmus of Rotterdam was later to write), but because of the quality of his arguments (*In Novum Testamentum annotationes,* Letter by Erasmus, *Opera* 1.802a).

His greatest political coup—both in the context of his philological work and in the interests of the king of Naples—was the demonstration that the so-called Donation of Constantine, on which the secular rule of the papacy was based, is a forgery. He hastened to affirm that he had written what no one other than himself had known up to then, not out of hatred of the pope, but for the sake of truth, of religion, and of fame (*Epistole* 22, p. 248). The defense of the truth is at least as important as the fight for one's fatherland, since the goal is to win the heavenly fatherland.[1] And this truth consists not only in uncovering the forgery, but also in showing that the church has been harmed by the possession of the church state. He argues on the basis of historical facts, ecclesiastical and civil law, and political and moral considerations. The principal argument is that Emperor Constantine could not have wanted to make the Donation, nor was he entitled and empowered to do so; likewise, Pope Sylvester could not have wanted the Donation, nor was he legally entitled to accept it. The best known arguments are the philological points made in the fourth part of the work: it is a mistake to read decrees (the *Decretum Gratiani*) and the biography of Sylvester as providing evidence of the Donation. Edward Gibbon described Valla's renown in this matter as follows: "This fictitious deed was transpierced by the pen of Laurentius Valla, the pen of an eloquent critic and a Roman patriot."[2] It is true that Valla's criticism was made against the background of the political situation of church and state in the period when Constantinople fell into the hands of the Turks, and that other authors (e.g., Nicholas of Cusa) disputed the legitimacy of the Donation at almost the same time. But it is Valla's merit to have employed lexicological and grammatical clues to expose the forgery as a poor concoction by liars. He blames an unknown individual, and shows that language possesses the power to unmask itself as falsehood. At the same time, like the sixteenth-century Reformers, he emphasizes that the church should confine itself strictly to its spiritual tasks and abandon all political and military ambitions.[3]

1. *De donatione,* ed. Setz, 57; ed. Coleman, 22; cf. *Retractatio* 56.
2. Edward Gibbon, *The Decline and Fall of the Roman Empire,* ch. 49 (Chicago, 1952), 2.206.
3. Cf. Celenza 2004, 85–100.

The argumentation that Valla applies in all the delicate questions of church politics is genuinely theological, but also refers to real persons, and it put his political critics in the wrong. Through his arguments, he strengthened the anthropocentric orientation of the humanists to substantive questions, by emphasizing more strongly that the individual was the ultimate authority in the evaluation of fundamental issues. That which one knows is worth communicating, and if it corresponds to the truth, it must in the long term benefit everyone.

In the introduction to his biography of King Ferdinand, Valla underlines that a personalized doctrine (*institutio illa sapientiae sub persona*) possesses greater authority, and that this applies not only to historical persons, but also to the author himself, who gives an example by means of his text (*Gesta Ferdinandi*, p. 4). Valla wrote to Cardinal Bessarion, an influential Byzantine theologian who propagated the study of Plato in Italy: "Follow your nature, listen to your own counsel, be like your own self. For if you are second to none in the virtues, you will surpass everyone in humaneness, mildness, and kindness" (*Epistole* 53, p. 385). And he admitted to the humanist Francesco Barbaro: "I would rather be and appear to be a good man, than be and appear to be a learned man" (*Epistole* 51, p. 379).

Valla's approach to the New Testament on the basis of the history of language (which became the academic standard only later, thanks to Erasmus) was viewed as a provocation. The humanist's self-consciousness finds expression in the affirmation that he did not reject the Architect of the Bible, but would really prefer himself to be the master builder (*Collatio*, ed. Perosa, 6ff.). He also demanded that theology should speak *eleganter,* that is, with an appropriate power of conviction,[4] since "[i]t is our desire to decorate the house of God in such a way that those who enter it will not feel contempt for what they see there, but will instead be moved to religious reverence by the majesty of the place" (*Elegantiae* Book 4, *praef.,* p. 303).

He claimed that the theologians of his day applied theoretical concepts to theological truths in such a manner that the specifically human concern of theology, namely, the religion of human persons, was lost to sight: above all, they appealed too glibly to pre-Christian classical authors, without tak-

---

4. T. Albertini, "Elegantia," in *Historisches Wörterbuch der Rhetorik* 2 (Tübingen, 1994), 998.

ing heed of the specifically Christian message in its distinctiveness. This accusation was leveled particularly at the late classical author Boethius, whose *Consolation of Philosophy* was repeatedly attacked by Valla, on the grounds that Boethius argued exclusively in the manner of pagan philosophers, not in Christian terms. This led Valla to demand that philosophical theology be replaced by a rhetorical theology *(Elegantiae 4, praef.)*; "rhetoric" denotes here the way in which truth speaks out of language to human beings, so that the truth can have a meaning for them. Rhetoric is the basis of Valla's philosophy, since "[b]asically, philosophy is only a soldier who fights for the truth under the generalship of speech. [. . .] Rhetoric is the queen who puts the swords into one's hand. This is why the orator is entitled to take his arguments from every source, and if someone opposes him, he may use the arguments to attack the philosophical crooks" *(De voluptate* 1.10, §3, pp. 14f.). The strength of rhetoric consists in "presenting many divergent arguments, as well as examples and comparisons, so that the orator compels the concealed truth to emerge" (3.12, p. 113).

The humanist Poggio Bracciolini accused him of heresy, because he understood the concept of "person" in such a way that it applied equally to God and to animals, since it really denoted only a quality and not a substance. Valla was accused of expounding the Trinity as a threefold quality of God. Valla on his part claimed to be pursuing precisely the interests of Christianity.[5] He held that the accusations were based on a typical misunderstanding: the words may lead to erroneous conclusions, but he is writing "about the matter itself, not about the individual words."[6]

The pièce de résistance of Vallas's linguistic argumentation is presented in the dialogue *De vero falsoque bono* (On the True and False Good) or, to use the title he himself preferred, *De voluptate* (On Pleasure). Throughout the Middle Ages and into the early modern period, Epicurus had been regarded as the embodiment of an immoral and antireligious life, until Cosma Raimondi (+ 1436) undertook his defense. He sees the concept of *voluptas* as the synthesis of the human striving for happiness, so that not only the soul, but the body too is entitled to demand happiness. At roughly the same time as Valla, Francesco Filelfo too had discussed the Epicurean

---

5. Camporeale 1972, 340 and 358; cf. Trinkaus.
6. Zippel, "L'autodifesa," §1, p. 82.

theory of pleasure in a number of letters. Both authors attempt to unite the happiness of the soul and the happiness of earthly human actions.[7] This makes *voluptas* a key concept for the interpretation of earthly activity. In his discussion of this concept in the three books of *De voluptate*, Valla lets the Stoic and Epicurean moral principles argue against each other, in order then to present a new Christian solution. Book 1 presents the Epicurean thesis that pleasure is the only good; Book 2 defends the Stoic ideal of virtue as honor; and Book 3 shows that *voluptas* is in fact the highest good, but in a special sense.

First, Valla disqualifies Aristotle by making the doctrine of *mesotês* appear ridiculous. In the *Nicomachean Ethics*, Aristotle writes that virtue consists in the correct middle point between two vices. This, however, means that each virtue has two foes—and that is not logical. From an Epicurean perspective, the reason is that there are more virtues than vices, and Valla reduces this to the thesis that there is only one single good, which all human actions follow, namely, pleasure (1.4, pp. 7f.; cf. *Retractatio* 1.10). Aristotle's intention was to set out the structure of human activity, but Valla concentrates the discussion on the point that human beings always act as the result of an impulsion that generates the individual actions and virtues. Valla disqualifies the Epicurean ethics with witty and provocative theses, for example, that adultery is a professional risk of husbands, so that adulterers who are caught deserve punishment—for their stupidity (1.42 §2–3, p. 37). He criticizes the Stoic doctrine as basically only a hidden form of the striving for pleasure: were this not the case, it would be impossible to explain why someone would be willing to die for his native land.

Valla's solution is both conceptually acute and Christian. Pleasure is the instinct in the human person that drives us to act, and thus pleasure is also the principle that guides our striving for that which lies beyond death. Accordingly, the important distinction to be drawn does not concern virtues on the part of the human person: it concerns the good. Pleasure is not the good; rather, the good is that by means of which one hopes to attain pleasure. This good is twofold, both earthly and heavenly. This means that God is not the *highest* good, but the *true* good. When the human per-

---

7. Raimondi in the English translation by Martin Davie in Kraye, ed., 1997, 1.238–44; a letter of Filelfo, translated by Luc Deitz, 1.234–37. Cf. Fois, 124 ff.

son strives to attain this good, he does not cease to be human. He enjoys the good *as* a human person—for otherwise there would be no pleasure in striving to attain the true good.

Normally, it is held that the highest good is in God. At this point, Valla makes a distinction between a highest good per se (which is indubitably God himself) and that which is good for the human person. God would be the highest good for the human person only if he could become God—but this is impossible. What the human person can attain is to know and enjoy *(frui)* God. It follows that this *fruitio* is the highest good of the human person, and is a pleasure. The heavenly happiness is a continuation of the earthly happiness with other means. It remains a happiness for the human person, when described from the perspective of the acting person (not from the perspective of an absolute God).

The specifically humanistic approach to the philosophical problems was a result of the anthropocentric perspective that used language as a medium to grasp and to describe the meaning of the world and of the human person, and their "dignity." The critique of language always went hand in hand with the solution to substantial questions such as freedom, science, the good, and so on on the basis of language.

In his *Dialectic* (the *Repastinatio dialecticae et philosophiae,* according to the title of one of the various versions), Valla proposes a completely new structure of philosophical systematics with rhetoric as the governing science. Once again, he works step by step from the grammatical analysis of the technical vocabulary under the influence of Quintilian. On the basis of the Aristotelian categories, this work discusses the substances and principles (Book 1); rhetoric, which also includes the forms of words and statements (Book 2); and finally dialectic in the narrower sense, that is, the rules governing logical inferences (Book 3).

Valla's initial question is: What do people actually want when they discuss a matter? They want to get to know the matter as it is. They do not want to get to know Being, nor the modes of Being: they want to get to know what something is. It is clear that people acquire the knowledge that they want by means of language and in language. Accordingly, the act of speaking is not located "alongside" the truth and right thinking. On the contrary, it shows precisely what we want to get to know about something—and this is not its Being (what it *is*), but the thing itself (*what* it is).

Human language reveals how objects always occur, as beings or as things. Late medieval logic assumed a number of "transcendentals," which accounted for everything that there is. "Being," "good," "true" were the most important transcendentals. On the ground of his language approach Valla reduced the transcendentals to one alone, namely, *res* (thing), thus undermining the Scholastic ontology.

One philological argument is suggested by a difference between Greek and Latin. Aristotle had made the present participle *on* (from *einai*, "to be"), which can be declined in all three grammatical genders, an abstract term by prefixing the article *to* ("the": *to on*, "the existent"). In this way, he was able to present *to on* as something that could basically only have the meaning "factual matter" *(pragma)*, a term used by rhetoricians to designate the subject of an oration (*Retractatio* 1.2, pp. 12 and 17f.). Aristotle had also introduced a duplication to the effect that the existent must be investigated "as that which is" *(to on ê on)*. However, this duplication causes ontological confusions, since in *ens prout ens*, the "existent" appears first as a noun and then as a verb, so that it is not longer the original "factual matter," but the *Being* of the existent that is thematized and thus becomes the goal of philosophical knowledge. The scholar must, however, thematize the *fact* of the existent. This argument is also found in the logical-pragmatic criticism of metaphysics in the modern period; but Valla adds a theological argument. The link to the Being of the existent itself excludes everything that is not Being; but the expression "'the thing that is' is appropriate only to God" (*Retractatio* 1.2, p. 14). Valla concentrates on the object of what we intend when we seek knowledge, in order to clarify the sphere of competence of logic and of knowledge. Leaving metaphysics out of account, Valla concedes validity only to that which can be thematized in language. Accordingly, the task of philosophy is not to open up and investigate the ditch that lies between word and the object, between thinking and what would later be called "extramental reality." Rather, philosophy must assume that things always exist in words and objects always exist in language.[8] Valla employs the same strategy to dissolve the structure of substance and accident. Of the ten Aristotelian categories, he accepts only substance, quality, and action, from which all the others are derived (1.13–17).

8. Cf., however, Monfasani 1989, 317f.

Unlike the Neoplatonists and the later natural philosophers of the Renaissance, Valla does not seek a real universal principle of the world. His intention is to slim the theory down by analyzing the ways in which it is spoken of. He thus intentionally and consciously takes a different line from the Scholastic nominalists (Nauta, "Occam," 2003). The content of thinking is revealed in the speech acts and in the classical philological models.

Valla acquired a certain measure of fame with a text about the freedom of the will. The starting point is the voluntaristic question about the will of God, the knowledge of human action, and grace. Divine freedom interests the human person for his own sake: this is the argument with which Valla believes he can refute Boethius, who maintained in the *Consolation of Philosophy* that the meaning of God's freedom lay in the divine omniscience, which was supratemporal, so that the events of all times were in the present tense for God.[9] Valla regards this as a conclusive and philosophically correct judgment which however does not solve the problem of freedom— for he objects: "But can I, who am rational and know nothing outside of time, aspire to the knowledge of intelligence and eternity?" (*De libero arbitrio*, p. 15; *Dialogue on Free Will*, p. 160). Of what benefit to the human person is God's freedom? The human person is subordinate to the freedom of God, and since the human person is temporal and dependent, the analysis of the conditions of the divine freedom will give rise to the fear that human freedom will be lost in the course of the argumentation. This problem became particularly acute later on, in the discussion between Martin Luther and Erasmus.

From the late Middle Ages onward, the discussion about grace inquired whether there was any space for free human action within the framework of God's providence. This, however, leads either to an ill-concealed determinism or to a justification of the divine freedom on the basis of the freedom of the human person to act spontaneously. Lorenzo Valla heightens this antinomy by attributing foreknowledge hypothetically to one god (Apollo) and the will, in which God's freedom consists, to

9. Anicius Manlius Severinus Boethius, *Philosophiae consolationis libri V*, lib. 5, pr. 3. On the modern discussion, cf., e.g., Nelson Pike, "Divine Omniscience and Voluntary Action," *Philosophical Review* 74 (1965): 27–46; Alvin Plantinga, *God, Freedom, and Evil* (Grand Rapids, 1977), esp. 67–73; John M. Fisher, *The Metaphysics of Free Will* (Cambridge, Mass., and Oxford, 1984); Peter van Inwagen, *God, Knowledge and Mystery* (Ithaca, N.Y., 1995).

another god (Jupiter; *De libero arbitrio,* pp. 31ff.; *Dialogue,* pp. 169ff.). This doubling of the "functions" of God appears to show that no kind of freedom remains to the human person, since the God who has the knowledge cannot warn, and the God who has the will cannot in the future make undone what the human person will do. There is a contradiction between justice and grace, all the more so because in reality (at any rate, in Christianity) both potencies are united in one God. In that case, however, although the freedom of the human person is not demonstrable, it is at least possible. This leads Valla to postulate that the divine foreknowledge includes not only those events that have in fact taken place, but also those that failed to occur. This is because in freedom, all possibilities are genuine possibilities, although they are distinguished *post festum* into mere options and facts. In the divine foreknowledge, freedom is retained, since all the alternatives are equally true in an ontological sense (*De libero arbitrio,* p. 28; *Dialogue,* p. 168). Nevertheless, Valla's historical reputation has been that of a denier of divine and human freedom.[10]

Shortly before his death, Valla was invited to hold the annual memorial discourse in honor of Thomas Aquinas in the Dominican monastery of Santa Maria sopra Minerva in Rome.[11] This was probably one move in the controversy in the Dominican order about the gradual consolidation of Thomism as a Scholastic doctrine, since Valla was known to be a critic of Scholasticism. In this discourse, he criticizes both the Scholastic terminology of the Thomists and Thomas's endeavors to provide a metaphysical foundation for theology. This is why he portrays him as the most recent (i.e., the last) of the Church Fathers and closes with the confession (found in all his works) that the apostle Paul is the "prince and teacher of all theologians."

Valla repeatedly emphasized that he was fighting on behalf of the truth, and hence on behalf of Christianity. His disrespectful expositions of theo-

10. E.g., Luis de Molina, *Liberi arbitrii cum gratia (. . .) concordantia,* ed. Johannes Rabeneck (Madrid, 1953), pars 1, qu. 14, art. 13, disp. 1, n. 17, p. 11.

11. Lorenzo Valla, *Encomium Sancti Thomae Aquinatis.* Introduction and text in J. Vahlen, "Lorenzo Valla über Thomas von Aquino," *Vierteljahrsschrift für Kultur und Literatur der Renaissance* 1 (1886): 384–96 (reprint in Valla, *Opera omnia,* vol. 2); a French translation in Mesnard 1955. Cf. O'Malley 1974; Kristeller, *Le thomisme,* 1967, 72–79, and idem, *Medieval Aspects,* 1974, 63f.; Gray 1965; Fois 1969, 456–69; Di Napoli 1971, 115–22; Camporeale 1972, 3ff.; Camporeale 2002, 123–76.

logical doctrines, and above all his linguistic and human perspective, were an important factor in theology's loss of its rank as queen of the sciences. For in Valla's ethics, historiography, and ontology, the discourse about God is invariably only a test case. It is never a central concern.

Note: For further reading see Valla in the References; for secondary sources see Besomi and Regoliosi; Camporeale; Celenza; Di Napoli; Fois; Gray; Laffranchi; *Lorenzo Valla: A Symposium;* Kristeller 1967; 1974; Mack; Mesnard; Monfasani 1989; O'Malley; Nauta; Regoliosi; Setz; Trinkaus; and Zippel.

4

NICHOLAS OF CUSA

(1401–1464)

Squaring the Circle: Politics, Piety,
and Rationality

Detlef Thiel

It is certainly possible to draw a distinction between what Nicholas of Cusa (Nicolaus Cusanus) *was* and what he *is:* what he was in the apparently so distant epoch of the fifteenth century in Germany, Italy, and the Netherlands, and what he means for us today and for the future. Both cases involve conjectures, more or less speculative sketches or (re-)constructions.

It is not easy to say briefly what he was: a churchman, a curial cardinal, a politician and organizer in the service of the Roman church, a pastor and a reformer two generations before Luther—a practical man. At the same time, he was a theoretician: a theologian and philosopher, one who defined important issues, a systematic thinker, an autonomous developer of the Platonic tradition; one who studied questions of methodology, a visionary, a man who drew on literature from outside the borders of Europe; a passionate collector of books and philologist; a mathematician, historian, and jurist. (We note only in passing that he is also a symbolic figure, the trademark of an entire industry of popularization, whose name adorns numerous institutions, grammar schools, associations, reading circles, etc.)

The following overview of his life and work will fill out this sketch to some extent, but we must restrict ourselves to essential information—without forgetting the crises of his age and the urgent problems: the relationship between the church and the world, schism, the danger from the Turks, and reform. We shall seek to present as many facets of Nicholas as possible, without making a forcible separation between the various academic disciplines.

He was born in 1401 in the village of Kues on the Moselle, the son of the wine grower and boatman Hennen Kryfftz ("crab," the animal in Nicholas's coat of arms). He studied in Heidelberg in 1416/1417, and then in Padua, where he took his doctorate in canon law in 1423 and had his first contacts with Italian humanists, especially with the geographer and astronomer Paolo dal Pozzo Toscanelli. In 1425 he entered the service of the archbishop of Trier. As a law historian at the University of Köln, he was influenced by Heymeric de Campo (1395–1460; member of the Albertist school of theology). In Paris, he made excerpts from the manuscripts of Ramon Llull. He was appointed dean of St. Florinus in Koblenz in 1427, and began an intensive activity as preacher, although he was not ordained to the priesthood until 1436; in addition to this work, he was already much sought after as a mediator and investigator in legal cases. Almost three hundred sermons survive from the period between Christmas 1430 (1428?) and mid-1463. Many of these are very abstract, but we are told that large numbers of people heard him preach. In 1444 he declared in Mainz that just as a baker sometimes makes rough bread and sometimes fine bread from one and the same flour, so too a preacher cannot always supply the same quality. His endeavor to express himself as clearly as possible must be seen as an expression of the religious-pedagogical commitment that was one of his central concerns.

From 1430 onward, he was the personal secretary of Ulrich von Manderscheid and represented his interests. Ulrich laid claim to the see of Trier and was even willing to oppose the decision of the pope; Nicholas, who became a member of the college of the Council of Basle early in 1432, attempted to win support for the position that the consent of the laity (as a divinely ordained institution in a corporative societal ordering) should take precedence over the imposition of papal authority. Ulrich's endeavors were defeated in 1434; the council charged Nicholas to continue his work of mediation. He wrote several treatises: on the return of the Bohemian Hussites to the Catholic Church (*De communione sub utraque specie,* 1433), on the question who should preside over the council (*De auctoritate praesidendi,* 1434), on calendar reform (*Reparatio calendarii,* 1434/1435, a work drawing both on astronomy and on astrology), and above all *De concordantia catholica* (1433/34), an extensive programmatic text that summarizes in three books the medieval theories about society and councils, uniting the microcosm and the macrocosm in a tripartite division into spirit, soul, and body, or sacrament, priest, and laity. Nicholas answers the questions about authority, legitimation, and competence by proposing a *concordantia:* the *Ecclesia romana* is represented by the pope *and* council together.

These studies of canon law and church history were much acclaimed. In August 1437 Nicholas was a member of the delegation that sailed from Venice to the Greek imperial court at Constantinople in order to prepare the union of the Western and Eastern Churches at the Union Council of Ferrara/Florence (1438). On this occasion, he made the acquaintance of the most important representatives of the Greek tradition, especially Bessarion, archbishop of Nicaea, an expert in Plato and translator of Aristotle's *Metaphysics.* On his return journey, Nicholas received the insight that there is something incomparably more solid that lies beyond the antitheses, beyond the endless to and fro of selective rational knowledge, beyond the Aristotelian principle of contradiction: namely, the "learned ignorance." He wrote that thanks to a gift from heaven, he came to the point where he could embrace the incomprehensible in an incomprehensible manner *(incomprehensibile incomprehensibiliter complectens).*

Henceforth, this insight was to remain fundamental for Nicholas. He returns to it again and again, meditating on it, developing it, and applying it. He does so in detail for the first time in the *De docta ignorantia,* a text that he signed, not without a certain pride: "Kues, February 12, 1440." He discusses in three books God, the universe, and Jesus Christ; or, in his own terminology, that which is absolutely the greatest, that which is the greatest in a limited sense, and that which is the greatest and binds the two together. The themes are not new, but he grasps them in a new manner.

This work cannot simply be classified under theology; it is marked equally strongly by philosophical traditions (Plato, Aristotle, Eckhart; the motif of *docta ignorantia* is already found in Augustine and Bonaventure). The best way to understand it is probably as methodology: reflection on the goal and the path, on the intention and the means of human knowledge. According to the *regula doctae ignorantiae,* one cannot arrive at anything that is absolutely the greatest or the smallest because there is always something even greater or smaller. This has three implications: *(1)* The absolute is inaccessible to the human person—God remains hidden, that which is completely Other. *(2)* Every approach is irrevocably provisional and asymptotic, and the *adaequatio,* the alignment of the intellect with its object (to take Thomas Aquinas's definition of truth), is faced with an endless field of possibilities, an open horizon for investigation. *(3)* The aids to knowledge take on an inalienably analogical function. Again and again, Nicholas quotes 1 Cor 13:12: "For now we see in a mirror and enigma, but then face to face"; and he gives vivid examples that lead the seeker through his own self to that which he seeks *(manuductio).* For Nicholas, however, the true mediator between the human person and God is Christ. His anthropology is built upon Christology.

Two other works are closely connected to the *De docta ignorantia: De coniecturis* (written between 1440 and 1444) and *Apologia doctae ignorantiae* (1449). The former elaborates a detailed and often difficult complementary structure of Being, articulated in four stages: God, the intellect, the soul, and the body. At the center, in the absolute *complicatio,* is the ineffable God, and it is from this inaccessible place that the original unity unfolds in a different manner in each individual stage *(explicatio),* down to the remotest and smallest things. Nicholas illustrates the double movement of ascent and descent by means of the "figure P," two intersecting triangles (for *unitas* and *alteritas,* light and shadow, etc.), each of which touches with its vertex the baseline of the other. Since the absolute positions (the vertices, so to speak) remain unattainable, all human knowledge remains a conjecture *(coniectura).* Through this radical separation, Nicholas sets in motion (on this side of the boundary) the infinite combinatory play of signs, which includes the possibility of inventing paradoxical signs such as audacious figures of speech that point by analogy to their origin and to their goal.

The *Apologia* replies in the form of a discussion among students to the objections brought by the Heidelberg professor Johannes Wenck in 1442/ 1443, especially the accusation of pantheism. It justifies and defends the *De docta ignorantia*, repeating and commenting on selected portions of the earlier work. The *Apologia*, a skillfully constructed mosaic of quotations and literary allusions, is an example of the true *docta litteratura*, as opposed to Wenck's *ignota litteratura* ("neglect of learning"—such was the title of Wenck's book). Nicholas's literary mastery claims to go beyond the letter, while Wenck's merely bookish knowledge is based on insufficient reading: he seems to have read little and to have understood less. Wenck confuses himself "by reproaching unwritten words for having been written." It is here that we also find the well-known methodological instruction that it is fitting "that one who investigates the spirit of an author in some matter should read all his writings attentively and dissolve them into one single harmonizing sentence."

In the 1440s Nicholas took part as papal legate in the lengthy negotiations to change the neutrality that the German princes had declared vis-à-vis the curia at Frankfurt in 1438. He proved his value as a practical man in the "daily business of administering salvation" (E. Meuthen) at the Imperial Diets in Nuremberg and in countless other assemblies, conflicts, and decisions, both in local matters and in the great political affairs of Europe. For example, he and the Spanish cardinal Juan de Carvajal created the presuppositions that allowed the Germans to abandon their distance and to join the pope; the Concordat of Vienna, which regulated this matter in 1448, remained in force until 1806. As early as 1447, Nicholas was a potential candidate for the papal election; in 1451 and 1455, he was designated as a mediator between England and France.

In addition to all these obligations, he pursued his "theoretical" ideas. Between 1445 and 1447, he wrote four brief texts that are contemplative and theological in the literal sense of the term: they speak of God as origin and goal, of his hiddenness and the search for him, of the vision of God, and of the human person as God's child *(De Deo abscondito, De quaerendo Deum, De filiatione Dei,* and *De dato Patris luminum).* There is a strong link between the idea of *filiatio—deificatio, theosis*—and the higher evaluation of that which is individual and of the individual human being that occurred in Italian humanism, both in the treatises on the "dignity of the human person" and in the form of autobiography; this idea can, however, also be traced back to Plato's concept of the *homoiôsis theô(i)* (*Theaetetus* 176 b).

At the same time, Nicholas undertook mathematical studies (*De geometricis transmutationibus, De arithmeticis complementis*). He was to continue these studies for many years; more than ten treatises survive, and the value of these works should not be underestimated. It has been asserted that they are the idle speculative pastime of an unschooled mathematician, and this is true to the extent that *in mathematicis,* the spirit is busy only with itself, and can achieve perfection. But Nicholas senses here too the obligation to attempt the impossible, namely, the squaring of the circle (as the figure that symbolizes God), and of course also the circling of the square (the transcendence from the visible to the infinite, in a hyperbolic *modus tollens*).

Nicholas now reached the height of his career. The pope created him cardinal of San Pietro in Vincoli in December 1448, and he was ordained bishop of Brixen in April 1450. He spent this Holy Year, in which all the pilgrims were granted a plenary indulgence, in Rome, where he wrote his four books about the layman between July and September: *Idiota de sapientia* 1 and 2, *Idiota de mente,* and *Idiota de staticis experimentis,* thereby coining another of those examples that bring together a wealth of meanings and associations in a vivid figure from daily life. It is precisely his remoteness from book-learning that makes the layman closer to the origin than his dialogue partners, the orator and the philosopher. Because (almost like Socrates) he knows that he does not know, he is able to open the eyes of other people: to mystical theology (in the sense of Pseudo-Dionysius the Areopagite, whom Nicholas still regarded as a contemporary of the apostle Paul, but also in the sense of the *devotio moderna* and the lay theology); to the methodology of conjecture and the necessary linguistic skepticism (outside the primal divine word, nothing can ever be named appropriately; names and objects merely refer to one another in an infinite game); to the activity of the creative spirit as measurer or criterion (this spirit is not, as in Aristotle, merely the faculty of judgment, but is a specific living substance—and this entails a Copernican revolution *before* Kant); and to experimenting with, measuring, weighing, and gathering data in the realm of nature and of medicine (Nicholas has been seen as one of the founders of modern natural science).

On December 31, 1450, he set out as plenipotentiary legate on his great journey through Austria, Germany, Belgium, and the Netherlands, in order to proclaim the grace of the Jubilee indulgence to all who could not come in person to Rome, and in particular to enforce a thoroughgoing reform of church, clergy, and monasteries in the Benedictines, Augustinian canons, and mendicant orders. This journey lasted for fifteen months, but despite all his endeavors, it was not crowned with lasting success (just as the conciliar movement did little to help the church). At every stage on his journey, Nicholas repeated his urgent appeals to the faithful to gain indulgences for the salvation of their souls, that is, to hand over cash to the church—thus proving a very conservative representative of the medieval psychoeconomy. (By the way, the pattern of this institutionalized acquisition of money corresponds exactly to that of modern joint-stock companies: "Time is money!") On the other hand, he also fought against the excessive forms of the sale of indulgences, which were to explode two generations later in the Lutheran Reformation.

An event with far-reaching consequences for the entire West took place on May 29, 1453, when the Turkish sultan Mehmet II conquered Constantinople. Under the impact of this catastrophe, Nicholas composed a number of works between September and November 1453. The first, *De pace fidei*, takes the form of an account by an anonymous man of the *visio* he received in an ecstasy *(raptus):* seventeen representatives of the peoples assemble in heaven with Paul, Peter, and the divine Word in order to discover, in the multiplicity of rites, the one true, universal religion in which all share in some way *(una religio in rituum varietate)*. This religious dialogue, which is on a par with Abelard *(Dialogus inter Philosophum, Iudaeum et Christianum)*, Llull *(Liber de gentili et tribus sapientibus)*, and Lessing *(Nathan the Wise)*, is often regarded today as a great document of tolerance; but it is perfectly clear that Nicholas makes no concessions in his endeavor to establish the hegemony of motifs that are embodied in Roman Catholicism alone.

The second text, *De visione Dei*, is a reply to Nicholas's friends, the Benedictines of the abbey of Tegernsee in Upper Bavaria, who had asked whether the pious soul could attain to God without rational knowledge or thinking, but exclusively through emotion and the ground of the soul, through the so-called *synderesis*. The cardinal relates on September 14, 1453, that he is at present working on a booklet for Pope Nicholas V, *De mathematicis complementis*, in which he employs mathematics to clarify all that was hitherto unknown; in another text, *De theologicis complementis*, he is transposing mathematical figures to the theological infinity, and he has inserted a chapter about the manner in which we can be led to mystical theology from one particular type of image, from a painting of the one who sees both all things and each individual thing, by means of a certain sensuous experience *(sensibili experimento). De visione Dei* thus stands between mathematics and theology, between sensuous and suprasensuous knowledge, between the concrete and the general. Starting from a *vera icona* (Rogier van der Weyden, Dürer, and Raphael painted such pictures), Nicholas illustrates in the form of a prayer the motif of the *coincidentia oppositorum,* which he describes as the "wall of paradise." Behind or beyond this, he locates the origin of all things, God, who can be experienced only in the darkness, when the *ratio* falls silent. One should look for the truth at the point where one encounters impossibility.

Nicholas found no opportunities for literary activity between the close of 1453 and the summer of 1458, with the exception of further studies of how to square the circle *(Dialogus de circuli quadratura, De Caesarea circuli quadratura).* He devoted all his energies to the reform of the monastery and the diocese of Brixen, against the opposition of the nobles, for example, Abbess Verena, who did not shrink from a grave breach of the peace. Above all, the confrontation with the secular ruler of the territory, the Habsburg duke Sigismund of Tyrol, became ever more intense. This conflict too went beyond the internal affairs of the church; it was one element of the old controversy between the curia and the German princes, which had already been treated at Basle.

It was only in August 1458 that Nicholas was able to keep a second promise made to the monks of Tegernsee and complete the *De beryllo.* Once again, he develops the semantic potential of "seeing," elaborating a mirror and enigma *(speculum et aenigma).* A cut beryl that is partly convex and partly concave becomes "spectacles" that allow us to touch the "indivisible origin of all things." Supported by Plato, Proclus, Pseudo-Dionysius, and Albert, as well as by Aristotle and Averroes, this text leads the reader to the insight that this origin lies beyond the point where the opposites coincide.

Shortly afterward, Nicholas went to Rome. On January 11, 1459, the pope appointed him curial cardinal and vicar general, and commissioned him to reform the Roman clergy. In July he submitted the plan of a *Reformatio generalis,* once again recommending the conciliar idea. He attempted to resolve the various local conflicts in Italy and elsewhere, in order to make it possible for the pope and the emperor to take joint action against the Turks. He also wrote two short treatises on the concept of God, *De aequalitate* and *De principio*. Both have their starting points in biblical passages; the latter refers both to John 8:25 ("Who are you?") and to Proclus's commentary on Plato's *Parmenides*. The *Trialogus de possest* (February 1460) draws on the same source. The neologism in the title, a contraction of the indefinite *posse* ("can": shorthand for the infinite creative power) and the definite *est* ("is": that which is created), designates the pure act in which the dualism between act and potency (which goes back to Aristotle) coincides. After the *maximum absolutum* and the *idem absolutum,* this word is a further station in the sequence of divine names that Nicholas elaborates.

The conflict in Brixen soon intensified even further. On April 16, 1460, Duke Sigismund arrested the cardinal and forced him to surrender secular authority in his diocese. Nicholas returned to Rome for good, and devoted himself in the remaining four years of his life to the tasks of reform and to a number of writings in which he attempted to gain an overview and a conclusion. In the winter of 1460/1461, he completed the studies of the Koran which he had probably begun already in Constantinople, and wrote the *Cribratio Alkorani* in three books. His intention is to "sift through the Koran," that is, to cleanse it of its imperfections, in order to show where it agrees with the Christian message of salvation. This work of comparative religion is a *manuductio:* Nicholas seeks to lead the Muslims from their monotheism to the Trinity, and this leads him to discuss soteriological and eschatological questions.

About a year later, in 1461/1462, in his very abstract dialogue *De non aliud* (The non-Other) Nicholas takes a noun formed from a predicative pronoun and develops from this a name for an "absolute concept" (such as the concept of God must be). The formula *non aliud est non aliud quam non aliud* ("nothing other is nothing other than nothing other") affirms that the non-Other is always required when the Other is to be defined. The negation of the negation generates an infinite definition. Trinitarian formulae such as Father, Son, and Holy Spirit are dismissed as confusing. Nevertheless, *non aliud* is as yet a rather static name. It is understood dynamically in *De venatione sapientiae* (1463), as the ability to act *(posse facere)* which is antecedent to every possibility of becoming *(posse fieri)* and every possibility of having come into existence *(posse factum)*. In this treatise, which explicitly owes its composition to his reading of Diogenes Laertius, Nicholas seeks to describe three different levels and specific places on these levels, thus leading the hunter for wisdom to specific fields. This is a systematic overall view of all the topics he has treated in his earlier works, and it has almost a mnemotechnical structure. In the tenth and last field, he writes that we strive for wisdom in order to be immortal: the necessity of dying is as it were transmuted into a will for immortality and into a virtue *(virtus)*.

In 1463 Nicholas also completed the two books *De ludo globi*. Once again, a vivid example illustrates the position of the human being in the cosmos, in the great "play" of the spheres of Earth and heaven. Each cast of a bowl that is hollowed out on one side—every life of a fragmented individual—is only an approximation to the ideal spiral. The central point of the playing surface that is formed by concentric circles is Christ. The game serves as a structural model for all the thought and action of what Nicholas (with Hermes Trismegistus) calls the "second god," the *homo creator* or *deus humanatus* which every human being can release in himself.

These extensive texts are followed only by two brief summaries. The *Compendium* (1463/1464) gives an overview of the various manifestations of the first origin *(primum principium)*. Affirmative theology and negative theology are equally inadequate; every more appropriate answer must remain in the oscillation between yes and no. God neither is nor is not; nor is he both Being and nothing. This leads Nicholas to elaborate a new divine name: *posse*. He now develops what he had written about immortality in the *De venatione sapientiae* as an explicit theory of signs; this is also a testament for his intellectual heirs. A gift from God is the perfection of a science of such signs *(perfectio scientiae signorum)* that enable people to exchange and preserve their ideas. In comparison with the divine *ars* and *scientia*, all human arts and sciences are deficient. The *ars scribendi* was invented by the reason, like the numbers, concepts, games, works of art, and other artistic products; but it is only writing that can guarantee the continuing existence of all these products—the tradition of the theory of the tradition of a theory. The hospital that the cardinal founded in Kues in 1458 still exists today.

The final text, *De apice theoriae* (Easter 1464), explains the last divine name at which Nicholas arrived: *posse ipsum*, "ability itself," the ability that underlies every ability and is the presupposition of every ability to exist, to live, and to understand *(esse, vivere, intelligere)*. This absolute superlative, the most concise and simple linguistic expression, is the high point of Nicholas's endeavors to write a *theologia brevis et facilis* which is accessible to all—just as the layman in the *"idiota* dialogues" emphasizes that Wisdom cries out everywhere in the streets and squares. Nicholas had already written in *De coniecturis* that theology is clear and short, and is not capable of being unfolded in a discourse *(sermone inexplicabilis)*, for since God, the absolute unity, admits neither of a yes nor of a no, the art of investigating the truth can "be written on three lines in the *complicatio* of its simple unity" for the one who is able to keep silent and see beyond all rationality. This ease and openness is the inversion of the darkness and falling silent of mystical theology, just as the light that makes possible all colors and all seeing itself remains invisible. In its self-reflection, the spirit sees that, like everything else, it is only an image of that *posse ipsum*, one mode of manifestation of a dynamic that is per se incomprehensible. This extremely brief text closes once again with a Christology.

In the summer of 1464, Nicholas left Rome in order to assemble in Ancona the scattered participants in the military campaign that the pope planned against the Turks, and to bring them to the Venetian fleet. En route, he succumbed to a fever and died on August 11 in Todi.

When we look at the chronological sequence of his texts, we notice the restless transition between phases of fruitful activity and sometimes lengthy pauses. The irregular rhythm has pragmatic and biographical reasons: it is astonishing to note the concentration and intensity that Nicholas of Cusa repeatedly achieves despite his continual journeys and his many practical tasks. All his texts, which he consistently refers to as "booklets" *(libelli)*, were written in very specific situations for specific readers. Although they are unsystematic and hence somewhat "nomadic," and have a strongly dialogical character, they retain an objective coherence. Like many of his contemporaries, especially among the Italian humanists and men of letters, Nicholas reflects explicitly on his authorship and therefore on his individuality, in an incessant attempt to speak simultaneously of the individual and the general. He came from a bourgeois family and had an excellent business sense; he belonged to no school or university, but moved in the highest circles of the nobility, the clergy, and scholars (e.g., he was a friend of Popes Nicholas V and Pius II, as well as of the Sforza and Gonzaga families). As E. Meuthen writes, he was "ambitious for responsibility."

His position at the point of intersection of so many contemporary tendencies, the powerful tension in his principal theses, his polyhistorical knowledge, his intensive activity in church politics and scientific organization—all this led at an early date to the tendency to see him as the founder or the decisively important forerunner of numerous later achievements. Here, however, we must exercise caution. S. Meier-Oeser has accurately summed up the later influence of Nicholas of Cusa as the "presence of a forgotten man." This refers to what we might call an "underground" reception of some of his theorems, in particular the idea of the *coincidentia oppositorum*. He clearly influenced Bruno, Kircher, Comenius, Descartes, Spinoza, Leibniz, and others up to the period of German speculative idealism. It is only since the Theological Faculty of Tübingen offered a prize for an essay in 1831 that Nicholas's life and work has been investigated more thoroughly, initially by Catholic church historians such as J. A. Möhler, F. A. Scharpff, and J. Uebinger, and then toward the end of the nineteenth century by some neo-Kantians such as H. Cohen and E. Cassirer. From the late 1920s onward, the Heidelberg Academy encouraged studies by E. Hoffmann, J. Ritter, and R. Klibansky.

This brief survey does not really do justice to the entire spectrum of Nicholas of Cusa, because too many fields of knowledge, sources, and intellectual constructions are linked to these topics. Let me mention two aspects.

First, although—or rather because—he held fast to the principle of the *coincidentia oppositorum,* Nicholas, like Ficino or Pico, links his philosophical activity to the tradition, mediated through Neoplatonism (Plotinus, Proclus, Eriugena) of the ancient academic thinking about methodology (the "unwritten doctrines"): a system of derivations; a hierarchical construction of Being; the henological link to an ultimate principle that nevertheless remains inaccessible and ineffable, and can be expressed (if at all) only in very concise linguistic terms; and the ontological priority of the numbers (which points ahead to Galileo and Kepler). Nicholas formulates the Platonic idea of "dialectic" differently from Hegel. He demands what he himself demonstrates, namely, the construction of antitheses until the enigmatic, "mystical" point is reached at which they coincide. However, they are not left lying on the ground like shattered potsherds, but work together in the sum total of their highest powers, in order to signal the existence of the *tertium* that must be beyond them both. (This *coincidentia* may also be the effect of a mutual deconstruction.) Without looking at a being and making a claim upon it—whether the being of the object or process under discussion, or the being of Being itself (God)—it is impossible to conduct a dialectic that will get to work on the contradictions and controversies in "theory" and "praxis," in methodological theory, both in the naming of the origin and in the labors of (ecclesiastical) politics, in the struggle of life.

Secondly, despite working all his life in the service of the Roman church, Nicholas is not unreservedly a theologian. He distances himself from Scholasticism, though without doing so explicitly: he published no *quaestiones* or *summa,* nor any continuous commentaries, but only exegeses of specific points. His entire oeuvre is marked by the tension between a historical consciousness, a strong interest in the empirical investigation of secular *singularia,* and an utterly intrepid intellectual concentration on the origin or on unity, as well as by tendencies to think in mathematical terms. Although it is necessary to draw a distinction between philosophy and theology and define these terms precisely, we must accept that they are closely intertwined in Nicholas (as so often in the Renaissance). This is particularly clear in a "special instance in the history of transmission" (V. Mertens, MFCG 30), namely, the two hundred and ninety-three texts commonly known as *Sermones.* It is only recently that a complete edition has been published. They amount to no less than a third of Nicholas's writings, and are roughly twelve times as long as the three books of the *Docta ignorantia.* They contain the entire spectrum of his interests—theology and philosophy, mathematics and natural sciences, politics and history. Each of the two series of texts forms as it were the other side, *recto* or *verso,* of the other series, but both strands are interwoven like a double helix. It is indeed true that strong emphases can be observed. The circa sixty texts that go back to Nicholas's journey as legate are marked by the church-political issue of the indulgence—*Faith without works is dead!*—and the principal theme of the one hundred and sixty-seven texts from the period in Brixen (1452–1458) is Christology. But precisely in the case of Nicholas of Cusa, the speech-act of preaching, with its homiletic foundation, does not in the least exclude philosophical analysis, a clear view of matters concerning life in the world, political events, the concern for the unity of the West, and details of natural science.

It is possible that neither the philosophers nor the theologians today will be willing to give up "their" Nicholas of Cusa. At any rate, this classic polarization will provide food for discussion for many years to come, and in such a *varietas rituum,* the only way to establish the *una religio* is probably the use of some kind of force.

This brings us to the question posed above: What is Nicholas of Cusa today, and what will he be in the future? Once again, let me mention two aspects.

First, he is an instructive example of how one can hold out under tensions, whether secular, societal, economic, spiritual, theological, philosophical, or scientific. His defense of a transparent order converges with an infinitism that remains optimistic despite all the sobering insight into human limitations and which inspires creativity—not as a trivial game, but as a reaction to the distress of the age.

Second, he is a paradigm of a universal semiotics in the light of infinity and immortality. If all knowledge is necessarily transmitted via signs, mirrors, and parables, and can be gained only by "symbolic investigation," this entails a disenchantment (with a nominalistic coloring) of false claims to power. Since the human person can never attain the *vocabulum praecisum* (the real term)—for that would be the object itself—all that remains is the reference (phonic, graphic, or of some other kind) of the signs to their origin, the human spirit. And this spirit should become an image of the absolute.

Despite prodigious scholarly endeavors, many aspects of Nicholas's work—sources and contexts, forms and intentions—remain insufficiently clear. Nevertheless, it is probably the union, and indeed the fusion, of antithetical tendencies that makes the writings of Nicholas of Cusa so interesting and fruitful an object of study both today and in the future.

Note: See *Acta Cusana* in the References. For secondary sources see André, Krieger, and Schwaetzer; Blum 2002; Casarella; Gandillac; Kremer and Reinhard; Machetta and d'Amico; Meier-Oeser; Meuthen; Senger; Vansteenberghe; Yamaki. Book series devoted to Nicolas of Cusa are *Mitteilungen und Forschungsbeiträge der Cusanus-Gesellschaft* (MFCG), Mainz, later Trier 1961 ff. (thirty-two vols. published so far); *Buchreihe der Cusanus-Gesellschaft,* Trier 1964 ff. (sixteen vols. and five separate studies published so far); and *Trierer Cusanus Lectures,* Trier 1994 ff. (fourteen vols. published so far).

5

LEON BATTISTA ALBERTI

(1404–1472)

Philosophy of Private and Public Life and of Art

Michaela Boenke

ALBERTI'S LIFE

Battista Alberti, who later added "Leon" to his name, was born in Genoa on February 14, 1404, during the exile of the Alberti family, and grew up in northern Italy. After a humanistic education and the study of classics under the celebrated humanist Gasparino Barzizza in Padua (1415–1418), Alberti began the study of canon law in Bologna, where he took his doctorate in 1428; he also studied mathematics, physics, and optics. Initially, he made a name for himself as a writer. He wrote his first literary work, the *Philodoxeus fabula,* circa 1424 and published it as the work of "Lepidus," an alleged author of late antiquity. This name means "comic" or "ridiculous," and Lepidus became the main interlocutor in Alberti's satirical writings. This work was followed by *De commodis litterarum atque incommodis* (1428), on the advantages and disadvantages of the scholarly life, and important treatises on moral philosophy and satires, including the satirical *Intercoenales*

(Dinner Pieces; ca. 1430–1449), table-talk composed in the style of Lucian, and the *Libri della famiglia* (1433).

In 1432 Alberti was appointed secretary for Latin correspondence at the papal court, a position he occupied under Popes Eugene IV, Nicholas V, and Pius II. In Rome, he was actively involved in the protection of antiquities and wrote a description of the city of Rome using a geodetic instrument that he himself had invented. After the dramatic flight of Pope Eugene IV from the Vatican, Alberti, as a member of the Curia, went to Florence, the center of cultural life, in 1434. After the Council of Ferrara moved to Florence, he spent a second period in his family's home town. He had amicable relations with famous humanists: with his curial colleague, the scholar Poggio Bracciolini, who had rediscovered Vitruvius's *Ten Books on Architecture* in 1414; with the physician, mathematician, and astronomer Paolo Toscanelli; with Christoforo Landino, who presents Alberti as the spokesman of the Platonists in his *Camaldolese Disputations;* and with the most important artists of his age—with Brunelleschi, who rediscovered perspective construction *(costruzione leggitima),* Donatello, the Della Robbias, Ghiberti, and others. He also became acquainted with works by Masaccio, who introduced the central perspective into painting.

During his time in Florence, he wrote the treatise *De pictura* (1435) on the theory of painting and another treatise, "On Perspective," which was first published in the nineteenth century; the attribution of the latter work is, however, uncertain. There followed a treatise, *De statua* (On Sculpture, 1436; sometimes dated ca. 1450), and other literary texts: the dialogues *Theogenius* (1440), one of Alberti's darkest works, and *Della tranquillità dell'anima* (1442). He also wrote the fourth book of the *Della Famiglia,* entitled "On Friendship" (1441), and presented it on the occasion of a poetry competition, the Certame Coronario, which he himself had founded. In this period, he also wrote the first textbook of the Tuscan language, the *Grammatica della lingua volgare.* As a Florentine born in exile, Alberti could rely on the help of Tuscan-speaking friends when he composed the first works written in the *lingua volgare.*

After the Curia returned to Rome in 1443, Alberti wrote two of his most important works, the *Treatise on Architecture* (completed ca. 1452; versions in Latin and Italian), which unites the theory of architecture with reflections on state and society, and its satirical counterpart, the allegorical novel *Momus sive De principe* (Momus, or The Prince, ca. 1444–1450). The *Ludi rerum mathematicarum* were written in 1450/1452, followed by the *Trivia senatoria,* a manual of rhetoric dedicated to Lorenzo de Medici. Alberti wrote the last of his Italian dialogues, *De iciarchia,* toward the end of his life (1469/1470).

From 1450 onward, Alberti was increasingly active as an architect. Pope Nicholas V made him his advisor on urban planning in the city of Rome, and in this capacity he directed the restoration of buildings, aqueducts, and fountains. He became one of the most sought-after architects of the fifteenth century, and set new benchmarks for Renaissance architecture. His harmonious and elegant buildings include the church of San Francesco (the Templum Malatestianum) in Rimini, the façade of Santa Maria Novella and the Palazzo Ruccelai in Florence, and the churches of Sant'Andrea and San Sebastiano in Mantua.

Alberti died in Rome in April 1472. The variety of his activities and the outstanding quality of his achievements earned him the name of the first *uomo universale,* the first universal genius of the Renaissance.

MORAL PHILOSOPHY

In his writings on moral philosophy, Alberti discusses the conditions necessary for a harmonious life guided by reason, in keeping with the commonplace of *bene et beate vivere* that goes back to Cicero. In the form of dialogues, the *Libri della famiglia* concentrate on the ethics of private life, taking up the relationships between old and young family members, questions of education and personal formation (Book 1); friendship, love, sexuality, and marriage (Book 2); the running of a household, including the various aspects of life in the city and in a country house, questions of clothing, how to treat servants, the administration and increase of private fortune, and the separation between family and business matters (Book 3). The fundamental economic principle of *masserizia* (thrift) is to govern the organization of the household, paying heed to what is *utile* ("useful"). "Virtue, benevolence, and sociability" add a further dimension of the *honestum* as superior virtue.

The ethics of private life are complemented by reflections on the ethics of public life in Alberti's treatise on architecture *(On the Art of Building*

in Ten Books). The ideal city should be built on the site that is climatical-
ly, economically, and strategically most favorable. The layout of the buildings reflects the hierarchically structured social classes; in this way, an ideal city plan promotes social peace. The public welfare is to be entrusted not
to the philosophers but to the architects, as Jupiter himself must acknowledge after his fruitless journeys to the philosophers in the novel *Momus*
(280). At the beginning of the "Ten Books on Architecture" Alberti writes:
"The conclusion is that for the service, honor, and ornament of the public,
we are exceedingly obliged to the architect; to whom, in time of leisure, we
are indebted for tranquility, pleasure, and health; in time of business, for
assistance and profit; and in both, for security and dignity."

Alberti the humanist does not ascribe any transcendental meaning
to life, nor subject it to the guidance of divine providence. He knows of
no demonic powers, and does not defend any religion. When he speaks of
God, he does so in a colloquial manner that takes God for granted. He is
far from elevating the human person to the *telos,* to the crown of the creation, which important humanists of his age found so natural—compare
the discourse *De dignitate et excellentia hominis* of Gianozzo Manetti, who
worked in Naples—and from the concept of the *copula mundi* ("knot and
bond of the universe"). By means of an implicit debate with Cicero, whose
anthropological theses in the treatise *De natura deorum* were widely dif-
fused in the Renaissance,[1] Alberti displays in the *Theogenius* the reverse
side of an attitude that identifies the dignity of the human person in his endeavor to create "as it were a second world in the natural world." Alberti rejected the anthropocentrism characteristic of Western thought as a whole.
The dignity of the human person lies not in a special ontological status inferred by metaphysical reasoning, but in his own nature. In the *Libri della
famiglia,* Gianozzo affirms that three things are the property of the human
person, bestowed on him by nature and inseparable from him: soul, body,
and time. The true preconditions for a good and happy life are mastery of
the body and the passions and the prudent conduct of life; and this can
only be successful by living in accordance with nature (56f.). The dispute
between *virtù* and *fortuna*—a Renaissance commonplace—is decided in
favor of prudent and virtuous action. At the beginning of "Della famiglia"
Alberti states: "Fate only triumphs over those who submit to it."

1. Cf. especially II, 60–63.

Nevertheless, a pessimistic undertone frequently breaks through in Alberti's writings on moral philosophy. The speeches of Gianozzo in *Della famiglia* already display a clear distance vis-à-vis public life, and Genipatro says in the *Theogenius* that he does not feel lonely in his withdrawn life, dedicated to science and to the investigation of nature, but enjoys the excellent and jovial company of satirical writers, of Plautus, Terence, Apuleius, Lucian, and Martial. This dialogue closes with the praise of death (*Opere*, ed. Grayson, 2.74 and 102ff.).

SATIRICAL WRITINGS

Satire is perhaps the most fascinating area of Alberti's literary production. In the "Dinner Pieces" (*Intercoenales,* written in the style of Lucian) and the novel *Momus, or The Prince,* Alberti depicts the shady side of the bourgeois moral philosophy and way of life. From the beginning of his literary activity, Alberti's works are permeated by the criticism of erroneous developments in public and private life, by the uncovering of abysses in the human soul (going as far as the reflection on cannibalism in the dialogue *Naufragium* [Shipwreck]), and by the unmasking of the incompetence and frivolity of those who hold political power. His writings typically employ the parallelism between construction and deconstruction, between the creation of an ideal and its satirical demolition. Construction is the work of the day, deconstruction the work of the night: in the genealogy of the gods, Momus, the hero of the novel that bears his name, is the son of the night, and Alberti writes in the prologue that this book is "the result of his nocturnal labors." It is a cynical, audacious, blasphemous work. In Alberti, construction and deconstruction always go hand in hand. On the one hand, we have the *Libri della famiglia,* and, on the other hand, the narrative of the life of Saint Potitus (*Vita Sancti Potiti,* 1433), which denounces bourgeois values as the work of the devil, and the first *Intercoenales,* in which the dialogue *Defunctus* and the bizarre visions of the dialogues *Fortuna* and *Somnium* stand out. In the *Defunctus,* the dead man observes his own funeral ceremonies from the roof of a neighboring house and must acknowledge that his life, which had been governed by *virtus,* was an illusion: he sees the infidelity of his wife and the joy his son feels at the freedom he has suddenly gained, and he sees how his business is ruined and his literary work destroyed. In the *Somnium,* a man dreams that he is wandering through the world of human passions and incompetences, a world that has congealed into a bizarre landscape. Ludovico Ariosto imitated this dream vision in the celebrated lunar scene in his *Orlando Furioso* (34, 72–92).

What Garin calls Alberti's "subtle and refined style"—which portrays the factors that determine reality by means of the antithesis between a constructive and a deconstructive, cynical, and satirical presentation— reaches its climax in the interplay between the treatise on architecture and the allegorical novel *Momus.* Its hero Momus is the Greek god of cynicism. He summarizes the experiences he has gained on earth by saying that public life is determined by dissimulation, the willful misrepresentation of facts, and the concealment of one's own egotistical motivations, which are hidden behind a mask of propriety and uprightness. After describing his wanderings on earth, Momus presents his praise of the vagabond life as the only form of life that is unaffected by deceit and self-deception and by the universal nexus of cheating, *simulando et dissimulando* (2.131ff.). Each in its own way, both *Momus* and the architectural treatise depict the structures of societal-political life. The antithesis to the *demonstratio diurna,* the image of the "good government" in the *Art of Building,* is the *demonstratio nocturna* of the bad government of Jupiter. In *Momus,* the gods appear as participants in the human tragicomedy in the "world theater." The spectacular culmination of the novel is a grotesque Götterdämmerung and the flight of the gods from a world that has lost all virtues and ideals (4.218ff.).

TREATISES ON THE THEORY OF ART

Alberti's writings on painting, sculpture, and architecture provided a theoretical basis for artistic activity and thereby founded a new academic discipline, namely, the theory of art. His treatises include both philosophical reflections on the status of art and of the artist and technical instructions for the creation of a work of art. They offer the artist the theoretical means that allow him to create harmonious works on the basis of mathematical laws. The relationships of musical consonance and the rules of rhetorical composition (following Quintilian and Cicero) serve as the models of harmonious proportions; the prototype of beautiful art is that which is beautiful in nature. Traditionally, artists had had the low status of a handworker *(faber)* who often remained anonymous; now, they are freed from this role and acquire the status of a scholar and creator who combines both theoretical knowledge and practical activity. As an observer and investigator of nature and of its laws, and as the author of works that realize these laws in new creations, the artist is "a second god."

The treatise *On Painting*—composed in a Latin version (1435) for scholars and in an Italian version, dedicated to Brunelleschi (1436), for the use of artists—is the first modern treatment of this subject. Book 1 contains the earliest theoretical formulation of the linear perspective for portraying three-dimensional objects in accordance with the laws of optics and geometry. Here, Alberti could appeal to his own optical experiments and to perspectivist studies by Brunelleschi, although he made decisive alterations to these. Alberti's chessboard method constructs the optic pyramid from the painter's or viewer's eyepoint; at the same time, he inserts a vanishing point at the same height in the picture itself. The exact geometrical construction includes both the lines that run from this vanishing point (which indicates infinity) to the base line and the lines (optic beams) that run from the eyepoint to the surface of the painting. Book 2 discusses the composition of pictures. Its three main parts deal with alignment, composition, and light and color. Book 3 discusses the artist and his relationship to the other *artes*.

According to Alberti, the division of painting into three parts is based in nature itself, like the activity of painting, which imitates the reflection of physical nature in the flat surface of springs of water. This recourse to nature is fundamentally important for Alberti: it denotes a mimesis in keeping with the laws of seeing: "If painting wishes to portray something visible, we must pose the question how we see something." What is involved here is not the copying of objects by painting them on a flat surface, but the principles of construction that lead to the creation of a concrete object in the picture itself—which is understood as a "window" in a new sense foreign to the medieval understanding. The three-dimensional object in nature, which occupies a space, appears in the picture first of all as an outline, a limitation of space in the surface. The spatial depth comes about through the mathematical division of surfaces in accordance with the perspectivist construction of vanishing point and eyepoint. After the completion of the formal composition, the appearance of the objects in their apparently three-dimensional physicality is brought about through the material of painting, that is, through colors, light, and shade. Colors must be used in keeping with the principle of friendship between contrasting colors. Alberti elaborated his own theory of color, which affirms that white and black symbolize the presence and absence of light, while the colors blue, red, green, and gray symbolize the elements sky, fire, water, and earth. (Later, Leonardo was to replace the gray of the earth with yellow.)

Book III deals with the *historia* or subjects of painting. As M. Baxandall has shown (1971), the composition of a painting is constructed in a manner analogous to the art of rhetoric. According to rhetorical tradition, clauses are formed from words, and sentences are formed from clauses. A sentence becomes a whole by means of the full stop at the end. Similarly, members come into being by drawing the outlines of the planes, and bodies come into being by joining the members. The bodies join together to form the *historia* of the picture. This is the objective of *pictura* (painting, figuring): the painter represents events, actions, that is, *historia* (story) by way of transforming movements of the soul into those of bodies. In order to identify the means necessary for this transformation and to find the right theme *(inventio)*, and in order to evoke in the viewer the desired effect, namely, *voluptas*, Alberti recommends that painters take up anew the themes of classical antiquity and study ancient rhetoric, since the rules governing its composition are also the normative aesthetic categories of the art of painting, namely, *varietas, copia* (to be employed with dignity and moderation), and *decorum*.

The treatise *On Sculpture*, which Alberti likewise understands as *pictura*, takes up the idea of mimesis as laid down in the treatise on painting: a sculpture is the imitation of an archetype, both in the Platonic sense of the idea of the object represented (of a living being, and by preference of the human being), and with regard to the specific form. Here too "imitation" does not mean the copying of an object that exists in nature, but a constructive proceeding that brings about ideal ratios and proportions. By removing material, the sculptor allows the form or shape to appear which—in the Aristotelian sense—was already present in the material in a hidden way, as a potential. The form is constructed on the basis of exact measurements with *exempeda* and a *definitor*, instruments invented by Alberti for calculating proportions and variables produced by movement.

The treatise *On Architecture,* the fruit of an intensive study of Vitruvius, is Alberti's chef d'oeuvre in the theory of art and philosophy. His theory of architecture is based on philosophical presuppositions that point above all to Platonic sources. He requires the ideal city to resemble Plato's ideal state as closely as possible; and both the basic aesthetic concept of *concinnitas* (harmonious proportions) and the relationship to musical art go back to Plato's *Philebus.* The idea of beauty is an innate idea *(ratio innata)* in the Platonic sense: the physical beauty is the imitation of an archetype of the beautiful mediated by mathematical-musical laws. An exact calculation is needed in order to discover these laws: Plato's *Timaeus* and the Pythagorean doctrine of harmony lie behind the musical and mathematical calculations of the treatise *On Architecture.*

There is a convergence between the aesthetic harmony deriving from beauty and ornament (which Alberti defines Platonically as the splendor of beauty) and the concept of utility transcending the work of art. Alberti defines beauty, the idea of which is innate in the human person, as *concinnitas:* "Beauty is a form of sympathy and consonance between the parts within a body, according to definite number [*numerus*], outline [*finitio*], and position [*collocatio*], as dictated by *concinnitas,* the absolute and fundamental rule in Nature" (*Art of Building,* Book XI, ch. 5). Alberti writes that *concinnitas,* defined in Platonic terms as the "spouse and soul of reason" and as *ratio innata,* governs both nature and the entire life and thought of the human person.

Number defines the quantity of the elements of a building on the analogy of the structure of the human body. The "limbs" of a building must be even numbers, and the "limbs" of the openings (doors and windows) must be uneven. The proportions of columns and pilasters are oriented to the proportions in living beings, especially in human bodies. This "aesthetic anthropometry" (to use Panofsky's phrase) is also found in the structure *(collocatio)* of the elements of a building in terms of their spatial position: the correct structure is based on symmetry and proportions, which are calculated with the help of laws of harmony in music or arithmetic means.

Finitio, defined as "a certain mutual correspondence of those several lines by which proportion is measured," is the central element of Alberti's architectural theory. "Understanding and reflection" are required for establishing the basic lines *(lineamenta);* this procedure is based on an intellectual outline *(conjectatio in mente)*. The calculation of the length, breadth, and height of buildings, and of the proportions between surfaces and ornamentation, follows the laws of the Pythagorean doctrine of harmony and geometrical calculations. Once again, Alberti's equation of musical with spatial proportions is based on nature, since according to Pythagorean-Platonic teaching, natural harmony is based on musical proportions: "The very same numbers that cause sounds to have *concinnitas,* pleasing to the ear, can also fill the eyes and mind with wondrous delight."

With the help of these factors, it is possible to calculate a "musical" ratio of the planes of the building, as well as the ideal height (or third dimension).[2] The geometrical calculation is to be used when the dimensions cannot be calculated in natural numbers. The arithmetical calculation to establish the *finitio* works out the mean proportion from given quantities. The task of discovering the mean ratio is directly related to Alberti's ethics, which gives the central position to the idea of *mediocritas,* the correct mean, and to the satirical texts, which present the deviation from the mean in sometimes bizarre forms and sequences reminiscent of dreams.

Alberti's buildings, constructed in keeping with *concinnitas,* the principle of harmony, are the primary evidence of the great importance that he attached to the exact calculation of harmonious proportions. For example, the form given to the façade of Santa Maria Novella is based on the perfect cube and the ratio 1:2, or octave. The treatise *On Architecture* affirms that *concinnitas* also means structuring the various parts upon an elaborate plan in such a way that they are pleasant to look at; accordingly, *concinnitas* concerns also the harmonious union of old and new. This can be seen in Alberti's first architectural project, the musical modulation of his remodeling of the church of San Francesco in Rimini, with its façade based on Pythagorean harmonies (the octave and the fifth).

The well-thought-out program of Alberti's philosophy of art integrates art into the framework of the humanistic *artes:* art, which is based on the humanistic sciences of the *trivium* (rhetoric) and the *quadrivium* (arithmetic, geometry, and music), is a science, not merely technical skill. Alberti identified the place of art within the humanistic sciences; the artist is a student of nature, a scientist and a craftsman at one and the same time.

2. There are exact calculations by Karvouni, Naredi-Rainer, Morelli, and Ghirardini in the catalogue to the 1994 Alberti exhibition in Mantua; cf. Rykwert and Engel.

SUBSEQUENT INFLUENCE

Alberti's posthumous fame is based especially on the *Libri della Famiglia* and the treatises on painting and architecture, as well as on his own architectural creations. His writings on the theory of art were always available. After A. Bonucci had published his editions of the *Opere volgari* (1843–1849), the nineteenth century discovered Alberti the civic humanist, the theorist of civic morality. The satirical writings remained largely unnoticed; Ariosto integrated the "dinner piece" *Somnium* into his *Orlando Furioso,* and Giordano Bruno revived the figure of Momus in his *Spaccio della besta trionfante* (The Expulsion of the Triumphant Beast, 1584).

The cynical zeitgeist circa 1500 led not to the rediscovery, but to the first discovery of *Momus,* which Alberti himself had never published. It went through two editions in Rome in 1520, and was translated into Spanish and Italian in the course of the sixteenth century. A German translation—very free and done without love—was published by the Kaiser Verlag in Vienna in 1790. It was only in the second half of the twentieth century, especially thanks to the intensive editorial and interpretative work of Eugenio Garin, that Alberti the satirist was rediscovered.

Alberti's theory of art formed the starting point and often the basis of the rapidly growing number of treatises on art theory in the fifteenth- and sixteenth-century Renaissance. Sometimes, scholars had direct recourse to Alberti, but sometimes his theories were transmitted or criticized without specifying the sources. Ludovico Dolce's *Dialogue on Painting,* composed circa 1550, places Alberti's arguments on the lips of Aretino; Piero della Francesca's treatise *De prospectiva pingendi* (ca. 1485) betrays the influence of Alberti. The most important followers of Alberti's theory of painting are Leonardo da Vinci, who had studied Alberti's treatises on painting and architecture very closely and very probably possessed copies of them (in addition to other works by Alberti), and Dürer. Leonardo also adopted (with some modifications) Alberti's theory of colors, which otherwise found few adherents; centuries later, it influenced Goethe's theory of color. The treatise *On Architecture* was published posthumously in 1486; previously, it had been available in a few manuscripts. It influenced Filarete's *Treatise on Architecture* (1461/1462). Giovanni Paolo Lomazzo's *Idea of the Temple of Painting* (1590) and Henry Wotton's *Elements of Architecture*

(1624) still refer to Alberti's doctrine of proportions and give an account of the symmetry between musical and spatial proportions that was the basis of his work.

Alberti left a lasting impression on Renaissance art. His treatise on painting had an exceptionally strong influence on the painting of Andrea Mantegna and found its perfect pictorial representation, in terms of both form and content, in the Camera degli Sposi in the Palazzo Ducale in Milan. Works by Piero della Francesca, Pisanello, and Jacopo Bellini were likewise inspired by Alberti's treatise on painting. His buildings, above all his ingenious designs for façades, became the most influential archetypes of Renaissance architecture in the fifteenth and sixteenth centuries; his musical theory of architecture exerted particular influence on Andrea Palladio's theory of art and architecture.

Note: See the works by Alberti in the References. For secondary sources see Aiken; Baxandall; Borsi; Gadol; Garin; Grafton; Jarzombek; Mitrović; Rykwert; and Tavernor.

6

GIOVANNI PICO DELLA MIRANDOLA
(1463–1494)

The Synthetic Reconciliation of
All Philosophies

Stéphane Toussaint

Giovanni Pico della Mirandola, prince and philosopher, was celebrated for the rare coincidence of his intellectual and physical beauty as the "Phoenix,"[1] that is, an emblematic and unique talent in the philosophical landscape of the fifteenth century. He was born on February 24, 1463, in the ancient fief of Mirandola and Concordia in northern Italy, the son of the knight Gianfrancesco I (who died soon afterward) and the learned noblewoman Giulia Boiardo, whose nephew wrote the *Orlando Innamorato*. According to one tradition, a sudden flash of lightning surrounded his mother during her pregnancy, presaging a great fate for the child, and a wet nurse, under divine inspiration, predicted that the child would have extraordinary gifts.[2] Giovanni Pico was destined at an early age for an ecclesiastical career, and he studied canon law in Bologna until the death of his mother in 1478. However, he was much

---

1. Sixtus Senensis, *Bibliotheca Sancta* (Venice, 1566), 4.422.
2. G. F. Pico 1994, 32–34.

more interested in literature. In the following years, we find him first at the court of the Este dynasty in Ferrara, then in Padua and Pavia.

It was now that Pico's real intellectual apprenticeship began. From 1480 to 1483 he studied Aristotelian philosophy, which was dominant at the universities of that period, under the guidance of two celebrated teachers, Nicoletto Vernia and Elia del Medigo. In 1483 he studied logic and mathematics in Pavia, but he also kept up the contacts that he had made in Florence during his first visit in 1479, as we see in his first letter to Angelo Poliziano (1454–1494; cf. Pico 1942, 3–4), where he asks for an evaluation of his elegies *De amoribus*. Other letters written in 1483 show that Pico was fascinated by the Florentine poetical model. Similarly, his lifelong friendship with Girolamo Benivieni[3] and the more problematic friendship with Marsilio Ficino, the author of the *Theologia Platonica* (1482), went back to this first visit to Florence. It was probably at that time that Pico had his first contact with the *famiglia platonica,* since he refers in a letter written to Ficino in 1482 to the advice the latter had given him years before with regard to his philosophical studies.[4] According to this letter, Ficino had encouraged Pico to read Aristotle as a preparation for the study of the higher Platonic wisdom. On July 15, 1484, Pico wrote a letter to Lorenzo de' Medici about the poetry of Dante and Petrarch. His emphasis here on the relationship between philosophy and poetry, truth and style, anticipates the principal theme of the letter he was to write in June 1485 to the Venetian Ermolao Barbaro (*De genere dicendi philosophorum; Opera* 351f.; and Bausi 1998). This first genuinely philosophical text by Pico already contains the profundity of thought and the irony that are characteristic of his more mature works.

This was preceded in December 1484 by other letters to Barbaro in which Pico expressed the wish to move on "from Aristotle to the Academy," in order to achieve a synthesis between Aristotle and Plato. "Their words could not be more antithetical, but in the substance, they could not be more in agreement," he writes in a passage which recurs in the *Conclusiones (Nine Hundred Theses)* and in the *De Ente et Uno.* The letter *De genere dicendi philosophorum* defends the philosophical knowledge of the "Pari-

---

3. Municipal Archive, Florence, Archivio Leonetti-Manucci-Gianni, ms. 43, c.35.
4. Viti 1994, 127.

sians," that is, the medieval teaching, against the claims made by the classical rhetoric that Barbaro prized so highly. Pico presents this defense brilliantly, in the form of a debate between the two styles of intellectual life, namely, the dialectical search for the truth and the emulation of the eloquence of antiquity.

Ermolao Barbaro, who had translated Themistius, a commentator on Aristotle in late antiquity, was himself regarded as a "Peripatetic" of the avant-garde, a man whose inclinations lay not so much in the Aristotelianism of the Middle Ages as in a return to the sources and a philological reading of ancient philosophers. He criticized the teaching methods of some of his colleagues in Padua, including Pico's teacher Elia del Medigo, who was a radical adherent of the Averroist tradition.[5] Pico sought a commitment to the investigation of an underlying structure of knowledge which went further than the humanistic projects of the immediately preceding generation of scholars such as Lorenzo Valla or Leonardo Bruni, and this made it difficult for him to reach a consensus with Barbaro on the question whether the language of philosophy ought to be exclusively "Greco-Latin" or (as Pico demanded) a purely conventional statement of the truth that was indifferent to the "elegances" of the grammarians. This position did not, however, entail any return to pre- or antihumanist values, nor the denial of the most recent philological and rhetorical achievements of the "grammarians": when Pico praised the translation of Themistius, he was in complete agreement with Barbaro. He does not criticize grammar as the *first* stage of the knowledge of things, but beautiful writing as the *ultimate* goal of intellectual endeavor.

Pico was not disturbed by the acute reply of Barbaro, who accused him justly of making use of poetic and "fabulous" (i.e., humanist) arguments in order to defend a "barbarous" (i.e., Scholastic) philosophy. In his constant search for solidity and substantiality in philosophy, Pico traveled to Paris immediately after this debate, in the summer of 1485. All that we know about his first visit to that city was that the "dialectical tournaments" and *quodlibeta* at the Sorbonne inspired him to begin his ambitious project of a great philosophical disputation in Rome, his celebrated *Conclusiones* or *Theses*.

5. Cassuto 1918, 284f.; Geffen 1973–1974; Fornaciari 1992.

Pico returned to Florence in 1486 and reflected on what he had learned in his studies in Padua, Pavia, and Paris. In addition to a mystical Averroism that he never denied,[6] there was now a strong influence from Paris, from his reading of Plato and Plotinus (which he had studied with Ficino), and from the mysterious Jewish tradition of the Cabbala. The rationalist Elia del Medigo regarded this last element with scant sympathy. His famous letter[7] about Averroes's *Physica* and *De substantia orbis* does indeed also discuss the infinity of the En Sof of the Cabbalists, but it speaks disparagingly of "that blessed Cabbala" *(isto benedicto Chabala),* as if he already was afraid of the new esoteric direction that his pupil was taking; however, Elia was in fact the first to note the important equivalence between the *Zephiroth* and the *numerationes . . . fluxa ab Infinito,* which Pico later develops further in the *Commento* and the *Conclusiones.* Pico found a counterweight to Elia's criticism in the person of another teacher, Guglielmo Raimondi di Moncada, also known as Flavius Mithridates, the translator of "very ancient" and valuable Hebrew texts, the most significant of which was the commentary on the Song of Songs by Levi ben Gershom.[8]

Pico displayed a striking intellectual vigor in the months between the spring of 1486 (the period of an unhappy erotic adventure, the "abduction" of the beautiful Margherita de' Medici in Arezzo) and the publication of the *Conclusiones* on December 7 of the same year. In these months, he read the Cabbalists, newly discovered Hebrew philosophers such as Levi ben Gershom, Maimonides, Nahmanides and others, Plotinus, Hermes Trismegistus, the Chaldaean Oracles, Simplicius, Themistius, Philostratus, Iamblichus, Averroes, Avicenna, Thomas Aquinas, Duns Scotus, Henry of Ghent, among others, and the number of *Conclusiones* grew from seven hundred to nine hundred. In this short space of time, Pico not only composed the *Conclusiones,* but also the *Commento sulla Canzone d'amore,* in which he developed an independent theory of the nature of the beautiful in Plato, and the celebrated *Oratio de Hominis Dignitate,* which is regarded as the manifesto of the new Renaissance thinking. Pico himself calls this a moment of glory under the sign of the Egyptian sphinx (Pico 1942, 581), in which, inspired

---

6. Nardi 1958, 127–46.

7. Contained in the Paris Latin codex B.N.F.lat.6508. Published in Pico 1942, 68–71. On Pico and Kabbalah, see Wirszubski, Idel, and Copenhaver 1999; Busi; and Campanini.

8. Viti 1994, 171f.

by the ideal of freedom and of an all-encompassing harmony, the message of the secret "poetical theologians" of the pagans agrees with the most hidden aspects of the Hebrew and "Chaldaean" tradition.

The *Oratio de Hominis Dignitate,*[9] in which Pico formulates the essence of his philosophy of human nature and of the freedom of the creation within the universe, was meant as a prelude to the disputation of the *Nine Hundred Theses* in Rome. Pico sees in the human being, Adam—who is called a "great miracle" in keeping with the Hermetic tradition of the address to Asclepius—an ontological miracle. This, however, owes its existence to a miracle of philosophical-literary fusion. Here, the God of Genesis speaks like Hermes Trismegistus, and this entails a radical shift from the perspective of the biblical creation, with the associated concepts of nature and person (cf. Boethius and Thomas Aquinas), in the direction of a gnosis similar to that found in Evagrius and Origen, whose doctrinal orthodoxy Pico defends in the *Theses.* As the son of a God who is seen against the background of a new cabbalistic Hermeticism as the "divine architect," the human person can become the *plastes et fictor sui,* the "producer" of his own self in a dynamic that is either regenerative or degenerative.

The divine Logos no longer speaks in the terms of a logic that possesses an existential character for the economy of the entire creation, but in dynamic concepts that accordingly are "free" of any preexistent model or archetype. It is not enough to call this freedom "existential" (where the human becomes what he wants) or "moral" (where the human person himself chooses what he wants), since it is a higher freedom in which the old model of a hierarchical nature is replaced by the *rationes seminales* of a discourse about the human person qua human person, who is given a place both in the world and outside the world. Pico is speaking here of the human person per se, considered in his ability to transcribe the plan of the creative word in the architectonic discourse of many various philosophies. Pico presented this position with great effect to the Roman theologians who were to have discussed his *Nine Hundred Theses.*[10]

---

9. Cf. Bori, De Pace, and the critical edition by Bausi: Pico 2003

10. At ego ita me institui, ut in nullius verba iuratus, me per omnes philosophiae magistros funderem, . . . omnigenae doctrinae placita in medium afferre volui, ut hac complurium sectarum collatione ac multifarie discussione philosophiae, ille veritatis fulgor, . . . animis nostris quasi sol oriens ex alto clarius illusceret (Pico 1942, 138–42). The *Nine Hundred Theses* are available in English in the edition of von S. A. Farmer 1998.

This is why the tendency to isolate the introductory discourse about Adam from the *archana sapientia* which runs through the *Conclusiones* risks reducing this discourse to a mere "philosophy of life." The metaphysics of the *Oratio* is much more demanding because Adam's infinite malleability is praised in the context of a project that seeks to demonstrate the "concord" of all ancient and modern systems. The basic idea in the discourse about the human person is thus generated by the ability to reshape the history of Western and Eastern thought in accordance with a mental process typical of the new epoch, a process aiming at the unity and infinity of all human knowledge. At the heart of Pico's "tripartite philosophy" (moral, dialectical, contemplative), the "winged lovers" inspired by Apollo (Pico 1942, 124) must discover the innermost structure of reality, which presents itself in "numerical" and harmonious laws through which it is possible to distinguish the various levels of the hidden "harmony" between Aristotle and Plato, Averroes and Avicenna, Thomas and Scotus, or the Cabbala and Christianity. This means that the central position of Adam as *protoplastes* in the world corresponds to the central position of the new intellectual in Pico's universalistic thinking.

It is therefore unsurprising that the numerical structure of the *Nine Hundred Theses* is both the expression of a mystical perfection and a comprehensive view of philosophy that unites in itself both the theological-philosophical conclusions according to the philosophers of each school and Pico's own conclusions "according to his own opinion."

Pico not only extends the traditional Scholastic commentary, which is the basis of his philosophy, by means of new authors such as Zoroaster, the "Chaldaean theologians," or the "sages of the Cabbala" (cf. Idel 2000), but also follows up the commentary as such, consisting of roughly four hundred conclusions, with nearly five hundred theses of the "new philosophy," which adduce other arguments such as the "paradoxical theses of reconciliation" and the theses on theology, magic, and the Orphic hymns. When we look at the total architecture of the *Conclusiones*, we can see the genuine speculative breadth of this work, which is entirely oriented to a progressive speculative resolution with its high point in the esoteric schools of the Greeks (Pythagoras and Orpheus), the Chaldaeans (Zoroaster and the Chaldaean theologians), and the Jews (the Cabbala).

Let us summarize the structure and divisions of this work. Of the first

402 theses, 115 are concerned with Scholasticism from Albert the Great to Giles of Rome; 82 with the Arabian Aristotelians from Averroes to Ibn Bagia; 29 with the Greek Peripatetics from Theophrastus to Themistius; 99 with the Greek Platonists from Plotinus to Proclus; 14 with Pythagoras; 6 with the Chaldaean theologians; 10 with Hermes Trismegistus; and 14 with the Cabbalists. This compilation is followed by 498 theses of Pico "according to my own opinion, which . . . are divided into conclusions about physics, theology, Platonism, mathematics, dogmatic paradoxes, theses which reconcile the paradoxes, Chaldaean and Orphic theses, magical and cabbalistic theses," that is, 17 theses that reconcile paradoxes; 80 theses that contradict the widespread philosophy; 71 paradoxical dogmatic theses; 29 theological theses; 62 theses on Platonism; 10 theses on the *Liber de causis;* 11 mathematical conclusions and 74 mathematical *quaestiones;* 15 Chaldaean theses; 26 magical theses; 31 Orphic theses; and 72 cabbalistic theses.

This impressive compilation allows us to gauge the complexity of Pico's project of presenting all known philosophies synthetically in the framework of a reconciliation based on the antithesis between "profane" and "esoteric" knowledge. Pico's conviction that he could decipher doctrines of the most various kinds, which were sometimes mutually contradictory, and reconcile them with one another led him to elaborate a doctrine of his own, often very subtle, in which the metaphysical discourse does not lead into the mysticism of Nicholas of Cusa (which is, however, without any doubt one of the sources of Pico's *concordia discors*), but rather into a dialectical revolution, or at least a unique formal metaphysics. Pico often arrives at surprising results, for example, the equation of the Aristotelian *intellectus agens* with the cabbalistic "angel Metatron" in the second thesis "according to Themistius."

The ideal fusion between the *metaphysicus* and the *dialectus* of which Pico dreamed, and which he presented in what is almost a self-portrait in the eighth thesis according to Alexander of Aphrodisias, evoked incomprehension and fears in the papal commission, which immediately declared some of the theological, magical, and cabbalistic theses to be excessively obscure, paradoxical, and open to the suspicion of heresy.[11] Thirteen the-

---

11. Dorez and Thuasne, 1976, 114f. Cf. Biondi; Paul Richard Blum: "Pico, Theology, and the Church," in Dougherty 2008, 37–60.

ses were at once condemned by Innocent VIII, and the condemnation of
the entire work followed. Despite his vain attempts at a clarification before
the commission, and the publication of an *Apologia,* Pico was arraigned
before the court of the Inquisition. The main points of the accusation were
his theses about the descent of Christ to the underworld, the eucharist, the
justification of Origen, magic, the Cabbala, the nature of the divine intellect, and the freedom of belief. The philosopher was compelled to flee, but
was arrested in Savoy and imprisoned in the jail at Vincennes in Paris.

After interventions by Lorenzo de' Medici, Ficino, and some French
friends, Pico was able to return to Florence in 1488. He concentrated on
the redaction of his commentary on the Psalms and on the *Heptaplus* (i.e.,
a "sevenfold" exegesis), in which he presents the various levels of interpretation of the first part of the Book of Genesis.

Pico remains faithful to his new cabbalistic hermeneutic and to the
"poetic theology" of the pagan myths (about Saturn, Venus, Eros, and
Janus) which he had begun to elaborate in the *Commento,* and concentrates in the *Heptaplus* on the hidden meaning of the words of Moses, in
which he finds esoteric links to other metaphysical traditions about the
nature of the divine creation of the cosmos and of the human being. This
work is closely related to the cosmological treatises of Eriugena, the school
of Chartres, and Alain of Lille. In the ensuing period, Lorenzo de' Medici endeavored in vain to have the Roman condemnation revoked; in this
situation, Pico attempted to demonstrate that the substantial agreement
in the cosmogonic knowledge of all the ages began with the figure of Moses. The underlying methodology may have been essentially the same as
that in the *Conclusiones,* but he had rethought the perspective. This new
perspective began with Scripture, and returned to it after lengthy chapters
in which the Pythagoreans, Chaldaeans, Platonists, and others made their
appearance—as if Pico secretly wanted to counter the accusations leveled
by Pietro Garzia, who had been commissioned by the pope in 1488–1489
to write the *Determinationes magistrales* in rebuttal of the *Apologia,* especially as regarded Pico's interpretation of Scripture.

The topics discussed in the *Heptaplus* are the unity of the indwelling
wisdom, the unbroken tradition of those truths that endure through all
ages, and the deep mystery of creation. In his foreword, Pico declares that
Moses himself showed the way to "the wise men of old" who incline by na-

ture to veil their intention while writing, as was the case with Plato later on (Pico 1942, 172).

The idea that the divine creation is revealed through contemplation of the archetype hidden in the heart of the prophetic words is what truly fascinates Pico, and this was to take on considerable importance in "esoteric" and prophetic literature from the sixteenth to the eighteenth century. Obvious examples of this influence are Francesco Giorgi Veneto ("Zorzi"; 1466–1540) or, in the eighteenth century, Johann Georg Hamann.

In the *Phaedrus*, Plato (in agreement with the Jews) testifies that the creation is articulated in three realms, the intelligible, the heavenly, and the sublunary. Pico observes in these three realms or worlds such a harmony that a secret affinity of nature binds together the objects and the names in each part of the universe. But after the ontological coherence of the secret analogies of the three worlds has been posited, there is yet a fourth world, which reflects this harmony and manifests it in a marvelous way, namely, the human person in his microcosm.

With these premises, Pico's commentary is unfolded in seven books, recalling the days of creation. In the course of his work, he does not refrain from veiled allusions to the Cabbala; indeed, one could say that the cabbalistic wisdom of the "alphabetical transformation" *(ars combinandi)* reaches its zenith in the celebrated close of the *Heptaplus*, which is entirely based on the permutation of the sequence of letters in the first word of Genesis, *Bereshith* ("in the beginning").[12] Here, Pico gives expression to one of his favorite philosophical ideas, the dissection and the new arrangement of formulae and words which in their innermost marrow contain "the knowledge of all arts, of all divine and human wisdom." Ultimately, he discovers in *Bereshith*, in which "the *ratio* of the world and of all things is revealed," the organization of macrocosm and microcosm, the mutual relationship between the cosmos and the heavenly human being, and the verbal seal placed on the entire creation (Pico 1942, 374f.).

In the *Heptaplus*, Pico could still entertain the illusion of a revocation of his condemnation for heresy, but this hope seems no longer to exist in the *De Ente et Uno (On Being and the One)*, probably his most metaphysical work, which he composed in Florence in 1490. It is immediately obvi-

12. Wirszubski 1989, 172f., 233f. Cf. Black 2006.

ous that this treatise, which developed out of a dialogue with Lorenzo de'
Medici and Angelo Poliziano, is a return to the stricter and more abstract
forms of philosophical discourse. Looking back to the disputes between
the Byzantines Gemistos Plethon, George of Trebizond, and Bessarion,
Pico wished to investigate the measure of agreement between the systems
of Aristotle and Plato, that is, between ontology and henology (philosophy of the One). This experiment, unique for its learning and its dialectical
acuteness, begins with an interpretation of Plato's *Parmenides* and *Sophist,*
in which Plato discusses being and nonbeing, and then goes on to Aristotelian metaphysics. He follows the *Quaestio de ente, essentia et uno* of Elia
del Medigo in mentioning the Arabs Averroes and Avicenna in the course
of his discussion.

Here too, in agreement with some Peripatetic and Platonic *Conclusiones,* Pico looks for the meaning that is hidden under the "bark" of the
words, but now he moves on the level of the ideas, of the universals, and of
the divine attributes. The clear and essential concepts employed in the discussion of being, the true, the good, the something and the one, as well as
the virtuosity of the treatment of its subject matter, make Pico's *De Ente et
Uno* the prototype of later investigations of the highest principles by Giordano Bruno, Francesco Patrizi, and the Jesuits of Coimbra. Pico takes a
position against the transcendence of the universals, that is, of being and
of the one, and seeks to demonstrate that in reality these two absolutes are
equivalent, for the precise reason that they belong to historically parallel systems, to Aristotelianism as the philosophy of substance and to Platonism as the philosophy of unity. He denies the purely theological function of Plato's *Parmenides* (which is a vital concern of Ficino, as a reader of
and commentator on Proclus) and undertakes a comprehensive and metic-
ulous investigation of the meaning that should be attached to the designa-
tions of the divine in the central texts of Scholasticism and of ancient philosophy. Here, he appeals inter alia to the *Commentary on the Sentences* and
the *De ente et essentia* of Thomas Aquinas, the *Proslogion* of Anselm, the *De
Mystica Theologia* of Pseudo-Dionysius, the *De vita Pythagorica* of Iamblichus, and to Plotinus. He then makes the canonical distinction between
the divine attributes *quatenus in se* and *quatenus causa,* and moves step by
step to the interchangeability of being and the one.

This led immediately to a dispute with the Thomist *magister* Antonio

Cittadini, to whom Pico sent three letters between 1491 and 1494 with observations and criticisms. This exchange of views makes it clear that Pico
is far from assuming a "logical" interchangeability that would see a *reduc-
tio* of being *ad unum* in the one, or else see being as the only substance that
constitutes that which is real. Rather, his intention in the *De Ente et Uno* is
to reflect on the interchangeability of being and the one with regard to the
infinity of God, or with regard to the question: "What is God?" The answer is that God is called neither being nor one, but "superbeing and su-
perone" *(superens et superunitas).*[13] Pico explains several times to Cittadini
that one must regard the various categories of human speech about that
which is incomprehensible as equivalent signs of the various perspectives,
which are only apparently contradictory. These must be integrated into a
metaphysics of the original unknowability or of the greater infinity of God
(ibid. 173–81, 262, 272–74). During the last years of his life, Pico was close
to his friend Poliziano and to the Dominican Friar Girolamo Savonarola
from Ferrara, who had been invited to Florence by Lorenzo de'Medici on
Pico's recommendation. Travels in search of valuable manuscripts, and polemics and discussions with other humanists at San Marco, did not prevent him from working on his great project: a treatise against astrology. In
his retreat in Fiesole, he wrote his *Disputationes adversus astrologos,* which
were summarized in Italian by Savonarola and published in 1496 by his
nephew Gianfrancesco Pico.

In twelve books, Pico formulates very precise criticisms of "soothsaying" astrology. The breadth and the extremely learned character of this
work, which presents all the astrological schools known at that time (from
the Chaldaeans via the Egyptians to the Arabs, from Petosiris to Ptole-
my, from Albumasar to Manilius), should not cause us to overlook some
fixed points of his philosophy: the freedom of the human being to "form
himself," in opposition to every astral determinism; and the truth that the
human reason succeeds in acquiring when it lets itself be guided by the
search for knowledge of the hidden causes. Pico opposed the fondness for
astrology which was widespread in his days. In his polemic against many
of his humanist friends, such as Giovanni Pontano (1429–1503) and Ficino, he professes a "skepticism" that redimensions much of his earlier be-

13. Toussaint 1995, 150–52.

lief in Hermeticism and magic. On the other hand, we should not forget the numerous contemporary testimonies by his nephew, the philosopher Nifo, and other acquaintances, which show us a Pico who continued to be convinced of the prophetic power of the Cabbala and was fascinated by the idea that the human person could return to his angelic origin by means of an interiorized mysticism.

As we should expect, given the briefness of the space of time, the Pico of the first months of 1486 is not completely different from the more mature and stricter Pico of the years 1490–1494, when his contacts with the "reformer" Savonarola, the Aristotelian Poliziano, the Jew Jochanan Alemanno, and Ficino, the commentator and editor of Pseudo-Dionysius, generated a climate of extreme intellectual tension and intensive metaphysical investigation.

On November 17, 1494, while Charles VIII was encamped at the gates of Florence, Pico died at the age of thirty-one. He was probably poisoned by his secretary because of his sympathies with Savonarola (see Edelheit). He left many notes and memoranda that are difficult to decipher—a metaphor of the puzzle he has posed to posterity.

Pico was a brilliant fifteenth-century personality with many of the traits of the Renaissance white magician. He stands out through his view of philosophy's ideal as the search for the hidden causes and as the realization and liberation of the human person. He was certainly one of the first Western philosophers to aim at a "new philosophy" that went beyond the canons of the Scholastic tradition, although he grasped this tradition in all its complexity. With Gianozzo Manetti, Girolamo Benivieni, and Savonarola, he was one of the initiators of Hebrew studies in the West, and he stands at the beginning of the Hebraizing and cabbalistic trend of the sixteenth century, from Johannes Reuchlin to Francesco Giorgi Veneto, down to Athanasius Kircher at a later period. With their profound intuition and their poetic power, their "poetic theology" that lies between the Cabbala and pagan mysteries, texts such as the *Oratio* or the *Commento* remain unique and valuable testimonies to an extraordinary world, to the epoch of Sandro Botticelli, Leonardo da Vinci, and Poliziano. Besides this, his receptivity—which borders on the miraculous—makes Pico a forerunner of encyclopedianism, and his equally admirable skill in imposing a dialectical order on the various philosophical views ensures for him, together with Agostino Steuco (1497–1548) and Francesco Patrizi, the first place among the inventors of a *philosophia perennis*. Pico shows his authentically metaphysical mind in the formulation of his ideal, namely, the fundamental unity of all human knowledge.

Against this background, the various recent attempts to reduce Pico's work to a purely humanistic scholarship and rhetoric,[14] or to a Scholastic[15] or even "reactionary"[16] interpretation, must be regarded as a thorough watering down of the philosophical Renaissance that Pico embodies, and as a gradual philosophical dumbing down of his thinking.

14. Craven.   15. Chomarat.
16. Simonsohn.

Note: See Bausi 1998; Pico della Mirandola, Giovanni; Farmer; Garin 1952; Toussaint 1995. For secondary sources see Biondi; Black, Crofton; Bori; Busi; Campanini and Busi; Cassuto; Chomarat; Copenhaver; Craven; De Pace; Dorez and Thuasne; Dougherty; Edelheit; Fornaciari; Garin; Geffen; Idel; Kristeller 1963; Lelli; Nardi; Pico della Mirandola, Gianfrancesco; Viti; Simonsohn; Toussaint; Valcke; Wirszubski.

The following Internet sites may be helpful: *Pico in English: A Bibliography. The Works of Giovanni Pico della Mirandola (1463–1494) with a List of Studies and Commentaries,* compiled by M. V. Dougherty: http://www.mvdougherty.com/pico.htm; Progetto Pico Project: De hominis dignitate: http://www.brown.edu/Departments/Italian Studies/pico/; Centro Internazionale di Cultura Giovanni Pico della Mirandola: http://www.picodellamirandola.it.

7

MARSILIO FICINO

(1433–1499)

The Aesthetic of the One in the Soul

✧

Tamara Albertini

INTELLECTUAL DEVELOPMENT: THE DISCOVERY OF A PHILOSOPHICAL GIFT

Marsilio Ficino was born in Figline Valdarno in 1433. Through his father Diotifeci, who was the personal physician of Cosimo de' Medici, he came as an adolescent into contact with the Medicean circle. His early years were marked by the political rivalries that dominated Florence at that period, and it is probably in this context that we should read the Italian translation of Dante's *De monarchia* which he made in 1468, since the dedication to Bernardo del Nero and Antonio Manetti mentions previous discussions about similar topics. Ficino followed his father's wish and studied medicine. At an early age, he developed a keen interest in Plato. He himself relates that this was connected with the visit of the Byzantine Platonist Georgios Gemistos Plethon, who came to Florence in 1439 with the entourage from Byzantium to the Union Council and who had made a lasting impression on learned Florentine circles through his public lectures on the compatibility of Aristotelian and Platonic philosophy. Later, the question of the

Concordia Platonis et Aristotelis became a problem for Ficino himself, in connection with the concept of the immortality of the soul.

Still without having read Plato in the original, Ficino wrote the *Institutiones platonicae* in 1456. This text is now lost; judging by the reactions to it, it was an apologia for the great classical philosopher. The intellectual climate in Florence was, however, unpropitious for this work, and the humanist Cristoforo Landino and other benefactors advised Ficino against its publication. Cosimo de' Medici, who had also seen the *Institutiones,* was nevertheless convinced that Ficino possessed philosophical gifts, and he encouraged him to undertake a deeper study of Plato. Although he continued his medical studies for the rest of his life, this was the beginning of Ficino's career as the leading expert on Plato.

In 1463, Cosimo furnished a villa in Careggi for Ficino's studies, and this became the seat of the "Platonic Academy." This "community of the liberal arts" *(liberalium disciplinarum communio)* brought together humanists, philosophers, artists, poets, musicians, physicians, astronomers, and mathematicians.[1] Its illustrious members included such outstanding names as Ficino's benefactor Landino, Leon Battista Alberti, Giovanni Cavalcanti, Angelo Poliziano, and Giovanni Pico della Mirandola. The major task entrusted to Ficino by Cosimo, the translation of Plato's entire oeuvre into Latin, was finished circa 1469 (printed in 1484). *De christiana religione,* a work in which Ficino reconstructs history in keeping with a *pia philosophia,* appeared in 1474. Other authors translated by Ficino included Hermes Trismegistus (1471), Plotinus (1492), Dionysius the Areopagite (1496/97), and Iamblichus (1497). He also turned his attention to less well-known philosophers such as Athenagoras, Psellus, Alcinous, Speusippus, Xenocrates, Synesius, Priscianus Lydus, and Hermias of Alexandria, a pupil of Proclus, and wrote commentaries on selected Platonic Dialogues or parts of Dialogues.[2] His commentary on the *Symposium,* also known under the title *De amore* (1469), is particularly significant, since it forms an important preliminary stage leading to his chef d'oeuvre, the *Theologia Platonica—De immortalitate animarum* (1482). Another preliminary

1. Cf. however Hankins 1991. Ficino's works are cited as *Op.* according to the *Opera* 1576; and as *Platonic Theology* with volume and page numbers in the volumes edited and translated by Raymond Marcel, 1964–1970.
2. Translations of some prefaces are available in Farndell 2006.

work is the even earlier *De voluptate* (1457), which examines the concept of desire. Ficino's most successful medicinal work was the *De vita libri tres* (1489). Another important source for the study of his philosophy is his volume of correspondence, published in 1495, which attests his fame throughout Europe.

Ficino witnessed much turbulence in his beloved Florence, but despite invitations to work at other courts, he never left this region. In 1478 he experienced the terrible consequences of the Pazzi conspiracy, and in 1494 the renewed exile of the Medici family and the invasion of French troops under Charles VIII. Finally, there was the episode of Girolamo Savonarola (of whom Ficino had no high opinion), culminating in his public burning at the stake in 1498. The deaths of four men who had watched over his early philosophical studies was particularly painful: Lorenzo the Magnificent (1492), Poliziano (1494), Pico della Mirandola (1494), and Landino (1498). There can be no doubt that when he himself died in the Villa Careggi in 1499, the most intellectually stimulating period of the Renaissance came to an end. Even today, his unique position in the history of ideas as the one who brought the Platonic philosophy back into the Western tradition is unchallenged. This position is due not only to his importance as the scholar who made available a wider textual basis for the study of Platonism and Neoplatonism, but also to the fact that Ficino successfully employed Platonism as an instrument to renew philosophy and culture in general.

THE ORGANIC WORLDVIEW:
MAN AS "INTELLECTUAL HERO"

Ficino looks at the world with a physician's eyes. Just as all the organs of the body affect one another, so too the parts of this world "all depend, like the limbs of a living being, on one Author and are connected with each other through the nature which they share" (*De amore* 6.10. p. 243f.). He describes nature as a female being that is self-sustaining. It is endowed with an inner creative life; it gives birth "spontaneously" to offspring and nourishes them.[3] Man is embedded in the totality of the world, and this means that he is exposed not only to physical, but also to mental and spiritual in-

---

3. *Platonic Theology* 4, 1, vol. 1: 144f.

fluences. Like a child in its mother's womb, he absorbs all the currents; he "pulsates," so to speak, in the rhythm of the great world-organism. Nevertheless, Ficino sees Man as a being who moves freely in the relational web of Nature (since all bodies are linked), of Fate (since souls refer to one another), and of Providence (since all rational beings form a fellowship). Thanks to his soul, Man influences the bodily world. Through his mind (*mens*), he rules the intellectual world and ultimately his own self.[4] Typically, the image of this "sovereignty" is the figure of Hercules. His twelve labors not only crown him as "the conqueror of the Earth, the favorite of the stars," but also represent the conquest of the twelve houses of the zodiac system, which makes him the one who overcomes fate. Hercules is interpreted as an intellectual hero who, precisely because he is united to everything, understands the world and thereby necessarily also transcends it. Despite many points of contact in the anthropology, this is certainly very different from the mostly nonmetaphysical orientation of humanism.

PSYCHOLOGY: THE SOUL AS "THE MIDPOINT OF EVERYTHING"

Although Ficino's philosophy is concerned with the assimilation of the soul to the mind, the center of attention is the soul rather than the mind. He writes that through its unifying movement between the individual and the universal, the soul "reestablishes the world which once was shaken."[5] The rational soul is able to achieve this because it is the midpoint of a world which, from an epistemological perspective, otherwise falls apart into antitheses. Ficino operates in several passages with gradations of orders which usually begin with matter and ascend to God. In all these sequences, the soul is regarded as the one movable member: its rational activity ensures the continuity between everything that exists. The *descensus-ascensus* motif of late antiquity, which is employed here in a wider context, strengthens the idea that the soul, which links everything to everything else, ultimately reflects the entire universe and thus represents the universe in itself. The fivefold sequence that is introduced at the very

4. *Platonic Theology* 13, 2, vol. 2: 206–14.
5. *Platonic Theology* 16, 3, vol. 3:118.

beginning of the *Theologia Platonica* has the preeminent position: "We shall compare these five stages of all things with one another, namely the bodily matter, the quality, the soul, the angel, and God. Since however the species of the rational soul occupies the middle place between these stages and can be seen to be that which binds together the whole of nature, ruling the qualities and the bodies and uniting itself to the angel and to God, we shall show that it is entirely indissoluble, as it unites all the stages of nature; that it is the most excellent of all things, as it heads the structure of the world; and that it is the most blessed of all things, as it joins itself to the divine."[6] Accordingly, the soul fulfills its true function when it unites everything with everything else from a middle position—and thereby breaks open the hierarchically gradated order of being. We find a similar sequence of five members in the early *De amore*, where matter, nature, the soul, and the angelic mind are presented as concentric circles that all revolve around the divine midpoint and endeavor to become like it. The motive force that sets everything in motion is the soul, which resides in the very center and thereby mediates between the immortal (God, angel) and the mortal (nature, matter). Ficino's commentary on the *Timaeus* shows that he favors a sequence of five members not only because this permits a numerical midpoint; it is thus linked, for example, to the number of the five Platonic species (being, identity, otherness, rest, and movement). Ficino also emphasizes that since the soul is the center of the universe—which is symbolized by the "ten"—it is best represented by the midpoint of this number.[7]

EPISTEMOLOGY: THE MIND AS
"INFINITE POWER"

Ficino reverses the Aristotelian principle that nothing can be in the reason without first having been in the senses. He affirms that without the intellectual measure that is already present in the act of perception, nothing can be grasped. Thus the human mind receives "from the bodies the occasion [*occasio*] for knowledge"[8] and learns thereby how to relate the

6. *Platonic Theology* 1, 1, vol. 1: 39.					7. *Op.* 2, ch. 28, 1451.
8. *Platonic Theology* 15, 2, vol. 3:19.

particularity that is established through the knowledge of the senses to the universality that is present in itself. Ficino gives a vivid description of this "intellectual art" *(ars intellectualis)* in an optical example (which must be reconstructed from the text). Two spherical lights touch each other: one represents the transition from the universal to the individual, the other the path from the individual to the universal. The point at which the tips of the two spheres meet represents the rational soul, which does not simply link the two, but has the function of "contracting" the universal to form something particular, and "sees" the universal through the particular. The mind possesses the universal in the form of "imprints" *(sigilla)* or (to use Augustinian language) *formulae* that "tend toward" the individual. The act of knowing has recourse to these imprints or formulae when it tests the sensuous images *(simulacra)* to see whether they are "congruent" with the universal. In the light of these formulae, the mind sees not only true objects, but also "makes the truth."[9] Confronted with both individual and universal, the mind makes its own images *(species),* through which it visually assimilates the world to itself. It also applies its congenital formulae to its own self, in this way undertaking self-evaluations and self-corrections. As with Nicholas of Cusa, therefore, we can observe in Ficino an epistemological turning point, or an "epistemological overthrow." It is not the spirit that follows the objects; rather, the objects are accommodated to the cognitive power that measures them in an act of comparison. However, the mind does not hold fast to what it has once recognized. It tests it again and again by means of its congenital "formulae." In this way, the mind continuously renews "the face of things" and ultimately discovers itself as the infinite epistemic power in the infinite relational context that it itself has created: "It is quite certain that this power has no specific stage of order in nature, since this power itself pulsates upwards and downwards through all the stages of order. It has no specific location, since it never stands still anywhere. Its power is not determined (in the sense of 'limited'), since it has the same effect upon all things. And if I may say so, this seems to me to be the principal proof of the unlimited power of the mind: it discovers that infinity itself exists, it defines what infinity is and how infinity is."[10]

9. *Platonic Theology* 12, 2, vol. 2: 159.
10. *Platonic Theology* 8, 16, vol. 1: 330.

METAPHYSICS: THE MIND-SOUL AS "INTELLECT AND WILL"

Ficino's metaphysics, which mediates between the inner world and the outer world, is based on a unified theory of the intellect. The distinction, deriving from the Aristotelian tradition, between the active and the receptive intellect is superseded by understanding these as parts of one and the same process, which presents objects in a luminous manner: "If we want a handy illustration of these two powers of the intellect and of how they are united, we can consider the eye of a cat as it chases mice. In this eye— almost in the same way as in our mind—there are likewise two powers, a crystal-clear brightness and the gleam of the look. The former is receptive power, the latter active power. The gleam of the look radiates into the night and takes from the bodies which it encounters an image of one color or another and imprints this image upon the receptive brightness of the cat's eye, which sees the entire body through its act of looking."[11] The text goes on to say that the mind sees itself in its own ray of knowledge which reflects the objects. A characteristic element in Ficino's theory of the intellect is that it also includes the will. This is implicitly present in the hunting cat, since its brilliant act of looking, which represents the optic beam of the mind, has a volitional orientation. This brings us to what Ficino regards as the real conceptual challenge: not how to unite intellectual activity and passivity, but how to describe the antithetical powers of the intellect and the will as dynamic and complementary epistemological powers. In the first version of his commentary on the *Philebus,* he writes: "The former [the intellect] draws the objects to itself, the latter [the will] is drawn by the objects. For the intellect does not grasp the objects as they are in themselves, but in its own manner: it grasps many objects in one way, it grasps the mobile objects in a stationary manner, it grasps the individual objects in a general manner, etc. And with its formulae, it straightens out whatever is defective in the objects. The will, on the other hand, tends to possess the objects as they are in themselves, and it is captivated by them after the idea has been conceived. It does not change them; rather, it itself is changed and leaves its rest for movement."[12] Ficino elaborates different ways of present-

---

11. *Platonic Theology* 11, 2, vol. 2: 96.   12. 1 ch. 37, *Op.* 2, 1251.

ing these antithetically operating powers. The intellect separates, interior-
izes, "sees," and preserves the necessary optic distance from the objects; its
mode of knowledge is presented by means of optic constructions. The will
is the exact opposite of this: it unites, it moves outward, it "desires," it overcomes the distance from the objects, and thus Ficino very appropriately
makes use of innumerable metaphors of love to describe the epistemological power that makes for the objects.[13] Throughout his lifetime, Ficino
pondered the question which of these two intellectual powers had the primacy. Initially, he gave the preference to the intellect, but later he spoke in
favor of the will. Finally, he sought a solution that would do equal justice
to both powers, and he succeeded in portraying this equality in his commentary on the *Timaeus*, where he locates the two intellectual powers in
a harmonious triangle and writes: "Although we have spoken elsewhere of
the same relationships in the soul, we did not mean *an arithmetical parity,
but harmonious equality*."[14] Unlike medieval thinkers who were also preoc-
cupied with the problem of the superiority of the intellect or the will, Ficino translates it into the question whether the inner or the outer dimension
has precedence. In other words, do the intellectual formulae have supremacy over the objects, or does the world of objects have supremacy over the
mind that measures them? As a subtle metaphysician, Ficino could not re-
nounce either of these possibilities. The only solution lay in the harmoni-
zation of subjective *and* objective ordering.[15]

AESTHETICS: THE SOUL AS "ARTIST"

According to Ficino, human beings are endowed with an appreciation
of proportions, symmetry, and regular forms, and that is linked to the intellectual formulae: "Every mind praises at once the round form which
it sees in the objects, and does not know why it praises. In the same way,
when it sees buildings, it praises the rectangularity of the rooms, the even-
ness [*aequalitas*] of the walls, or the arrangement [*dispositio*] of the stones,
the corners which match one another, the form and the position of the windows. It also praises in the same way a certain proportion [*proportio*] in the

13. Albertini 1997, 246.   14. *Op.* 2, ch. 34, 1460.
15. Albertini 2001.

limbs of the human body, or the harmony [*concordia*] of rhythms and voic-es."[16] Despite the great importance that Ficino attaches to the intellectu-ally attractive proportions, he states clearly that the well-shaped form (*fig-ura*) is not per se beautiful; nevertheless, it is the precondition of beauty (*pulchritudo*). The primary aesthetic object for Ficino (as for the artists of his day) is the natural body, especially the human body, which he concep-tualizes as a physician by stating that the rational soul can form only the healthy body in which the fluids are "well tempered." In keeping with the principles laid down by Vitruvius, he then points out: "This means for ex-ample that three times the length of the nose amount to the length of the face as a whole, and that the two half-circles of the ears, taken together, are equal to the circle of the opened mouth; the same should be true of the eyebrows when they are joined together. The length of the nose should be equal to the length of the lip and likewise to the length of the ear. The two curves of the eyes should be equal to the opening of the mouth. Eight times the length of the head, and likewise the extension of the arms and legs, should equal the length of the entire body" (*De amore* 5, 6, 155). Sym-metries and proportions serve the predisposition of the body, so that beau-ty can shine in it. Since it is an expression of the divine goodness in the world, it is also described as a ray of light or as luminous splendor. Quot-ing an Orphic poem that calls the Graces *Splendor* (luminous splendor), *Viriditas* (the bloom of youth), and *Laetitia* (cheerfulness), Ficino com-ments that "luminous splendor" refers to the attractiveness and beauty of the soul, "the bloom of youth" refers to the gracefulness of figure and color, and "cheerfulness" denotes the joy that is given by music. Although beauty transcends the mathematical formulation of the principles that govern the aesthetic order, it nevertheless remains dependent on them. Beauty con-sists "in a certain actuality, liveliness, and gracefulness" (ibid.), and can therefore be detached from the bodily appearance.

It is impossible to emphasize too strongly the aesthetic dimension of Ficino's philosophy, which goes beyond the contemplation of the beautiful to embrace epistemology and metaphysics as well. The mind-soul, which measures everything and compares everything with everything else, im-plicitly brings about a restoration of the beautiful. Ficino's thinking, which

16. *Platonic Theology* 11, 5, vol. 2: 128.

is presented in optic-geometrical figures, can itself be seen as active and living, and thus as *graceful*.

THE HISTORY OF THE
RECEPTION OF FICINO

Even during his own lifetime, Ficino was famous far beyond the borders of Italy. He received letters from Spain, France, England, Germany, and Hungary. The most celebrated visitors to the Academy included Jacques Lefèvre d'Étaples, John Colet, and Johannes Reuchlin. Ficino's philosophy enjoyed a long-lasting reception. It would be difficult to find any philosophical text of the sixteenth or even the seventeenth century—whether Aristotelian or Platonic in its approach—that shows no traces of influence by Ficino.[17] Giambattista Vico (1668–1744) recommends him in his autobiography as a model metaphysician. Not only philosophers, but also physicians, astronomers, historians, artists, musicians, men of letters, and poets found much to stimulate them in his work. His most influential text is undoubtedly the *De amore*, without which much of the Renaissance Italian and French literature would be simply unthinkable.

17. Cf. Mahoney 1982.

Note: For further reading see Farndell 2006; Shaw 1978. For Ficino's Commentaries on Plato see Ficino 1975; Allen 1981, 1989, 1994; Ficino 1985. See also the works by Accademia; Albertini; Allen; Blum 1999; Chastel; Edelheit; Farndell; Garfagnini; Gentile, Niccoli, and Viti; Gentile and Toussaint; Granada; Hankins; Kristeller; Mahoney 1982; Marcel; Otto; Toussaint 2002; and Vasoli 1999.

8

PIETRO POMPONAZZI
(1462–1525)

Secular Aristotelianism in
the Renaissance

Jill Kraye

Pietro Pomponazzi was one of the most important and influential Aristotelian philosophers of the Renaissance. Working within a philosophical tradition whose central themes, methods, and terminology had been established in the thirteenth century, Pomponazzi nevertheless managed to challenge received opinion and to put forward bold and innovative ideas.

SECULAR ARISTOTELIANISM

In the twelfth and thirteenth centuries, a substantial increase in the number of Aristotelian treatises available in Latin translation prepared the way for these works to become the basis of the philosophy curriculum in European universities. During the course of the thirteenth century, above all at the University of Paris, two contrasting approaches to Aristotelianism evolved, both of which would continue to shape the study of philosophy until well into the seventeenth century. On the one hand, there was Christian Aristotelianism, best exemplified by Thomas Aquinas (ca. 1225–1274). This approach appropriated Aristotelian doctrines as the philosophical foundation of Christian theology, emphasizing the areas of compatibility between the two, while not denying that there were certain issues where divine revelation transcended the reason-based principles of Aristotelian philosophy. On the other hand, there was secular Aristotelianism, developed by natural philosophers such as Siger of Brabant (ca. 1240–1284). Their main concern was to determine what Aristotle had thought on a given issue, staying solely within the bounds of human reason and not taking account of theological considerations. When it came to issues such as the personal immortality of the soul and the eternity of the world, where Aristotle and reason led to conclusions that did not agree with Christian dogma, they did not declare—as has often been claimed—that that there were two equally valid and contradictory truths, one grounded in philosophy, the other in religion. Instead, they maintained that all philosophical conclusions were merely probable since they were based on fallible human reasoning, and that absolute truth belonged only to the divinely revealed and sanctioned dogmas of Christianity. These philosophers insisted, nevertheless, that they should be allowed to pursue their own investigations, using their own tools (Aristotelian philosophy and reason), without interference from the theologians, whose truths they accepted as a matter of faith but did not believe were necessarily susceptible of rational or philosophical demonstration.

The universities of northern Italy provided a conducive environment for the development of secular Aristotelianism. The study of philosophy there was preparatory not to theology, as in Paris or Oxford, but to medicine. Some Italian universities did not even have theological faculties, since they specialized in training physicians and lawyers rather than theologians. This encouraged an atmosphere in which philosophy could operate as an autonomous discipline, guided solely by rational criteria, and in which Aristotelians were able to explain natural phenomena according to philosophical principles, without recourse to theological arguments. From time to time, however, the Catholic Church challenged thinkers whose single-minded pursuit of natural explanations was perceived to encroach on the sacred domain of faith. When, for instance, Biagio Pelacani da Parma (ca. 1365–1416) dared to argue that the soul was material and hence mortal, he was quickly forced to recant by the ecclesiastical authorities. Yet, while these Aristotelians were willing to subordinate the relative truth of philosophy to the absolute truth of theology, they were as insistent as their Parisian predecessors on the need to keep the two realms separate and on their right to use arguments based solely on Aristotle and on reason in philosophical contexts. Just as it was necessary, Biagio Pelacani affirmed, when discussing matters of faith to leave behind one's philosophical mentality, so when discussing philosophy one had to set aside one's Christian beliefs.[1]

Aristotelian philosophers employed the expository techniques, methods, and vocabulary of the larger intellectual movement known as Scholasticism. Scholastic treatises had a rigidly logical format: arguments for and against a particular proposition were set out, often in the form of syllogisms; a solution was reached; possible objections were raised and appropriate responses supplied. These treatises employed a highly technical Latin terminology, which had developed during the Middle Ages and which continued to be one of the hallmarks of Scholastic treatises produced during the Renaissance. Aristotelian works were read and studied in word-for-word medieval translations written in this same Latin style. The philosophy professors of northern Italy were expected to expound these Latin versions of Aristotle, usually in conjunction with the interpretations of the Arabic philosopher Averroes (1126–1198), whose commentaries were so highly regarded in the West that, just as Aristotle came to be known as "the Philosopher," Averroes was referred to as "the Commentator."

A LIFE DEVOTED TO PHILOSOPHY

Pietro Pomponazzi (1462–1525) was a secular Aristotelian who spent his life teaching philosophy in various northern Italian universities. Born in Mantua, he studied philosophy (receiving his master's degree in 1487) and then medicine (receiving his doctorate by 1496) at the University of Padua. Even at this bastion of secular Aristotelianism, Pomponazzi's teachers included a Dominican, who lectured on Thomist metaphysics. More important for his education, however, was Nicoletto Vernia (1420–1499). The leading Averroist of the day, Vernia, like Biagio Pelacani a century ear-

---

1. *Quaestiones disputatae de anima* (1385), in Pelacani 1974, 71.

lier, came into conflict with the church for his views on the sensitive issue of the personal immortality of the soul. Pomponazzi himself began teaching philosophy at Padua in 1488, rising steadily in the academic hierarchy until 1496, when a dispute with Agostino Nifo (ca. 1470–1538), his *concurrens* (an official opponent appointed by the university to lecture at the same time, in order to stir up competition among professors), led him to abandon Padua for Ferrara.

Pomponazzi spent the next three years attached to the court of Alberto Pio (1475–1531), prince of Carpi, who was in exile in Ferrara. The nephew of Giovanni Pico della Mirandola and the dedicatee of the Aldine edition of Aristotle in Greek (1495–1498), Alberto Pio was closely associated with humanist Aristotelianism, which encouraged the study of Greek philosophical texts in the original, the production of new translations in classical Latin, and the use of philologically sophisticated techniques of editing and exegesis. Pomponazzi, though a beneficiary of this movement, which gave him valuable access to ancient Greek commentaries on Aristotle and provided him with more accurate translations of Aristotelian treatises, was by no means a humanist himself: he never learned Greek and wrote treatises that were thoroughly Scholastic in both format and style. Together Alberto Pio and Pomponazzi studied a non-Aristotelian form of logico-mathematical physics developed in fourteenth-century Oxford, which had become fashionable among northern Italian philosophers but which neither the humanist prince nor his Scholastic tutor found to his taste. Nonetheless, Pomponazzi's first published work concerned problems related to this so-called calculatory tradition and was dedicated to Alberto Pio.[2]

In 1499 Pomponazzi returned to the University of Padua to take up the position of his recently deceased teacher Vernia as the main professor of philosophy. From surviving lecture notes taken down by his students, known as *reportationes,* we can reconstruct his teaching from this period, during which he expounded the *libri naturales* of Aristotle (including *De anima, De caelo,* and the *Physics*), together with the commentaries of Averroes, whose cosmological treatise *De substantia orbis* he also taught in 1507. His lectures, though rigidly structured and delivered in a turgid Scholas-

---

2. Pomponazzi, *Tractatus utilissimus in quo disputatur penes quid intensio et remissio formarum attendatur nec minus parvitas et magnitudo* (Bologna, 1514).

tic Latin, were occasionally enlivened by light-hearted remarks in the ver-
nacular and anticlerical jibes—among Italians, then as now, by no means
a sign of religious disbelief or insincerity. His philosophical expertise, as
well as his caustic sense of humor, made Pomponazzi a popular lecturer
with the Paduan students, who endorsed his performance so consistently in the annual votes held by the university officials that in 1504 he was
given the right to teach without submitting to the student ballot. When,
however, the War of the League of Cambrai forced the University of Padua
to close down in 1509, Pomponazzi accepted the invitation of Duke Alfonso d'Este to return to Ferrara, this time as professor in the university. The
war soon closed down the Ferrarese university as well, so he returned for
a year to his home town of Mantua. In 1511 he was invited to teach natural
and moral philosophy at the University of Bologna. He took up the post
the following year. A highly acclaimed and well-paid teacher, he continued
to lecture on Aristotle's treatises, adding the zoological works to his reper-
tory, until his death, from kidney stones, in 1525.

This essentially tranquil and successful existence, dedicated to the
study and teaching of philosophy, was disrupted by one period of notoriety, when Pomponazzi found himself at the center of a hotly debated
controversy, which was to alter the future balance of power between philosophy and theology. It all began when he published a treatise on the immortality of the soul, an issue that had long been a stumbling block in the
relations between secular Aristotelians and the Catholic Church.

THE IMMORTALITY OF THE SOUL

In the late fifteenth century, the right of secular Aristotelian philosophers to use their own methods and to draw their own conclusions, free
from theological constraints, as long as they ultimately deferred to the absolute truths of Christianity, came under threat. A new intellectual climate
was developing, in which philosophical arguments were increasingly expected to confirm religious doctrines, making it difficult to maintain the
traditional lines of division between philosophy and theology. In the Aristotelian camp, Pomponazzi's teacher, Vernia, after renouncing his Averroist views under pressure from the church, proclaimed that the Christian
belief in the personal immortality of the soul was demonstrable in philo-

sophical terms.[3] On the Platonic front, Marsilio Ficino (1433–1499) rejected the separation of reason and faith, calling for a "pious philosophy" in
which Platonism would provide the rational foundation for many Christian beliefs. To demonstrate the fundamental compatibility of the true philosophy, Platonism, and the true faith, Christianity, Ficino, in his *Platonic
Theology* (1474), drew on Platonic principles to present rational proofs for
the immortality of the soul.[4]

The culmination of this challenge to the autonomy of philosophy was
the bull of Pope Leo X, "Apostolici regiminis" (December 19, 1513), which
was published in the eighth session of the Fifth Lateran Council. It condemned as dangerous heretics philosophers who dared to defend, even on
purely philosophical and rational grounds, views of the soul that denied
personal immortality.[5] Philosophy professors, when discussing the issue
in their own classrooms, would hereafter be obliged to make every effort
to establish the truth of the Christian belief in immortality and to refute
any philosophical arguments that ran counter to it. Only two members of
the council voted against the decree, one of whom was Tommaso de Vio
(1468–1534), minister general of the Dominican Order and soon to become
Cardinal Cajetan. A former colleague of Pomponazzi at Padua, Tommaso
de Vio had maintained only a few years earlier, in his commentary on *De
anima* (1509), that although the doctrine that the soul dies with the body
was false, according to faith and to the true principles of philosophy, which
must be in agreement with faith, it was nonetheless the view held by Aristotle.[6] What he objected to now, however, was the idea of entrusting philosophers to teach the truths of faith.

The belief that the human soul, like that of animals, was the material form of the body, and therefore perished along with it, was associated with the ancient Greek commentator on Aristotle, Alexander of Aphrodisias (ca. 200 A.D.). Alexander's treatise *On the Soul* became available

---

3. Vernia, *Contra perversam Averrois opinionem de unitate intellectus et de anime felicitate*, 1516. Cf. Mahoney 1968.

4. Ficino, *Platonic Theology*, 2001–2006.

5. For the decree and the objections raised against it, see G. D. Mansi et al., *Sacro-
rum conciliorum nova et amplissima collectio*, 54 vols. (Venice, 1759–1798), 32, cols 842–43.
Text available in Norman P. Tanner, *Decrees of the Ecumenical Councils* (London: Sheed &
Ward, 1990). Cf. Constant 2002.

6. Tommaso de Vio 1938–1939.

in Latin translation only in 1495, but medieval philosophers had been par-
tially familiar with his views through a few passages quoted by Averroes
and through a twelfth-century Latin version of another work, attributed to
him, on the intellect. Pomponazzi, in his courses on *De anima* at the University of Padua in the early years of the sixteenth century, argued that Alexander's mortalist account of the soul was neither valid in itself nor an accurate representation of Aristotle's position. According to Aristotle (*De
anima* I.1), the question of immortality hinged on whether the body was essential for all the soul's operations, including thinking. Pomponazzi at this
time still accepted the position that had been worked out by medieval Aristotelians: although the soul could not think without the images or *phantasmata* created by the imagination from the raw material of sense data, the
process of intellection did not take place in a corporeal sense organ, in the
way that vision, say, was located in the eye. The soul's separability from the
body, and hence both its immateriality and immortality, was therefore preserved, since it needed the body not as its subject, but only as its object.

A further problem with Alexander's belief that the soul was material
was that it was unable to account for the intellect's capacity to understand
immaterial universals. The Averroist thesis, which in these years Pomponazzi regarded as the authentic interpretation of Aristotle, was able to explain the intellect's comprehension of universals, but at the unacceptable
cost of severing the essential unity of body and soul, since it postulated a
single immaterial and immortal intellect for all mankind, which temporal-
ly guided the rational activities of individual bodies rather than serving as
their substantial form. This theory was not based on an analysis of the way
in which human thought functioned in practice, but instead was logically
deduced from the Aristotelian principle that there is only one immaterial
being per species. Although Pomponazzi thought that Averroes had accurately interpreted Aristotle's position, he did not regard it as philosophically respectable, let alone tenable: "Averroes's opinion seems to me to have
been that of Aristotle; nevertheless, I can in no way support it, and it seems
to me the most flagrant nonsense. Say what you will, I for one am more
repelled by Averroes's opinion than I am by the devil."[7] For all his com-

---

7. *Quaestio de immortalitate animae* (1504), in Kristeller, "Two Unpublished Questions on the Soul of Pietro Pomponazzi," 1955, at 93: "De opinione . . . Averrois mihi videtur quod fuerit opinio Aristotelis, tamen nullo pacto possum illi adherere, et videtur mihi

mitment to Aristotelian philosophy, Pomponazzi placed reason and experience above the pronouncements of any human authority, including "the
Philosopher." While never doubting that even reason and experience must
ultimately defer to divine authority on a question such as the immortality
of the soul, he remained undecided for many years as to the correct solution of the problem on purely philosophical grounds.

The turning point came during a series of lectures Pomponazzi gave at
the University of Bologna in 1515–1516 on *De caelo*. In discussing the eternity of the world, in book 1, chapter 10, Aristotle establishes that generation
and corruption are convertible: that which is generated inevitably suffers
corruption and perishes, while that which is not generated is incorrupt-
ible and eternal. Pomponazzi realized that, following this principle, if the
soul was immortal, it did not have a beginning in time; and if it did have
a beginning, it was not immortal. Since, according to Aristotle, the soul
comes into existence at a particular point in time, it cannot be immortal.
Consequently, the most accurate interpretation of Aristotle, as well as the
most satisfactory answer to the question of immortality in terms of philosophy, was neither the belief, formulated by Thomas Aquinas, that the
soul was created by God, functioned temporarily as the substantial form
of an individual human being, and then went on to an immortal afterlife,
nor Averroes's theory of a single immortal intellect, but rather Alexander
of Aphrodisias's view that the soul was both material and mortal. The Lateran Council, however, had outlawed both Alexander's position and that
of Averroes, demanding that philosophers not only support the Christian
belief but also put forward the strongest possible arguments against both
these doctrines. Consequently, if the long-standing right of philosophers
to treat philosophical issues philosophically, without interference from
theologians, was to survive, it was imperative to defy the council's pro-
nouncement.

This is precisely what Pomponazzi did in his treatise *On the Immortality
of the Soul* (1516). In this work he set out to answer two questions concerning the soul's immortality put to him by a Dominican student of his: "First,
leaving revelation and miracles aside, and staying entirely within natu-

---

maxima fatuitas. Dicat autem quisque quicquid vult, ego magis abhorreo opinionem Averrois quam diabolum."

ral limits, what is your opinion in this matter? And, second, what do you think Aristotle's view was on the same issue?"[8] Pomponazzi now rejected his former belief that Averroes had correctly understood Aristotle, declaring that the Arabic commentator's interpretation was "unintelligible and monstrous and totally alien to Aristotle. Indeed, I think that Aristotle never even thought of such nonsense, much less believed it."[9] Recognizing the unavoidable consequences of Aristotle's empirical epistemology, he now maintained that even though the process of intellection required the body only as object, that is, as the source of the sense data from which *phantasmata* were generated, the fact that human thought (unlike that of the celestial intelligences or the Unmoved Mover) could not take place without these *phantasmata* meant that the body was essential to the soul's ability to think. Therefore, based solely on philosophical premises and Aristotelian principles, the probable conclusion was that the soul was essentially mortal. It was, however, immortal in the limited sense that intellection was an incorporeal act, performed by the soul without a bodily organ and entailing some degree of participation in the immaterial realm through the human mind's ability to comprehend universals.

In characteristic Scholastic fashion, Pomponazzi proceeded in the penultimate chapter of the treatise to consider and answer various objections that might be raised to his conclusion. This was by no means an easy task, he admitted, since belief in the survival of the soul after death was commonplace and, as Aristotle had made clear in *Metaphysics* II.3, "it is difficult to speak against conventional wisdom. But insofar as I am able," he continued, "I shall endeavor in this matter to speak at all events with probability,"[10] thus underlining the point that arguments based on reason, as opposed to divine revelation, could not hope to be definitive. To the objection that it was impossible for mankind to achieve happiness in the present life and that therefore, as Ficino had announced in the opening chapter of his *Platonic Theology:* "Were the soul not immortal, no creature would be more miserable than man,"[11] Pomponazzi replied that human happi-

---

8. Pomponazzi, *On the Immortality of the Soul,* in Cassirer et al., eds., *The Renaissance Philosophy of Man* (1948), 280–381, at 281 (here and elsewhere I have modified the translation); Pomponazzi, *Tractatus de immortalitate animae* (1954), 36.

9. Pomponazzi, *Immortality,* 286; *Tractatus,* 48.

10. Pomponazzi, *Immortality,* 350–51; *Tractatus,* 180.

11. Ficino, *Platonic Theology,* 1.14 (1.1).

ness consisted in morally virtuous behavior, which could be achieved by everyone in the present life. Rejecting the view put forward by Aristotle in book 10 of the *Nicomachean Ethics,* Pomponazzi did not place the supreme good in the intellectual virtue of contemplation, attainable only by a few philosophers or mathematicians, but instead in the practice of moral virtues such as prudence and temperance, which were within the grasp of all human beings.

As for the objection that mortality would spell the end of morality, since no one would behave virtuously without the hope of rewards and the fear of punishment in the afterlife, Pomponazzi adopted the Stoic position that virtue was its own reward and vice its own punishment. Only men of a truly philosophical disposition, however, could be expected to pursue virtue on account of its inherent nobility; the mass of mankind needed to be led to virtue by the carrot of heavenly rewards and the stick of infernal punishment. It was for this reason that the founders of all religions had invented the pious fiction of immortality. Since they had no concern for the truth, but desired solely to lead men to virtue, their unanimity did not constitute a serious philosophical objection to the doctrine of mortality. This cynical argument, which reduces religion to a device for social control (in the manner of his contemporary, Niccolò Machiavelli), has provided powerful ammunition, from Pomponazzi's own day to the present, for those who distrust the sincerity of his consistent protestations of orthodox Christian belief, regarding these as tactical statements, designed to protect himself from ecclesiastical censure.

One of the most controversial of these protestations comes in the final chapter of the treatise, where Pomponazzi states that despite all the probable philosophical arguments he has put forward in the treatise in favor of mortality, his belief in the absolute truth of the Christian doctrine of personal immortality remained unshaken, since it was sanctioned by the God-given authority of the church, which must be preferred to any fallible human reasoning. Citing Plato's *Laws* (641D), Pomponazzi says that "to be certain of something when many are in doubt is for God alone. Since therefore such distinguished figures disagree with each other, I think that this matter can be decided with certainty only by God."[12] As an article of

---

12. Pomponazzi, *Immortality,* 377; *Tractatus,* 232.

faith, however, the immortality of the soul could be proved only by the means appropriate to faith, which were revelation and Scripture, not reason or philosophy.

There was an immediate reaction on the part of those theologians and their philosophical allies who felt threatened by Pomponazzi's stand, which effectively ruled out Aristotelian natural philosophy as a means of providing rational support for the Christian dogma of immortality: his treatise was publicly burned in Venice; he was denounced by the suffragan bishop of Mantua, Ambrogio Flandino (1462–1531); and attacks on him and his work issued from the presses. Pomponazzi's first response to this onslaught was an *Apologia* (1518), cannily dedicated to Cardinal Sigismondo Gonzaga, in which he restated his position that immortality was not rationally demonstrable since it was contrary to the principles of Aristotelian natural philosophy. As an article of faith, it could—and should—be founded solely on divine revelation. Next, he wrote a *Defensorium* (1519), in reply to a treatise written against him by his former Paduan rival Agostino Nifo, in which Pomponazzi pointed out that, as a professor of philosophy at the University of Bologna, he had been commanded by the city officials and by the pope (since Bologna was part of the Papal States) to explicate Aristotle's views according to natural principles; therefore, in the treatise on immortality he was merely "following orders and obeying his oath of office."[13] Pomponazzi's powerful backers in Rome, including Pietro Bembo (1470–1547), secretary to Leo X and a future cardinal, saw to it that he was merely asked to comply with the Lateran decree by retracting his statement that, according to Aristotle and to his own philosophy, the soul was mortal.[14] And even though he never made the retraction, nothing further happened to him—the crisis brewing in Wittenberg may have distracted the Catholic Church's attention. Furthermore, in 1518, when the controversy was at its height, the University of Bologna granted Pomponazzi the extraordinary privilege of lecturing without a *concurrens* and of deciding for himself which books of Aristotle he would expound in his courses.

13. Pomponazzi, *Defensorium sive Responsiones ad ea quae Augustinus Niphus adversus ipsum scripsit de immortalitate animae*, 1519, fol. 104r: "Mandata sequor, iuramentum observo."

14. The demand for a retraction is quoted in L. von Ranke, *Die römischen Päpste in den letzten Jahrhunderten*, 3 vols. (Leipzig, 1889), 1.48, n. 1.

The Inquisition had refused to allow Pomponazzi to publish his *De-fensorium* without an accompanying refutation of his arguments. He had therefore agreed to have Crisostomo Javelli (ca. 1470/72–ca. 1538), regent of the Studium of the Dominican Order in Bologna, write the required tract. Javelli argued that the immortality of the soul was rationally demonstrable, but not according to the principles of Aristotelian natural philosophy. Instead, Javelli transferred the arena of debate to metaphysics, a discipline where theological considerations were still allowed to hold sway. Pomponazzi's bold move had forced theologians and Christian Aristotelians to shift their ground, so that they turned increasingly to metaphysics and gradually abandoned natural philosophy. Secular Aristotelians, less hindered by interference from theologians, were freer to interpret Aristotle as they chose and to develop an autonomous science of nature. While the Inquisition could still investigate philosophers for failing to teach the immortality of the soul, this was a rare occurrence and, as in the case of Galileo's Paduan colleague Cesare Cremonini (1550–1631), the charges were often dropped.[15]

THE NATURAL CAUSES OF "MIRACLES"

Pomponazzi's next substantial work was a treatise entitled *On Incantations*, in which he excluded supernatural explanations from the domain of nature by establishing that it was possible to assign purely natural causes to those extraordinary events commonly regarded as miracles. Completed in July 1520, it circulated in manuscript but was not printed until 1556, a quarter of a century after his death. Having been the center of one cause célèbre, Pomponazzi was unwilling to risk publishing another controversial treatise—wisely, in the event, since the book was placed on the Index of Prohibited Books in 1590,[16] the only work of his to be formally censored by the church.

Pomponazzi states at the outset that he accepts the Christian belief that certain miraculous events occur through the intervention of angels and de-

---

15. The documents are published in A. Poppi, *Cremonini e Galilei inquisiti nel 1604: Nuovi documenti d'archivio* (Padua, 1992).

16. *Index de Rome 1590, 1593, 1596*, ed. J. M. Bujanda et al. (Sherbrooke and Geneva, 1994), 163 (no. 413).

mons. The question he is attempting to answer, however, is whether there is any place for such supernatural forces in the Aristotelian universe—a similar perspective to the one he had adopted when examining the immortality of the soul. He goes on to argue that according to the principles of Peripatetic philosophy, spiritual beings such as angels and demons cannot bring about the "miraculous" effects that are attributed to them, since, as immaterial substances, they are incapable of having any physical contact with material objects. Moreover, in Aristotle's system, everything that happens in the sublunary realm—the region stretching from the Earth to the Moon, characterized by continual change and by an endless flow of coming into being and passing away—is governed by the heavenly bodies in the celestial spheres. These spheres are located in the supralunary realm—the region above the Moon, characterized by eternal immutability and by constant, regular, and unvarying circular motion—and are moved by the separate intelligences or minds, which do the bidding of Aristotle's god, the chief of these intelligences, known as the Unmoved Mover. Since every conceivable event that happens in the sublunary world, whether considered to be ordinary or exceptional, is controlled by the stars, acting according to invariable laws of nature, it is superfluous, in Aristotelian terms, to postulate any supernatural agents such as angels and demons.

Since the heavens, acting as the instruments of the celestial intelligences, which, in turn, were agents of divine providence, operated according to unchanging and predictable laws of nature, astrology appeared to be constructed on a firm rational foundation. It was therefore traditionally regarded by secular Aristotelians as a science. Its scientific validity, for Pomponazzi, was reinforced by the fact that expert astrologers were frequently able to predict the occurrence of future events, even so-called miracles or prodigies.

Pomponazzi was not himself skilled in astrology, as he admitted, with his customary intellectual honesty, to the students attending his lectures at Bologna.[17] In contrast to this enthusiastic proponent of astrology, who

17. In his lectures on Aristotle's *Meteorology*, Pomponazzi stated: "I do not understand astrology" ("Ego non intelligo astrologiam"); and, when lecturing on *De generatione et corruptione*, he confessed that he could not resolve a problem "because I am not an accomplished astrologer" ("quoniam ego non sum bonus astrologus"); cited in Graiff 1976, at 339, 347.

knew little of its intricacies, Giovanni Pico della Mirandola (1463–1494), a fierce opponent of astrology, possessed a profound knowledge of the science of the stars. Pico's *Disputations against Divinatory Astrology*, left incomplete at his death but printed two years later in his *Opera* (Bologna, 1496), is an extremely learned attack on divinatory or judicial astrology. Pico carefully distinguished between, on the one hand, the genuinely scientific study of the general effects produced by the movement of the stars and, on the other, the superstitious and worthless belief that astrologers could predict what would happen in specific cases to particular individuals.[18] Since the influence exerted by the stars and planets was the mainstay of Pomponazzi's conviction that all sublunary phenomena, both general and specific, could be explained in terms of natural causality, he was keen to discredit Pico's penetrating criticism of astrology. Though not mentioned by name, Pico is clearly the target of Pomponazzi's disparaging comments about "certain modern writers who attack astrologers with lengthy and elegantly phrased arguments. . . . Either they understand nothing about astrologers, or, if they do understand, they are seriously mistaken. I myself certainly find only arrogance and impudence in their books, which contain nothing worthwhile apart from the elegant style."[19]

While for Christians, miracles are the result of direct divine intervention in earthly affairs, the Aristotelian divinity cannot directly produce any event in the sublunary world, since to do so would entail internal change and movement in him, which is an impossibility for the Unmoved Mover: "That God does not act directly in this lower world," writes Pomponazzi, "is clear from Book VIII of the *Physics*, Book II of *De caelo*, and Book II of the *Metaphysics*."[20] So although Aristotle's God is the first cause of everything that happens in the universe, he can only operate in our world through intermediate and secondary causes, that is, the heav-

18. Giovanni Pico, *Disputationes adversus astrologiam divinatricem*, 1946–1952.

19. Pomponazzi, *De naturalium effectuum causis, seu De incantationibus liber*, 1970, 266–67: "quidam recentes multis verbis ornatis insectantes astrologos . . . aut enim astrologos non intelligunt, aut si intelligunt, graviter errant, et certe in illis suis libris non video nisi arrogantiam et petulantiam, et praeter ornatum nihil boni contineri." Pomponazzi did name Pico in his lectures on the *Meteorology*: "Pico della Mirandola, in finding fault with astrologers, was ignorant of Aristotle's principles" ("Picus Mirandulensis reprehendens astrologos ignoravit principia Aristotelis"): cited in Graiff 1976, 350.

20. Pomponazzi, *De incantationibus*, 134: "Quod . . . deus in haec inferiora immediate non agat, patet ex 8. Physicorum, secundo De coelo, et secundo Metaph[ysicorum]."

enly spheres, guided by the celestial intelligences. Nor can this divinely controlled movement of the stars, which totally determines the course of events here on Earth, be altered by any actions on our part, either magical incantations or—far more damagingly from a Christian perspective— prayer. But although our prayers will not be answered, the act of praying does have subjective value, according to Pomponazzi, since it engenders in us "piety and reverence for God."[21]

The mass of humanity, for whom Pomponazzi had nothing but contempt, readily believes that everything out of the ordinary was miraculous; and they are encouraged in their credulity by the theologians, who employ fables about angels and demons in the same way that they use the myth of immortality: as a means of inducing virtuous behavior and discouraging vice. Even Plato had resorted to such stories, not because he believed them, but "because his aim was to instruct the ignorant."[22] By contrast, those philosophers who are single-mindedly dedicated to discovering and disseminating the truth do not regard exceptional events as "miracles" which "run completely counter to nature or are at variance with the course of the heavenly bodies," but rather believe that they "are only said to be miracles because they are unusual and rare."[23]

Pomponazzi's astral determinism further threatened Christian belief in that he held the stars to be responsible for all of human history, as well as for natural phenomena. Not only was political change, such as the emergence of a great leader or the overthrow of an empire, governed by the heavens—for ancient historians invariably recorded that such occurrences were presaged by a celestial portent—but so too were the rise and fall of religions. Earlier secular Aristotelians had advanced the notion, taken over from Arabic astrologers such as Albumasar (ca. 790–886), that it was possible to cast the horoscope of a religion. The theory was that each time a particular conjunction of constellations occurred, as part of the endlessly recurring cosmic cycle set in motion by divine providence, a prophet was infused with a highly potent combination of natural forces, enabling

21. Ibid., 249: "pietas et in Deum religio."
22. Ibid., 202: "sed quoniam suum fuerit propositum homines rudes instruere."
23. Ibid., 294: "non sunt autem miracula, quia sint totaliter contra naturam et praeter ordinem corporum caelestium, sed pro tanto dicuntur miracula, quia insueta et rarissima facta."

him to produce the extraordinary effects or miracles necessary to convince people to adopt a new religion. In Pomponazzi's view, such power is concentrated in these prophets "by the gift of God and the intelligences, that they are plausibly believed to be the sons of God."[24] According to this philosophical explanation, all religions, including Christianity, were destined to follow the same pattern of birth, growth, and decay, determined by the eternal cycle of stellar movement. That Christianity was now in its final phases was apparent, since the flow of celestial power to the earth had dried up: "[E]verything grows cold in our faith, and miracles have ceased, except those which are false and fraudulent; for the end seems near."[25]

Although Pomponazzi argued that certain biblical miracles performed by Moses or by Christ and the Apostles could be explained in natural terms, he nevertheless maintained that for others, such as the stopping of the sun by Joshua or the unusually long eclipse at the time of Jesus's crucifixion, there was no conceivable natural cause. "Such miracles," he concluded in the final chapter of the treatise, "which go beyond the course of created nature and which only God can make happen, and which do sometimes happen, provide a truthful demonstration of the inadequacy of Aristotle's teaching and that of the rest of the philosophers, and clearly proclaim the truth and reliability of the Christian religion."[26] He had, of course, adopted the same stance at the end of his treatise on the immortality of the soul, denying the validity of the probable hypotheses of Aristotelian philosophy, which he had explained and defended throughout the work, in the face of their incompatibility with the unshakeable truths of Christianity.

DETERMINISM AND HUMAN FREEDOM

The astral determinism that provides the foundation of Pomponazzi's case for natural causation in *On Incantations* also plays a key role in his

24. Ibid., 283–84: "ex Dei et intelligentiarum munere, adeo quod Dei filii creduntur rationabiliter."
25. Ibid., 286–87: "in fide nostra omnia frigescunt, miracula desinunt, nisi conficta et simulata; nam propinquus videtur esse finis."
26. Ibid., 315: "Talia miracula quae sunt praeter ordinem naturae creatae, et a solo Deo fieri possunt, et fiunt aliquando, veraciter demonstrant insufficientiam doctrinae Aristotelis et caeterorum philosophorum, ipsamque veritatem et firmitatem religionis Christianae aperte declarant."

treatise *On Fate, Free Will, and Predestination,* which he completed a few
months later, in November 1520, and which, like the earlier treatise, remained unpublished during his lifetime, reaching print only in 1567. In
both works the universe is shown to be governed by constant and eternal laws, emanating from the Unmoved Mover and put into operation by
the celestial intelligences and the heavenly spheres that act as their instruments. What Pomponazzi explores in *De fato* are the implications for human freedom of this rigidly determined cosmos, in which each earthly
event can be traced through a chain of causation back to the heavens and
ultimately to the divine first cause.

In defending astrology as a scientifically valid vision of the universe,
Pomponazzi did not attempt to deny its deterministic consequences: "sublunary matters are governed by the heavenly bodies,"[27] nor can the stars
be deflected from their predetermined course; therefore, "what happens,
happens inevitably."[28] Not only was the lifespan of Socrates determined
by the astral and planetary influences exerted on him while he was still in
the womb, but so too was his character.[29] And the fate imposed on him at
birth could not be eluded; for history showed that the more one attempted
to escape one's destiny, the more unavoidable it became.[30]

Although Pomponazzi accepted the mortalist interpretation of Aristotle developed in Alexander of Aphrodisias's *On the Soul,* he rejected the
Peripatetic critique of Stoic determinism put forward by the Greek commentator in his treatise *On Fate,* which was translated into Latin in 1516.
Alexander objected to the Stoic doctrine of fate because it eliminated any
possibility of free will. Pomponazzi, who supported the Stoic position
against Alexander, pointed out that this arch-Aristotelian, in arguing for
the existence of contingency, had failed to take into account the fundamental Aristotelian principle that, apart from the Unmoved Mover, movement must be initiated from outside. Since no secondary cause can move
if it is not itself moved, the human will, in opting for one choice instead of
another, must be determined by some external force. We may have the illusion of free choice, but this is simply because we are ignorant of the real

---

27. Pietro Pomponazzi, *Libri quinque de fato, de libero arbitrio et de praedestinatione,* ed.
R. Lemay (Lugano, 1957), 158: "ista sublunaria a superioribus gubernari."
    28. Ibid., 35: "quod evenit inevitabiliter evenit."
    29. Ibid., 211, 213.   30. Ibid., 44.

cause of our decisions. The Stoics were therefore right to find no room for either contingency or human freedom in a sublunary realm controlled by the ineluctable movement of the heavenly spheres.

Not only were the Stoics more faithful to Aristotle than Alexander was, they were more Aristotelian than Aristotle himself. For "the Philosopher," as Pomponazzi noted, had contradicted his own principle, expounded in *Physics* 8, that motion cannot be self-initiated, when in works such as the *Nicomachean Ethics,* written to promote moral responsibility among the general population, he held that we have free will.[31] Indeed, the doctrine that Pomponazzi attributed to the Stoics was in many respects more Aristotelian than Stoic. By presenting his own version of Peripatetic astral fatalism in the guise of Stoicism, which was generally thought to have much in common with Christianity, Pomponazzi was not only able to demonstrate that this doctrine was the "opinion least likely to be contradicted,"[32] but also to highlight its superiority, in purely philosophical and rational terms, to Christian providentialism, on the grounds that it had a more acceptable theodicy. While the omnipotent Christian God is open to the charge of injustice because he can eliminate evil and sin from the world but chooses not to do so, Stoic providence is determined not by a personal God, capable of direct intervention in human affairs, but rather by the eternal and immutable structure of the universe, to which even the divinity is subservient.[33] "Since," however, as Pomponazzi consistently affirmed, "human wisdom is almost always in error, nor can man attain the genuine truth, especially in relation to divine mysteries, by means of purely natural reasoning, one must in everything stand by the determination of the Church, which is guided by the Holy Spirit."[34] Therefore, Stoic fate is to be rejected in favor of Christian divine providence, which must be firmly embraced as the absolute truth.

Yet the church's position was not itself without problems, as generations of theologians had discovered when trying to reconcile divine providence with human free will. Unsatisfied with any previous attempts to re-

31. *De fato,* 274–75.

32. Ibid., 451: "nulla . . . opinionum est magis remota a contradictione quam opinio Stoicorum."

33. Ibid., 202.

34. Ibid., 453: "cum sapientia humana quasi semper sit in errore, neque homo ex puris naturalibus potest attingere ad sinceram veritatem et praecipue archanorum Dei, ideo in omnibus standum est determinationi Ecclesiae quae a Spiritu Sancto regulatur."

solve this dilemma, Pomponazzi formulated his own solution in the second half of *On Fate*. Like the humanist Lorenzo Valla (1406–1457) in his *Dialogue on Free Will* (1437), Pomponazzi recognized that there were two sides to God's providence—his omniscience and his omnipotence—and that while the former was, in principle, compatible with the existence of free will, the latter presented seemingly intractable difficulties. Valla had taken the view that as pious Christians we should not delve further into this impenetrable mystery and should instead humbly accept that the answer was not accessible to the meager powers of the human intellect; our failure to understand this matter was, in any case, of no importance, for "we stand by faith, not by the probability of reason."[35] Rather than follow Valla down this fideistic path, Pomponazzi attempted to find a rational solution to the problem of human freedom, rescuing it, if not from the philosophical determinism of the Stoic doctrine of fate, then at least from the theological determinism of the Christian dogma of divine omnipotence. He did this by arguing, on the one hand, that God, in order to preserve the distinction between past, present, and future time, had limited his own omnipotence by predetermining the future as contingent, and, on the other hand, that the human will had a purely negative power of suspending its act of choice, that is, of refusing to make a decision between the alternatives presented to it by the intellect. However weak and unsatisfactory this resolution may seem, it had cost Pomponazzi dearly, as he made clear in his heartfelt lament for the philosopher who attempts to comprehend the mysteries of God: like Prometheus, "he is eaten away by perpetual cares and thoughts; he feels no thirst or hunger; he does not sleep, he does not eat, he does not spit; ridiculed by everyone and regarded as foolish and impious, he is persecuted by inquisitors and made into a public spectacle. These then are the wages earned by philosophers, this is their reward."[36]

Although Pomponazzi took the precaution of not committing *On Fate* to print, the work circulated in manuscript and, as he predicted, left him

---

35. Lorenzo Valla, *Dialogue on Free Will*, in E. Cassirer et al., eds., *The Renaissance Philosophy of Man* (Chicago and London, 1948), 155–82, at 180; Lorenzo Valla, *Über den freien Willen. De libero arbitrio*, ed. and trans. E. Kessler (Munich, 1987), 140.

36. Ibid., 262: "perpetuis curis et cogitationibus roditur, non sitit, non famescit, non dormit, non comedit, non expuit, ab omnibus irridetur, et tanquam stultus et sacrilegus habetur, ab inquisitoribus prosequitur, fit spectaculum vulgi. Haec igitur sunt lucra philosophorum, haec est eorum merces."

open to attack, though not on the scale of the controversy over his treatise *On the Immortality of the Soul.* The chief persecutor was Bishop Ambrogio Flandino, who had earlier denounced his treatise on immortality.
Flandino, in his polemic against *On Fate,* completed in 1524 and dedicated to Pope Clement VII, not only accused Pomponazzi of every vice from
hypocrisy and arrogance to lust and gluttony but also insinuated that his
philosophical defense of Stoic determinism was, in effect, clandestine pro-
paganda for the Lutheran doctrine of predestination. Pomponazzi was
thus an agent of the devil, secretly supporting Luther's rebellion against
the Catholic Church, which would, if successful, destroy Christendom.[37]

POMPONAZZI'S LATER REPUTATION

In his *Elogies of Learned Men* (1546), the historian Paolo Giovio (1486–
1552), who had studied under Pomponazzi, admitted that his teacher, "who
took first place among distinguished Peripatetics," had attempted to prove
that, according to Aristotle, the soul died along with the body, a harmful
theory that corrupted the youth and undermined Christian discipline.
Giovio nonetheless pointed out that the "most holy and erudite" Cardinal
Cajetan had agreed with Pomponazzi's writings.[38] Far from dying down
in the seventeenth century, the controversy surrounding Pomponazzi es-
calated into full-scale notoriety. This was to some extent a matter of guilt
by association: the Neapolitan philosopher Giulio Cesare Vanini (1585–
1619), who was burned at the stake in Toulouse on the charges of atheism,
blasphemy, and impiety, gave pride of place among recent thinkers who
had inspired him to Machiavelli and Pomponazzi, describing the latter as
"the prince of philosophers in our times" and referring to him as a "god-
like teacher."[39] Though more skeptical about astrology than Pomponazzi,

37. Flandino's *De fato contra Petrum Pomponatium pro Alexandro Aphrodisio apologia*
is preserved only in manuscript; see R. Lemay, "The Fly against the Elephant: Flandinus
against Pomponazzi on Fate," in *Philosophy and Humanism: Renaissance Essays in Honor of
Paul Oskar Kristeller,* ed. E. Mahoney (Leiden, 1976), 70–99.

38. Paolo Giovio, *Gli elogi degli uomini illustri (letterati, artisti, uomini d'arme),* ed. R.
Meregazzi (Rome, 1972), 96: "Petrus Pomponatius, Mantuanus, in philosophia praeceptor
meus, inter Peripateticos illustres primum suggestus locum obtinuit"; "vir sanctissimus
atque doctissimus, Thomas Caietanus Cardinalis."

39. Giulio Cesare Vanini, *De admirandis naturae reginae deaeque mortalium arcanis*

Vanini took over his emphasis on finding natural causes for all phenomena, even so-called miracles, and his belief that all earthly events, including the rise and fall of religions, were determined by universal laws of nature.

The prominence given to Pomponazzi by Vanini led the French Jesuit François Garasse (1585–1631) to condemn his writings sight unseen. Giving thanks to God that he had not had to waste any time reading the impieties of Pomponazzi, having been sufficiently informed about them through the works of Vanini, Garasse, in a polemical tract simultaneously directed against Protestants and contemporary French freethinkers, declared Pomponazzi to be a "very wicked man," who must have been "some kind of a devil incarnate."[40] Toward the end of the century, the German scholar Daniel Morhof (1639–1691) laid at his feet the blame not only for Vanini but also for the Spinozas and Hobbeses of his own day, whose arrows, he claimed, had come from Pomponazzi's quiver.[41]

While the conviction that Pomponazzi was a freethinker *avant la lettre* brought him discredit in some quarters, within the Republic of Letters it earned him a certain respect. The ambiguity of his reputation is well illustrated by the account of him in the *Naudeana*, a posthumously published collection of anecdotes and sayings attributed to Gabriel Naudé (1626–1653): "Pomponazzi was an atheist or at any rate a dangerous freethinker, because he was clever."[42] The second edition of the *Naudeana* was edited by the Protestant scholar and champion of toleration Pierre Bayle (1647–1706), who devoted a substantial and sympathetic article to Pomponazzi in the enlarged 1702 edition of his *Historical and Critical Dictionary*. Accepting at face value Pomponazzi's declarations at the end of his treatise *On the Immortality of the Soul*, Bayle wrote: "He did not call into doubt the immortality of the soul; on the contrary, he maintained that it was very certain dogma, of which he was firmly persuaded. He maintained only that the

---

(1616), in his *Opere*, ed. G. Papuli and F. P. Raimondi (Galatina, 1990), 469: "Pomponatio, nostri saeculi philosophorum principe," "divinus praeceptor."

40. François Garasse, *La Doctrine curieuse des beaux esprits de ce temps* (Paris, 1624), 1010: "Pour le Pomponace je n'en puis dire autre chose, sinon que c'est un tresmeschant homme . . . je dis que cet homme devoit estre quelque Diable incarne."

41. Daniel Georg Morhof, *Polyhistor, literarius, philosophicus et practicus . . .*, 4th ed. (Lubeck, 1747), 55–56, at 56: "Pomponatius, omnium magister, e cujus pharetra omnia illa tela desumta sunt, quibus nunc utuntur Spinosae et Hobbesii . . ."

42. *Naudeana et Patiniana*, , 2nd ed., ed. Pierre Bayle (Amsterdam, 1703), 33: "Pomponace étoit un athée ou du moins un libertin très-dangereux, parce qu'il avoit de l'esprit."

natural reasons given for it were neither solid nor convincing."[43] Pomponazzi's denial that Aristotelianism could be used to demonstrate the Christian dogma was a view, moreover, which present-day Cartesians would
support, since they held that no philosophical system previous to that de-
vised by Descartes was capable of providing an ironclad proof of immortality.[44] In Bayle's eyes, Pomponazzi was an innocent victim of the bigotry
and hypocrisy of the Catholic Church: since it accepted that dogmas such
as the Trinity, the Incarnation, and Transubstantiation were based on revelation rather than reason, why should Pomponazzi be suspected of irreligion for saying the same thing in relation to the immortality of the soul?[45]
It was absurd for theologians to accuse a philosopher of impiety simply
because he declared that in those areas where natural reason leaves us in
doubt, we must turn to the word of God: "This is what Pomponazzi did,
and for having done so, he saw himself cruelly persecuted by the monks.
What a fine state of affairs!"[46]

Jacob Brucker (1696–1770), author of the monumental *Critical History
of Philosophy,* first published between 1742 and 1744, expressed admiration
for Pomponazzi's philosophical learning but contempt for his "barbarous,
inept, and garbled" Latin style, which reeked of the "Scholastic stable."[47]
Far worse for Brucker, a devout Lutheran, was Pomponazzi's impiety: "he
preferred to pursue Aristotelian nonsense than to philosophize in a pious
and restrained manner," putting forward monstrous notions, especially in
his *On Incantations,* "which were completely at variance with sound learning and which did harm to the Christian religion."[48] In his treatise *On Fate,*

43. Pierre Bayle, "Pomponace," in his *Dictionnaire critique et historique,* 16 vols. (Paris,
1820–1824), 12.226–44, at 227: "[I]l n'a point révoqué en doute l'immortalité de l'âme; il a
soutenu au contraire que c'était un dogme très-certain, et dont il était fermement persua-
dé. Il a soutenu seulement que les raisons naturelles que l'on en donne ne sont point sol-
ides et convaincantes."

44. Ibid., 236.

45. Ibid., 229.

46. Ibid., 236: "C'est ce qu'a fait Pomponace, et pour l'avoir fait il s'est vu persecuté
cruellement par la moinerie. Que cela est beau!"

47. Jacob Brucker, *Historia critica philosophiae . . . ,* 2nd ed., 6 vols. (Leipzig, 1766–1767),
4.1, pp. 158–82, at 161: "in stilo barbaro, inepto, confuso, et Scholasticorum stabulum redo-
lente."

48. Ibid., 167: "fatendum omnino est, valde suspectum eum esse impietatis, qua Aris-
totelicas nugas sequi, quam pie sobrieque philosophari maluit, adeo monstrosa et a sani-
tate doctrinae abhorrentia inque ipsam Christianam religionem iniuria sunt ea maxime,
quae in libro *de Incantationibus* suggerit."

moreover, Pomponazzi had pushed aside St. Paul in order to put Aristotle triumphantly on the throne. It would therefore take a heroic act of faith to believe in the sincerity of his professed veneration for, and obedience to, the dogmas of the Catholic Church.[49]

This image of Pomponazzi was disseminated during the Enlightenment through the article on "Aristotelianism" in the *Encyclopedia*, which, like many of the entries on the history of philosophy, was strongly colored by Brucker's views. The author, Abbé Claude Yvon (ca. 1720–ca. 1790), a second-rate man of letters, stated that Pomponazzi had "no God other than Aristotle" and that "he laughed at everything he saw in the Gospels." Yvon was unable to fathom how Pomponazzi's defenders could claim that his views on immortality, miracles, and determinism were offered solely in his capacity as a philosopher and that, as a Christian, "he believed in all the dogmas of our religion."[50] He was convinced that while Pomponazzi paid lip-service to Christianity, "he was impious in his heart."[51]

The conviction that Pomponazzi's deference to the Christian religion was a calculating gesture, aimed at protecting himself from persecution, continued to be voiced during the nineteenth and twentieth centuries. Instead of tarring him with the brush of irreligion, however, it helped to transform Pomponazzi into a radical philosopher and forerunner of Galileo. Yet this positive account is no less biased than the negative one from which it derives, since it reflects an anachronistic approach both to Pomponazzi's secularism and to his methods of philosophical enquiry. He did not want to challenge or abandon Christian beliefs but to set them aside temporarily, in an effort to determine what precisely the pagan philosopher Aristotle had thought on a given issue. And although he was willing to question Aristotle's authority on the basis of experience and eyewitness observations—often reported secondhand—Pomponazzi's philosophy was not constructed on a foundation of empirical, and still less experimental, data. Rather, it was grounded in an acute and critical reading of Aristotle and his commentators, enabling him to draw out implications and to identify contradictions

---

49. Ibid., 169.

50. "Aristotélisme," in *Encyclopédie*, 35 vols. (Paris 1751–1780), 1.652–73, at 665: "[I]l n'eut d'autre dieu qu'Aristote; il rioit de tout ce qu'il voyait dans l'Evangile"; "[I]l croyoit tous les dogmes de notre religion."

51. Ibid., 667: "[I]l étoit chrétien de bouche, et impie dans le coeur."

that eluded other exegetes. To understand Pomponazzi we need to see him not as a pioneer of modern attitudes toward the separation of reason and religion nor as a harbinger of the Scientific Revolution but as one of the foremost representatives of a tradition that stretched from the late Middle Ages to the end of the Renaissance: secular Aristotelianism.

Note: For further reading see Pomponazzi; Ferri; Kristeller 1955; Pagnoni Sturlese; Perfetti 1998. For secondary sources see Bakker; Bianchi; Blum 2007; Caroti; Casini 2007; Céard; Cuttini; Di Napoli; Doni; Douglas; Eberl; Galimberti; Gilson 1961; Graiff; Granada; Innocenti; Iorio; Jadin; Kessler 1988, 1993, 2008; Kristeller 1956, 1964, 1968, 1983; Lemay; Lohr; Mahoney 1968; Maurer; Mojsisch; Nardi; Oliva; Olivieri; Perfetti; Perrone Compagni; Pine; Pluta; Poppi 1970, 1988; Raimondi; Ramberti; Randall; Salatowsky; Scribano; Suarez-Nani; Tavuzzi; Treloar; Vasoli 1995; Wilson; Wonde; Zambelli; and Zanier.

9

NICCOLÒ MACCHIAVELLI

(1469–1527)

A Good State for Bad People

Heinrich C. Kuhn

Niccolò Machiavelli (1469–1527) was for many years employed in the administration of the commonwealth of Florence and was later dismissed.[1] He was a military theoretician, the author of accounts of political travels, a dramatist, and a man of letters who even today is celebrated for the lucidity of his prose style.[2] His works contain so many contradictions, startling leaps of thought, inconsistencies, and obscure passages that a conclusive interpretation has proved impossible up to the present day and will most likely continue to do so in the future. He offers his readers much that is extraordinary. The secondary literature is both rich and various (to put it mildly).[3]

1. Bertelli 1979 gives information about editions from the sixteenth to the nineteenth centuries.

2. De Grazia 1994, 3, calls him Italy's "greatest writer of prose."

3. Examples of inconsistencies between individual works are the clearly divergent remarks about fortresses in *De principatibus* and the *Discorsi* (e.g., *De Principatibus* ch. 20 [Machiavelli 1994, 287f.—on the use of *this* edition in the present essay instead of the edition by Martelli and Marcelli (Machiavelli 2006), see below, note 4, paragraph 2] in comparison to *Discorsi* II ch. 24 [Machiavelli, 2001a, 463ff.].). Cf. the assessments of the political order in Florence in the *Provisione della ordinanza* 1 and the *Provisioni della repubblica di Firenze*

Despite all the contradictions and inconsistencies—some of which are due to shifts in perspective, while others are explained in the secondary literature as the author's development of his theses—we encounter some points again and again. First, there is the close link between the political and the military order (see below); and second, there is the impetus to set up an ideal state. In view of Machiavelli's widespread reputation as a cynical advocate of tyranny (Buck, 129ff.), this may surprise some readers.

According to Machiavelli, there is no greater source of honor than the good reordering of a state. When this truly succeeds, the one who has reordered the state is wonderful and worthy of admiration.[4] Indeed, "Never is a man as highly praised for any of his actions, as are those who have reformed the commonwealth and the realms with laws and institutions: it is they who are, after those who were Gods, praised most. And because there were few who had the chance to do so, and very few who did know how to do it, the number of those who did it is small. And this glory has been considered as so prestigious by the men—who ever cared for anything else besides glory—that as they could not create a commonwealth in reality, they did create it in writings, as did Aristotle, Plato, and many others. . . ."[5]

---

per istituire il magistrato de' nove ufficiali dell' ordinanza e milizia fiorentina . . . Provvisione prima (Machiavelli 2001b, 477ff.; Machiavelli 1961, 101ff.) in comparison to the parallel passage in *La cagione dell'ordinanza dove si trovi e quel che bisogni fare* 1 in the *Discorso dell' ordinare lo stato di Firenze alle armi* (Machiavelli 2001b, 470ff.; Machiavelli 1961, 95ff.). Cf. the remarks about Francesco Sforza in the *Arte della guerra* I (Machiavelli 2001b, 42f.) in comparison to what we read in *De principatibus* ch. 7 (Machiavelli 1994, 208). On internal contradictions in the *Discorsi* (and an attempt to resolve these by reflections on the chronology of the genesis of the texts), see Bausi 1985 (and also Bausi's *Introduzione* to Machiavelli 2001a).

4. *De principatibus* ch. 26 (Machiavelli 1994, 309). Cf. also the "Non dà adunque, il cielo maggiore dono ad uno uomo, né gli può mostrare piú gloriosa via di questa [viz., to establish or impose order upon a society in real life]" in the *Discursus florentinarum rerum post mortem iunioris Laurentii Medices* (Machiavelli 2001b, 640).

N.B.: For the *De principatibus*, I continue to quote *Inglese's* text (Machiavelli 1994) rather than the new edition by Martelli and Marcelli (Machiavelli 2006). Too much space would be required here to explain the various reasons that have led to this decision; I hope that I can do so on another occasion. My reservations about the text established in Machiavelli 2006 (and about parts of the commentaries that accompany it) do not mean that I dispute the presence of much suggestive and useful material in the commentaries on Machiavelli, etc. Even one who (like myself) continues to prefer the *text* of Inglese should at the very least also consult the edition by Martelli and Marcelli for the sake of their commentary on the questions discussed.

5. *Discursus florentinarum rerum post mortem iunioris Laurentii Medices* (Machiavelli 2001b, 640: ". . . non è esaltato alcuno uomo tanto in alcuna sua azione, quanto sono quegli che hanno con leggi e con istituti reformato la republica e i regni: questi sono, dopo

But Machiavelli is not interested in a merely *ideal* state. He does not want to write about something imaginary, but about something real: "But as I intended to write something useful for him who understands me, I considered it more convenient to go directly for the real truth of the thing than for its phantasy. And many have imagined republics and principalities which never were seen nor known in real existence. Because how one lives is that distant from how one should live, he who sets aside what one does in favor of that what one does, will learn about his ruin instead of learning about his preservation."[6] In other words, his subject is not utopia, but politics in the real world.

The people in Machiavelli's world are not very good. They do good only when they must.[7] Nature makes few of them decent *(gagliardi)*.[8] Property means more to them than honors.[9] One who does good will be completely submerged among all the wicked persons.[10] Against this background, Machiavelli does not offer a theory of politics that is primarily orientated to an abstract "common good." The "common good" remains empty of contents; in one place, Machiavelli uses "common good" as an equivalent to a military leader's own view, which he must convince his subordinates to accept.[11] Otherwise, it remains vague.[12]

Machiavelli's subjects are different. Among the best known are the acquisition of power by the new prince in *De principatibus*.[13] This ruler has at-

---

quegli che sono stati Iddii, i primi laudati. E perché e' sono stati pochi che abbino avuto occasione di farlo, e pochissimi quelli che lo abbino saputo fare, sono piccolo numero quelli che lo abbino fatto. E è stata stimata tanto questa gloria dagli uomini che non hanno mai atteso ad altro ch'a gloria, che non avendo possuto fare una republica in atto, l'hanno fatto in scritto; come Aristotile, Platone e molt'altri. . . ."

6. "Ma sendo l'intenzione mia [stata] scrivere cosa che sia utile a chi la intende, mi è parso più conveniente andare drieto alla verità effettuale della cosa che alla immaginazione di essa. E molti si sono immaginate republiche e principate che non si sono mai visti né conosciuti in vero essere. Perché gli è tanto discosto da come si vive a come si dovrebbe vivere, che colui che lascia quello che si fa, per quello che si dovrebbe fare, impara più presto la ruina che la preservazione sua" (*De principatibus* ch. 15 [Machiavelli 1994, 253]).

7. *Discorsi* 1, ch. 3 (Machiavelli 2001a, 30).

8. *Dell'arte della guerra* 7 (Machiavelli 2001b, 278).

9. *Discorsi* 1, ch. 37 (Machiavelli 2001a, 18; cf. op. cit., 185 n. 69).

10. *De principatibus* ch. 15 (Machiavelli 1994, 253f.).

11. *Dell'arte della guerra* 4 (Machiavelli 2001b, 184).

12. Cf. *Discorsi* 2, ch. 2 (Machiavelli 2001b, 13).

13. On the choice of the title "De principatibus" instead of "Il principe" (the widespread title since the first printing [cf. Inglese's introduction to Machiavelli 1994, 26]), cf.

tained power neither by election[14] nor by hereditary succession,[15] but either by virtue *(virtus)*, by Fortuna, or by villainy.[16] Aristotle had discussed
such "tyrants," their path to rule, and their specific instruments of rule, in
the fifth book of his *Politics*,[17] and he is not wholly condemnatory: he too
employs language that can at least in part be understood as advice.[18] Similarly, Giles of Rome had explicitly discussed the subject of the new prince
in his immensely influential[19] *De regimine principum,* where he writes that
the behavior of such a ruler tends to be tyrannical.[20] Most of Machiavelli's
counsels for a new prince are unexceptional; if they seem extraordinary,
this is due either to ignorance of the tradition in which he stands or to the
formulations he chooses when he hands on his advice.

Nevertheless, there are astonishing things in *De principatibus.* The
book insinuates that it is giving its dedicatee (Lorenzo de' Medici, duke
of Urbino) recipes that will enable him to make himself lord of all Italy.
One glance at a political-historical map of Italy at that period[21] suffices to
show that there was little probability of such a project being realized; and
the advice to disarm all the territories that had been conquered by military

---

Inglese's information about the choice of title in the manuscripts that do not depend on
printed sources (esp. Machiavelli 1994, 39, 41, 43, 50; on this, cf. also Machiavelli 2006, 49
n. 45 [although I cannot accept the argumentation in the latter work, which argues that
the use of "De principatibus" as a title is likely to confuse nonspecialists]; and last but not
least, cf. Machiavelli's own reference to this work in his *Discorsi* [2, 1: Machiavelli 2001a,
309: "nostro trattato De' principate"]). The reference to this work as "De Principe" in 3,
42 (Machiavelli 2001a, 767) seems more likely to be the result of an unintentional abbre-
viation or an abbreviating reading than vice versa; besides this, in this passage, two of the
manuscripts (B and G) have information about the contents ("*del* Prencipe") rather than a
title. And I do not believe that any text offers support for the idea that Machiavelli himself
called this work "*Il* Principe."

14. *De principatibus* ch. 19 (Machiavelli 1994, 282); but cf. also *De principatibus* ch. 9
(Machiavelli 1994, 224ff.).

15. The discussion of inherited rule in *De principatibus* is extremely brief, and relates
only how easy it is to retain such a rule (ch. 2; Machiavelli 1994, 184f.).

16. Cf. *De principatibus* ch. 8 (Machiavelli 1994, 217).

17. Especially from 1313a34.   18. Cf., e.g., 1314b1 ff.

19. Cf. Canning 1996, 133.

20. On this, cf. *De regimine* 3, pars 2, ch. 5 (Ægidius, 1607, 462f.); cf. also 3, pars 2, ch. 15
(Rule 3: Ægidius, 1607, 490f.)—note that this lists the requirements for the conduct of
good kings, not of wicked tyrants. For the "genuinely" tyrannical measures undertaken
in order to hold onto power, cf. 3, pars 2, ch. 10 (Ægidius, 1607, 477ff.); but one should also
note the statement in ch. 11 of the same part that all rulers who are not at least demigods
employ at least some of the "specifically tyrannical" measures (Ægidius, 1607, 481).

21. For a simplified overview, cf., e.g., Marino 1994, 332.

force (instead of using their inhabitants to reinforce the conqueror's own army)[22] shows that it was completely unrealizable. It is impossible to say whether Machiavelli was serious about his call for the unification of Italy under Medicean rule; but he was certainly serious when he insisted that the ruler must make it his *first priority* to assemble troops of his own, a military force consisting of the ruler's own subjects.[23]

The connection between the political and the military spheres, and the dependence of the political order on the military, is one of Machiavelli's principal themes. He writes in chapter 12 of *De principatibus*: "The basic fundaments of any state, be it new or old or mixed, are the good laws and the good military. And because there can be no good laws where there is no good military, and as it happens that where there is good military there are good laws, I'll skip reasoning about laws and will speak about the military."[24] For Machiavelli, a good military is never one that owes obedience to other rulers;[25] still less does it consist of mercenary troops.[26] It must always consist of "one's own" troops, recruited from subjects of the commonwealth or of the ruler and deployed by it or by him.[27] The artillery

22. *De principatibus* ch. 20 (Machiavelli 1994, 284).

23. *De principatibus* ch. 26 (Machiavelli 1994, 310).

24. "E principali fondamenti che abbino tutti li stati, così nuovi come vechi o mixti, sono le buone legge e le buone arme: e perché non può essere buone legge dove non sono buone arme, e dove sono buone arme conviene sieno buonne legge, io lascerò indietro el ragionare delle legge e parlerò delle arme" (Machiavelli 1994, 236). I am grateful for a discussion of this passage in the late 1990s with John Sloan, John Leonard, Luc Borot, Ray Lurie, and (last but not least) Walter Stephens. Cf. also the *Cagione dell'ordinanza, dove la si trovi quel che bisogna fare* / the *Discorso del ordinare lo stato di Firenze alle armi* (Machiavelli 2001b, 470ff.; Machiavelli 1961, 95ff.) as well as the toned-down version of this, accommodated to the actual circumstances of government: *Provisione della ordinanza* (Machiavelli's draft) / *Provvisioni della repubblica di Firenze per istituire il magistrato de' nove ufficiali dell' Ordinanza e Milizia fiorentina, dettate da Niccolò Machiavelli. Provisione prima per le fanterie, del 6 dicembre 1506* (official version) (Machiavelli 2001b, 477ff. / Machiavelli 1961, 101ff.), and the Preface to *Dell' arte della guerra* (Machiavelli 2001b, 27ff.), *Discorsi* 1, ch. 4 (Machiavelli 2001a, 33), and *Discorsi* 3, ch. 31 (Machiavelli 2001b, 720), where we are told that the reader will find similar passages everywhere in the *Discorsi* ("ad ogni punto, nel leggere questa istoria").

25. Cf. e.g. *Discorsi* 2, ch. 20 (Machiavelli 2001a, 440ff.), *De principatibus* ch. 13 (Machiavelli 1994, 244ff.), *Dell' arte della guerra* 3 (Machiavelli 2001b, 132).

26. Against mercenary troops: e.g., *De principatibus* chs. 12 and 13 (Machiavelli 1994, 235ff.), *Discorsi* 1, ch. 43 (Machiavelli 2001a, 213f.), *Dell' arte della guerra* 1 (Machiavelli 2001b, 56f.), *Dell' arte della guerra* 7 (Machiavelli 2001a, 284ff.).

27. Cf. e.g. *Dell' arte della guerra* 1 (Machiavelli 2001b, 55ff.), *De principatibus* ch. 13 (Machiavelli 1994, 244ff.), *Discorsi* 1, ch. 21 (Machiavelli 2001a, 124ff.).

is largely useless,[28] and the cavalry has relatively little significance.[29] The most important part of the army is the largest in terms of numbers, namely, the infantry.[30] Soldiers should be recruited from all the professions.[31] And the soldiers are to remain in their professional work: the formation of a professional army is rejected as detrimental to the order of the commonwealth.[32]

The establishing of such an "army of subjects" has political consequences. Commands cannot be issued to the people, and it is no longer so easy to rule it.[33] The consequence of having "one's own" army and arming the populace—which is a necessary precondition for every extension of one's rule—is that precisely this populace can no longer be manipulated by the ruler as he pleases.[34] Once the populace has been armed, anyone who attempts to disarm it puts his rule at risk.[35] In any case, Machiavelli advises the individual ruler always to behave in such a way that "the people" *(populo)*, that is, the broad masses of the populace,[36] will take his side.[37] Machiavelli sees the wish of the *populo* not to be oppressed as "more honorable" *(più onesto)* than the wish of the great men to oppress it.[38] When this people is kept in a state of repression and is unarmed, this leads to a danger-

28. Cf. *Dell' arte della guerra* 3 (Machiavelli 2001b, 138–145), *Discorsi* 2, ch. 17 (Machiavelli 2001a, 406ff.). On this context, cf. also Fachard 1996, 161f.

29. Cf. *Discorsi* 2, ch. 17 (Machiavelli 2001a, 417f.) and *Discorsi* 2, ch. 18 (Machiavelli 2001a, 419ff.).

30. Cf. the passages on the cavalry in n. 30 above, and *Dell' arte della guerra* 1 (Machiavelli 2001b, 48).

31. Cf. *Dell' arte della guerra* 1 (Machiavelli 2001b, 64). (Such a general arming of all the groups in the population is very different from what we find in the classical political theory of Aristotle and Plato.)

32. Cf. *Dell' arte della guerra* 1 (Machiavelli 2001b, 45–50).

33. Cf. *Dell' arte della guerra* 1 (Machiavelli 2001b, 49; 59).

34. *Discorsi* 1, ch. 6 (Machiavelli 2001a, 45).

35. *De principatibus* ch. 20 (Machiavelli 1994, 283f.). Such an attempt makes the people hate the ruler; but a ruler must attempt at all costs to avoid being hated (cf. *De principatibus* ch. 17 [Machiavelli 1994, 261ff.]).

36. Machiavelli includes himself in this category: cf. the close of the second-last paragraph of the dedicatory epistle in *De principatibus* (Macchiavelli 1994, 182).

37. Cf., e.g., *De principatibus* ch. 9 (Machiavelli 1994, 225ff.), ch. 19 (Machiavelli 1994, 270ff.), ch. 20 (Machiavelli 1994, 288), *Discorsi* 1, ch. 16 (Machiavelli 2001a, 103), ch. 40 (Machiavelli 2001a, 207f.), *Discorsi* 3, ch. 6 (Machiavelli 2001a, 589). In some of these passages, as well as in other texts (cf. e.g. *Ritratto di cose di Francia* [Machiavelli 2001b, 546ff.]), Machiavelli's attitude to the grandees and nobles *(magni)* is clearly less friendly.

38. *De principatibus* ch. 9 (Machiavelli 1994, 225). Cf. also *Discorsi* 1, ch. 4 (Machiavelli 2001a, 35f.).

ous weakness and makes lasting rule impossible.[39] But this is not all. The people is morally superior to the prince;[40] although it is ignorant, it has the capacity to perceive the truth.[41] The mass of the people is wiser and more reliable than a prince.[42] The people is a suitable guardian of the constitution,[43] and it makes fewer mistakes than a prince in allocating public offices.[44] Thanks to a hidden power *(per occulta virtù)*, the people sees what is bad for itself and what is good.[45] Whether or not it possesses laws, it is superior to a prince in the same situation.[46]

Machiavelli attempts to show the Medicis, who ruled Florence (more or less directly) like princes, that a republic is the only form of government that is in any way suited to Florence.[47] A republic can be stable only when it takes account of the populace as a whole.[48] In a well-ordered republic, it is impossible for an individual with sinister intentions to do any harm.[49] Municipalities in which the *popoli* rule make great progress in a short time, because rule by the people is superior to rule by princes.[50] Municipalities become great when the common good is superior to particular interests— and this is the case only in republics.[51] According to Machiavelli, the power and the fickleness of Fortuna are great,[52] and it is important to be able to adapt to changing times.[53] In these circumstances, republics are lon-

39. *Discorsi* 1, ch. 6 (Machiavelli 2001a, 45).
40. Cf. *Discorsi* 1, ch. 29 (Machiavelli 2001a, 145ff.).
41. *Discorsi* 1, ch. 4 (Machiavelli 2001a, 36).
42. *Discorsi* 1, ch. 58 (Machiavelli 2001a, 276ff.).
43. *Discorsi* 1, ch. 5 (Machiavelli 2001a, 37ff.).
44. *Discorsi* 1, ch. 58 (Machiavelli 2001a, 283); *Discorsi* 3, ch. 34 (Machiavelli 2001a, 737f.).
45. *Discorsi* ch. 58 (Machiavelli 2001a, 283).
46. *Discorsi* ch. 58 (Machiavelli 2001a, 285).
47. *Discursus florentinarum rerum post mortem iunioris Laurentii Medices* (Machiavelli 2001b, 631f.).
48. *Discursus florentinarum rerum post mortem iunioris Laurentii Medices* (Machiavelli 2001b, 636).
49. *Discorsi* 3, ch. 8 (Machiavelli 2001a, 601).
50. "Vedesi, ortra di questo, lle città dove i popoli sono principi, fare in brevissimo tempo augumenti eccessivi e molto maggiori che quelle che sempre sono state sotto uno principe; [. . .] Il che non può nascere da altro se non che sono migliori governi quegli de' popoli che quegli de' principi": *Discorsi* 1, ch. 58 (Machiavelli 2001a, 384).
51. *Discorsi* 2, ch. 2 (Machiavelli 2001a, 313).
52. Cf. e.g. *Dell' arte della guerra* 4 (Machiavelli 2001b, 160), *La vita di Castruccio Castracani da Lucca* (Machiavelli 1981, 486), *De principatibus* ch. 25 (Machiavelli 1994, 302–306).
53. Cf. e.g. *Dell' arte della guerra* 1 (Machiavelli 2001b, 36ff.), *De principatibus* ch. 25

ger lived and more favored by Fortuna than principalities because the rich diversity of their citizens allows republics to adapt better to the times in which they live.[54] The peoples are so much superior to the princes when it is a question of keeping things in order that those who set up the rule of the people are praised for doing so.[55]

Machiavelli spoke of the high honor accruing to those who had reordered the commonwealths and of those who had not had the opportunity of doing so, but had nevertheless made suggestions about how this ought to be done. He claimed that he had written about politics in accordance with political reality. He had written about the intimate connection between the military and the political orders, and had located the efficient cause in the military order. He had sought to show that the only good military orders are those where the army consists of one's own subjects. He regarded the republic as the political order that corresponded to a good military order of this kind.

If the powerful men who read him had followed his advice, and if this had led to the outcome that Machiavelli had hoped for, his place would assuredly be *between* those who reorder commonwealths and those who only write about the ordering of commonwealths. And yet it is indeed true that in his own estimation, Florence had never been a genuine republic in all the period for which reliable traditions existed;[56] and in all the period of its existence as a more or less autonomous political unit, it never became a genuine republic (the only exception being at most the episode from 1527 to 1530).[57] Nevertheless, there is a considerable difference between the theories about the ideal political state proposed by other utopists and Machiavelli's comprehensive investigation of human nature, concrete circumstances, the meaning of government, military and political orders, and his endeavor to influence the political realm. His writings exercise a unique fascination.

(Machiavelli 1994, 300), *De principatibus* ch. 25 (Machiavelli 1994, 304ff.), *Discorsi* 3, ch. 9 (Machiavelli 2001a, 607ff.).

54. *Discorsi* 3, ch. 9 (Machiavelli 2001a, 610).
55. *Discorsi* 1, ch. 58 (Machiavelli 2001a, 284).
56. *Discorsi* 1, ch. 49 (Machiavelli 2001a, 236f.).
57. For a brief overview of the history of Florence after Machiavelli, cf., e.g., Capelli 1988, 410–12, or, e.g., *http://www.storiadifirenze.org/*.

Note: For further reading see Machiavelli in the References. For secondary sources see Bausi; Bertelli and Innocenti; Buck; Canning; Capelli; De Grazia; Granada; Fachard; Marino; and Vasoli 2006.

10

AGRIPPA VON NETTESHEIM

(1486–1535)

Philosophical Magic, Empiricism, and Skepticism

Wolf-Dieter Müller-Jahncke and Paul Richard Blum

Agrippa von Nettesheim, whose real name was Heinrich Cornelius, was born in Cologne on September 14, 1486. He began his studies in Cologne in 1499 and left the university in 1502 as master of arts. Apart from a period in Paris, his whereabouts are unknown until 1507. In 1509 he lectured at the University of Dôle on Johannes Reuchlin's *De verbo mirifico*, but the clergy had him expelled; Agrippa complains about this in several of his writings (*Opera* 2.492–501). After staying with John Colet in London, Agrippa went to Italy on military business in 1511, and was knighted there as *eques auratus* in 1512. He attended the University of Pavia, where he probably took his doctorate in medicine. In 1518 Agrippa took a post as lawyer in the free imperial city of Metz, where he defended before the Inquisition a woman from a village who had been accused of witchcraft. This defense led to accusations against Agrippa himself, and he left Metz and returned to Cologne in 1520. He became the municipal doctor in Geneva in 1522, and occupied the same post in Fribourg (Switzerland) from 1523. In 1524 he obtained a post at court as physician to Louise of Savoy, the mother of the French king. By mid-1526, however, his position at the French court had deteriorated to such an extent that he felt obliged to flee via Paris to Antwerp, where he worked as a doctor from 1528. Thanks to his merits as "plague doctor" during the outbreak of the "sweating sickness" *(sudor anglicus)*, he was appointed court historian in Mechelen in 1530, but pressure from the theological faculty of the University of Louvain forced him to abandon this position in the following year. Leaving Mechelen, Agrippa went to the court of Archbishop Hermann von Wied in Cologne, and later moved to Bonn with him. After travels through Germany, Agrippa returned to France in 1535, and was arrested in Lyons. In the same year, he died in Grenoble and was buried in the Dominican church in that city.

The first version of Agrippa's first major work, *De occulta philosophia* (On the Hidden Philosophy), was complete by 1510, and was dedicated to Johannes Trithemius, abbot of the Benedictine monastery in Würzburg. Since incorrect copies soon began to circulate, Agrippa decided in 1530 to revise the work and have it printed. The first book of *De occulta philosophia* was published by Johannes Graphaeus in Antwerp in 1531; all three books were published, in two typological variants, by Johannes Söter in Cologne in 1533. A fourth book, published by Andreas Kolbe in Marburg in 1559, should not be ascribed to Agrippa. In *De occulta philosophia*, which was later often described as a "compendium of magic," Agrippa drew principally on Neoplatonism and Hermeticism, but also on astrology, numerology, and the Cabbala as instruments for acquiring knowledge and mastery of the cosmos. His second major work, *De incertitudine et vanitate scientiarum atque artium* (On the Uncertainty, Indeed the Emptiness of the Sciences, Arts, and Crafts), was published by Graphaeus in Antwerp in 1530. With stylistic brilliance, Agrippa demonstrates here the contradictions of scientific doctrines and describes the controversies of the professors. Later historians have seen this text as a high point of his attacks on the established academic community, or else as a *summa* of his personal experience of life, and they have drawn attention to Agrippa's skeptical or even agnostic attitude. Agrippa's philosophy is reflected above all in his concept of *magia* in the *Occulta philosophia*. In both the 1510 version and the printed version of 1533, Agrippa divides magic into three sections, to each of which he dedicates a book. In the first book, he discusses natural magic, in the second book heavenly magic, and in the third book ceremonial magic. He defines the *magia naturalis* in the sense of Marsilio Ficino, namely, that magic can help the human person to know the properties of things and of the stars, and that one can make use of magic in soothsaying. Agrippa thus follows Pico della Mirandola in seeing magicians as the most exact investigators of nature. Consequently, magic is one section of the *philosophia naturalis*.

According to Agrippa, magic can be practiced only by one who fully grasps the system of the "emanational form of physics," which is elaborated in the framework of the traditional ideas about microcosm and macrocosm. Like other Renaissance philosophers, he sees a hierarchical order in the cosmos, in which a world-soul *(anima mundi)* is at work as the unifying principle. The world-soul transports the ideas of the archetype and brings these as "rational seeds" *(semina rationalia)* into the matter of the natural, intellectual, and heavenly worlds. In this matter, the rational seeds become visible as "forces" *(virtutes)*. The world-soul passes through various stages on its path from the archetype to matter. The first stage that it reaches is the spheres with the heavenly bodies; it either penetrates these directly or else unites itself to them, so that its mediatory task can be taken over by the world-spirit *(spiritus mundi)*. In this theory, Agrippa adopts Stoic ideas about *pneuma,* but he links these ideas to demons and intelligences, who occupy a prominent place in the texts about ceremonial magic *(magia caeremonialis)* which were available to him. Unlike Marsilio Ficino, Agrippa does not avoid listing the names of these demons and intelligences; but he agrees with Ficino in seeing them as autonomous forms of the world-spirit. Agrippa underlines the role of the stars and planets and the zodiac through his detailed exposition of their *virtutes* and of their influence on the sublunary world. Ultimately, the reason for this close link between astrology and magic lies in the transport of ideas from the archetype to matter, and Agrippa maintains that only the man who masters astrology as an art *(ars)* will be able to practice magic as natural philosophy. Through the mediation of the intelligences and demons, the world-soul and the world-spirit can imprint on matter a sign *(signum)* of the idea of the archetype. This signature reveals the *virtutes* of each thing and indicates its place in the cosmos. The world-soul dynamically unites the upper world with the lower world, and vibrations can arise (as when one touches the strings of a well-tuned lyre [*cytara*]) that can move both the upper world and the low-er. Agrippa sees the "forces" as the central problem of magic or of natural philosophy, since these are ultimately the active dynamic transfers of the ideas of the archetype in matter. It follows that every thing in the cosmos is endowed with a force, which may be elementary *(virtus elementaris)* or hidden *(virtus occulta)*. The elementary forces are linked to the constitution of the elements, which are present in the archetype itself, but also in the microcosm and macrocosm. The hidden forces denote the property *(proprietas)* of those things that are no longer to be counted as belonging to the element, but only to matter. The hidden forces are brought into action by the "rational seeds."

In the first part of the first book of *De occulta philosophia*, Agrippa supports his theory with numerous examples from the three natural realms and thus explains through his "magical system" phenomena that were regarded up to that time as "miraculous." The same applies to the hidden forces of the numbers. Here, Agrippa draws especially on the doctrines of the Cabbala, as these had been handed on by Giovanni Pico della Mirandola (1463–1494), Johannes Reuchlin (1455–1522), Giovanni Zorzi (Giorgi; died 1540), and other authors of the Christian Cabbala. He writes that the mathematical abstract concepts of the stars and particular figures or square numbers possess an even higher force than the stars themselves, so that the mathematical magic *(magia mathematica)* can become a heavenly magic *(magia coelestis)*. Not only numbers, but words and names too possess a hidden force *(virtus occulta)*, which, however, takes an intellectual form, since it is able to describe the system of emanations and, as in Hebrew, includes symbolically the name of the archetype itself.

In the third book of *De occulta philosophia*, Agrippa draws on the sources of the most ancient theology *(prisca theologia)*, that is, on those texts concerning the Cabbala, Hermeticism, and Neoplatonism that were available to him, to describe the ceremonial magic *(magia caerimonialis)*, which can be explained only through knowledge of the forces *(virtutes)* of the human soul. As in the other natural objects, the world-soul *(anima mundi)* is able to bring the ideas that originate in the archetype into the human body which is attached to matter. In this case, it makes use of an ethereal chariot of the soul *(vehiculum etherium animae)* which is closely related to the stars, a heavenly and airy structure that it is able to bring into the very center of the heart. The world-soul now becomes a bodily soul *(anima hu-mana)* and awakens the forces *(virtutes)* in the seven external and internal senses that are oriented to the elements. The inner senses form one part of the human soul *(anima humana)*; the other part is made up of the under-standing *(ratio)* and the natural disposition *(mens)*. Through their forces, the soul and its components can change the body of the human person. With the help of these forces, one person can also influence another. Be-sides this, the soul of the human person is capable of elevating itself to God through self-knowledge; this corresponds to the natural striving *(appeti-tus naturalis)* of the human soul to unite itself to God. The human person can support this natural striving through burning incense, praying, or ob-serving a particular diet. When the soul detaches itself from the body, thus overcoming matter, it is capable of ruling over both microcosm and mac-rocosm. With the aid of the forces of the stars, words, or numbers, the soul discerns the future by practicing the auspices, by casting lots, or by means of oracles. When it is completely detached from matter, it can predict the future in dreams, in states of madness, or in the throes of death.

The *De occulta philosophia* of Agrippa von Nettesheim can be seen as a Renaissance philosophical conception that offered an explanation of all the natural and spiritual phenomena of magic, and of the astrology that was linked to this. Thanks to the soul's capacity for knowledge, the entire cosmos lies open to the human person, so that the hidden forces *(virtutes occultae)*, whether these proceed from objects, abstract concepts, stars, spirits, intelligences, or demons, can be known and mastered. According to Agrippa, this knowledge is revealed to the human person only through the texts of the most ancient theology *(prisca theologia)*, but not through the texts of medieval or Arabic authors.

Agrippa's *De occulta philosophia* is a turning point in the understand-ing of the place of natural magic *(magia naturalis)*, although the question of the way in which the forces *(virtutes)* worked ultimately remained open: Were the forces communicated to the sublunary world through the media-tion of the stars, or was this mediation to be attributed to the demons, or even to the devil himself?

Subsequent authors who discussed these topics suggested many new approaches to an explanation of the hidden forces *(virtutes occultae)* in the cosmos. This discussion led to a leveling down of natural magic, culminating in the fairground hucksters of the eighteenth century; on another trajectory, the hidden forces *(virtutes occultae)* were transformed into instruments of the demons and of the devil, and this idea ultimately led to the witchcraft trials of the late sixteenth century.

Agrippa himself not only accepted that it was possible to doubt his theory; in his *De incertitudine,* he dismissed all academic endeavors in view of the finitude of human experience, which comes to rest only in faith in revelation. It was in this context that he then published his "occult philosophy." In the preface, he calls it a "work of his youth" that would repay reading. In their substance, the two works complement each other, for the treatise on the "emptiness of the sciences" is also an encyclopedia that uses and quotes all the standard authors and gives an accurate presentation of the various disciplines (though always with a view to demonstrating the contradictions in which the authors get entangled, and the potential misuse of what they write). For example, in the chapter on the soul (52), Agrippa presents the contemporary discussion with its problems, but then refers to his own *Occulta philosophia* for the phenomenon of appearances *(appa-ritiones).*

He expands his discussion of the seven liberal arts to include the art of memory and Lullism, applied sciences, the fine arts, and architecture. This is followed by the occult sciences and the philosophical disciplines of natural philosophy, metaphysics, ethics, and politics; then come the history of religion and of the church, economic sciences, agriculture, medicine, law, and finally theology. The encyclopedia closes with a "Praise of the Ass" which is influenced by Erasmus of Rotterdam *(Praise of Folly)* and was later taken over by Giordano Bruno *(Cabala del Cavallo pegaseo).* With this conclusion, Agrippa positions himself and his work squarely in the reforming endeavors of humanism. Between jurisprudence and theology, he appropriately inserts a sharp critique of the Inquisition and of the persecution of witches, based on his own experience (ch. 96). He accuses the authorities of a misuse of logic and of the law, and claims that they are corrupt.

Agrippa explains his methodology in the first chapter of *De vanitate sci-entiarum.* Since it is traditionally assumed that thanks to the sciences, human beings "oftentimes, beyonde the limites of Humanitie, they may be reckened amonge the fellowship of the Gods" (Sanford's translation), he intends to reverse the perspective and to show the dangers of the sciences, for example, the trust in language ("for the seat of Trueth is in the harte, and not in the toungue"), the search for happiness, the capriciousness of the tradition, and above all the trust in rationality with regard to faith: "For every Science, hath in it some certain Principles, which must be believed, and can not by any meanes be declared." Although Agrippa appeals here to a well-known rule of the Aristotelian philosophy of science—namely, that a science cannot demonstrate its own principles—he employs this in the sense of Reformation piety, by giving the good life, respectability, and trust in God precedence over every form of human knowledge. Agrippa joins in the choir of humanist critics of a merely logical Scholasticism, and declares that only two theologies are legitimate, namely, the exposition of Scripture (*theologia interpretativa*; ch. 97) and prophetic theology (ch. 98). He holds that the exposition of the Bible includes its application to political circumstances, as exemplified in the Florentine preacher Girolamo Savonarola (*Opera* 2.288). Prophetic theology sees the world as the work of God, and hence as a mediated vision of God. Here, Agrippa inserts a positive list of possible visions, which does not differ from his occult philosophy (*Opera* 2.292–94).

The reference to Savonarola (1452–1498) is interesting, since he is regarded as the founder of a direction of skepticism that called human knowledge into question not on the basis of the philosophy of science but for religious reasons, while at the same time summoning people to take theocratic action. The unity between Agrippa's occult philosophy and his quasi-skeptical critique of science can be seen clearly in his brief treatise *De triplici ratione cognoscendi Deum* (On the Threefold Way of Knowing God; *Opera* 2.454–81), in which he speaks of three books: the book of nature, the Old Testament which contains the Law, and the New Testament which makes God known through his Son Jesus Christ. The metaphor of the "book of nature" had a long tradition, and had recently been taken to a deeper level by Raymond of Sabunde (d. 1436) in his *Theologia naturalis seu Liber creaturarum* (published in Lyons ca. 1484); this work also influenced Michel de Montaigne. This did indeed agree with some of the Reformers in the way in which the Word of God was given precedence over academic investigation; at the same time, however, this justified the investigation of the occult working of God in nature.

The comparison shows that Agrippa in his reception promoted both the spiritualistic and the empirical views of nature. The occult philosophy is in fact philosophically inconsistent in its combination of trust in the divinity of nature with a technical or practical approach. But despite all the differences from the scientific thinking of the modern period, we should respect Agrippa's philosophical intention and his empirical approach. Agrippa wants to bring the various occult sciences together in one unified theoretical system and to overcome the mutual isolation of the various theoretical models such as the doctrine of substance, the doctrine of the soul, mathematics, astronomy, and physical science. The deepest gulf separates the philosophical theories of nature from the empirical phenomena and the practical experiences of doctors, alchemists, or astrologers, and this gulf can be overcome only when one assumes a unity of nature which is not merely a good theory, but is a real foundation for the unity between scientific thinking and the objects of the theory. Although Agrippa's presuppositions are different, he formulates the modern desideratum of a holistic nature in which every technical intervention of human beings is considered in the total context and in the light of its consequences for the totality. For Agrippa, as for many Renaissance thinkers, the totality was brought about by the spirit-soul, which can permeate and govern all things and preserves the harmony of the various levels. There dwells a force in the spirit-soul that reveals itself in an infinity of forms and is also the basis of all technical activity. It was therefore only logical that Isaac Newton (1643–1727) should have made an intensive study of magical theories of this kind while he was developing his purely mathematical concept of force, which was to be the unifying principle of the unity of scientific physics until the twentieth century.

The empirical aspect of the occult philosophy also points toward the modern period. Observation and hypothesis are the heuristic principles of scientific magic, since the hypotheses (no matter how abstruse they may appear) govern the observed data; but these hypotheses are valueless if they are not empirically confirmed. The astromagical worldview demanded empirical observation and experiment. This is why some Renaissance natural philosophers were also inventors and discoverers. Giovan Battista Della Porta (1535–1615), author of a *Magia naturalis,* elaborated a physiognomy, a systematic study of the character traits that could be read in a person's face, and invented a telescope. Girolamo Cardano (1501–

1576) made "subtlety" a universal natural concept and studied mathematics and the natural sciences; he is famous as the discoverer of Cardano's wave. However, the modern scientific-technical worldview is profoundly marked by mathematical-rational theory and empirical observation. This worldview is usually held to have begun with Galileo Galilei (1564–1642), who arrived at new results with new astronomical instruments, with technical experiments, and through the application of calculation (as in the discovery of the moons of Jupiter, or the laws of falling bodies). Galileo's celebrated dictum that the book of nature is written in numbers denotes the radical change from a theological-speculative to an empirical-experimental investigation of nature. From this perspective, the magical theories and practices are not superstition or mere nonsense. Rather, they represent a transitional phase from mere speculation to systematic research. Francis Bacon (1561–1626) offered the following explanation: when the philosophers abandoned the Scholastic-Aristotelian doctrine of substance, which was based only on a slender empirical basis, they did indeed come seriously close to experience, but they drew overhasty inferences about universal principles in objects (*Novum Organum* 1, Aphorism 64)— here, he has the Renaissance magicians in mind. Bacon demanded a systematically organized empiricism.

Note: For further reading see Agrippa von Nettesheim in the References. For secondary sources see Keefer; Lehrich; Müller-Jahncke; Nauert; Van der Poel; and Zambelli.

11

JUAN LUIS VIVES

(1492/93–1540)

A Pious Eclectic

🙪

D. C. Andersson

BIOGRAPHY

Juan Luis Vives was born on March 6, 1492 (or 1493), in Valencia, Spain.[1] His parents were clothmakers and Jewish converts to Christianity. He left the country of his birth in 1509, partly due to the increasing vigor with which the Inquisition, who had arrived in that part of Spain only a few years earlier, pursued their anti-Semitic policies. He was never to return to Spain. Moving first to France, he attended the University of Paris, which had a high reputation for the speculative disciplines (philosophy and theology) of the late medieval curriculum. Despite this, he was later to decry the intellectually hidebound approach of these faculties, in similar terms to those used by Erasmus, who was famously lukewarm about his own time in Paris.[2] Vives himself said that

---

This essay is for Eckhard Kessler, with belated thanks.

1. There is a doubt in the birth year according to Perez-Garcia, 23–24.

2. The key text is his famous *Contra pseudodialecticos*. For a reliable translation, see Guerlac, *Against the Pseudodialecticians* (though Guerlac's introduction says that Vives's metaphysics show that he had fully "absorbed" the Scho-

it was members of the Spanish nation who were particularly responsible for the continuing backwardness of the university. His college was the famous College Montaigu, one of the constituent colleges of the arts faculty.[3] Of his philosophical tutors, we know a good deal about Jan Dullaert, who was an expert in the Scholastic treatment of natural philosophy.[4] Vives stayed in Paris until 1514 and appears to have involved himself in the publishing industry there, as Erasmus had done with Aldus Manutius.[5] After Paris, Vives moved to to Bruges, where he found a position as the private tutor to Guillaume II de Croy, a young nobleman. He was then appointed to a professorship in the University of Louvain (in the *Collegium castrense*) in 1519. He returned to Bruges in 1522, where he stayed until his death, though there were important trips to other areas, for example, a stay in Corpus Christi College, Oxford, where he wrote his interesting account of what should be done about the "Turkish question."[6] His association with England took, however, an unhappy turn when in 1527 he was imprisoned for six weeks by Henry VIII for having opposed the king's divorce

---

lastic thought of, *inter alios,* Jan Dullaert and Marsilius of Inghen—this may overstate matters). See now Rummel, 153–92.

3. This was the college that John Calvin attended and as a result a great deal of work has been done on its intellectual and institutional life; see the classic work of Renaudet, and Ganoczy; see also *History of Universities* 22, no. 2 (2008), special issue on the College Montaigu.

4. He wrote an obituary for Dullaert in the autumn of 1513: *Vita Ioanni Dullardi,* in Vives, *Early Writings* (*Selected Works,* vol. 5), 2:10–15. It must be said that the *vita* does not mention much in the way of Vives's connection with Dullaert, though only so much personal information was permissible in such a genre. Further speculation on the extent of Vives's relationship with Dullaert may be found in Tournay.

5. See Schepper. How much time Vives actually spent studying the traditional curriculum in Paris after 1512 until his departure is not clear (see Gonzalez, ch. 2). Casini, "Freedom of the Will," 2006, in a lucid account of the similarities in conception between Jean Buridan's *Quaestiones super libros decem Ethicorum Aristotelis* and Vives's own *De anima et vita,* suggests the similarities gain force now that we know that Vives stayed in Paris longer than the traditional account allows. A dating issue occurs here, however. *De anima et vita* was finished in 1538 (published in Basel), some twenty-four years after Vives had left Paris. One may quibble whether the Scholastic influence of the curriculum in those last two years really made such a difference all that time later, especially given Vives's certainly increasing disillusionment with the Scholastic style of study, and his involvement in the publishing trade. Casini should also have mentioned the slighting reference to Buridan's logic in the *De causis corruptarum artium,* in Juan Luis Vives, *Opera omnia,* ed. Mayans (Valencia, 1782; hereafter M), M 6.117. All citations of Vives's works are taken from this edition, unless otherwise indicated. I have repunctuated the texts.

6. *De Europae dissidiis et de bello Turcico dialogus,* M 6.452–81.

from Catherine of Aragon.[7] After his release he returned to Bruges, where he remained until his death, probably from a gallstone-related cancer, on May 6, 1540.

THE SCOPE OF VIVES'S WORKS

Vives was a voluminous, sometimes rather diffuse, writer. He was certainly not a systematic writer, either by practice or (as far as we can tell) by inclination. Furthermore, his interests lay much more in the reformation of church institutions and schooling and in the promotion of piety through these institutions than in academic philosophy.[8] The key philosophical texts are the *De anima et vita,* first published in 1538, and the *De prima philosophia,* first published in 1531, dealing with psychology and metaphysics, respectively (modern commentators have tended to focus on the former to the exclusion of the latter, an emphasis that will be rebalanced here). Other works, in particular his attack on Scholastic logic *(Contra pseudodialecticos)* and his educational works (especially the *De tradendis disciplinis*), cast interesting sidelights on the set of presuppositions that undergird these texts but are more remote from both the philosophy of the Schools and from that which has most interested modern commentators.[9] In this width of interests and unsystematic approach, Vives had much in common with his mentor, Erasmus. His eclectic influences should not blind us to the fact that he was in essence an Aristotelian; the Swiss philosopher Johannes Thomas Fregius (1543–1583) explicitly lists him as a "modern Peripatetic."[10] All of these factors led him to delimit the systematic nature of the philosophical enterprise. One has little sense in Vives (as with other humanists) that philosophy functions as an end in itself; the purpose of philosophy is the better to live the human life that God has enjoined. The culmination of the *De anima* is an injunction against pride, and *De prima philosophia* closes with a discussion of the limits of human knowledge,

7. For the most up-to-date synthesis of Vives in England, see the entry on Vives in the *Oxford Dictionary of National Biography* (2nd ed.).

8. This is well emphasized by Monsegú, 59–64.

9. Casini, *Psychology,* 2006, and Noreña 1970 are the most accessible studies in English.

10. Johannes Fregius, *Mosaicus, continens historiam ecclesiasticam . . .* (Basel, 1583), sig. A8r.

which causes one to stray from the inbuilt rule of *conservatio sui*.[11] This lack of interest in the Scholastic style of philosophy makes an assessment of Vives as a philosopher difficult.[12]

The humanist impetus in Vives's work is strong. Questions concerning the difficulty of translation of philosophical terms from Greek into Latin abound. With Seneca's famous letter (and Lorenzo Valla) in mind, he discusses the difficulties in translating the Greek word for being *(to on)* with the Latin word *res*.[13] This is not the first sign of the influence of Valla: he even quotes, with some disapproval of Valla's polemical tone, however, the discussion from the *Dialectica* on the innate capacity of animals to reason.[14] The Italian humanist's concern with proper Latin style was keenly imbibed by Vives. The emphasis too on translation and its problems is particularly strong, and sits easily with the Vives's concern for utility—for a poor translation into an idiom too far removed from the normal (if equally moribund) fluent Latin of Cicero would prevent people from understanding the text aright. This comes out strongly in his attack on the translation of Averroes's translation of one passage of the *Metaphysics*.[15]

DIALECTIC AND SKEPTICISM

Mention of humanism carries dialectic in its wake. For Vives is often seen, along with Philipp Melanchthon, as one of the most influential promoters of the brand of Agricolan humanist dialectic that became so marked a feature of the intellectual landscape in the sixteenth century.[16] Certainly, any account of him that leaves out his typically Renaissance fondness for classification in general is misleading. He is the enthusiastic inheritor of the Renaissance emphasis on finding the appropriate box for

11. *De prima philosophia*, M 3.296–97. Translation of this term is difficult: "self-preservation" needs to be purged of its Benthamite connotations, but it will do.

12. Noreña (255) says that Vives was not very good at thinking a problem through to the end.

13. *De prima philosophia*, M 3.288.

14. *De anima et vita* 2.4; M 3.358. This passage, together with the passage in Valla's *Dialectica*, should be read now in the light of the stimulating discussion by Serjeantson, "The Passions and Animal Language."

15. *De causis corruptarum artium*, 5.2; M 6.192–94.

16. Still the most general and readable survey of humanist dialectic is Lisa Jardine in Schmitt and others, 1988, 173–98.

one's word or thing, so that one may better employ the techniques of argumentation, analysis, and generation of discourse. Nature, he writes, has provided in dialectic something akin to the apothecary's shop window where every medicament and potion has a label affixed to it.[17] The classification system that he was talking about was, of course, dialectic. Rudolph Agricola had already attempted to emphasize one area of the *Organon,* the topics, at the expense of the others, and his version of dialectic included as many available modes of argumentation as possible.[18] These "topics," to which Agricola attached such importance, were the numerous different aspects under which a given term can be viewed to facilitate the creation of a speech, but which also enabled what one might term a greater "cognitive fluency."[19] They had already been the subject of treatments by Aristotle and Cicero and Boethius before Agricola, to name but the most influential figures. Vives was one of the many early sixteenth-century humanists influenced by Agricola who promoted topical invention, upon whom he heavily depends. His enthusiasm for the topics as a purely dialectical tool led Vives to delimit the scope of the metaphysical content of Aristotle's *Categories* and even of those basic class terms (*genus, species, differentia, proprium,* and *individuum*) on which the *Categories* depend.[20] At a more general level, each of these systems of classification (the topics, the *quinque voces,* the *Categories*) was simply a means to negotiate the division

17. *De explanatione cuiusque essentiae,* M 3.121.

18. See Mack.

19. Vives's own defintion is (*De instrumento probabilitatis,* M 3.86): "est enim locus nomen instrumenti, quo rationem probabilem rimamur, sunt horum nomina tamquam lemmata nartheciorum apud pharmacopolas, et unguentarios, quis illi admonentur quid in quoque insit narthecio."

20. *De Aristotelis operibus censura,* M 3.28: "Opus hoc desumtum est ex prima philosophia, quae meta ta phusika nominatur: sed haec tractantur illic ut res, in categoriis autem ut voces res illas significantes, idcirco categoriae nominantur, quasi praedicationes, aut vulgo vertunt, uno autem verbo Latine dicere, per difficile: sunt autem haec modi quidam, et velut rationes, queis primas essentias, hoc est singular rerum denominamus, consignamus, configuramus, convestimus, seu quod aliud vocabulum magis placet, aut si quod est istis aptius; dicimus enim Socratem animans esse, et album, et procerum, et maritum, et Athenis, et quae sunt ejusmodi: sed denominationes istae ex rebus pendent atque ut res separare ac segregare operosum est, et arduum, ita et categorias istas: multum tamen ab Aristotele est profectum, plurimum confectum viae uno decursu." Vives's enthusiasm for the Agricolan topics stopped him from ever seeing the long lists of topics as equally difficult to separate from the things in relation to which they stood, since the topics had a more obvious practical end (for both Aristotle's and, to a much greater extent, Agricola's books are filled with examples).

between the desire to analyze discourse statically (and hence have a formal or empty account of the relations of word to the world) and the desire
to produce discourse: some of course had stronger institutional footholds
than others, and following the strongly rhetorical cast of his own ideas on
education, Vives was less likely to see his enthusiasm for topical invention
from this perspective.

Distaste for the traditional questions of metaphysics (along with the
more rarefied aspects of Scholastic logic) was, of course, en vogue among
humanists in the early sixteenth century. Vives's account, however, of this
distaste is strongly influenced by his views on the scope of man's abilities
to know. Aristotle's *Metaphysics,* he says, is a difficult and obscure work in
places because it deals with the most abstruse of questions which only a
very few people have the wit to penetrate.[21] This comment should be lin-
gered over because it stands on all fours with two other aspects of Vives's
thought. On the one hand, he holds the idea that some forms of knowledge are, if not impossible, then difficult for everyone to achieve, an idea
to which we will return in a moment. On the other hand, he believes the
notion that the enquiry that one adopts will be dependent on the sorts of
things that one is discussing. This second notion derives from the deeply
practical cast of Vives's thought; a more historically specific genealogy is
to be found in the Renaissance rediscovery of rhetoric.

There is plenty of material in Vives that emphasizes the limits of the
possibility of human understanding. Truth, for Vives, always seems to be
hedged round with metaphors of inaccessibility and darkness. At a less
general level, one finds in *De prima philosophia* an interesting discussion
of the ways in which the "crude" human mental capacity warps the nature
of the thing that is being considered.[22] Aristotelian knowledge, characterized in Latin by the *scientia,* only counted as knowledge to the extent that
it dealt with essences, otherwise one was dealing simply with histories,
which existed in particularity and from which no "true" knowledge could
flow.[23] Now, throughout his works Vives scatters statements about the dif-

---

21. *De Aristotelis operibus censura,* M 3.32: "ad quas in abditis et abstrusis Naturae posi-
tas perpauca possunt ingenia penetrare."

22. *De prima philosophia,* M 3.210: "Ita enim crasso judicio crassa sunt objicienda,
quae censeat, tum in latitudine illa tanta varietas judiciorum et sententiarum comprehen-
datur."

23. Like many humanists, Vives's interest in the classical past led him to place particu-

ficulty of knowing things as they really are, and the weakness of human judgment. We can distinguish this vague skeptical underpinning from statements that are more tightly connected to an elaboration of a given branch of philosophy. Vives certainly makes the point that the key terms in traditional logic (such as "necessaries" or "first propositions" and so on) are ill-suited to the cognitive capacities of man, whose nature it is always to make error-laden judgments.[24] Here one may contrast those persons (such as Petrus Ramus) who believed that their structures actually were, in some sense, "in" the mind.[25] If there was a purported lack of fit between our actual mental functioning and the concepts within traditional logic that bring knowledge, then this would suggest certain consequences for the theory of knowledge. One may see Vives less as a skeptic than as a naturalist in the same way that Hume is now seen as a naturalist but was seen at the time as a skeptic, though he would anxiously differentiate himself from the purely human naturalistic conception of happiness that he found in Aristotle.[26]

To return to the theory of knowledge, Vives starts with an aside that whatever ability man has to discern truths is not so much an innate capacity, but a gift from God.[27] He then discusses human judgment. Vives argued that if one required knowledge to derive from universals, our ability to attain such knowledge was impossible since particulars are potentially infinite and one cannot therefore know all particulars. Knowledge, then, can only be "probabilistic," though this is not a Renaissance term.[28] This is the first element of Vives's skepticism and is best decribed as a general critique of Aristotelian scientific epistemology. This logical problem is compounded by a secondary problem of method, at least as regards certain aspects of human life. For the true nature or essence of some things is

---

larly high regard on history, despite its noninstitutional status in the arts course and its inability to produce "true" knowledge in the Aristotelian sense of *scientia;* see Bejczy.

24. *De causis corruptarum artium,* 3.3; M 6.118: "respicis nos et captum nostrum, an rerum naturam . . . natura habet intelligentiam non errantem."

25. For this idea that Ramus's structures were in some sense viewed as being part and parcel of the human mind, see S. Kusukawa in this volume and Meerhoff, 208.

26. Vives, *De causis corruptarum artium,* M 6.213: "Aristotelicam felicitatem contrariam esse Pietati nostrae, atque adeo rectae rationi, neminem puto dubitare. Nam pietas non in vita hac brevi, et imbecillo corpore, casibus et calamitatibus objecto, sed in illo immortali corpore nostro, injuriae omnis experti, ad immutabilem firmitatem reficto."

27. This is important because Vives is perfectly explicit about our fallen nature and distance from God.

28. Certainly "probabilitas" does *not* mean probability.

more difficult to ascertain than that of others. In particular, knowledge of
the soul, because it is knowledge of something that is not fully empirical, is
very difficult.[29]

The question to ask ourselves here is *What sort of claim is Vives making?*
Or rather, *How "philosophical" a claim is it?* There are at least four different
ways of answering this question:

- Vives's approach derives from metaphysics (and hence is "strongly"
  skeptical)
- Vives's approach derives from rhetoric (and hence is only "weakly"
  skeptical)
- Vives's approach derives from medicine or some other "empirical"
  knowledge practice (and hence is only "weakly" skeptical)
- Vives's approach is an unstable and unclear mix of some or all of the
  above approaches (bearing in mind too the fact that skepticism
  includes what we would today call naturalism)

His work on metaphysics, *De prima philosophia,* provides some ammunition for the first answer. There was a long-standing tradition in Aristotelian
metaphysics of discussion about the relation between substance and accidents.[30] Vives's own discussion certainly allows us to suggest some limits
on the scope of Vives's skepticism, but the broad position that there is a
difficulty in obtaining certain knowledge will be recontextualized according to one's more specific intellectual and disciplinary presuppositions.
For example, those involved in the teaching of rhetoric saw Vives's claims
about the scope of knowledge in their own disciplinary terms, namely, an
emphasis on the enthymeme[31] at the expense of the syllogism: at least one
English sixteenth-century reader thought so, John Rainolds (1549–1607).[32]
In addition to these purely philosophical delimitations of skepticism, we
should be aware of an additional explanation for this emphasis on the difficulty of obtaining true knowledge, and that is a religious one (to which we
return at the end of this essay).

---

29. *De anima et vita,* M 3.299.

30. The most recent treatment of this Aristotelian background is Casini.

31. For Vives's definiton of this term (usually translated as "the imperfect syllogism"),
see De censura veri, book 2; M 3.166.

32. See Green in Rainolds, *Oxford Lectures,* 75–76.

THE TEXTURE OF MAN

The question of the scope of this skepticism is subtly different in his work on the soul, *De anima et vita,* where much of the most influential aspects of Vives's thought lie, and which is his most original act of philosophical synthesis. There is less emphasis on the impossibility of the knowledge of essences than on the relative weight accorded to such knowledge. It is one thing to say that perfect knowledge is unobtainable because of the way our minds are constituted; it is another to say that one is simply not interested in coming up with a metaphysical account of the soul, preferring instead to concentrate on the way in which the soul's manifestations, especially emotions, appear to the subject. Here we have the well-established Renaissance tradition of "prudential reasoning" exercising an influence on Vives. This tradition was deeply connected with the status of the truths accorded to rhetoric.[33] In accordance with these prudential inclinations, and distaste for Scholastic essentialist epistemology, the nature of the soul is for Vives less important than how it operates:

Knowing what the soul is does not concern us at all; however, knowing in what way it is and its functions is of great interest to us. He whose orders were that we should know ourselves made reference not to its "essence" but to the actions which tend toward the formation of character.[34]

Knowing ourselves, that eminently classical and humanist maxim of self-knowledge, entails knowledge of function rather than of essence. One remembers at this point the earliest work that Vives wrote, the entertaining (and almost card-carryingly humanist) little sketch *Fabula de homine,* in which man is set free by the gods to shape his destiny as he sees fit.[35] For all that, Vives is not breaking with tradition entirely here. The nature of medieval faculty psychology was that there were different aspects to the soul (sometimes referred to as different souls: the vegetable soul, the appetitive soul, the intellectual soul—the precise status of these souls, whether ontologically separate entities or merely "modes" or aspects is controversial). Each of these aspects of the soul possessed a mode of functioning ap-

33. Fernandez-Santamaria and Kahn.
34. *De anima et vita,* M 3.332.
35. English translation of this piece in Cassirer and others, eds., *The Renaissance Philosophy of Man* (1948).

propriate to it.[36] Vives can thus be seen as drawing on, if not standing in, this functionalist rather than essentialist tradition, albeit in a rather submerged fashion.[37] The continuity, however, should not be overstated. Although there was a tradition in late medieval psychology that also stressed its functioning rather than its essence, Vives's account appears more emphatic in this direction.[38] There is no viewpoint on introspection that does not include the introspecter himself:

What these actions of the soul are, their number, how they are, where they come from, their development, their growth and decline, their end—to peer into such matters is very arduous and very difficult. Furthermore, we do not have another mind above this one which could look down and judge the one below.[39]

Where Vives departs further from tradition than by these worries about the scope of man's ability to attain sure knowledge of his own nature through introspection is his innovative account of cognitive psychology and its relation to a theory of action, or in the less modish terminology of Carlos Noreña, in the description of "the mechanism of human actions to its completion in the decision of the will."[40] This account has attracted much attention and it is rightly considered one of the more innovative aspects of *De anima et vita*.[41] For this he needs to be viewed against the great late medieval debate on the freedom of the will, which was viewed from two disciplinary backgrounds, theology and philosophy, though there was considerable interpenetration between the two. Within philosophy, there were furthermore two rivals for the proper explanation of the functioning of the will. One, the "intellectualist" position, held that the will was the

36. The argument in favor of continuity between Vives and his medieval forbears (e.g., Pierre d'Ailly) is made by Casini, "Freedom of the Will," at 401, relying in particular on the work of Jack Zupko, "What Is the Science of the Soul?: A Case Study in the Evolution of Late Medieval Natural Philosophy," *Synthèse* (1997): 297–304.

37. A still important study of the medieval background to Vives's psychological terminology is Hoppe 1901.

38. For this tradition, see the work of Zupko cited above.

39. *De anima et vita*, M 3.332: "Quae sint harum facultatum actiones, quot, quales, qui earum ortus, progressus, incrementa, occasus, perscrutari longe arduissimum ac difficilimum, plenissimum intricatae obscuritatis; propterea quod supra mentem non habemus aliam, quae inferiorem possit spectare ac censere."

40. Noreña 1970, 255.

41. On Vives's theory of the will, see Casini, "Freedom of the Will," who discusses Vives's proximity to Calvin and the intellectualists and the voluntarists.

servant of the intellect. This position is associated with Aquinas, but can be found in many of the different strands of late medieval thought. The alternative explanation was that the will operated as a sort of independent faculty, potentially acting against the intellect's dictates. This view was associated with Bonaventure, but also with many others influenced by the long shadow of Augustian "voluntarism," both within and without the Franciscan order.

Vives's account is complicated by eccentric terminology and is perhaps in the end conceptually confused. However, its broad thrust is clear. The will can only act in accordance with that which the intellect has judged good. The will has two different modes of acting, one acting in favor of the object *(approbatio)* and one rejecting the object *(refutatio)*.[42] The key passage, however, presents a phenomenologically very interesting account of willing: the will cannot, it would appear, will something that is bad nor will against something good, but the will can not only will for and will against, but it can also decide "not to will" and also to "not to will against."[43] The question, as so often with a syncretic writer, is the scope, and allegiance, of this claim and its vocabulary. There are, of course, other contexts. Lexicographical work throws up, for example, a legal usage.[44] It is important to be able to decide the precise lineage of Vives's thoughts, but not as important as recognizing the distinctive attempt by Vives to do justice, first and foremost, to how the experience of willing appears to the subject.

Certainly, for all of this underlying Scholastic conceptual undergirding and the humanist emphasis on dialectical precision, there is much truth in the traditional picture of Vives as concerned above all with observation, experience, and phenomenology. One example may be taken from his account of reason (in the sense of ratiocination). The soul, according to Vives's at this point quite traditional account, first uses the power of intel-

---

42. *De anima et vita,* 2.11; M 3.386–87.

43. *De anima et vita,* 2. 11; M 3.383: "Voluntatem enim humanam liberam jussit esse auctor suus, et quasi sui juris ac mancipii. Obtemperat quidem illa semper rationi, sed nulli uni est alligata. Sequitur autem quamcunque libuerit ex propositis. Liberam quidem animo inter actum et orbationem, velle non velle, nolle non nolle, non inter duos actus contrarios. Quando enim vis haec nihil potest velle nisi sub aliqua boni facie, nihil nolle nisi sub mali, ostensa boni specie, non mali, potest quidem non velle, sed non potest nolle, hoc est, aversari et odisse; vicissim quoque, objecta mali specie, non boni, potest non nolle, sed non potest velle, hoc est, amplecti et amare."

44. See Dante, *De mon.* 3.2.6.

ligence to apprehend objects and then it (and here Vives's teminology is eclectic) "considers and collates" those apprehensions before transferring them to the "reason."[45] His definition of reason is the "progression of [the] collation" from one thing to another.[46] The alternative name, again not without Scholastic precedent, that he gives for this procedure is "*discursus*," or "discourse." This term (deriving from the Latin for "to run about") is an accurate one, he then argues, because it well captures the fact that our experience of reasoning is that we often do not proceed by a smooth progression but by little jumps from one thing to another, coming to a conclusion despite gaps.[47]

One is reminded of a passage dealing with volition. Vives comments that one never really has time in life to settle fixedly on what the good object truly is.[48] Vives is the theorist of the naturally mercurial. Book 3 of the *De anima et vita* continues this tendency toward the empirical and contains the most striking departure from the late medieval and Renaissance commentary tradition on Aristotle's *De anima*. It consists of a series of descriptions of the passions or, in Vives terminology, the *"affectiones."* Vives is insistent that emotions interact with each other, and gives much greater space than previous theorists to the notion that emotions are "mixed." He is particularly concerned with the physiological aspects of the emotions.[49] Again and again, the frustratingly unclear conceptual undergirding is less important than the attempt to adequately capture the nature of experience.

---

45. *De anima et vita*, 2.4; M 3.353: "quae intelleximus, consideravimus, contulimus, omnia sunt parata in usum rationis."

46. *De anima et vita*, 2.4; M 3.353: "ea vero est collationis progressio ab uni in aliud."

47. *De anima et vita*, 2.4; M 3.352: "nec perturbet nos quod discursum diximus, nam interdum ratio non tam cursu ingreditur, quam salticulis per diversa delibando, est enim ratio alia per suos gradus continua serie discurrens, est alia transiliens, et medios aliquos gradus intermittens vel ex ignorantia recti ac congruentis progressus, vel quod illos attingere minime existimat necessarium."

48. *De anima et vita*, 2.11; M 3.383–84: "in tanta autem rerum varietate nihil venire potest sub consultationem, in quo rationis vis non et bona et mala deprehendat, quae suadeat, quae dissuadeat, pro locis, temporibus, personis, qualitate, et eiusmodi."

49. For discussion of one such example, see Andersson.

THE SEARCH FOR A PIOUS PHILOSOPHY

Dealing with a Renaissance philosopher normally involves thinking seriously about the relationship between constructive metaphysics and whatever other sort of enquiry he is being engaged in. This connection between the descriptive enterprise and the metaphysical one is usually not considered very profoundly. The disciplines of metaphysics, ethics, and natural philosophy were partner and product of a range of intuitions about the levels or orders of reality. Most of these intuitions became the object of academic or intellectual discussion only once they were ordered through a form of systematic organization. The question of the different branches of philosophy and indeed of knowledge in general is relevant here. This segmentation of reality clearly demarcated the physical, the logical, and the theological one from another.

In a very revealing image, Vives says that the diversity of existence, the *"ordines rerum,"* were created by God partly in order to help mortals understand the nature of reality in the same way that there are different disciplines in the arts course.[50] The increasing emphasis on the disciplinary divisions, and the professionalization of knowledge as the sixteenth century wears on, meant that it became a critical question for some in the sixteenth century what sort of connection existed between these different orders.[51] In other words, the problem that Vives's account discloses, however, by his rigorously descriptive and nonmetaphysical account of the soul is simple, and is one that continues to divide philosophers today.[52] It would perhaps be less of a problem if he had not been so attached to the pious possibilities in his metaphysics. What need is there of a vertical unifying metaphysic if all that is necessary for good human life can be captured by reference to a

50. *De prima philosophia,* M 3.294. "non aliter quam doctus quispiam qui artes omnes pernovit, alium librum de Grammatica scribit, alium de Dialectica, alium e Philosophia naturae, libri vero simulacrum quoddam sunt illius mentis."

51. Nicholas Jardine, "Keeping Order in the School of Padua."

52. For one recent attempt to argue for a connection between these two sets of intuitions (the natural/metaphysical and the moral), see Iris Murdoch, *Metaphysics as a Guide to Morals* (London, 1992). One might contrast the arguments of the evolutionary biologists who argue that consciousness is in essence nothing more than a mistake, or, at best, the wake that is created by the requirement for a high level of processing power in the human brain.

descriptive enquiry? The notion is that without such a unifying account, man would be a wholly wretched and miserable creature, and God inexplicably perverse. A similar drive, rooted in a Platonic Christian account of metaphysical principles, can be seen in the works of that understudied pupil of Pietro Pomponazzi, Gasparo Contarini. Pomponazzi had famously produced a naturalistic account of the soul that left a rather reduced space for the top-down action of the divine on the natural world.[53] Contarini followed his teacher in the *De elementis* written, perhaps, in 1530 (though not published until many years later) in that he emphasized an explanatory theory of the mutual interaction of elements and physical mixtures based on a purely physical property: heat. However, in his compendium of metaphysics, Contarini is explicit that there is indeed a unifying metaphysical principle of goodness that flows down from the uncreated One to the created Many.[54] Vives himself, equally interested in some of the Galenic theories that motivated Contarini's account, also finds time for the unifying principle of heat, though his immediate source is Plato's *Theatetus*. This principle of heat is simultaneously a metaphysical and a physical entity.[55]

Vives's philosophical output, then, manages uneasily to maintain the almost therapeutic comfort of a vertical integration of the orders of reality with an introspective account of the phenomenological properties of the emotions and their connections with the virtues that was distinctly ambivalent about the metaphysical status of the soul. It was certainly this latter aspect of his work that was most original and which found the greatest diffusion—Juan Huarte's famous *Examen de ingenios para las ciencias* derives largely from Vives's *De anima et vita* and was soon translated into English.[56] Despite Vives's hostility to Averroes's starkly nonrational basis for belief in a deity, it was this unstable conjunction of the descriptive

53. See Jill Kraye in this volume and Kraye, "Immortality," 2000, 51–68; cf. Blum, "Immortality," 2007.

54. This appears to be in essence a Platonic thought, since the clear division between celestial and sublunary is one of the major (and from the point of view of the development of such key concepts as gravity, regrettable) changes wrought by Aristotle to the Platonic system. The influence of Avicenna on Contarini's thought is asserted, with almost nothing in the way of textual proof, by Giacon. Cf. Mulsow, 90: "Contarinis Thesen zeigen, dass auch nach Pomponazzi 'vertikale' Begründungsmuster keineswegs passé waren."

55. *De prima philosophia*, M 3.279–80, esp. 280.

56. Juan Huarte, *Examen de ingenios*. This work found an interesting *fortuna* in the tradition of Puritan practical divinity.

and the metaphysical that led easily to the more providentialist fideism of Philipp Melanchthon, as well as to such examination of subjective states as that found in the works of Montaigne.[57]

57. The precise relationship between Vives and Melanchthon deserves a monograph. Melanchthon himself does not mention Vives. For further bibliographical orientation on Vives, see Noreña 1990.

Note: For further reading see Vives; Guerlac in the References. For secondary sources see Bejczy; Casini; Cruselles Gómez; Fernandez-Santamaria; Gonzalez; Jardine, Nicholas; Monsegú; Noreña; Perez-Garcia; Renaudet; Rummel; Schepper; and Tournay.

12

PHILIPP MELANCHTHON

(1497–1560)

Reformer and Philosopher

✑

Günter Frank

Whether Philipp Melanchthon is indeed one of the Renaissance philosophers and should be acknowledged as such depends
on the answer to a number of complex problems which can give
rise to controversial discussions. One may legitimately ask whether this humanist and scholar of the Reformation should be classified under the philosophy of the Renaissance; but this depends
decisively on whether one recognizes his thinking as "philosophical" at all. After all, Melanchthon's thinking is concerned essentially with the truth of a Christian doctrine which consciously concentrates, in the context of the history of salvation, on the
theology of the cross and soteriology, which Luther had made
central; and at least in the case of Luther, this had led to a far-
reaching rejection of all the possibilities of the speculative and
practical reason. Here, however, one should not let oneself be distracted by Luther's own antiphilosophical attitude. As long as
Melanchthon was interpreted de facto on the basis of Luther—as
one can see in the countless essays written in the twentieth century under some such title as "Melanchthon alongside Luther"—it

was not possible to give the philosophy of this scholar more than a cursory attention. To take one example of the Lutheran interpretation of Melanchthon: Luther's theology of the cross emphasizes the lost state of the human person as a sinner. How could this be compatible with the anthropocentric implications that were central to the endeavors of the humanists at that time, whose principal representatives were Erasmus of Rotterdam and Melanchthon? But we must take a different path, setting him in the larger contexts of the debates of his age. These are not only the Europe of the Reformation movement, but also the Europe of humanistic scholarship, that is, the age when the knowledge of classical antiquity was acquired anew and transformed under the presuppositions of the image of the world and of the human person in the early modern period.

Where they have studied his philosophy, scholars have repeatedly presented Melanchthon the Aristotelian. Johann Jacob Brucker, the first great German historian of philosophy, celebrated him as the greatest Aristotelian in the age of the Reformation.[1] This is not at all surprising, since Melanchthon wrote commentaries and textbooks on almost all the scientific disciplines of Aristotle, and described himself, with an emphasis that cannot go unnoticed, as *homo peripateticus* (CR 3.383). Up to now, this interpretation of Melanchthon in terms of Aristotelianism has not basically changed.[2]

Naturally, Melanchthon's Platonic ambitions did not pass entirely unremarked, and it is in fact indisputable that he appeals to no authority other than Plato in questions that are significant for the understanding of philosophy, such as the knowledge of God or the concept of God, and the immortality of the individual soul. It is well known that he also wrote a number of revisions of Cicero's writings on the philosophy of law and of the state; as yet, little research has been done into these works. It appears extremely difficult to unite these different approaches under one system, and this too makes it problematical to describe Melanchthon as a philosopher.

1. *Historia critica philosophiae* 4 (Leipzig, 1743), 102–16.
2. For a detailed discussion of this interpretation in terms of Aristotelianism, cf. G. Frank 1995, 16–23. For an assessment of recent Melanchthon studies, see Günter Frank, "§ 56 Melanchthon," in *Grundriss der Geschichte der Philosophie. Humanismus und Renaissance,* ed. Enno Rudolph (Basel: Schwabe, 2010).

MELANCHTHON BETWEEN THE HUMANISTIC
AND THE REFORMATION MOVEMENTS

Melanchthon was born on February 16, 1497, in Bretten near Heidelberg, in the Electoral Palatinate.[3] We are well informed about his life,
thanks to his first biographer, Joachim Camerarius (1500–1574).[4] He was
named Philipp Schwartzerdt after his father. He began his education at
the Latin school in Pforzheim. One of his fellow pupils, who remained
his close friend until his death, was Simon Grynaeus (1493–1541), later to
achieve renown as a humanist in Basle. It was in Pforzheim that his relative Johannes Reuchlin (1455–1522) finally gave him the humanistic name
"Melanchthon." His studies led him via Heidelberg, where he was awarded the degree of bachelor of arts in the Scholastic *via antiqua* in June 1511,
to Tübingen. The story that he became a nominalist in Tübingen is only
a legend. It was told already by his first biographer Camerarius, and research into Melanchthon has largely accepted this assertion; but as other
studies of the philosophical traditions of the University of Tübingen have
shown, there are no differences worthy of mention between the two alleg-
edly principal representatives of the *via antiqua* (Konrad Summenhart)
and the *via moderna* (Gabriel Biel).[5] Nor is it possible to demonstrate that
G. Biel (whom Melanchthon himself calls the clearest of all philosophers;
CR 4.407) was a nominalist. Besides this, exact analyses of what Melanchthon says about the question of nominalism reveal that he is completely
uninterested in the relevant problems (CR 20.714f.; CR 1.142f., 145f, 165f.,
519f., 529, 750f.).[6] These problems become meaningful only in an ontological context in which metaphysics is the first philosophy, and this played a
significant role in the Latin reception of Aristotle. But as we shall see in detail, the starting point of Melanchthon's philosophy is not this tradition of
metaphysics.

It was, however, in Tübingen that he formed his plan of a critical edition of Aristotle. With this plan, and thanks to a recommendation by
Reuchlin, Melanchthon came to the University of Wittenberg as a promis-

---

3. On Melanchthon's biography, cf. especially Scheible 1992 and 1997.
4. *De vita Philippi Melanchthonis narratio*, 1566 (ed. G. T. Strobel), Halle 1777.
5. J. Haller, *Die Anfänge der Universität Tübingen 1477–1535* (Stuttgart, 1927), 1.173.
6. For detailed information on this debate about nominalism, cf. Frank 1995, 33–37.

ing educational reformer. His inaugural address on August 28, 1518, *De corrigendis adolescentiae studiis* (On the Improvement of the Studies of Young People), breathed this spirit of a renewal based on wide-reaching humanistic studies. In the following years, Melanchthon fell completely under the spell of Luther's personality. He adopted Luther's understanding of justification, which was to remain constitutive for his own theological writings for the rest of his life, although he gave a different interpretation of some aspects that were linked to the doctrine of justification, for example, the question of the freedom of the will. He attended Luther's lectures, and after only one year took the degree of *Baccalaureus biblicus,* in order to be able to give exegetical lectures.

It was in these years that he spoke most harshly against philosophy. The young Melanchthon's criticism of philosophy in the first eventful years of the Wittenberg Reformation has often led scholars to pose the prickly question of how his "return" to philosophy, which began no later than 1527, is to be evaluated—especially since Luther had definitively excluded philosophy from theology. However, the statements critical of philosophy—which are in fact rather scattered[7]—show that Melanchthon agreed with Luther in rejecting one particular philosophical tradition, namely, metaphysics as the first philosophy in the sense meant by Aristotle and by his Latin commentators. This is made clear by his most detailed exposition of metaphysics, which he published under a pseudonym in 1521 in his celebrated apologia for Luther, *An Address by Didymus of Faenza against Thomas of Piacenza for the Theologian Martin Luther.*[8] Melanchthon defends Luther against the accusation by the Roman professor Tommaso Rhadino (1490–1527), which was already circulating in these years, that Luther rejected all philosophy. He argues that Luther does not reject the whole of philosophy, but merely the metaphysics and moral philosophy of Aristotle. The decisive point is the reason Melanchthon adduces for the exclusion of the Ar-

7. In addition to the defense of Luther, the basic texts are his inaugural lecture in Wittenberg in 1518 (CR 11.17–19) and his preface to the edition of the *Clouds* of Aristophanes in 1520 (CR 1.273f.), in which, like many humanists, he pokes fun at the hair-splitting of Scholasticism. Melanchthon's works are cited according to the volumes and pages in *Corpus Reformatorum* 1834–1860: "CR."

8. *Didymi Faventini adversus Thomam Placentinam oratio pro Martino Luthero theologo,* in Stupperich 1951, 1.72–75 (hereafter MSA). Note: Didymus means "twin brother," so the pseudonym suggests Luther's favorable brother.

istotelian metaphysics and moral philosophy: "I reject the metaphysical theories because I consider it dangerous to investigate heavenly mysteries with the methods of our reason. And I reject the ethics because it obviously is diametrically opposed to Christ" (MSA 77f.). Like Luther, Melanchthon understands the Aristotelian metaphysics as a human attempt to employ the methods of the reason to seize hold of the divine mysteries; he likewise agrees with Luther that the doctrine of grace is incompatible with the Aristotelian doctrine of the virtues. He did in fact reverse his verdict on Aristotle's ethic later on, but he affirmed throughout his life that metaphysics as the first philosophy must be excluded from the curriculum of the academic disciplines.

However, these criticisms of philosophy—more precisely, of metaphysics—were not Melanchthon's last words on the subject of philosophy. In his celebrated *Commentary on the Letter to the Colossians* (1527)[9] and in a programmatic discourse "On Philosophy" (1536),[10] he offered a new systematic definition of the relationship between theology and philosophy, thereby laying the foundations for the inclusion of all the nontheological academic disciplines (with the exception of metaphysics) in the curriculum of the sciences. The decisive starting point for a new systematic definition of philosophy is the theology of creation, for Melanchthon defines philosophy as a "true and good creature of God" in the field of societal affairs and of human nature (MSA 4.230). Later, he extended the sphere of philosophy to include the knowledge of God. His second systematic starting point, which he put forward as a kind of fundamental theological prolegomenon to all his later academic commentaries, is the Lutheran distinction between Law and Gospel, which he transferred in principle to the relationship between all the academic disciplines and theology (ibid.). This distinction has a soteriological relevance, since the priority of the theology of salvation was the central aspect of the renewal of the Reformation movement. From a soteriological perspective, therefore, anything that may be accessible in the academic disciples is completely irrelevant. With these

9. MSA 4.209–303. Commentary on Col 2:8: "See to it that no one makes a prey of you by philosophy and empty deceit, according to human tradition, according to the elemental spirits of the universe, and not according to Christ."

10. CR 11.278–84. For a commentary and German translation, cf. G. Frank, *De philosophia*, in Melanchthon 1997 (*Melanchthon deutsch*; Leipzig, 1997), 1.125–35.

two theological doctrines as his basis, Melanchthon could address the task of reforming the sciences—and reforming philosophy.

MELANCHTHON'S PHILOSOPHICAL WRITINGS

Writings on Dialectic

Even in the first years of the Wittenberg Reformation, despite his criticisms of metaphysics and the undeniable exaggerations in his polemic, Melanchthon was not philosophically inactive. In 1520 he published his extraordinarily influential work *Compendaria dialectices ratio,* a short summary of logic (CR 20.711–64). In his early dialectical works, he still looked to the dialectic of Rudolf Agricola (1442/44–1485). In his *Inventio dialectica,* first printed in Louvain in 1515, Agricola had united late medieval logic to the rhetoric of the Italian Renaissance; this work was particularly influential among Reformation scholars. However, Melanchthon's principal work on dialectic, the *Erotemata dialectices* (Logical Inquiries, 1547), makes it clear that he regarded a dialectic orientated to the study of the *loci communes* as incapable of providing sufficiently sure knowledge in the sciences.

There can be no doubt that the *Erotemata dialectices* was the most influential textbook on dialectic among Reformation scholars until the second half of the seventeenth century.[11] Melanchthon's ambitious program in this book was to propose a *fundamental science* for all the scientific disciplines. He responded here to the demand made by Raymond Llull (1232–1315) for a fundamental philosophy for all the sciences (philosophy, natural philosophy, anthropology, and theology), a demand that remained influential until Leibniz. Scholasticism offered no methodology for the discovery of those scientific principles that would ultimately belong to a fundamental science. Melanchthon holds that a fundamental science would have as its object all the theoretical and practical themes (CR 13.514), and would formulate a general methodological doctrine for all these subject areas (ibid. 515). His dialectic offers this in two parts: first, the judicative analysis, which is the real core of Melanchthon's dialectic, and second, the *inventio* which belongs under the study of the *loci communes,* since it leads to the

11. On this, cf. Hartfelder 1889, esp. 211–20; Risse, "Die Melanchthonschule," in Risse 1964, 79–121; G. Frank 1995, esp. 162–81.

discovery of the objects. The judicative analysis helps to evaluate the concepts and their links, and establishes the connection between the members in a syllogism and in other forms of argumentation (ibid. 641). The dialectic of 1547 is a general epistemology that basically takes the form of an analytics expanded to include the *loci communes.*

For Melanchthon this syllogistic demonstration is a path to discover knowledge. Its evidential power and conclusiveness is based on his three criteria of certain knowledge: (1) universal experience *(experientia universalis)*; (2) principles or "natural notions" *(notitiae naturales)* with which the human spirit is endowed in the form of principles and of natural clarity of this spirit *(lumen naturale),* and from which the individual sciences take their origin; (3) and the knowledge of the structure that correctly links the members in a syllogism (ibid. 647f.). According to Melanchthon, these criteria of certainty apply to all the scientific disciplines: to anthropology,[12] natural philosophy,[13] moral philosophy,[14] and even theology, which, however, possesses a further criterion of certainty in the divine revelation and in the testimonies of the biblical writings. The human person must assent in faith to this criterion, even if it were to diverge from the verdict of the reason (CR 13.650; 21.603–6).

Like many scholars in the early modern period who endeavored to elaborate a unified methodology for a universal epistemology, Melanchthon's unified methodology formulated a "syllogism in which we draw a necessary and immutable conclusion either from principles known from nature, or from universal experience, or from a definition based on the results of correct deduction. In other words, either we demonstrate that specific results come from obvious causes, or we take precisely the opposite path" (CR 13.652). These two methodological steps are now explicitly identified with the two paths of geometrical demonstration: "[T]he customary and very well known concepts in geometry are the *compositio* or synthesis, which is generated by that which goes before, and the *resolutio* or analysis, which leads back to the principles on the basis of that which follows" (ibid.). It was his study of Euclidean geometry that suggested to Melanchthon this unified methodological ideal of synthesis and analysis, which was

---

12. *De anima* (1553; CR 13.149–53).
13. *Initia doctrinae physicae* (1549; CR 13.185–90).
14. *Philosophiae moralis epitomes libri duo* (1546; MSA 3.158f.).

unknown to the medieval Scholastic writers on logic. His friend Grynäus published the first edition of the Euclidean *Elements* in Basle in 1533, and this work inspired the composition of a large number of methodological treatises in the sixteenth century.[15] Melanchthon was the first scholar to employ Euclid's mathematical-geometrical methodological model for his dialectic. Drawing on Grynaeus's edition, he set forth in detail in two treatises the fundamental significance of the geometrical methodology for establishing a basis for knowledge and science. His *Praefatio in geometriam* (August 1536; CR 3.107–13) is a continuous "praise of geometry" *(laus geometriae)*. In the *Oratio de studiis veteris philosphiae* (1557), he emphasizes that a scientific demonstration is achieved only on the analogy of the geometrical proofs (CR 12.246), since the true origins of all the sciences consist of correctly developed and appropriate proofs, or else are derived in a methodical sequence from the sources of the proofs, as discussed in Euclid's *Elementa* (ibid. 248).

The Commentary on Aristotle's *Physics*

Melanchthon's *Initia doctrinae physicae* (1549)[16] is the first Lutheran treatment of Aristotle's *Physics*. He himself affirms that his natural philosophy is Aristotelian; he sometimes calls it *Aristotelica* or *Initia Aristotelica* for short (CR 13.183f.; 7.475). On closer examination, however, an investigation of the specific and central ontological elements of his elaboration of the *Physics*, for example, the understanding of movement, causality, and finality, shows that all the ontological dimensions in natural philosophy are eliminated and that it is overlapped at the decisive points by Platonism. The image of nature that Melanchthon presents in his treatment of Aristotle's *Physics* is that of a *machina mundi* (CR 206f.) or a *universa machina* (ibid.) which displays a universal causal nexus (which does not, however, place limitations on divine and human freedom) and is marked by mathematical structures. This *machina mundi* is not, however, separated from the divine fundament of the world; as *machina mundi*, it is the work of a structuring and intelligent reason, and can be recognized by the human spir-

15. On the reception of the Euclidean *Elementa*, cf. above all H.-J. Engfer, *Philosophie als Analysis. Studien zur Entwicklung philosophischer Analysiskonzeptionen unter dem Einfluß mathematischer Methodenmodelle im 17. und frühen 18. Jahrhundert* (Stuttgart, 1982).
16. CR 13.179–412. Cf. Kusukawa 1995.

it. This metaphysical optimism in Melanchthon's view of the world and of nature is firmly established thanks to the two theological doctrines of the creation and of the human person as the image of God. Despite the absolute precedence of soteriology, therefore, Melanchthon also acknowledges that the world possesses both rationality and intelligibility. It is clear that this establishes a kind of competition between the theology of creation and the theology of salvation: for even outside of revelation (and here Melanchthon takes up Augustine's motif of the "book of nature"),[17] nature is a book or a mirror in which God shows himself (CR 13.198).

We find this metaphysical optimism, which had a great influence on the worldview of the early modern period, in many scholars of the sixteenth and seventeenth centuries, for example, Copernicus, Galileo, Newton, Boyle, and Vico. At the same time, this metaphysical optimism was linked to the return of the Platonic myth of creation from the *Timaeus*. Almost all modern scholars agree that this Platonic conception, which in its core is a "natural theology," superseded the Aristotelian natural philosophy and became dominant on the threshold of the early modern period. Melanchthon too postulates that the first beginnings of natural philosophy are not to be sought in Aristotle's doctrine of the elements, but in Plato's *Timaeus* (CR 13.195), and he interprets the intelligibility of the world by means of mathematical structures that constitute the ordering of the cosmos. Just as the "Pythagorean" Timaeus[18] had spoken of the composition of the world-body in accordance with the mathematical proportions between numbers, so Melanchthon (like Plato) speaks of God as a geometer in whom the wisdom of the divine architect can be seen (CR 12.246f.).

The Platonic superseding of Aristotle's *Physics* and these allusions— which are not exceptional[19]—pose once more, with a renewed urgency, the question that has given rise to so much scholarly controversy: To what extent should Melanchthon properly be interpreted as a Platonic philosopher? The provenance of this Platonism is not the tradition of Ficino's *Cor-*

---

17. *De Genesi ad litteram*, MPL 34 (*Op. omn.* 3.1), 219–22.

18. Plato, *Timaeus* 31c–32b, 53b–54c.

19. For example, Melanchthon declares in his preface to *M. Luther, De novissimis verbis Davidis* (May 1, 1550), that Plato's insight must be taken seriously, although (like all pagan insights) it needs to be complemented (CR 7.581–85). In the preface to *M. Luther, In librum Mose enarrationes* (1544), he explicitly elaborates the story of creation from Plato's *Timaeus* (CR 5.258–68).

pus hermeticum, but the second large-scale edition of Platonic writings, which his friend Simon Grynaeus published in the house of Johannes O. Valder in Basle in March 1534; and it is to this edition that Melanchthon's praise refers in his letter to the Basle humanist in November 1534 (CR 2.815). Melanchthon always had recourse to Platonic theories from this tradition where they seemed merely compatible with the antecedent data of theology (in this instance, with the theology of creation) than with the bases of the Aristotelian natural philosophy. And precisely this Platonism is the decisive foundation of the metaphysical optimism that is basic to Melanchthon's view of nature and of the world.

The Two Commentaries on the *De anima*

Melanchthon's commentary on Aristotle's *De anima* (1553), the first treatment of this Aristotelian work in Germany since Albert the Great, was one of the most successful writings in his extensive theological-philosophical oeuvre.[20] It was published in at least forty editions and eight commentaries in the sixteenth century, and it was still being used as a textbook in the teaching of philosophy in the eighteenth century.[21] The extraordinary importance of Melanchthon's commentary, to which its historic success witnesses, is due to the position held by Aristotle's *De anima* in the philosophical curriculum, thanks to its treatment of questions of metaphysics, theology, noetic theory, and epistemology.[22] Although Melanchthon broadly follows Aristotle's order in his treatment of the *De anima,* the content of his commentary presents a completely new concept of psychology, which we could also call a comprehensive theory of the human person, or "anthropology."

At the center of this comprehensive theory of the human person is the definition of the essence of the human soul. This definition is a systematic network of various theological and philosophical theorems by means of which Melanchthon attempts to achieve a synthesis between the concern

20. The commentary on the *De anima* had its origin in Melanchthon's studies of the *Physics* and in the lectures he gave. On the theological-philosophical aspects of this commentary, cf. E. Kessler, "The Intellective Soul," in Schmitt et al. 1988, 516–18; G. Frank 1995, 159–81; cf. Salatowsky.
21. Kessler, "The Intellective Soul."
22. For details, cf. K. Park and E. Kessler, "The Concept of Psychology," in Schmitt et al. 1988, 455–63.

of theology, especially Reformation theology, and attempts to provide a
basis for philosophy. The fact that the doctrine of the soul is the center of
his anthropology has a number of theological implications. First of all, it is
based on the theology of creation, which portrays the human person as the
creature of a divine architect: the principal goal of this creature is to recognize the traces of God in the human soul (CR 13.5). The second theological
implication of Melanchthon's anthropology is the link between this goal,
namely, the knowledge of God, and the theological doctrine that the human person is made in the image of God (ibid. 169). This means above all
that "imprinted upon the human spirit are *notitiae* which show that God
exists and reveal how he is. . . . And the first degree of this condition of being the image of God is the possession of an intelligent ability and living in
accordance with wisdom" (ibid.). Like most of the Latin writers of the patristic age and the Scholastics, Melanchthon did in fact teach that the human person is the image of God in an abiding, structural sense—and this
means that he does not at all agree with Luther that the consequences of
the fall were so far-reaching that a philosophical knowledge of God was
impossible. It is obvious that Melanchthon's anthropology takes an unam-
biguously optimistic view of the human ability to acquire knowledge, not
only achieving the knowledge of the existence of God, but penetrating to
the predicates of God's being, which are already contained in the Platonic concept of God (CR 21.610). Finally—and this is the specifically Reformation aspect of this theological anthropology—Melanchthon transposes
onto his doctrine of the soul the Lutheran dialectic between Law and Gospel as a criterion of discernment. This means that whatever may be accessible to the human spirit in the knowledge of God is insufficient and irrelevant from the perspective of soteriology and of the theology of revelation
(CR 13.7).

Melanchthon once again has recourse to Platonic theorems insofar
as they are compatible with theology. The Platonic theory of exemplar-
ism corresponds to the theological doctrine of the human person as the
image of God. The relationship of "archetype and image" between the divine spirit and the human spirit is a relationship of participation (CR 13.5;
11.941). Therefore the human spirit and the *notitiae naturales* which are imprinted upon it not only display a light of the divine wisdom: in the powers
of the soul, the human spirit shares in God's governance of the world (CR

11.942; 13.6). With this theory of the *notitiae naturales,* which is borrowed from Cicero but is now interpreted in an exemplaristic context, Melanchthon has formulated principles of philosophy that are fundamental for his understanding of philosophy and of science. These function as principles of the philosophy of spirit, in which the human spirit participates in the divine spirit. They also constitute the origin of human knowledge, thus determining those aspects of his anthropology that concern the psychology of knowledge and the noetic theory. In union with the *lumen naturale,* that is, a natural clarity of the human spirit in the act of knowledge, the *notitiae* are also the gnoseological aspect of the theory of cognition. And finally, in the manner of mathematical-geometrical axioms, they form the ultimate principles of the theory of cognition.

Writings on Practical Philosophy

It is thanks to Melanchthon that despite Luther's criticism of Aristotle's *Ethics,* the Aristotelian *Ethics* and *Politics* became so influential in Protestantism. Melanchthon's writings on Aristotle's *Ethics* and *Politics* offer paraphrases of selected teachings, which he illustrates by means of the teachings of ancient schools of thought and explains in the context of the practical questions posed by his contemporaries; accordingly, he never dealt with all the books of the *Ethics* and *Politics.* The paraphrases he makes of the *Ethics* and *Politics* of Aristotle are guided by topoi or central concepts of Reformation theology. Basic questions of the *Ethics* and *Politics* are discussed in terms of the fundamental Reformation dialectic between Law and Gospel, and of theologically determined central concepts such as *finis hominis, virtus,* and *iustitia.* Here, it is theology that defined the contours of the *Ethics* and *Politics,* above all the Lutheran dialectic between Law and Gospel which Melanchthon had applied to all the academic disciplines. The structural principle that developed from this dialectic means that for Melanchthon's practical philosophy, nothing that the human person can will and do in the sphere of ethics or politics has any soteriological significance whatever.

The definition of the goal of human life—that is, the question of the Aristotelian *eudaimonia*—is a further demonstration of the fundamentally theological perspective of the practical philosophy. In his moral philosophy of 1538, Melanchthon draws a distinction in the chapter about the goal of the human person between the *finis principalis* ("principal goal"), which lies in the knowledge of God and in obedience to God, and the *fines minus principales* ("less principal goals"), subordinate goals of the human person that are to be achieved in the acts of virtue (CR 16.30f.). In order to understand the "less principal goals" correctly, we must bear in mind that Melanchthon—in what he took to be the Aristotelian manner—relates these to the natural law (on this, cf. the chapter *Quae est ratio sententiae Aristotelicae?*, CR 16.31). It is true that allusions to the natural law are also found in Aristotle (*NE* V 10,1134 b 18–21), but the Greek philosopher sees the path of habituation as the ethical center (*NE* II 1103 a 17). Melanchthon concedes that the basis that Aristotle proposes for ethics is derived from principles of natural philosophy, but he affirms that the source of argumentation must be the true and solid principles of natural philosophy which are established in nature by divine ordinance, namely, the law of God— and these are nothing other than the natural laws *(leges naturae)* qua divine laws *(leges divinae)*, that is, the practical principles that are established in nature by divine ordinance (CR 16.31). This is why the doctrine of the natural law plays a preeminent role in the task of establishing a basis for the practical philosophy. His own proposal finds the natural law in the *lex Dei* and in the *lex divina* or *leges divinae* which manifest the law of God; these are transmitted in the Books of Moses and the Gospel. Melanchthon also calls these *leges divinae* the *leges mosaicae,* which he divides into three groups: the *leges morales,* which are revealed most clearly in the Decalogue; the *leges iudiciales* or *forenses,* which refer to positive laws concerning matters such as marriage, property claims, and penalties; and the *leges caerimoniales,* which refer to rules of worship and rites. Melanchthon's teaching on the natural law is elaborated in detail in the two *Loci theologici* of 1535 (CR 21.388–406) and 1543 (CR 21.685–719).

Melanchthon's textbook on books 1–3 of Aristotle's *Politics* follows the same procedure as his writings on the *Ethics.* He presents paraphrases of individual teachings, which are discussed in keeping with the presuppositions of theology and against the background of contemporary political events, especially the emergence of Wycliffe, the Anabaptists, and some theologians from Switzerland and Strasbourg who are accused by Melanchthon of failing to make a clear distinction between the state and the Gospel (CR 16.419). The basis of the state in natural law is fundamental to Melanchthon's understanding of the state, for as he underlines, "The *Politics* treats of civil society and of the obligations which apply to this society, and deduces the causes of society from nature" (CR 16.421f.). Like all the academic disciplines, politics has its origins in primary, very general principles that are known to us from nature. The primary principles of politics are the following: the human person is naturally created for society, and the first society is the legitimate union between man and woman (CR 16.423). Further general principles are then derived from such principles. In keeping with the natural law explanation of the origin of society, Melanchthon identifies these general principles of politics with the natural law, which he equates with the divine law *(ius divinum)*. It is noteworthy that Melanchthon completely abandons the traditional definition of the goal of the human person, and identifies *utilitas* as the goal of politics. "For the state," as he defines it, "is a legitimately erected community of citizens with the goal of a common usefulness, though mostly with the goal of defense" (CR 16.435). He thus avoids tackling the theological problem of harmonizing *eudaimonia* as the goal of the state (as Aristotle had understood this) with the goal proclaimed by the theology of revelation—a goal that the human person cannot achieve by his own efforts, but is given to him in faith.

MELANCHTHON'S INFLUENCE

The history of the influence of Melanchthon's theology and philosophy is still to be written, and is an urgent desideratum. The permanent temptation, mentioned above, to interpret him on the basis of Luther, and hence to perpetuate the suspicion that early Reformation scholars in general were hostile to philosophy, has led to a distorted picture of the philosopher Melanchthon. Let me mention at least two aspects here. Melanchthon's textbooks and commentaries, which won a secure position in the emerging Protestant universities, made a decisive mark upon the discourses of the educated elite in the early Reformation period. His wide humanistic learning, leading him to rediscover radical philosophical alternatives such as the Platonic creation myth or the idea of participation, led in conjunction with Calvin and Calvinist scholars to the optimistic worldview and the theological anthropology that were to become characteristic of the early modern period. In the history of philosophy, this was significant above all in the philosophy of spirit, in a model (known in the tradition as innatism) of the principles governing the knowledge of God's existence and being. These principles are usually called *notitiae naturales, communes, koinai ennoiai, prolepsis,* or *anticipationes.* This model found no consensus among the scholars of the Reformation, as the vigorous controversy about Daniel Hoffmann at the end of the sixteenth century was to show.[23] This innatism played an important role in the early discussions of the philosophy of religion by Hugo Grotius, Lord Herbert of Cherbury, and the Cambridge Platonists, as the starting point for the philosophical attempt to formulate a general idea of religion. But these epistemological principles for religion and philosophy proved highly ambivalent in the course of the theological controversies between the rival camps, since they had the character of a purely natural condition, something existing a priori—and this was ill-suited as the basis of a philosophical approach to theological themes. John Locke perceived the dilemma of a naïve innatism of this kind and formulated its presuppositions in the following thesis: "It is an established opinion amongst some men, that there are in the understanding certain innate principles; some primary notions, *koinai ennoiai,* characters, as it were stamped upon the mind of man; which the soul receives in its very first being, and brings into the world with it."[24]

23. This controversy, which led to the description of Daniel Hoffmann as "the patriarch of the heretics," concerned the possibility of a philosophical knowledge of God on the basis of the *notiones communes, koinai ennoiai* or *prolêpsis,* which had been taught since the time of Melanchthon—and which Hoffmann or his pupil Caspar Pfafrad vehemently rejected.

24. John Locke, *Essay Concerning Human Understanding* (Heidelberg, 1904), 1.1.30f.

Note: For further reading see Melanchthon; Stupperich in the References. For secondary sources see Frank; Hartfelder; Kessler 1988; Park and Kessler; Kusukawa; Risse; and Scheible.

13

PETRUS RAMUS

(1515–1572)

Method and Reform

Sachiko Kusukawa

The significance of Ramus's thought is a much debated issue, partly because of the complex and evolving nature of his thought, and more importantly because of the heterogeneity of the claims made by those who purported to follow him. It is thus important to assess Ramus's reputation as well as his thought.[1]

Ramus was born in Cuts, Vermandois, in 1515 and entered the Collège of Navarre, University of Paris, in 1527. There he first gained public notoriety in 1536 when he defended a master's thesis that claimed whatever Aristotle taught is wrong ("Quaecumque ab Aristotele dicta essent, commentitia esse"), but it would be misleading to assume that Ramus was a thorough-going anti-Aristotelian. After a short teaching spell at the Collège du Mans, he moved to the College de l'Ave Maria. There, inspired by the works of Johann Sturm (1507–1589) and Rudolph Agricola (1444–1485), he developed his ideas to reform the arts curriculum and

1. For Ramus's biography, see Hooykas 1958 and Sharrat 1975. For his publications, see Ong, *Inventory,* 1958, and Bruyère 1984; for studies on Ramus and his impact, see *Pierre de la Ramèe* 1986, Meerhoff and Moisan 1997, and Feingold, Freedman, and Rother 2001.

methodology of learning. As a result, in 1543, he published the *Aristoteli-cae animadversiones* and the *Dialecticae partitiones sive institutiones.* These works echoed earlier humanist calls to place dialectics, a subject tradition-ally regarded as teaching the procedures for probable arguments useful for rhetoric (rather than for demonstrative sciences), at the heart of the arts curriculum. Ramus argued that dialectics in general had three compo-nents, nature, art, and exercise: God had endowed humans with the gift of "natural dialectic," an innate power of knowledge; art or "artificial dialec-tic" was the teaching of procedures that mirrored operations of this natural reason; and exercise was practice by examples. Ramus criticized Aristotle, especially his commentators (both ancient and modern) for not anchoring their methods in practice and examples. Following Agricola's division of Ciceronian dialectics, Ramus divided his (artificial) dialectics into inven-tion (finding arguments) and judgment (ordering arguments). Judgment was further divided into proposition, syllogism, and method. Ramus be-lieved the last to be the Platonic method of definition and division and *the* single method of presenting material by proceeding from the more gener-al and prior in nature to the more concrete. To ensure inclusion of all rel-evant material, Ramus adopted three rules, taken from Aristotle's *Posteri-or Analytics:* the propositions have to be universally true, essentially true, and as general as possible. He also encouraged students to practice this di-alectics by analysis (the exploration of disputations already made) and by genesis (the production of new disputation). Ramus considered this dia-lectics to be applicable to all areas of knowledge, from poetry to mathe-matics. Though the emphases and structure of his dialectics evolved and changed subtly in successive editions of his textbooks, Ramus was clear that his method united logic and textual analysis.[2]

Ramus's anti-Aristotelian pronouncements prompted swift responses from Joachim Perionius *(Pro Aristotele in Petrum Ramum orationes 1543)* and Antonius Goveanus (António de Gouveia; *Pro Aristotele responsio ad-versus Petri Rami calumnias, 1543).* Goveanus, in particular, succeeded in procuring from François I a royal edict to ban Ramus from teaching phil-osophical matters in 1544. The next year, Ramus moved to the College de Presles, teaching mainly rhetoric and mathematics. In 1547, on the acces-

2. Mack 1993, 334–55. See Meerhoff 1991 for Ramus's debt to earlier humanist reforms in dialectics.

sion of Henry II, the ban was lifted through the intercession of Ramus's patron, Charles de Guise. In the same year, Ramus published the second edition of his dialectical manual, *Institutionum dialecticarum libri II*. In 1551 Ramus was named the professor of eloquence and philosophy in the Collège Royale, where he advocated a humanist reform of the arts curriculum at Paris, which placed dialectics as the foundation of reading classical texts. From 1554, he was embroiled in an extended dispute with Jacobus Carpentarius (who had published the *Animadversiones in libros III Dialecticarum institutionum Petri Rami*) over his idea of "method." In 1555 he published the third and definitive edition of his *Dialectics*. After attending the Colloquy of Poissy in 1561, Ramus enthusiastically supported Calvinism.

In 1562 Ramus proposed the establishment of chairs in mathematics, botany, anatomy, pharmacology, and the teaching of Hebrew and Greek. He criticized the shortcomings of contemporary teachings of natural philosophy and metaphysics in the *Scholarum physicarum libri VIII* (1565) and the *Scholarum metaphysicarum libri XIV* (1566), respectively. In the area of natural philosophy Ramus argued that the mixed sciences, such as mechanics and optics, Aristotle's *Meteorology*, and his works on animals were far more useful than his *Physics*. Ramus's own teaching on natural philosophy seems to have been confined to agricultural maxims and natural historical material taken from the works of Virgil and Pliny the Elder. Ramus argued that metaphysics was virtually superfluous and could be replaced by dialectics. However, he never published textbooks setting out alternative ways of teaching natural philosophy or metaphysics.

During 1568 and 1570, he toured Strasbourg, Basel, Heidelberg, Nuremberg, Augsburg, Geneva, and Lausanne. While at Basel, he befriended Theodor Zwinger the Elder and Johannes Thomas Freigius, who both became his enthusiastic followers, and he also published the *Scholarum mathematicarum libri XXXI* (1569), which contained the *Prooemium mathematicum*, published earlier in 1567. In these writings, Ramus set out to defend mathematics as the theoretical basis of natural philosophy as well as a practical tool for mechanics, astronomy, and trade. At the same time, he criticized contemporary mathematical instruction for ignoring practical application and for presenting Euclid's *Elements* in syllogistic form. In his earlier textbooks on arithmetic (1555) and geometry (1569), Ramus had tried to remedy these shortcomings by grouping material by the types of problems it could solve. Although Ramus himself seems to have lacked the necessary skills to pursue the connection, he further suggested in the *Scholarum mathematicarum libri XXXI* that there was a link between algebra and Greek analysis. For reforming astronomy, on the other hand, Ramus actively solicited help from others: from 1563, he exhorted the astronomer Georg Joachim Rheticus as well as the young Tycho Brahe (whom he had met during his sojourn to Augsburg) to initiate a reform of astronomy. Seeing all mathematical and physical hypotheses as fictitious, Ramus said he would give up his chair for the person who could construct a mathematical astronomy as they are observed—an astronomy without hypotheses.

Ramus returned to Paris in 1570. He was murdered in the St. Bartholomew's Day Massacre in 1572. His *Commentary de religione Christiana libri IV,* an attempt to reduce theology to an art, was published posthumously in 1576.

The appeal of Ramus to later generations is complex and multifaceted. Through bitter controversies with several renowned philosophers of the time (Joachim Perionius, Jacob Schegk, Jacobus Carpentarius, etc.), Ramus's name came to stand for anti-Aristotelianism, though Ramus himself was dependent on the ideas of the Stagirite and other classical authors as he was on his humanist predecessors such as Agricola and Philip Melanchthon.[3] Although Ramus's own religious position supporting a congregational Reformed Church with lay ecclesiastical authority made him far from a "perfect" martyr in the eyes of Genevan propagandists, the gruesome manner of his death seems to have transformed the reputation of the irascible and petulant Regius Professor into that of an authority of serious contention in matters of learning in other Protestant regions.[4] It is indeed after his death that textbooks bearing the title of "Ramist" started to appear in large numbers, some of which purported to synthesize the dialectics of Ramus and that of Melanchthon (the "Philippo-Ramists"). One must beware of assuming widespread popularity of Ramus's works simply from the number of editions of his work, since the printer Andreas Wechel deliberately tried to flood the market with Ramus's works in order to retain monopoly of the market.[5] As Freedman's examination of these textbooks shows, there appears to have been no common cause or shared ide-

---

3. For Aristotelian defenses against Ramus, see Ong, *Inventory,* 1958, 374–80, and Matton 1986.

4. Kingdon 1967, 96–113.　　　　　5. For Wechel, see Maclean 1990.

ology among the authors of "Ramist" textbooks.[6] Ramus certainly became an important pedagogical authority for the teaching of dialectics and rhetoric, and for producing bureaucrats for the early modern state.[7] His pedagogical success, however, appears to have been limited largely to schools in countries such as England and the Netherlands, as his method was regarded as too limited and unscholarly for more advanced discussions.[8]

By the late sixteenth century, Ramism seems to have been equated with the pedagogical tendency of simplifying and reducing all branches of knowledge through diagrammatic partitioning, particularly by dichotomies. It should be remembered, however, that diagrammatic tabulation itself was a well-known way of organizing information on a page known well before the age of printing, for instance, in logical manuals, and continued to be used in medical works in the sixteenth century, with increasing sophistication.[9] Further studies on the implication of Ramist and other diagrammatic printing are still required to assess to what extent the penchant for dichotomies attributed to Ramus, as Ong has argued, with the spread of printing technology transformed the European mind from a dialogical (and aural) approach to a spatial and essentially visual approach to organizing knowledge.[10]

In the sciences, Jean Pena, who obtained the Regius chair of mathematics with Ramus's support, translated Euclid's *Optics and Catoptrics* (1551) in which Pena made an effort to raise the status of the optics, stressing its usefulness for astronomy, natural philosophy, and religion. An effort to raise the status of mathematics by stressing its utility was also repeated by Frederick Risner, who occupied the chair in Paris, established by the will of Ramus, in the *Opticae libri quatuor ex voto Petri Rami* (1572). Ramus's call for astronomy without hypothesis was taken up in different ways by Tycho Brahe, Christoph Rothmann, and Johannes Kepler.[11] Any attempt to assess Ramus's legacy must understand how Ramus could stand for different things to different people.

6. Freedman 1993.
8. Feingold 2001 and Verbeek 2001.
10. Ong, *Method*, 1958.

7. Meerhoff 2001 and Sellberg 2001.
9. Höltgen 1965 and Maclean 2001.
11. Jardine and Segonds 2001.

Note: For further reading see Ramus in the References. For secondary sources see Bruyère; Feingold; Feingold, Freedman, and Rother; Freedman; Höltgen; Hooykas; Jardine and Segonds; Kingdon; Mack; Maclean 1990, 2001; Matton; Meerhoff; Meerhoff and Moisan; Ong; *Pierre de la Ramèe*; Sellberg; Sharratt; and Verbeek.

14

BERNARDINO TELESIO

(1509–1588)

New Fundamental Principles of Nature

Cees Leijenhorst

Bernardino Telesio was born into an aristocratic family in Cosenza, in Calabria in southern Italy, in 1509.[1] In 1517, he moved to Milan, where his uncle, the humanist Antonio Telesio, was his first teacher. In 1527, he followed his uncle initially to Venice; subsequently, he studied natural philosophy, astronomy, and mathematics at the celebrated University of Padua. He did not, however, set out upon an academic career.[2] Clearly dissatisfied with the academic formation he had received up to that point—above all with the Aristotelian philosophy, which "contradicts the facts perceptible to the senses, its own self, and the Christian religion" (1.20)—he withdrew to a Benedictine monastery, probably to the Grancia della Seminaria near Mileto in Calabria,[3] with the inten-

---

1. Telesio, *De Rerum Natura iuxta Propria Principia,* is cited in the critical edition by Luigi De Franco by volume and page. I am indebted to my Nijmegen colleague Christoph Lüthy for his valuable help.
2. Cf. De Franco 1989, 4.
3. Ibid., 5.

tion of studying the Greek natural philosophers in the original language.

Telesio seems to have worked at several of the more important Italian courts in the 1540s and 1550s, inter alia as secretary. In circa 1552 he married the noblewoman Diana Sersale. The impact of her early death in 1561 made Telesio resolve to concentrate on his scholarly research; accordingly, when Pope Pius IV offered him the post of archbishop of Cosenza, he declined in favor of his brother Tommaso. Telesio completed the first draft of his natural philosophy as early as 1563, but since he had doubts about the cogency of his arguments against Aristotle, he first submitted his manuscript to an examination by the Aristotelian Vincenzo Maggi, whom he probably knew from Padua. After Maggi had confirmed that the criticism was justified and that the theses he put forward against Aristotle were well founded, Telesio had the first two books of his work printed in Naples in 1565 under the title *De Natura iuxta Propria Principia, Liber Primus et Secundus*. In 1570 the second version of the first two books was published in Naples *(De Natura iuxta Propria Principia, Liber Primus et Secundus, Denuo Editi)*, together with three shorter studies of concrete natural-scientific questions that were closely linked to this work. At this time, Telesio gathered a circle of pupils and friends around himself in Naples and became the leader of the Accademia Cosentina, a small coterie of humanistic scholars. Under his direction, they discussed concrete questions of natural philosophy and the empirical observation of nature. He also developed friendly relations with important members of the higher clergy, including Pope Gregory XIII (famous for his reform of the calendar). These friendships made it possible for him to publish and diffuse his strongly anti-Aristotelian and strikingly unorthodox work in a period increasingly marked by the Counter-Reformation.

In 1586, two years before his death, Telesio published the definitive version of his work in Naples under the title *De Rerum Natura iuxta Propria Principia Libri IX*. This work was well received by many scholars—for example, the young Tommaso Campanella,[4] Giordano Bruno,[5] and even

---

4. In 1591 Campanella published in Naples the *Philosophia Sensibus Demonstrata,* a detailed defense of the Telesian philosophy against the attack by the Aristotelian Jacobus Antonius Marta, *Pugnaculum Aristotelis adversus Principia Bernardini Telesii* (Rome, 1587).

5. Bruno speaks of the *giudiciosissimo Telesio* in the third dialogue in *De La Causa, Principio e Uno* (London, 1584).

Francesco Patrizi, although he had written to Telesio as early as 1572 to express not only admiration, but also criticism.[6] *De Rerum Natura* was, however, also the object of vigorous attacks by Scholastic philosophers of various schools, and this culminated in the condemnation of the book by the Congregation of the Index in 1596. This decree could not prevent Telesio's philosophy from receiving a broadly positive evaluation and reception by the first generation of "modern" philosophers. Bacon called Telesio "the first of the moderns."[7] Pierre Gassendi[8] and René Descartes[9] expressed similarly positive judgments, and Telesio's philosophy even seems to have left its traces on Thomas Hobbes.[10]

In the present essay, I will analyze only the final version of his work, in which Telesio elaborates a philosophy that encompasses the whole of nature and is based exclusively on sense perception. The first, general part consists of books 1 to 4. Book 1 describes the general principles of natural events and the way in which these principles generate all the natural bodies. Books 2 to 4 present a detailed critique of the relevant Aristotelian doctrines. This general part is followed by a special part that seeks to analyze "the constitution of some natural things" (2.206), but is basically limited to an investigation of human nature, which Telesio understands as composed of the body and a material soul, the so-called *spiritus*.[11] Book 5 is a more thorough discussion of this *spiritus,* while book 6 deals with the human body. The other parts analyze the activities of the *spiritus,* especially perception (book 7) and rational knowledge (book 8). The ninth book contains a reinterpretation of ethics: Telesio holds that ethics should be understood as the investigation of the instincts and virtues of the *spiritus.*

6. Cf. Patrizi's *Obiectiones,* in Telesio 1981, 463–74.

7. Francis Bacon, *Works,* ed. Ellis, Spedding, and Heath (Stuttgart–Bad Canstatt, 1963) [= London 1857 ff.], 3.114; 5.495.

8. P. Gassendi, *Opera Omnia* (Stuttgart–Bad Canstatt, 1964) [= Lyons 1658], 1.245b.

9. R. Descartes, Letter to Isaac Beeckman, October 17, 1630 (*Correspondance,* ed. Adam—Tannery, 1.158).

10. Cf. Schuhmann "Hobbes," 1988.

11. To a large extent, Telesio abolishes the distinction between animal nature and human nature. Accordingly, his remarks about human nature refer explicitly to animal nature too. He also declares that he will discuss phenomena from the inorganic world (e.g., the essence of comets and the way in which rainbows come into existence) "in separate studies" (2.208). Most of these studies were published by his pupil Antonio Persio in Venice in 1590, after Telesio's death (Telesio 1981).

THE FUNDAMENTAL PRINCIPLES
OF NATURE

Telesio recognizes two fundamental powers, warmth and cold, which he calls "active natures" *(naturae agentes)* because of their ability to diffuse themselves continuously. The warm principle makes bodies mobile and fluid; under the influence of cold, bodies becomes thick and rigid (1.40). The experience of the senses identifies the Sun as the seat of warmth, but the Earth as the seat of cold (1.30). Under the "activating" influence of warmth, the Sun moves with exceptional rapidity through the sky, whereas cold makes the Earth immobile. These fundamental powers diffuse themselves in all directions, each from its own location, and all the objects of nature are generated by the aggressive collision between heat and cold which takes place above all on the surface of the Earth; the specific properties of these objects are to be ascribed to the quantities of warmth and cold that constitute them (1.30). This might suggest the possibility of a "modern" (i.e., exact and purely quantitative) knowledge of nature; but Telesio does not actuate this possibility because he holds that our sense perception is not capable of attaining a precise knowledge of the quantities of warmth and cold that are contained in the objects of nature (1.152).[12]

The two active principles, warmth and cold, are incorporeal and therefore need matter as a substratum for their activities (1.150). These activities need only be understood as the disposition and figuration of parts of matter by means of thickening and thinning (1.60). Unlike the two "active natures," this third natural principle is purely passive (1.50). Matter always remains the same in terms of its quantity (1.60); it must also be understood as homogeneous, a characterization that runs counter to the customary Aristotelian distinction between heavenly and earthly matter. Since matter is passive, it lacks the ability to act upon our organs of perception. Accordingly, it is per se imperceptible and colorless; for Telesio, this means black (1.74).

Because of its fundamental formlessness, its inactivity, and the fact that we never perceive it as something existing independently, Telesio calls matter "almost a nonexistent" (1.324). On the other hand, matter must be un-

12. Cf. De Franco 1989, 148.

derstood as something independent, since one of its constitutive qualities is corporeality *(corporeitas)*, and this means in theory that it could exist on its own. It can therefore be regarded as a substance, that is, as something that exists per se, although this title belongs in the true sense only to the concrete natural object that is composed of a specific quantity of warmth, cold, and matter (1.322).

Whiteness and light, which Telesio calls the "nonphysical face" or *species* (2.52) of warmth, work actively against the darkening of matter. This means that every color must be understood as the outcome of a specific quantitative superiority of whiteness over darkness (1.138). In this case, therefore, the antithesis is not between warmth and cold: in a certain sense, matter takes on the role of cold here. According to Telesio, cold has no *species* or "face" of its own; all it does is to block the sense of sight (1.56). It thus has the same effect as blackness. At this point, the asymmetry in Telesio's thinking between the two "active natures" can be clearly seen.[13] Warmth must be regarded as the genuine active principle. Telesio frequently affirms that warmth is the creator of all the objects in nature, and the bearer of their positive qualities and activities. The only function of cold is to "temper" the activity of warmth (1.50); this means that it comes very close to the pure passivity of matter.

Telesio presents his three natural principles as alternatives to the triad of matter, form, and privation in Aristotelian physics (1.376). Telesio rejects *privation* as a sheer fiction (1.386f.). He affirms that natural processes of change do not take place between the two poles of the positive quality and its lack; rather, there is always an active contrariety of two forces that work actively against each other. The second Aristotelian concept, *the principle of form,* is likewise given a fundamental reinterpretation by Telesio. In Aristotelianism, the incorporeal form has the function of substance. In other words, it constitutes the essence of things and is the independently existing bearer of their qualities and activities. In this context, primary qualities such as warmth and cold possess only an instrumental function. According to the teaching of the Aristotelians, for example, the substantial form of the fire (substance) burns the wood by means of the warmth that dwells in it (accident). Telesio liberates the "active natures" from their

13. Cf. Schuhmann 1990, 123, and De Franco 1989, 146f.

merely subordinate instrumental function, and elevates above all warmth to the genuine substance of the objects in nature (1.322f.). This means that the essence of the Sun is not some abstract form, but the warmth that is irradiated by the Sun and is perceptible to the senses. As for the third Aristotelian concept, *matter,* this too must be understood as the background to Telesio's concept of matter, since the Telesian description of matter as an actually existing physical substance is formulated in the framework of some Averroist and Ockhamist tendencies in Paduan Aristotelianism. In a development that begins already with Zabarella, the concept of matter in Telesio loses most of its metaphysical significance, and becomes a physical component of natural bodies.[14]

This clear reference to Paduan Aristotelianism is nothing exceptional in Telesio. Both his views on the relationship between light and warmth, and the link between the antithetical pair of warmth and cold, on the one hand, and the concept of self-preservation, on the other (see below), should be understood as transformations—indeed, often as simplifications—of the Paduan theories which were elaborated above all in the commentaries on Aristotle's *Meteorologica.*[15]

Francis Bacon was correct to assert that Telesio had merely "turned their own weapons against the Aristotelians."[16] He was correct since Telesio developed the empiricist and materialistic elements that he found in the *Corpus Aristotelicum,* and especially in the "concrete" physics of the *Meteorologica* (which he frequently quotes), and played these off against the more formal and metaphysical teaching about principles in the *Physics.* As we shall see in greater detail, however, Neoplatonic and above all Stoic elements were also to intervene in this process of transforming Aristotelianism. It has often been affirmed, from Patrizi and Bacon onward, that Telesio's teaching on principles is a restoration of Parmenidism,[17] but it is much more than this. Like his natural philosophy as a whole, it is the result of a detailed debate with the Scholastic Aristotelianism of his age.

14. Cf. Lerner 1985, 836, and Schuhmann 1990, 128.
15. Mulsow 1998.
16. Bacon (see n. 7) 4.359; cf. Giachetti Assenza 1980.
17. On this, cf. Lerner 1992.

SPACE, TIME, AND MOVEMENT

According to Telesio, natural events described above occur within a three-dimensional space that is defined in a manner opposed to the traditional Aristotelian concept of place. Aristotle defines the place of a body as the first immovable boundary surface of a body that surrounds this body (*Physics* IV, 4, 212 a 20). This means that his concept of place is relative: the place of a body can be determined only in relation to other bodies that surround this first body. From an ontological perspective too, this place is relative, since it remains bound to the surface of a body and can never appear on its own.

Against this "relative" concept of place, Telesio defends an "absolute" concept of space. The place *(locus)* of all natural bodies is the space *(spatium)* that exists per se, devoid of form and qualities (1.188). Unlike the Aristotelian cosmos, which is made up of qualitatively differentiated places, Telesio's space is qualitatively homogeneous and undifferentiated. It has a three-dimension extension, is incorporeal, and is immovable. This is why it remains completely indifferent to the natural objects that move in it (1.196). Whereas therefore the objects are dependent on space for their existence and movement, space is *per se existens* and is independent of the objects not only ontologically, but also physically (1.216). Although we normally never find space without the bodies that fill it, it is possible with the aid of experiments to bring about a vacuum that is empty of objects (1.188f.). It is striking that, notwithstanding the independent way of being of space, Telesio does not explicitly ascribe to space the status of a substance, but defines it rather negatively as "quasi nonexistent" and as "nothing other than the mere capacity to receive bodies" (1.216).

Despite its dependence on the commentary on the *Physics* by the sixth-century Neoplatonist Johannes Philoponus, which had been rediscovered by the Italian Renaissance, Telesio's concept of space is novel and original, and it had a corresponding historical influence. Via Patrizi, Gassendi, and Henry More, it led to the concept of "absolute space" in Isaac Newton.[18]

Telesio's concept of time has a similarly innovative power. Once again, a "relative" Aristotelian definition—in this case, that of time as "measure

18. Schuhmann 1992, 163f. and 143.

and number of movement with regard to earlier and later"—is rejected, and an "absolute" concept is elaborated in opposition to this. Although time seems to be indissolubly linked in our consciousness to movement, time is something that exists of itself, is independent of movement, and is not an accident inherent in movement; it resembles a substance. Time, exactly like space, is incorporeal and completely uniform (1.220f.). In a manner parallel to Telesio's concept of space, his concept of time led via Patrizi and Gassendi to Newton's "absolute time." Also the credit for the parallelization of these two parameters must be attributed to Telesio.[19]

Telesio also rejected the teleology and final causality that the Aristotelian worldview held were immanent in nature, and this too points to the future; indeed, it seems protomechanistic. The Sun does not warm the Earth's surface because it intends to create living beings there. This is only the necessary consequence of its warming nature, and Telesio argues that this effect is to be understood only in terms of efficient causality (2.170).

In this way, Telesio develops the picture of a fundamental necessity of nature for which God has created only the "parameters,"[20] by creating the three principles and the two primary bodies (the Earth and the Sun). Everything that occurs in nature after this act of creation is autonomous, and follows its course to all eternity without any direct intervention on God's part. In order to make an independent functioning of this kind possible, God has equipped the "active natures" with a fundamental instinct for self-preservation and a primitive capacity for perception that is at the service of this instinct. Thanks to this, the "active natures" are able to distinguish between the pleasant processes that promote their self-preservation and the unpleasant processes that damage their self-preservation (1.64f.). This explains, for example, why normally no vacuum exists: the self-preservation of bodies is best assured when they form a material continuum, and this is why they always try to remain as close as possible to each other (1.66).

Telesio also endeavors to reconcile this physical necessity of nature with the concept of a divine finality: he writes that God, in his infinite wisdom, has determined the distance between the Sun and the Earth in such a way that the Sun does not burn up the Earth, but is rather able to promote

19. Schuhmann "Entstehung," 1988, 38f.
20. Kessler 1992, 28.

its growth. Although the Sun merely obeys the necessity of its own nature, not any goals "foreign" to its own self, it nevertheless accomplishes a higher, God-willed purpose or finality, and this permits us to see the wisdom of God shining forth from the whole of nature (2.168). It is, however, impossible for our limited human understanding to grasp the way in which God has created the world (1.90).

Although the world appears in Telesio's writings as a kind of machine that has merely been set in motion by God, he holds fast in his explanation of the functioning of this "machine" to an organic model in which the individual bodies appear as quasi-living beings with an active capacity for perception. This concept of movement takes very different anti-Aristotelian paths from the mechanistic concept of movement. Thus, Telesio goes so far as to ascribe to warm bodies a capacity for self-movement, whereas the mechanicism of a thinker like Hobbes, who followed Aristotle on this point, excludes a priori the self-movement of any body. Unlike Hobbes and Descartes, Telesio also sees movement as an effect of warmth, not as its cause.[21] Nor does he reduce (as does Hobbes) Aristotle's qualitative alteration and other kinds of movement to local movement; indeed, he makes a much stronger distinction between them than does Aristotle (2.142f.).

THE *SPIRITUS* AND ITS ACTIVITIES

Telesio's consistent naturalism explains the nature of the human person by the same principles as that of the inanimate objects of nature. Specifically, all the human acts of knowing are understood as real motion, which is evoked in the human soul by external objects. All living beings have their origin indirectly in the "active natures," that is, in the "seeds" created by these active natures. The specific active principle of living beings (including the human person) is the *spiritus*, a subtle body resembling fire or light that is completely determined by warmth (2.260). It resides in the nervous system and uses the body in the manner of a shield or garment (*tegumentum*) against harmful influences from the external world (2.474).

Just like the "active natures," the activities of the *spiritus* are driven by the instinct for self-preservation. The most important activity of the *spiri-*

21. Schuhmann "Hobbes," 1988, 119.

tus consists in sense perception that allows us to recognize what is beneficial or unfavorable to our self-preservation, by showing us the sources of
pleasure and of pain. An act of perception occurs as soon as the *spiritus* is
set in motion by external bodies. The peripheral parts of the *spiritus,* stimu-
lated by the external bodies, transmit these stimulations to the central part
of the *spiritus,* which is located in the brain; this central part then analyz-
es this information and stores it. Since perception fundamentally involves
a setting in motion of the *spiritus,* all the different kinds of perception,
with the exception of the act of hearing,[22] can be reduced to the sense of
touch (3.30).

Perception means, however, more than the passive suffering or being
set in motion of the *spiritus,* since it also includes the reaction to the movements that come from outside. The *spiritus* either contracts or spreads out
(2.260f.), and Telesio understands this as the activity or *operatio* that is
specific to the *spiritus* (3.28). This active aspect can also be seen in Telesio's opinion that perception consists primarily in becoming aware of the
changes in the *spiritus* that are caused by the objects (3.6).

Perception is the basis of every other kind of knowledge, including rational knowledge, which consists of a renewal or recollection of the *spiritus* movements (3.294). We require this form of knowledge only when the
perception of an object is incomplete, for example, when the object that we
perceive appears too far off (3.164f.). In this process, reason succeeds in ex-
trapolating from those parts of the object that are perceived, on the basis
of comparisons with what it has already experienced, to the nature of objects that are incompletely grasped, or even of objects that in principle cannot be perceived. The act of comparison is in fact the principle of universal knowledge, which is nothing other than a kind of generalization of the
similarities that are perceived between a number of objects (3.170). From
this perspective, accordingly, rational knowledge appears to be merely a
substitute for perception by the senses—which in Telesio's eyes is far superior to every other form of knowledge (3.170).

In keeping with this view, Telesio also writes that "all the sciences, including mathematics, derive their principles from perception" (3.174). Nev-

---

22. Hearing takes place indirectly, by means of the air that is between us and the external body (3.138).

ertheless, there are fundamental differences between the various sciences here. While physics has its basis in the perception of the natural bodies and of their qualities, and makes it possible for us to have a direct insight into the essence of these bodies, mathematics refers to objects that are not perceived, but are derived from perception, namely, to the so-called signs (*signa*). Mathematics must therefore be termed a merely hypothetical science, one that is subordinate to physics (3.180f.). Similar reasons explain why Telesio has a partly negative attitude to astronomy, since this discipline too deals with objects that are scarcely perceptible (1.316).

Like his natural philosophy, Telesio's psychology and epistemology must be understood in the context of a profound debate with Aristotelianism. For example, his idea of the soul as a material, though extremely subtle, substance that is present in the body in the same way as a sailor is present in a boat (2.124) is explicitly directed against the Aristotelian idea of the soul as the nonphysical form or entelechy of the body. Telesio also refuses to see perception and other processes of the psyche as the actualization of potential and hierarchically structured capabilities of one or even several nonphysical souls (3.258); he defines perception, as we have seen, exclusively as the processes of movement within the unified *spiritus* in reaction to external stimuli. This definition runs directly counter to the Aristotelian teaching of a reception of nonphysical forms or formal aspects of the external world (3.266).

Since this *spiritus* is common to all living beings, there is no fundamental distinction between human and animal nature, but only a difference of degree. The human *spiritus* is merely "purer" than that of the animal, and is better protected in the brain from harmful influences: this explains why human beings receive and analyze information better than the animals (3.226, 232). Nevertheless, there is one essential characteristic that distinguishes the human being from the animal: in addition to the bodily *spiritus* that proceeds from the seed (*spiritus e semine eductus*), the human person also possesses a nonphysical, immortal soul that God has poured into the body (*anima a Deo infusa*) and which Telesio defines as the "form of the *spiritus*" (3.232). The existence of this soul explains why the human being, unlike the animal, is not content with the finite objects of sense perception and the momentary, earthly, bodily self-preservation, but has an infinite urge for knowledge of divine, immortal things that are not accessible to perception by the senses, and thereby yearns to work for his eternal self-preservation (3.234).

However, the nonphysical soul is completely tied to the material *spiritus* and to the body (3.360). The existence of the *anima* thus makes no fundamental difference to the explanation of the "earthly," normal human activities of knowledge, and this has led many commentators to dismiss the *anima* as an alien element inserted into the Telesian doctrine merely as a concession to the Catholic Church. On the other hand, the *anima* corresponds to Telesio's methodological requirements, namely, that one must study the essence of things on the basis of their behavior: an infinite urge oriented to the nonphysical sphere points to the existence of a nonphysical soul that in some sense is infinite.[23]

Understood in this way, Telesio's teaching about the *anima* is not an alien element, but is in one sense the very heart of a "pessimistic anthropology."[24] Despite its divine origin, the human soul that is darkened by original sin no longer has access in this life to the knowledge of divine things—it depends entirely on the perception of the senses. Although Telesio employs here metaphors of Platonic provenance, such as that of the "imprisoned" soul (3.360), recent scholarship has shown that his doctrine of two souls is essentially of Aristotelian (more precisely, Albertinist-Averroist) provenance.[25]

Telesio's teaching on the *spiritus* must be seen above all in the context of the debates generated by the tension between Aristotelianism and Galenic medicine.[26] Here too Telesio attempted to play off some empiricist and materialist elements of the *Corpus Aristotelicum*, above all from the *Parva Naturalia*, against the Scholastic psychology with its more spiritualistic orientation. We can also see the clear influence of Epicureanism and in particular of the Stoic doctrine of the *pneuma*.[27]

The doctrine of the *spiritus* is completed by an ethics of self-preservation. Telesio derives differences in intelligence and in moral virtuousness from climatic and other material circumstances to which the *spiritus* is exposed (3.324f.). Self-preservation is the true and only "highest good"

23. Schuhmann "Hobbes," 1988, 116.   24. Mulsow 1998, 287.
25. Spruit 1992.   26. Mulsow 1998, 201f.
27. Mulsow 1998, 19.

(summum bonum) that the human person can strive to attain (3.170). Joy comes from the perception that one has successfully preserved oneself; pain comes from the perception that self-preservation has been destroyed (3.342). The human instinct for self-preservation has, however, a higher goal than the mere continuance of one's existence: it strives for the good or "comfortable" life (3.342), and this goal can best be achieved in society, where we can count on the help and assistance of other persons. Our need for security in such a community requires us to practice justice, the most important societal virtue (3.354). For precisely this reason, justice is as it were engrained upon the *spiritus*. It is justice that best guarantees our self-preservation, in the sense of a good or "delightful" life in the collective. Telesio (like Baruch Spinoza at a later date) sees the virtues as temperate emotions or passions that contribute most to self-preservation; the vices are intemperate passions that militate against self-preservation (3.346).

Telesio's fundamental principles of nature take up the current discussion of the Renaissance and reach original solutions that were to prove successful in the philosophy of the Baroque period and of the Enlightenment.

Note: For further reading see Telesio in the References. For secondary sources see Badaloni; De Franco; Giachetti Assenza; Kessler 1992; Lerner; Mulsow; Schuhmann; and Spruit.

15

JACOPO ZABARELLA

(1533–1589)

The Structure and Method of
Scientific Knowledge

Heikki Mikkeli

LIFE AND WORK

Jacopo Zabarella, the eldest son of Count Giulio Zabarella, was born on September 5, 1533, in Padua, and died in the same city at the age of fifty-six, on October 15, 1589. He studied the humanistic disciplines, logic, natural philosophy, and mathematics at the university in his home town, and was awarded the degree of doctor in 1553. He spent his entire career at this university, and was appointed to the first chair of logic in 1564. In 1568 Zabarella was appointed to the second chair in the extraordinary Department of Natural Philosophy; in 1577 he was appointed to the first chair in this department. In 1585 he was appointed to the second chair in the ordinary Department of Natural Philosophy, which he held until his death.[1]

In 1576 a severe plague afflicted the Veneto region, and Zabarella and his family left for the countryside. Freed from his

1. Edwards 1960, 1–61.

teaching duties, he had the time to write his collected works on logic, the *Opera logica* (hereafter cited as OL; Venice, 1578). In 1580 Zabella's manual of Aristotelian logic, the *Tabulae logicae,* was published in tabular form in Padua. *In duos Aristotelis libros Posteriores Analyticos commentarii,* his commentary on Aristotle's *Analytica posteriora,* appeared in Padua in 1582. His *De doctrine ordine apologia* (On the Order of Instruction; Padua, 1585) was Zabarella's response to his colleague Francesco Piccolomini in the dispute about the structure of the teaching of the various disciplines. In 1586 his *De naturalis scientiae constitutione* (On the Nature of the Natural Sciences) was published in Venice; this work was also inserted as the introduction to the great work on the various fields of natural philosophy, *De rebus naturalibus,* which was published in Venice in 1590, after Zabarella's death. His sons also edited the unpublished commentaries of their father on works by Aristotle: *In libros Aristotelis Physicorum commentarii* (Venice, 1601) and *In tres Aristotelis libros De Anima commentarii* (Venice, 1605).

THE HIERARCHICAL STRUCTURE OF THE SCIENCES

Jacopo Zabarella was one of the most important Aristotelian philosophers of the sixteenth century. His collected works on logic begin with his treatise on the nature of logic *(De natura logicae).* He begins by presenting the separation, on which his philosophy is based, between the eternal and the necessary natural things, on the one hand, and the world of the contingent, which is conditioned by the human will. On this basis, and following the structure laid down by Aristotle in his *Nicomachean Ethics,* Zabarella divides the various academic disciplines into theoretical and practical sciences and productive arts (OL 2 a–3 c).

The sciences that aim at theoretical knowledge deal with the eternal natural things, while the practical sciences that aim at action deal with contingent matters conditioned by the will. In addition, there exist productive or mechanical arts for the manufacture or production of objects. The sciences deal with already existing objects in a manner different from the arts, which seek to bring something new into existence. Since it is possible to engage in theoretical sciences only by means of thought, Zabarella calls these contemplative sciences. Following Aristotle, he divides these into three genres: metaphysics, mathematics, and natural philosophy. The last of these held a special interest for Zabarella. Assured and demonstrative knowledge can be attained only from the objects of the theoretical sciences; and for Zabarella, it was precisely the certainty of knowledge that was the *conditio sine qua non* of scientific knowledge (OL 4 a–b).

For Zabarella, the structure of the sciences had a hierarchical nature. Ultimately, the goal of practical philosophy as a whole (ethics and politics) is the highest sphere of contemplation. He affirms that the ultimate goal of the human person does not lie in the activity of the practical life, since only the contemplation of the theoretical sciences can guarantee the perfection of the human being (OL 97 b). Since the goal of the productive arts is not the theoretical knowledge of their objects, it is unnecessary to possess a complete knowledge of the things that are produced. Nevertheless, the various branches of the arts are dependent on the knowledge of the theoretical sciences, which provide the basis of action and production.

The Renaissance Aristotelians structured the sciences hierarchically in keeping with two different criteria. First, they referred to the rank of the object of the science in question: thus, they regarded metaphysics, which deals with the divine, as more valuable than natural philosophy and mathematics. Secondly, they referred to the certainty of the demonstrative proofs of the sciences: and in this case, natural philosophy was regarded as more valuable than mathematics and metaphysics, which dealt with abstract objects.[2] Since Zabarella employed both these criteria, he gave no unambiguous answer to the question of the hierarchy of the theoretical sciences.

THE NATURE OF LOGIC

Throughout the entire sixteenth century, the Aristotelians in Padua devoted great attention to the question of the methods *(methodus)* and curricula *(ordo)* employed in the various academic disciplines. In Zabarella's philosophy, the discussions of methods and structure are closely linked to the distinction between sciences and arts. The different academic disciplines had different methods of attaining knowledge, as well as various

2. Zabarella 1605, 8 a–b; Olivieri 1983.

curricula, in order to teach in as comprehensible a manner as possible. For Zabarella, logic was not a genuine science, since it dealt, not with the eternal natural objects, but with the terms and concepts formed from these objects; indeed, he affirmed explicitly that logic was an instrument of the theoretical sciences (OL 21 a). The defense of the instrumental nature of logic kindled a debate between Zabarella and his pupil Ascanio Persio, on the one hand, and Bernardino Petrella, professor of logic at the University of Padua, on the other. Petrella wished to hold fast to the status of logic as a theoretical science: he and his pupils held that logic should deal not only with questions of truth or falsehood, but also with moral questions concerning good and evil.

According to Zabarella, logic was not a genuine science. Nevertheless, it played a central role for science, since it was possible to draw explicitly on the methods of logic in order to guarantee the necessary nature of knowledge that was demanded in the theoretical sciences. He held that scientific knowledge is related explicitly to the universal nature of the *genera,* which cannot be attained exclusively with the help of generalizations based on observations. Instead, a demonstrative inference is required in which, with the help of the rules governing syllogistic inferences in Aristotelian logic, we can convince ourselves of the necessary relationship between cause and effect.

In addition to demonstrative logic, Zabarella discussed other branches of instrumental logic. He held that dialectic and rhetoric were by their nature very closely related spheres; the central difference between them was the sphere of their application. While demonstrative logic is an instrument of the speculative sciences, and dialectic an instrument of the ethics that is based on probabilities, rhetoric is an instrument of politics as a science, and its goal is to convince people to behave virtuously (OL 95 b–97 d). Zabarella also included poetry among the logical academic disciplines, since, like rhetoric, it offers examples of virtuous activity in the field of politics. Among the humanistic disciplines, on the other hand, Zabarella had little appreciation of history, since he held that it is merely a narrative of things from the past, with no place for the will of the human person and his inventions (OL 100 d–101 a).

STRUCTURES AND METHODS OF
THE ACADEMIC DISCIPLINES

Zabarella discussed scientific methodology in the second treatise (*De methodis*) of his collected works on logic. In every academic discipline, the structure (*ordo*) must come before the specific discussion of methods. Here, "structure" denotes that way of presenting a matter which characterizes the academic discipline as a whole; the "methods" denote the way in which knowledge of individual matters is acquired. The goal of the appropriate methods is knowledge per se, while the structure suitable to each discipline aims to promote an easier and more thorough learning of the individual matters (OL 135 a–d).

According to Zabarella, there exist two structures, the compositive and the resolutive. In the theoretical disciplines, where the goal is knowledge per se, one moves from the first principles to perfect knowledge with the aid of the compositive structure. For example, in the presentation of the natural sciences, this means the progression from the *genera* to the *species*. In the artistic disciplines, on the other hand, the goal is action, and here one proceeds in the resolutive structure toward the first principles, in order to attain the desired goal. Zabarella takes as his example the art of building, where the house is the goal and the principles are the building materials such as bricks, stones, and wooden boards. He writes that in the structure of the art of building, one proceeds from the mental picture of the house (e.g. solidity, resistance to wind and water) to the material house, and one notes in so doing that bricks are the most appropriate building material (OL 190 d–192f.).

Zabarella's understanding of the structures led to a dispute with his colleague Francesco Piccolomini, who held that the structures should always imitate the cosmic and divine ordering of nature. Behind Piccolomini's philosophy lay the syncretistic idea of a union of the philosophies of Plato and Aristotle in which natural philosophy too would be at the service of the higher metaphysical goals, whereas Zabarella was unwilling to subordinate natural philosophy to metaphysics. He wished to emphasize the instrumental nature of logic, which became an instrument that made possible a natural philosophy independent of metaphysics.[3]

3. Poppi 1972; Vasoli 1985.

Zabarella discusses the methods in the third book of his treatise *De methodis*. He holds that there are only two methods: the demonstration (proof) from the effect to the cause *(demonstratio quod* or *demonstratio resolutiva)* and the demonstration from the cause to the effect *(demonstratio propter quid* or *demonstratio compositiva),* that is, the resolutive and the compositive methods (OL 230 e–231 a).[4] He did not regard the induction that proceeds from individual instances to a generalization as a separate form of inference, but only as a subspecies of the resolutive method (or the demonstration from the effect to the cause). Induction is peculiar in its results: While it is possible to employ the resolutive method to draw conclusions about causes that are not manifest, such as the Prime Mover (i.e., God) as the cause of the orbits of the heavenly bodies, induction can be employed only to deal with objects that are manifest to the senses, such as the conclusion that fire is the cause of smoke.[5]

Methods in the strict sense of this term are employed only in the contemplative sciences, because it is only in these that scientific knowledge is the aim. Ultimately, the resolutive method is a tool of the compositive method, assisting the demonstration of the principles of the compositive method. The true goal of the sciences is the progression from the knowledge of the principles to the total and clear knowledge of the consequences, with the aid of the compositive method. In those sciences in which all the principles are known, as, for example, in mathematics, the resolution is completely unnecessary. Rather, we can progress directly from the principles that are known with the help of the composition, to a clear knowledge of the consequences (OL 265 f–267 d).

THE METHOD OF *REGRESSUS*

The method of *regressus* results from the union of the resolution and the composition. According to Zabarella, this method can be employed to ascertain the certainty of the knowledge that is attained especially in natural philosophy. Zabarella was not the first Aristotelian in Padua to elabo-

---

4. The resolutive and compositive methods were predecessors of the later known analytical and synthetical knowledge (the terms are the Greek equivalents of the Latin terms used in the Renaissance).

5. OL 268 f–270 f.

rate the *regressus* method, but it reached a high point in his works. It consists of three phases. During the first phase (or resolution), one progresses with the aid of syllogistic inferences from an observed effect to the probable cause of this effect; as yet, however, this knowledge remains confused in the mind of the one who draws the inferences. This is followed by the so-called phase of mental negotiation *(mentalis negotiatio)*, in which thought assures itself of the necessary linkage between cause and effect. The final phase of the *regressus* method is the compositive demonstration, in which one returns from the assured cause to its effect. This means that the necessary relationship between cause and effect is proven and manifest (OL 488 d–489 d).[6]

The *regressus* was accused in the sixteenth century of being a circular argument, because the conclusion returns to the same effect that was the starting point. Zabarella and other Aristotelians reply that in the *regressus* method, our knowledge of the relationship between cause and effect is transposed to a new level and changes from a confused *(confusa)* to a clear *(distincta)* knowledge, so that certainty about the link between cause and effect is attained. This means that the phase of mental negotiation between two syllogisms—the phase in which the certainty of knowledge is confirmed—is relevant to the scientific character of the *regressus* method. The significance and function of the phase of negotiation lie in human intellect or reason (OL 494 b–496 a).

THE STRUCTURE OF THE INTELLECT
AND THE QUESTION OF THE CERTAINTY
OF KNOWLEDGE

The structure of the soul, which Aristotle had treated in his *De anima,* also played an important role in the discussion of scientific methodology. Following Aristotle, Zabarella makes a distinction in his collected works on natural science *(De rebus naturalibus)* between the so-called passive intellect *(intellectus patibilis)* and the active or acting intellect *(intellectus agens).* He held that the active intellect illuminates the universal nature

6. This method preceded the later developed hypothetical deductive method in science. Note the final section of this chapter.

of the individual sense observations during the process of thinking. Consequently, the active intellect can be equated with God, as that principle that alone makes comprehensibility possible. The passive part of the intellect—which, according to Zabarella, is not in fact passive, but is actively at work—meditates on the ideas that are illuminated by the active intellect. By means of selection and abstraction, it makes these ideas appropriate objects of knowledge for the theoretical sciences (Zabarella 1590: *Liber de mente agente*).

In this way, the *regressus* method gives scientific knowledge a divine guarantee, since the reason, through its active part, is connected to the higher intellect. However, Zabarella did not want to present the inferences of the intellect as a deterministic process in which the reason would react automatically to all the impulses that came from outside. Rather, he saw the inferences of the reason as a process conditioned by the will, a process essentially dependent on the intentions of the human person. He did not wish to take part in the lively discussion of the immortality of the soul which had been kindled by the writings of Pietro Pomponazzi and lasted throughout the entire sixteenth century. He left it to the theologians to resolve such questions, since Aristotle had not explicitly stated his opinion on this subject in his writings.

THE COMPLETION OF NATURAL PHILOSOPHY AND THE GROWTH OF KNOWLEDGE

The treatise about the structure of the natural sciences *(De naturalis scientiae constitutione)*, which stands at the beginning of his treatises on natural philosophy *(De rebus naturalibus)*, discusses the question of the completeness of the natural sciences. In the final chapter of this treatise *(De perfectione scientiae naturalis ac de eius ordine)*, he confirms that the Aristotelian system is perfect in terms of its structure and form, but imperfect because it does not mention all the natural objects. Zabarella holds that although Aristotle did not discuss everything, did not in fact know anything, and could even make mistakes, his system can be compared to Euclid's geometry, in which all the theorems of an academic discipline are mentioned. Euclid did not mention all the possible inferences, since a thoroughness of that kind would merely exhaust the reader. Similarly (according to Zabarella), the Aristotelian natural philosophy is complete in its basic structures, so that the only task remaining to scholars is to correct errors and fill in lacunae. For example, Albert the Great supplemented the Aristotelian system with a treatise on minerals, and it ought to be comple-mented in a similar manner on other incomplete points (Zabrella 1590: *De naturalis scientiae constitutione*, 119 d–120 c).

Zabarella's understanding of the nature of scientific knowledge poses the question of progress in the sciences. He held that science developed *within* the Aristotelian-Scholastic worldview which had its origin in classi-cal antiquity; accordingly, there was no creation of new knowledge as mod-ern science understands this. The development of science appears rather as an act of correcting and completing the already existing Aristotelian mod-el, which had boundaries and a framework that were basically known. In this case, science is a system of already known truths, which one can adopt and bring to intellectual completeness. The work of the scholar is there-fore to complete the Aristotelian explanation and structure of the world— not a search for hitherto unknown knowledge, and still less something like modern experimental research.[7] Although he presents observations of na-ture in his writings, Zabarella does not employ these as evidence of the correctness or falsehood of theories, but only as examples that illustrate the principles of Aristotelian natural philosophy.[8]

NATURAL PHILOSOPHY AND MEDICINE

Zabarella's view of the nature of science brought him into conflict with the medical tradition, which was strongly represented at the University of Padua in the sixteenth century. Anatomy, based on section and on ob-servations, had increasingly become the basis on which the other parts of medicine were constructed. Zabarella regarded all the theoretical parts— for example, physiology, which was situated on the border between med-icine and natural philosophy—as belonging to natural philosophy, since medicine itself was a branch of the arts, not a science in the genuine sense of the term. Medicine had a practical function, namely, to heal the sick and to keep people healthy; but it drew the theoretical instruments for this task

7. Mikkeli 1992, 40–44.   8. Rossi 1983, 146.

from the truths of Aristotelian natural philosophy, not in the least from empirical anatomical observations. No matter how exact and valuable medicine per se may be, it cannot be a science, since its goal is not a knowledge (OL 60 c–62 a).

Both natural philosophy and medicine deal with health and sickness, but natural philosophy discusses their universal attributes. When a doctor treats human beings, he should apply the natural philosopher's knowledge of the nature of animals and their attributes. In this context, Zabarella too quoted the aphorism that was so celebrated in the sixteenth century: *Ubi desinit philosophus, ibi incipit medicus* ("Where the natural philosopher stops, the doctor begins").[9] In addition to the diversity of goals and materials, different methods are also employed in these two academic disciplines. The use of the compositive method is appropriate to natural philosophy, since this is a theoretical science; the resolutive method is appropriate to medicine, since this is a branch of the arts (OL 193 e–197 f). In Zabarella's discussion of the boundary line between natural philosophy and medicine, we see clearly the sharp division between the theoretical and the practical spheres of science which was typical of his concept of science.

MODERN SCIENCE AND ZABARELLA'S
POSTHUMOUS INFLUENCE

The interpretation that I have presented of the Aristotelians' concept of science and of their relationship to the so-called Scientific Revolution in the seventeenth century is diametrically opposed to the so-called Randall thesis. According to the thesis that John Herman Randall put forward in the 1940s, it was in fact the Aristotelians in Padua who can be regarded as the ancestors of the modern science that began with Galileo Galilei. Scholars have subsequently shown that in the early texts that he wrote in the Collegio Romano, the Jesuit college in Rome, Galileo applies the same conceptual apparatus that is typical of Zabarella and the other Renaissance Aristotelians.[10] However, this line of interpretation, which emphasizes the modernity in the Aristotelians of Padua, fails to take account of three fundamental facts. First, the conceptual apparatus of Aristotelian

9. Schmitt 1985, 12.   10. Wallace 1992.

logic was in universal use at that period, when scholars wrote about scientific method. This means that we should not only look at the shared terminology: it is more important to investigate the *use* that is made of this terminology. Second, the methodology of Galileo and of the other pioneers of the "new natural science" of the early seventeenth century was essentially mathematical—unlike the natural-philosophical and methodological writings of the Renaissance Aristotelians. Third and most important, the Aristotelian framework of science was questioned ever more frequently in the seventeenth century, so that from the time of Galileo onward, the development of science took place by means of new observations and experiments, and no longer by means of corrections to the Aristotelian model. Theoretical constructions were made on the basis of observations and experiments, and the truth of such constructions was no longer checked against the Aristotelian worldview. Nevertheless, the Aristotelian scheme remained present in the basic university textbooks for a long time to come.

Nevertheless, Jacopo Zabarella can be considered one of the most important Aristotelians of the sixteenth century, thanks to his posthumous influence. His philosophy was a central source on which many textbooks of natural philosophy drew at the end of the sixteenth and the beginning of the seventeenth centuries. The publication of his collected works on logic at Basle in 1594 played a decisive role in the diffusion of his works north of the Alps. The Aristotelian logic that Zabarella presented in his works was particularly popular in the Protestant regions of Germany, where it was employed in the legitimation of the new theology.[11] In the seventeenth century, many universities experienced the rivalry between the Ramistic and the Aristotelian logic, and the latter was based precisely on Zabarella's interpretation of Aristotle's writings on logic. In the same century, Zabarella's commentary on Aristotle's *Analytica posteriora* was still regarded as one of the best commentaries ever written on this work.

11. Leinsle 1985.

Note: See Zabarella in the References. For secondary sources see Edwards; Kessler 1987; Leinsle; Mikkeli; Olivieri; Piaia; Poppi 1972; Randall; Risse; Rossi; Schmitt 1985; and Wallace.

16

MICHEL DE MONTAIGNE

(1533–1592)

Philosophy as the Search
for Self-Identity

Reto Luzius Fetz

MONTAIGNE'S LIFE

Michel de Montaigne was born in 1533 in the castle of Montaigne, about sixty kilometers inland from the French port of Bordeaux.[1] He came from a bourgeois family of merchants who had entered the ranks of the aristocracy when they bought this castle. His father took part in the French campaigns in Italy and returned as an enthusiastic humanist and devotee of the Renaissance. In order that his son might learn the language of ancient Rome as his mother tongue, so to speak, he employed a German tutor who was to speak only Latin with the child. At the age of six, he was sent to an aristocratic academy, the famous Collège de Guyenne, where he received instruction in the humanistic disciplines. Since his father had determined that he was to pursue a career in the administration, he studied law at the Universities of Bordeaux and Toulouse. From 1557 to 1570, from the age of twenty-four to thirty-seven, he

1. The best biography of Montaigne is by Frame 1965.

served as magistrate, parliamentary counselor, and judge in Bordeaux. In the chaotic times of the French wars of religion,[2] he maintained a Catholic and conservative position, behaved correctly, and was loyal to the king, without displaying an exaggerated zeal. He was happy to be sent as a delegate to the royal court in Paris, and he accompanied the court on its journeys into the provinces. At the age of thirty-two, he married a local noblewoman. He himself relates that this was due less to his own decision than to the advice of others: Montaigne sees marriage, like the state and religion, largely as a matter of conventions, of tradition and good manners, although he accepts only the personal conscience as the ultimate authority.

Montaigne had had passionate encounters and love affairs in his early years, but he felt the deepest bonds only to another man, Etienne de La Boétie, who was three years older and, like Montaigne himself, a parliamentary counselor in Bordeaux, where they met in 1558 when Montaigne was twenty-five years old. This close friend and intellectual guide, with whom Montaigne could reflect on all of life's questions in the spirit of Stoic philosophy, was carried off by an illness five years later, leaving a gap that was never filled.

In 1568, on his father's death, Montaigne inherited the family seat. Three years later, in 1571, he resigned from all his posts in Bordeaux and retired to his castle to lead a contemplative life far from the busy world. He installed his library in a room in the castle tower and had sentences from the wisdom literature of classical antiquity and from the Bible engraved upon the ceiling beams, to remind him continuously of his philosophy of life.[3] But Montaigne's spirit refused to submit to the regimen that he wanted to impose upon it: he writes that his spirit "gave birth to so many chimeras and fantastic monstrosities, one after another, without order or fitness, that, so as to contemplate at my ease their oddness and their strangeness, I began to keep a record of them, hoping in time to make my mind ashamed of itself" (1.8.31 [34]).[4] The books that were gradually written in this way

2. On the historical background to Montaigne's life and his *Essais*, cf. Nakam 1982, 1984.
3. The inscriptions on the beams can be found in the edition of Montaigne by Thibaudet and Rat, pp. 1419–25 (ed. Balsamo 2007, 1311–16).
4. The Arabic numerals indicate the book, chapter, and pages in the *Essais*; regular page references are to the English translation by M. A. Screech, page references in square brackets [ ] are to the French edition by Thibaudet and Rat.

are Montaigne's *Essais*. He published the first volumes in 1580, less than ten years after his withdrawal from public life.

Despite this withdrawal, Montaigne continued his political activity. He attempted to mediate between the contending parties in the French civil wars. In 1577 he noticed the first symptoms of a nephrolithiasis (kidney stones); Montaigne knew that this illness was fatal, since his father had died of it. In search of relief, he visited spas from 1580 to 1581, traveling via northern France, Switzerland, and southern Germany to Rome, where he was made an honorary citizen. Montaigne regarded this as the crowning of his world-citizenship. While he was returning, news reached him at Lucca that the city of Bordeaux had offered him the mayorship. On the insistence of the king, he accepted this post, and he was elected to a second term in 1583. He seems to have played a role in the conversion of Henry IV, which ended the civil war. All these new experiences are echoed in the third book of his *Essais*, which he published in 1588 together with a new edition of the first two books. He made new entries in his own personal copy until the end of his life. In 1590 he declined a salaried high position at the court. He died of his nephrolithiasis in his castle in 1592, not yet sixty years old.

INTELLECTUAL DEVELOPMENT AND PHILOSOPHICAL INFLUENCES

Montaigne's life falls into three clearly separate phases. The first is formed by the years of his youth and early manhood, until his withdrawal to the castle. This time is marked by dependence on his father and by the conduct of official business and activities at court, that is, by a rather superficial form of life. The second phase is marked by the death of his father, the attaining of full independence, and the decision to withdraw from public life. This withdrawal follows a Stoic ideal, which, however, soon proves unrealizable; and this leads, with the writing of the *Essais*, to the search for the authentic ego, as opposed to a preconceived image. The new selfhood that Montaigne attains opens the third phase of his life and gives him a new access to the world—his journeys to the spas and to Rome. His acceptance of the mayorship displays a new social involvement. This last phase is the period of the real Montaigne, who speaks to us in the third book of his *Essais* and in the additions he makes to the first two volumes.

A variety of philosophical tendencies influenced Montaigne in his intellectual development. Their impact can be seen above all in the transitions between the various phases of his life.[5] In La Boétie, he not only reveres the true and honest friend: he also admires the Stoic wise man who could face death with serenity and composure. This is why the Stoic attitude of a pure morality of will, calmness, and freedom from passion, which immovably defies every blow of fate, is the model that Montaigne initially seeks to imitate when he withdraws into private life. His favorite philosopher is Seneca, the author whom he quotes most frequently in his first *Essais*. However, the attempt at leading a life inspired by Stoicism soon proves to be artificial, something that does not correspond to Montaigne's own nature. In the debate with Stoicism, an ancient opponent of the Stoa now moves to center stage, and finally becomes Montaigne's favorite author, namely, Plutarch, whose *Oeuvres morales* were published in 1572 in Amyot's translation. In Plutarch, Montaigne finds biographies on a human scale. In this period, however, he also comes under the influence of the Skepticism that is flourishing in the France of the late Renaissance. The ancient Skeptic Sextus Empiricus has the strongest influence on him, and Montaigne has several of Sextus's aphorisms engraved upon the ceiling beams of his tower room. He made *Que sçais-je?* ("What do I know?") his motto, because Skepticism "can best be conceived through the form of a question" (2.12.591; cf. 562 f. [508]).

In the final phase of his life, where Montaigne has fully found his own self, he has often been regarded as an Epicurean, thus giving us the triptych of the initially Stoic, then Skeptic, and finally Epicurean Montaigne. This triadic structure fails to recognize that Montaigne was never genuinely a Stoic; all he did was to engage on the existential level with the Stoic ideals about life. It also overlooks the fact that Skepticism was not an intermediate phase, but an enduring element that had a very precise function in Montaigne's thinking. Thirdly, it fails to perceive that although Montaigne ended up as a philosopher of the art of life and displayed undeniable Epicurean traits, he does not borrow these from other sources, but develops them from ideas of his own. The presentation of his oeuvre and of his ideas will make this clear.[6]

5. The standard work on Montaigne's development and his sources remains Villey 1933.
6. The finest and most detailed interpretation of Montaigne's entire work remains

MONTAIGNE'S LITERARY WORK:
THE *ESSAYS*

In writing and publishing his *Essais,* Montaigne presents a new literary
genre, and precisely for this reason the title does not yet function here as
the concept of a literary genre, but has a purely methodological meaning.
Montaigne wanted to present "attempts" rather than assured knowledge
(still less, a "system"). As the various phrases including this noun show,
these are "attempts" in a threefold sense: the attempt to depict his own being (*essay... de ma peinture,* 3.9.1091 [941]: "this tentative essay, this... self-
portrait"), attempts at evaluation,[7] but also the list of the things Montaigne
had attempted in the course of his life (*régistre des essais de ma vie,* 3.13.1224
[1056]: "an account of the essays of my life"). Montaigne justifies the experimental character of his writings by appealing to the instability and mutability of his experience of his own self: "If my soul could only find his foot-
ing I would not be assaying myself but resolving myself. But my soul is ever
in its apprenticeship and being tested" (3.2.908 [782]).

The *Essais* seek to capture authentically, in the whole spectrum of its
variety, the ego, which is experienced as changeable, with the paradoxical result that Montaigne must confess: "I may happen to contradict myself but... I never contradict truth" (3.2.908 [782]). By means of this self-
description, Montaigne succeeds in rising above each individual moment
and getting an overview of his entire being. This makes the *Essais* a medium
for the totalization and objectification of the experiences of the self. Montaigne's own image contributes to the formation of his own self: "While I
formed this image in keeping with myself, I was so frequently obliged to
position myself and to strike a pose in order to depict myself correctly, that
the model thereby became consolidated and in a sense formed itself" (2.18.
[647f.]; cf. 755). There is a mutual process whereby the author and the *Essais* constitute each other: "*I* have not made my book any more than it has
made *me*" (2.18.755 [648]). This is why the book can be considered "consub-
stantial" with its author (ibid.).

Friedrich 1967. Starobinski 1989 is also valuable, not least for its information regarding
Montaigne's personal identity.

7. [289]: "Our power of judgment is a tool to be used on all subjects.... That is why I
seize on any sort of occasion for employing it in the essays I am making of it here."

With what self are the *Essais* concerned? Montaigne answers this question by underlining the novelty of his way of presenting himself: "Authors communicate themselves to the public by some peculiar mark foreign to themselves; I—the first ever to do so—by my universal being, not as a grammarian, poet, or jurisconsult but as Michel de Montaigne" (3.2.908 [782]). Montaigne wishes to present himself, not in his role identity, but in his personal identity with his universally human traits. According to Montaigne, all of moral philosophy can be constructed upon one single human life, no matter how nameless and devoid of splendor this life may be, since every human being bears in himself the entire image of humanity (ibid.). This must not be understood to mean the absorption of the individual into the generality, as if the individual human being were merely one instance of a species. One essay is devoted to the topic of the inequality that reigns among us, and Montaigne ventures to assert that there is a greater distance between this human being and that human being, than between this human being and that beast (1.42.288 [250]).

Montaigne's emphasis on human individuality must be seen against a background that is no longer that of antiquity and the Middle Ages. In Montaigne, the contrast is not so much between the individual and singular, on the one hand, and the general qualities of human nature, on the other; the decisive contrast is provided by the socialization of the human person. This makes Montaigne a precursor of the modern theory of identity. He discovers an individual self that is also aware of being a socialized self. "I have nothing of my own apart from my own self; and this possession too is in part imperfect and borrowed property [*empruntée*]" (3.9.[946]).[8]

The breakthrough to a personal identity, the abandoning of role playing in order to arrive at one's own authentic self, is manifested externally in the way in which the *Essais* are presented. On the title pages of the two first editions, Montaigne lists all his titles, declaring himself a member of an order of chivalry, chamberlain, and mayor. On the title page of the last edition, his name stands on its own. The human being Montaigne has put a distance between himself and the functionary and dignitary. This does not happen by chance. Montaigne's *Essais,* more strongly than any other

---

8. Cf. p. 1096: ". . . imperfect and defective." For a detailed study of these topics, cf. Fetz 1995.

sixteenth-century work, reflect the breakthrough from a role identity to a personal self-identity.

PHILOSOPHY AS A FORM OF LIFE

AND AN ART OF LIVING

Montaigne's *Essais* have won him an established place in the history of literature; the same cannot be said of his position in the history of philosophy, where he is often passed over or mentioned only peripherally. It is seldom that a whole section is dedicated to him. Hegel supplies one reason for this: he classifies Montaigne as one of the "remarkable men" of the Renaissance, who are indeed "customarily included in the history of philosophy too," but belong "in reality not to philosophy, but rather to culture in general."[9] Nietzsche's judgment is very different: "The fact that such a man wrote has increased the delight in living on this earth. . . . My choice would fall on him, if I were given the task of making myself at home on earth."[10] This divergence in the evaluation of Montaigne is only to be expected in two thinkers who represent such different forms of philosophical activity—systemic thinking, on the one hand, and a philosophy of life, on the other. Montaigne engages above all in a debate with the philosophical schools of classical antiquity, which were primarily interested in discovering and justifying the right form of life, rather than in sketching philosophical systems. Montaigne too belongs to this tradition of "philosophy as a form of life,"[11] since he says of himself: "All my effort has gone into the forming of my life" (2.37.885 [764]). But the true self-culture, or *culture de l'âme* (2.17.[642])—Montaigne adopts here Cicero's formula of the *cultura animi* (*Tuscul.* 3.13)—is impossible without philosophy, which is the real creator of judgment and of morals (1.26.184 [242]). Philosophy trains us in a life that follows freely chosen principles that one has appropriated internally, rather than external conventions, so that this life has the inherent ability to create structure (cf. 1.26, *passim*).

9. G. W. F. Hegel, *Vorlesungen über die Geschichte der Philosophie,* Part 4, ed. P. Garmiron and W. Jaeschke (Hamburg, 1986), 60.

10. Friedrich Nietzsche, *Unzeitgemäße Betrachtungen* III, 2, in *Sämtliche Werke. Kritische Studienausgabe,* ed. G. Colli and M. Montinari, Vol. 1 (Munich and Berlin, 1980), 348.

11. Hadot.

Philosophy, understood as a teaching about life, is put at the service of the highest goal Montaigne knows, namely, the correct way to lead one's life. "If you have been able to examine and manage your own life you have achieved the greatest task of all" (3.13.1258 [1088]). This is the real, indeed the only art for which Montaigne declares himself responsible: "My professional work and my art are: life" (2.6.[359]: "Mon mestier et mon art, c'est vivre." Cf. p. 424). The goal of this art is a life that is fulfilled in itself. This is the ancient *vive ut vivas,* life for its own sake; Montaigne praises this *vivre à propos* as "our great and glorious masterwork" (3.13.1258 [1088]).

The distinction between the art of living and the other arts is that it is not directed toward something external, something other than itself. It bears its goal in itself, in the life that is shaped by art (cf. 3.6.881). Accordingly, the "general main chapter" of the art of living affirms that life "must itself be its goal and its intention" (3.12.[1028f.]; cf. 191). The ultimate standard that the art of living acknowledges is only humanity, which must be exploited and enjoyed to the full. "Nothing is so beautiful, so right, as acting as a man should" (3.13.1261 [1091]). Fidelity to one's own being thus becomes the maxim of Montaigne's art of living. "It is an absolute and almost divine perfection to be able to rejoice honestly in one's own being" (3.13.[1096]; cf. 1268). Correspondingly, Montaigne knows only one real danger, that of alienation from one's own self. A human being sets out on this false path when he falls away from his own being, either by lowering himself to the level of the animals or by raising himself up above his own self and wanting to become an angel (cf. 3.13.1268 [1096]). It is only an "inhuman wisdom" that makes us despise our body and its pleasure (3.13.1256 [1086]). The spirit and the senses must penetrate each other, in order that we may attain those fully human joys which Montaigne describes as "spiritually sensuous, sensuously spiritual" (3.13.1087).

Montaigne saw alienation by society as the principal danger for a life in keeping with our own being. But the more he uncovers the societal dependences, the more does he also discover an autonomous self that is capable of eluding the clutch of these dependences. Here, Montaigne enters virgin territory, and his discoveries make him the forerunner of the modern theory of identity.

THE SEARCH FOR SELF-IDENTITY

Montaigne's art of living makes the care of one's own self the central concern, thus exposing itself to the risk that this may surreptitiously turn into a conceited care for one's image. Montaigne knows very well that the primary determinant of our life is not the relation to oneself, but the relation to other people. We attach more importance to how we are perceived externally than to how things are within ourselves (3.9.[932]). Thereby, however, we deceive both the others and our own selves. Our happiness does not depend on whether other people *think* we are happy, but on whether we ourselves genuinely *are* happy (1.14.[67]).

In a world that is oriented only to external ostentation (3.12.1174 [1014]) and in which what "seems" matters more than what "is," we must find a basis that can support our own form of life. Montaigne agrees with classical antiquity in finding this basis in human nature; but unlike the ancient authors, he no longer acknowledges the existence a priori of a general teleology in human nature. His thinking gives nature a stronger position as the principle of self-realization, since it must now hold its own against all those forms of socialization that trivialize us and make us superficial. Montaigne is convinced that every person has in himself a hidden motivating force that allows his life to rise above societal conditioning. "Provided that he listen to himself there is no one who does not discover in himself a form entirely his own, a master-form which struggles against his education as well as against the storm of emotions which would gainsay it" (3.2.914 [789]).

This nature, however, does not function as a principle of individuation without any activity on our part. It is only via life itself that this nature truly becomes our own; and each one must personally explore what corresponds to his nature and is beneficial to it. Only when nature is developed and tested in this way does it provide the criterion by which we can measure what belongs to our own self. This shows us the sphere in which we can lead the life that is appropriate to us. Only an activity that is reflexive—in the sense that it takes this sphere into consideration, and does not leave it—can preserve us from the confusions that follow upon alienation. Montaigne sees examples of this alienation in avaricious and ambitious persons whose unbridled desires lead them to aim at goals that lie outside the sphere of their own lives (cf. 3.10.[987f.]).

The quintessence of this attitude lies in the art of belonging to oneself, which Montaigne calls the greatest thing in this world (1.39.[236]). For a man of Montaigne's social class, the risk of defecting from one's own self takes the form of the role playing of high society, the desire for recognition by those in positions of power, the wish to receive public offices and dignities. Montaigne reflects on his own relationship to social roles, on the basis of his experiences as mayor of Bordeaux, in an *Essai* (3.10) in which he draws distinctions between a role-self and a personal-self that are far in advance of his contemporaries' understanding of role playing and anticipate the differentiations of the modern theory of identity.

Montaigne succeeds in uniting two apparently contradictory attitudes: commitment to a public office and an inner distance from this office. On the one hand, he prizes highly the public service that in extreme instances must be carried to the point of laying down one's life; on the other hand, he pleads for an inner reservation that keeps our personal self out of public business. This is possible only when one does not identify oneself with the role one has taken on. Montaigne attacks these false self-identifications with an incomparable irony, poking fun at those office-bearers who take their office with them onto the night commode and equate their own greatness with that of their official seat (3.10.1144 [989]), although even "upon the highest throne in the world we are seated, still, upon our arses" (3.13.1296 [1096]).

The author now claims that the mayor and Montaigne were always *two*, clearly and cleanly distinct from one another (3.10.1144 [989]). It is impossible to express more clearly the separation between the personal-self and the role-self. Montaigne's concept of the conscience shows that the former refers to an autonomous rather than to a conventional ego. Long before Nietzsche and Freud, he discovered that what people call "conscience" is usually nothing other than the internalized voice of external authority and conventions. "The laws of conscience which we say are born of Nature are born of custom; since man inwardly venerates the opinions and the manners approved and received about him, he cannot without remorse free himself from them nor apply himself to them without self-approbation" (1.23.130 [114]). However, he says of himself: "I have my own laws and my own courtroom to pronounce judgment on myself, and I have recourse to it more than to others" (3.2. [785]; cf. 911). This autonomous conscience is a part of our self, indeed the part "which alone truly determines who we are" (2.36.[735]). This does not prevent Montaigne from also pleading for respect for tradition and customs, provided always that the inner freedom is preserved (1.23.[117]). This means that his conservatism and convention-alism, which have often been emphasized and criticized, should not be seen as a defection from an autonomous ego. What we find here is the perception that conventions have the function of organizing and making life easier.

Although Montaigne is generally reserved with regard to relationships with other persons, there is one exception where he is willing to reveal ev-erything about himself, namely, friendship. Since, however, the kind of re-lationship he had with his friend Etienne de La Boétie is extremely person-al and private, it cannot be explained. All one can say is: "Because it was him: because it was me" (1.28.212 [187]).

SKEPTICISM AND TRUST:
MONTAIGNE'S WISDOM

Up to this point, we have said little about Montaigne the "skeptic." This is because his skepticism can be understood only when one also bears in mind the underlying attitude of trust that is an essential element of the comprehensive attitude to reality that constitutes Montaigne's wisdom.

In Montaigne, skepticism is primarily an antidote against the "natural inherited illness" (2.12.[429]) of our spirit, namely, the presumption (or the imagination) that we definitively know something (cf. 2.12.[467]). He trac-es this back to the "folly of measuring the true and the false in terms of our own ability to understand" (this is the title of *Essai* 1.27). Montaigne prais-es the Skeptics of antiquity for their realization that our ability to know is limited, and for their form of the search for truth, which suspends ev-ery absolute judgment (2.12.562ff. [482ff.]). In Montaigne, this critical res-ervation is compensated by a fideistic attitude that corresponds in the field of religion to his conservative conventionalism in the political sphere: the more we keep to earthly matters and leave the ultimate things to God, the better will we fare (2.12.[486f.]).

Montaigne's orthodox religious attitude of trust is a mixture of fideism and conventional belief, and includes an element of superficiality. Ulti-mately, the Catholic faith that Montaigne unquestioningly and respectfully professes is not really his thing. This superficiality vanishes in a paradigmatic manner when Montaigne struggles with that human question about meaning, which he experiences as the most universally human and at the same time the most personal of all, namely, death. Montaigne puts his trust primarily in another authority, which he experiences directly: at this point, the immanent nature takes the place of the transcendent God.

Montaigne does not speculate about death and immortality, nor does he discuss in any detail the Christian hope of a life beyond death. He is suspicious of the pathos with which the Stoics seek to master death; but he cannot accept the view of the Epicureans that death does not concern us. The decisive question is whether death can be integrated into one's life in such a way that life can be experienced *from its end* as a fulfilled life. This can be learned only if we understand death, in accordance with the "good counsels of Nature, our mother" (1.20.107 [94]), as something immanent in life itself, something that bestows on life the intensity that can be experienced ever more deeply, the shorter our life expectation becomes (3.13. [1092]).

There are several facets to what Montaigne calls "nature." First of all, it denotes the principle of organization of one's own individuality. It also forms a deep stratum antecedent to the consciousness and the will, a stratum to which Montaigne wishes to entrust himself in order to pass the test of death. Finally, as "mother nature," it is the ground that sustains all living beings, and thus the symbol Montaigne employs to speak of an ultimate principle that is both in and above the world. His skepticism is not least the expression of his conviction that one cannot get the better of this nature by means of discourses and argumentations—the contemporary controversies about concepts strengthened him in this belief. This, however, does not in any way diminish his attitude of trust. On the contrary, the one who has the most childlike trust in nature disposes his life in the wisest way (3.13.[1050]; cf. 1218). Behind this lies Montaigne's experience that his own being was revealed to him not through discursive thinking, but by a more or less accidental, but immediate, perception of himself in the authentic acts of his life (cf. 1.10.[41]; 3.13.[1074]).

This experience of nature within himself relativizes the discursively revolving ego, which proves to be superficial. Under the name of nature, he penetrates to a profound dimension that he experiences as his own authentic self and hence as the norm of his identity. Since this "nature" also denotes the maternal basis of all the beings in the world, Montaigne can associate with it the experience of being kept safe in an all-encompassing totality. He experiences this nature not only as a "gentle guide," but also as a "great and almighty giver" (3.13.1265 [1093f.]). Only one attitude is appropriate vis-à-vis such a giver, namely, the grateful acceptance of one's own life. "I for my part love life and cultivate it and care for it, just as it has pleased God to give it to me" (3.13.[1093]; cf. 1264). The cultivation of existence—Montaigne's art of living—thus ultimately becomes a quasi-religious act of worldly piety.

Note: For further reading see Montaigne in the References. For secondary sources see Andersson; Fetz; Frame; Friedrich; Hadot; Langer; Nakam; Starobinski; and Villey.

17

FRANCESCO PATRIZI

(1529–1597)

New Philosophies of History Poetry, and the World

Thomas Leinkauf

Francesco Patrizi was born in 1529 on the Dalmatian island of Cherso and died in Rome in 1597. In his youth, he traveled extensively with his uncle in the Mediterranean area. After attending school in Ingolstadt, he began his studies in 1547 in Padua, the stronghold of the humanistic interpretation of Aristotle. Initially, he studied medicine, and made the acquaintance of leading teachers of the Paduan Aristotelianism such as Bernardo Tomitano (1517–1576), the teacher of Jacopo Zabarella, and Francesco Robortello (1516–1567), a specialist in the discussion of the *Poetics* (LO 47). In 1551 Patrizi began studying philosophy. A Franciscan is said to have drawn his attention to Marsilio Ficino's *Theologia platonica*. He also read Ficino's commentary on the *Symposium* and Giovanni Pico's *Commento alla canzone d'amore di Benivieni*. Patrizi was in Venice from 1556 to 1571. Economic difficulties led him to enter the service of the Venetian count Contarini and others. He held lectures on Aristotle's *Ethics* for Contarini and was sent by him (and later by Archbishop Mocenigo) to Cyprus, where he purchased valuable books and manuscripts. Later, when he was the Venetian ambassador in Spain, he attempted to sell these. After this period, he moved to Modena, where he wrote *L'amorosa filosofia* in 1577. In the same year, he was appointed to lecture about Plato and Platonic philosophy at the Studium in Ferrara. In 1592 he became professor of Platonic philosophy at the Sapienza University in Rome. Here, while Giordano Bruno languished in the prison of the Inquisition, it seemed that Patrizi had reached the goal of his lifelong project, namely, the replacement of the Aristotelian philosophy and the overcoming of a formalized and misused theory of poetry and history through the reestablishing of a historically and philosophically based sapiential knowledge; but this program was blocked by the forces of the Counter-Reformation.

RHETORIC AND THE STUDY OF HISTORY

Patrizi's philosophical work begins with the study of the humanistic themes of language and history which had become increasingly important in the early sixteenth century, thanks above all to the study of the newly edited *Poetics* of Aristotle.[1] The debates in these fields concerned how one might attempt a "reorganization and *vulgarisation* of culture"[2] not against, but with Aristotelianism.

Patrizi is probably the first to inquire into a genuine truth of history, a *verità storica* (H V 25v ff.; VIII 45 r).[3] He wishes to demonstrate that "history," "rhetoric," and "poetics" each possesses its own certainty, evidential character, and precision, which are not in any way inferior to those of the mathematical-geometrical disciplines. He notes a loss of truth and of wisdom, thanks to the drifting apart of *res* and *verba*, "objects" and "words": "rhetoric" has lost its relationship to things and "history" has lost its relationship to reality. History does indeed affirm that it has a definite relationship to reality, but it has its reality outside its own self, since what is asserted to be "true" is measured, not against the *res gestae*, actions and facts,

---

1. Works of Patrizi are cited as follows: *Della retorica* (R); *La città felice* (CF); *Della historia* (H); *L'amorosa filosofia* (A); *Discussionum peripateticarum libri XIII* (DP); *Della Poetica* (P); *Della nuova geometria* (G); *Nova de universis philosophia* (NP); *Lettere ed opuscoli* (LO); *Emendatio in libros suos novae philosophiae* (E).

2. Vasoli 1989, 30.

3. On H, cf. Vasoli 1989, 25–90; Leinkauf 1998; Blum 2000.

but against intentions that lie beyond these and are attributed to them *ab extra.* The demand for knowledge of truth in history implies a claim to objectivity and certainty that is diametrically opposite to the claim made hitherto in the understanding of history. This understanding covers a spectrum from the simple act of retelling to the presentation of the praise of a prince with rhetorical refinement. Patrizi consistently rejects all prejudice and special interests (cf. H I, 4r). *First,* like the truth of poetic works and of language as a whole, the truth proper to history has its metaphysical basis in an original relationship between being and language; *second,* it has its fundament in a metaphysical history that forms the criterion of all innerworldly cosmic events established from the beginning of time; and *third,* it has its organ only in the *"memory of things"* which is accessible to the spirit.

Patrizi sees the meaning and function of history against the general background of the perfect fulfillment of human existence, that is, *felicità.* He argues that one can distinguish three modes of being: *essere* as the successful maintenance of oneself in existence; *bene essere* as the successful praxis of coexistence; and *sempre essere* as the state of the intellectual, theoretical vision of the ideas or of God (H IV, 23v; IX, 51r). History is orientated to *bene essere.* Patrizi criticizes the late humanistic theory of history, which regarded history as the area of the merely probable, of that which is "true to a large extent, or roughly," and conceived of history's power to impart moral conviction on the analogy of the poetic persuasion by means of *exempla* and *fabulae* (H V 26v–27r, 30r). Alongside philosophy, the science of causes and reasons, history ought to be the science of the effects of those realities that are based on causes (H II 7v–8v; VII 41 v ff.). Unlike the demonstrative-deductive construction of philosophy, logic, and mathematics, therefore, history shares the fundamental style of the hypothetical-inductive reconstruction of the structures of reality—a reconstruction accessible to the human person only through singular and contingent facts. But since it is a *scientia* rather than an *ars,* it ought to share with philosophy the character of a knowledge of causes (H II 8r). The proper object of history is not the facts, but the reference of these facts to their coming into existence or to their transmission through human activity. The inherent possibility of an action must be demonstrated, in order to give the fact a form of necessity (H VII 40v). For Patrizi, history becomes an integral of time, completely detached from the chronological structure

of the chronicle or narrative; this integral could be understood as a secu-
larized image of the similarly integral history of salvation. The totality of
this body of history is now completely immersed in the soul of the individual, in the *libro dell'anima* (H III 13r) in which *tutte le cose* are inscribed.
The historian and the one who hears or reads history must make a comparison that activates a rational relationship between the invisible inner book,
which contains all possible things, and all possible visible external "books"
that can be realized by human persons. Patrizi's argumentation here is oriented both methodologically and theoretically to the exact sciences:

First, history must proceed in a manner analogous to the scientific
method of dialectic or of natural philosophy, especially in dealing with the
individual event: here, Patrizi employs the image of the anatomist (H III
13r). The anatomist's scalpel cuts into history, looking for the intelligible
reason behind the action, a reason that lies in the soul and the spirit of the
human person. It makes use of a scientific-categorial conceptuality that is
derived from the ontological structure of the objects *(cose),* where these are
actions: the agent *(attore)* and the action *(attione)* each forms a substantial
unit, under which so-called *circonstantie* are classified: occasion, means,
time, place, manner, success, structure. These conceptual tools reveal the
internal and external structure of an action (H V 29v; VII 38r–40r; X 60v).
The historian is characterized by his "clear" narration or presentation of an
action by means of its constitutive elements. *Second,* historical knowledge
and historical understanding are linked to the realization of a proportional
correspondence or congruence between subjective certainty and the objective structure of the facts (H III 13r; *conformità/difformità*). The plurality of perspectives of historical truth is revealed by the fact that a sphere
of possibility can be filled out—like an intelligible, already existing sche-
matism—by the individual historian's application of objective, clear procedures (H V 25v).

BEAUTY AND LOVE

Although Patrizi's treatise *L'amorosa filosofia* is written with the Platonic tradition in mind, its intention is radically humanistic, moving from
the "words" to the structure of the things and developing a theory of "self-
referentiality" or "self-love" *(philautia).* It takes the idea of return or conver-

sion in the Platonic-Christian idea of love and applies this to the problem of self-preservation and self-perfecting. In this work, he lays the ground for his "new" metaphysics in the *Nova de universis philosophia* by presenting a *nuova filosofia vera et perfetta*, which is proclaimed by a new Socrates (Patrizi) and a new Diotima (Tarquinia), and in which the classical theme of Renaissance Platonism is reduced "naturalistically" to a universal principle, as can be gathered from the title of the third dialogue: all species of love originate from love of oneself *(tutte le spetie d'amore nascono dallo amore di se stesso).* The radicality of this reduction of love, even of the love of God, to self-love must not lead to the overhasty conclusion that Patrizi is arguing here in a non-Platonic and non-Christian manner: for in (Neo-)Platonic thinking too the origin of love consists precisely in the return into the One itself. Accordingly, absolute return and self-reference coincide in the highest One. Besides this, each existence possesses its existence only through being one with itself and in the affirmation of this unity, and this unity with itself is then the basis of the self-transcendence into the union with the Other, and ultimately with the One itself. As the *amore assoluto* of God (A 110–11), the One is the principle of every finite form of love (A 101f.). Self-love as self-preservation was a key term of Stoic ethics (cf. NP *Pancosmia* XXIII 123ra).

POETICS AND INVENTION

Between 1586 and 1588, Patrizi worked on an unfinished treatise *Della poetica,* in which he parts company with the Aristotelian and the (Neo-) Platonic tradition by defining the poet no longer as an "imitator," but as a "maker of the marvelous" (cf. P II 271ff., 284). The poet's power makes all the elements of the poetry representatives of the marvelous *(mirabile).* Patrizi distinguishes three forms of the production of reality (P II 285f.): *creare* ("to create"), *generare* ("to bring forth"), and *operare* ("to act with skill"), which have various authors: God, nature, and the human person (in arts and crafts). As a perfected image of reality, poetry unites in itself all three modes of production. The poet "creates" in cosmogony and theogony; he "brings forth" through mythology and invention; and he is "artistically active" in three basic modes, which he shares with the historian: "to make more out of less, to make as much from so much, and to make less from more" *(far di meno più, far tanto d'altretanto,* and *far di più meno;*

P II 289). The poet is a maker *(facitore)* in the same sense as the demiurge in Plato's *Timaeus* (P II 271–273), and his activity is "exalted above" other forms of human activity. This "poetics" attempts a synthesis drawn from the analysis of language and of activity, applying the categories that Patrizi had developed in rhetoric and the study of history: the true and the false (P III 14–15), the possible and the impossible, the necessary and the unnecessary, "that which happened" and "that which did not happen" *(avvenuto—non avvenuto)*, and above all the criteria of *furor* and *magia*. When the detailed list of these criteria and categories is set in relation to the basic authorities (God, nature, the human person) and modes (creating, bringing forth, acting), it is possible to posit a combinatory matrix of all possible "places" of poetic discourse, a matrix that follows the Llullism of Giulio Camillo and the humanistic topology of Petrus Ramus (P II 311–27).[4] The truth of poetry lies in the poet's ability to communicate his imagination directly to the human soul through the meter which is anchored in the eternal rationality of mathematics, through rhythm, and through the harmony of the verses. That which is imaged and communicated through this "instrument" of beauty itself is the *mirabile*. As a fabrication *(finzione)*, it is the positive counterpart of the negative deception, deceit, and the abuse of power (P III 23f.). The freedom of poetics unfolds in its *topoi*, which are demarcated by universal categories and by a combinatory understanding of science.[5] The traditional *imitatio*, which was oriented to something alleged to be real, is replaced by *renovatio* or transformation, which transforms that which was known into the unknown, the old into the new (P III 19,51), thereby constituting the *mirabile* or *maraviglioso* which the soul of the hearer/reader immediately grasps (P II 307). Patrizi defines this *mirabile* as a "mixture" or compenetration of the *credibile* and the *incredibile* (P II 310). The "marvelous" thing is that through poetry, the incredible becomes credible and the credible incredible (P II 315–16). The *mirabile* is the spirit or the omnipresent form of the poetry (P II 330). Patrizi believes that he is the first to have shown poetics the certain path for the production of the *mirabile*, through the union of poetics with the rationality of combinationism and of topology (P II 327). He ascribes both to the historian and to the poet an active, constructive, instructive position in the world.

4. Bolzoni 1980; Vasoli 1984, 263–70.
5. Bolzoni 1980, 124–29.

CRITICISM OF ARISTOTLE

Aristotle was the touchstone for the philosophical arguments of humanism as a whole, and for the non- or anti-Scholastic philosophy of the fifteenth and sixteenth centuries. From the second half of the fifteenth century onward, there was a debate between those who wished to reconcile and harmonize Aristotle with Plato (George of Trebizond; cf. DC 140), and those who strictly rejected this (George Gemistos Plethon). Read in this context, the detailed debate with Aristotle that Patrizi conducts in the *Discussiones peripateticae* displays an unprecedented philological and philosophical willingness to engage in radical criticism, indeed a destructiveness. Patrizi's project consists *first* in a reconstruction of the chain of transmission of the most ancient wisdom, wholly in keeping with the *topos* of *prisca sapientia* (ancient wisdom) that had played a determinative role since Ficino in the thinking of the humanists and the philosophers of the Renaissance (cf. DP I/6, 67–68); *second,* in a restitution of the philosophical core of this wisdom in the Platonic/Neoplatonic ontology and metaphysics, thus permitting *third,* the establishment of a new philosophy of nature, of language, and of history; *fourth,* this must be preceded by the destruction of the Aristotelian logic and ontology, as well as of the historical "myth" of Aristotle's originality. This fourth point is an application of the analytic-anatomic method, which Patrizi had developed with a view to the *verità storica,* to a philological-historical problem. The radical destruction of Aristotle presupposes, however, an equally thorough reconstruction of his writings, their structure and philosophical content. The *Discussiones peripateticae* are a philological and philosophical interpretation of Aristotle, and based on this, an extremely sharp criticism born of the conviction that Aristotle had "betrayed" Plato. One element in Patrizi's strategy is that his criticism of Aristotle very frequently becomes a springboard for extensive quotations from the "real" authors, that is, texts from the Corpus Hermeticum, the *Oracula Chaldaica,* the Neoplatonists, and the like (cf., e.g., DP 200).

On the ontological level, Patrizi identifies a central difference between the philosophy of Pythagoras, Parmenides, and Plato, on the one hand—who understood being as "that which is truly in accordance with the object," that is, the ideas and the immaterial, immovable, and immutable substances[6]—and the philosophy of Aristotle, on the other. Aristotle's central concept of the "existent" *(ens)* can mean only "that which is common to all predicates" (DP 106–7). Aristotle is thus alleged to have employed a concept of Being drawn exclusively from (linguistic) logic.[7] Hermes Trismegistus, Orpheus, Parmenides (and the Eleatic school), and Plato acknowledged the One as the divine *principium entium,* which is neither similar nor comparable to the existent, and does not fall under the number of the existent (DP 200); the greatest defect of Aristotle's concept of Being is that it thought of the One only on the level of categories. Similarly, Aristotle's concept of God is situated in the realms of physics and cosmology (on *De caelo* and *De caelo,* cf. DP 216; NP 3v, *Panarchia* 19vb–20ra), with three consequences. *First,* God is degraded to an "animate being"; *second,* the addition of the many movers of the spheres introduces a plurality of principles *(polyarchia);* and *third,* the relationship between God and the world remains undefined (the world has neither beginning nor end, and God is neither "creator" or "master architect" nor "father" (cf. NP, *Mystica Aegyptiorum* 49v–50r; DP III/1, 297–99).[8] This means that we cannot claim that Aristotle wrote a genuine theology. Patrizi's criticism of the Aristotelian philosophy is also directed above all to the concept of the *forma* or *eidos* or "substance," and to the form of the "soul." The Aristotelian *eidos* is not seen in relation to the *mundus intelligibilis,* the "ideal world" in the thought of the absolute first One (God), and thus the real subsistence of the ideas/forms and the universal participation of these ideas/forms cannot be deduced in the stages of Being (DP 334), but only in relation to an abstractive-linguistic "reality" that is anchored in thought. Patrizi concentrates here especially on *Met.* Z 6–8 (DP III/5, 334–35; NP *Panarchia* 26r–v): substance and accidence, form and matter are "unscrewed" from their false hierarchical opposition (where a reversible definition attributes the one only to the other, or bases the one only on the other) and are replaced by a new evaluation of a relational and intrinsically differentiated unity (DP 385–88; DP 199–200). Finally, Patrizi also

6. Patrizi traces the theory of the ideas back to a pre-Platonic origin in which they are given a theological significance antecedent to all ontological significance (cf. DP III/5, 324ff.).

7. Cf. DP III/5, 353 for the difference between the "real subsistence" *(huparchein)* of the universal (of the Forms) and the linguistic "existence" *(sêmainein, legein)* of the universal (of the Forms) which is grasped/understood by the intellect.

8. For a detailed discussion, cf. Muccillo 1975, 72–75; Leinkauf 1990, 77–82.

rejects the Aristotelian definition of the soul as a form or entelechy linked
to a material bodily substratum (*De an.* 412 a 19 f. and 27; *Met.H* 1043 a 35),
in favor of a substance of the soul that is in principle "separable" and therefore "immortal" (NP, *Pampsychia* 53r, 54r–v), since he affirms that the con-
finement of the universal world-soul (from Plato's *Timaeus*) to the segment
called "heaven" imposes an irreconcilable, monstrous dividing line on the
continuity of the world as a whole.

THE "NEW" PHILOSOPHY

The measure of a "new philosophy," conceived of as a system, must inevitably be the philosophical thinking of Aristotle, which Patrizi had criticized. Unlike the dialogue form of the *Poetics, Rhetorics,* and *History,* and
the critical-rhetorical form of the *Discussiones,* the *Nova de universis philosophia* takes the form of a dry, condensed system.

After a "new scientific ordering" of Plato's dialogues, the "new philosophy" receives a positive impetus from the appeal to the great Neoplatonists
of late antiquity, to Proclus and his *Elementatio theologica,* which Patrizi
himself had translated and published,[9] and to Damascius and his *De principiis.*[10] The new ordering of Plato's dialogues gives particular prominence
to the *Parmenides.* Patrizi is influenced here above all by the evaluations
of Proclus, who saw this text as a codification of Plato's "theology." This
means that Patrizi bases his affirmations in his *Nova de universis philosophia* on a theology that takes the idea of the One (*unum*) as its starting
point. After a dissertation on the theory of light (the *Panaugia*), the system
presented in this work is articulated in three main parts: (1) the *Panarchia,*
a theory of principles, the theory of the One and of God, the theory of the
spirit (*nous*) and of particular ontological structural principles (*essentia-
vita-mens, essentia-virtus-operatio*) that have their foundations in this spirit
and are the form in which the spirit is realized. Here, each of the two first
factors of the basic Neoplatonic structure—the One, the spirit, the soul—

9. *Procli Lycii Diadochi Platonici Philosophi Eminentissimi Elementa Theologica et Physica. Opus omni admiratione prosequendum quae Franciscus Patricius de Graecis fecit Latina* (Ferrara, 1583). The new order of Plato's dialogues is appended to NP 1591 and 1593. Cf.
"Dell'ordine de' libri di Platone," LO 178–88.

10. This was pointed out by Klibansky 1943, 326. Cf. the references in Leinkauf 1990,
25, 43, 46, 51–52, 58–59, 65.

is transformed into its Christian counterpart: the One is transformed into the triune God, and the spirit into the angelic spirits. This book closes with a chapter *De creatione*. (2) The *Pampsychia* is a theory of the soul. (3) The *Pancosmia* is a theory of nature. In all these fields, Patrizi consistently argues on the basis of the One or of the principle, and its immediate explications. The entire text is permeated with formulae drawn from the philosophy of Neoplatonism; in their concision, they mostly follow formulations by Proclus.

The ontology of the NP sets alongside the ontology of substances a dynamic ontology that has its essential object in the tension between *complicatio* and *explicatio,* and in the reference or relationship between substantial forms or areas. Again and again, Patrizi speaks of so-called intermediary *(mediae)* forms or existents, an existent that occupies a position between the purely intelligible and the purely sensory (NP *Panarchia* XXII, 47rb–va). An existent of this kind, such as the light or the ray of light, is in itself both distinct from that in relation to which it is intermediary, and not distinct from this in virtue of the fact that it is determined in its essence by the qualities of both the adjacent existents (*similis-dissimilis, incorporea & corporea simul;* cf. *Panaugia* IV, 10a; *Panarchia* XI, 23a; XVIII, 39va; *Pancosmia* IV, 74ab; XIX, 141rab; and *Panaugia* III, 7vb; IV, 10vb). It is neither substance nor accident; rather, it is the *pars essentialis* or *principalis* of the essential definitions of the substances, and a constitutive element of a substantial process (NP, *Panaugia* I 2ra). Such intermediary forms of Being, which are constitutive for ontological, psychological, and physical processes, can themselves be adequately described only by means of a dynamic form of process in which activities, events, or processes can be understood as explications of the substance itself. One such form is the ternary *essentia-virtus-operatio* (or alternatively: *essentia-vis/vita-actio*), since "[e]very activity proceeds from the powers, and the powers in turn proceed from the essence."[11]

"Life is nothing other than the essence which gives birth [*parturiens*] to activity partly in its own self, partly out of its own self. When it gives birth to activity in its own self, it does not go out from itself. It is in itself and re-

11. NP, *Panaugia* III, 6vb; IV, 10ra; *Pampsychia* II, 52ra; *Panarchia* II, 3rb; XVIII, 40va; *Pancosmia* IV, 74vb, VI 78vb, XIV 95rb, XX 113rb, XXI 115va. Cf. Leinkauf 1990, 39–44.

mains in itself, and gives birth to nothing other than its own self; but when it brings the activity out from its own self, it [the essence] is not itself idle in this activity" (NP, *Pampsychia* I, 59vb). The powers that express themselves as intermediary and mediating existents are that which is "really" meant by the concept of "substance." In their origin, they are infinite powers *(virtutes infinitae)*, explications of the infinite *potentia producendi* of the One itself (NP, *Panarchia* VII, 14ra; XXI, 45ra) which are limited only by their union to a material substratum (NP, *Panaugia* VIII, 19ra–b, 20ra). These powers are that which "opens" the substance and determines its activity and self-development. Since the powers are conceived in accordance with the paradigm of the psychical (NP, *Pampsychia* II, 52rv), and the soul—in accordance with the tradition of the world-soul *(anima mundi)*—functions as the *forma universalis* of the finite existence, of the world, Patrizi's cosmology, like that of Giordano Bruno,[12] must be understood as affirming a universal (not animistic or pantheistic) presence of the psychical, in the sense that all that exists is permeated by processual-dynamic structures (NP, *Pampsychia* IV, 55va, 56ra). Through the mediation of the activity of the soul (and of the psychical in all the individual existents), natural Being is elevated into a horizon of unity that can be seen to be consistency, duration, and (self-) preservation or the ability to relate to oneself *(Pampsychia* IV, 56vb). Accordingly, Patrizi sees the structure of the world as a "chain" of causes and effects (NP, *Panarchia* III, 5vb; XVII, 37va; XVIII, 39vb) and an "indissoluble bond" (NP, *Pampsychia* IV, 56va) that permeates everything that exists and confers an inherent structure on this (NP, *Pampsychia* III, 53v; *Panarchia* V, 9va; XI, 23ra; III, 6vb). As in Neoplatonism, the a priori substantial ordering of the "unities" is a living ordering that mediates both in itself and *ad extra* into the finite world (NP, *Panarchia* VI, 10va; *Pampsychia* I, 49va). The multiplicity that has gone forth *(progressa)* from its unity in the One *(Panarchia* XI, 23rab) is determined by the mutually compenetrating factors, and is thus the explication of the One. Consequently, Patrizi defines "nature" as "the one life of the whole world, which depends on the soul as its cause" (NP, *Panarchia* XII, 27rb).

With his theory of natural Being in the last part of the *Nova de universis philosophia,* the *Pancosmia,* Patrizi is on a par with other authors of his age,

12. Cf. *De la causa, principio e uno,* dial. II.

for example, Girolamo Fracastoro, Bernardino Telesio, Girolamo Cardano, Bruno, the Paduan school with its theory of nature, Galileo Galilei, Nicholas Copernicus, Tycho Brahe, and others. Patrizi discusses the problems of the concept of nature against the background of his theory of the One, of the metaphysics of spirit, and his doctrine of the soul: space, the first principles, the primary qualities, the position of the Earth in the world, and the question of a central point of the Earth. Patrizi treats of physics in the context of a radical philosophical and systematic questioning, but without excluding the dimension of the senses: *sensus* and *ratio* are complementary capabilities that (as in Telesio) bring forth a rationally structured *experientia* (NP, *Pancosmia* 61rb, 63ra, va). He makes the following options:

First, space is "a self-subsistent, hypostatic extension which is not inherent in anything other than itself" (NP, *Pancosmia* I 65rab). It is substance beyond all categorial definitions, and is both "an unbodily body and a bodily nonbody." It is the first of all (created) things and is present everywhere; it is both finite and infinite (ibid. 61v, 64r). With space, which itself is an existent, begins a sequence—*spacium-loca-corpora-qualitates*—for which space is the absolute basis and the bearer of all the individual objects that are realized in this sequence (ibid. 64ra, 65ra).

Second, the first principles of the finite being, which replace the elements of the Aristotelian tradition, are the following: *(a)* space *(spacium),* as a universal recipient; *(b)* light *(lumen),* as a universal *agens* that imparts structure and makes objects visible (NP, *Pancosmia* IV). Patrizi makes a distinction in the concept of light between its primary state of not being explicated *(lux)* and its secondary state of being explicated *(lumen;* cf. NP, *Panaugia* I, *Pancosmia* IV 73v), and he makes light, as the principle of knowing and being known, antecedent to all physical-biological perception. *(c)* Warmth (NP, *Pancosmia* V) is a universal principle derived from light (ibid. 76va) which mediates "life" (ibid. 77ra). Like the light, warmth is originally united to the divine principle, and is therefore understood in the self-differentiation between a primary state of not being explicated *(ignis)* and a secondary state of being explicated *(calor;* ibid. 76rb–va). *(d)* Fluid *(fluor* or *humor;* NP, *Pancosmia* VI, 78r) is a universal principle of bodily existence in space and time (ibid. 79ra; VII 82rb); through its activity, it mediates to this existence the factor of *resistentia (antitypia, antaeresis;* ibid. 78ra).

Corresponding to the processual triad of *essentia-virtus-operatio,* these constitute the first concrete object (the empyrean; NP, *Pancosmia* VII), the real, concrete, pure fire *(ignis)* with which the building of the cosmos begins (ibid. 80ra), and then all the following elemental areas: the ether, which is finite and includes all the spheres of the stars up to the Moon (NP, *Pancosmia* IX), fire (ibid. V, XV, XXII), air (ibid. XIV, XXIII), water (ibid. XXIV), and earth (ibid. I, 78 r–v; XIV 95v–96v; XXVI, XXXI). They are present to all the areas of Being and all the individual objects as dynamic principles. They participate in the bivalent "intermediary" mode of Being (*simul incorporea et corporea;* cf. NP, *Pancosmia* IV 74rb, V 77rb, VI 79rb). They are capable of a high degree of penetration and operationality (cf., e.g., NP, *Pancosmia* IV 74rb, V 77ra, XIV 95ra–va). Their ontological hierarchy corresponds to their affinity to the One or to simplicity itself. The principal discovery that Patrizi claims to be completely new is his insight into the way in which these principles work (ibid. XXII, 120vb).

Third, Patrizi localizes the Earth in the center of the world, as a planet which moves in this center and around it. Its circular movement is assured by the fact that the center of its own rotating movement and the center of the universe are identical (NP, *Pancosmia* I, 65vb; XVII, 104rb; XXXI, 149ra, vb).

Fourth, the extension of the world, created by God's infinite power, is infinite—but in such a manner that de facto only the empyrean space surrounding the Earth (in the middle of the world) is infinite (NP, *Pancosmia* IX, 85va: *empyreum mundum ad extera infinitum*), while the subempyrean space of the stars and planets, and so on, is finite but "almost infinite" (ibid., cf. NP, *Pancosmia* VIII, XIII).

Fifth, heaven, or the astronomical space, is a unified and continuous *totum & integrum* which is not segmented by means of separate spheres or heavens (NP, *Pancosmia* XIII, 92va, 94rb). This continuum, infinite *ad extra* and limited *ad intra,* is the "place" that makes possible the copresence and universal activity of the principles *lumen, calor,* and *fluor.* This permits us to say of the structure of the universe as a whole: *unum ergo corpus, totum est universum, partium locis tantum, in se differens.* The empyrean is that part that extends infinitely *ad extra,* and the air is that part which is limited *ad intra,* toward the center (NP, *Pancosmia* XIV 96vb).

INFLUENCE

The most influential of Patrizi's works was the *Pancosmia* in the *Nova philosophia,* but his writings on the theory of history and of poetry sometimes found a reception too. Bruno, Tycho Brahe, Johannes Kepler, Robert Fludd, innovators such as Pierre Gassendi, Thomas Hobbes, and probably Galileo, as well as the Cambridge Platonists knew and discussed his works. The precise manner of his influence on the philosophy and science of the modern period still awaits investigation.

Note: For further reading see Proclus in the References. For secondary sources see Blum 2000; Bolzoni; Brickman; Gregory; Henry; Klibansky; Kristeller 1970; Leinkauf; Muccillo; Plastina; Puliafito; Purnell; Schuhmann 1986; Vasoli 1989; and Wilmott.

18

GIORDANO BRUNO

(1548–1600)

Clarifying the Shadows of Ideas

Eugenio Canone

Filippo Bruno (who later took the religious name Giordano) was born in January or February 1548 in San Giovanni del Cesco near Nola in the kingdom of Naples. His father, Giovanni Bruno, was a military man. Filippo probably began his studies in Naples in 1562 (Firpo 1993, cited as "Proc."; Proc. 156). The courses he attended at the Studio publico included the lectures on logic by Giovan Vincenzo Colle, known as "Sarnese," and the private lectures of Teofilo da Vairano, an Augustinian priest whom Bruno calls his "most important teacher in philosophy" (Spampanato, cited as "Doc"; Doc. 40). Sarnese's Averroist, antihumanistic, and antiphilological orientation left its mark on Bruno; this also accounts for his aversion to the humanistic attempts to replace the Aristotelian logic by a new logic (e.g., Petrus Ramus). The lectures of Teofilo da Vairano will have given Bruno the opportunity to study the ancient and more recent Platonic tradition. It was probably in the mid-1560s that Bruno became acquainted with the radical Valdesian teachings (named after Juan de Valdés; died 1541) which interpreted Erasmus of Rotterdam in an extreme fashion and thus tended towards anti-Trinitarianism; this date is suggested by his testimony that he "had doubts about the name of the Person of the Son and the Holy Spirit . . . and I already held this view at the age of eighteen" (Proc. 170). At that period, Bruno also studied the *ars lulliana* and the *ars memoriae* (BOL II, 2 130). On June 15, 1565, Bruno entered the Dominican monastery of San Domenico Maggiore in Naples and received the name Giordano.

During his intensive years of study in the monastery, Bruno will have read not only the writings of the Averroists and Alexandrists, but also the work of Marsilio Ficino, who is the point of convergence of a number of components of the Platonic tradition and the theorist of a program (which Bruno did not share) to reconcile Christianity and the thought of classical antiquity. Bruno will also have had the opportunity in Naples to encounter the philosophy of Nicholas of Cusa and Nicholas Copernicus's *De revolutionibus orbium coelestium*. Besides this, there was a lively discussion in the cultural world of Naples in the late 1560s and 1570s about the works of Giambattista Della Porta and Bernardino Telesio, about the various spheres in which natural magic could be practiced, and about a new physics that had recourse to the Pre-Socratics.

In July 1575 Bruno was "promoted" to lector. The eleven years he spent in the monastery in Naples were a time of inner unrest, marked by tensions with his priors that are documented in two disciplinary proceedings. The second and more important episode began at the end of 1575, because it was then that Bruno, in a debate with his confreres, expressed some purely philosophical objections to the dogma of the Trinity, appealing directly to the position held by Arius and Sabellius. At the start of 1576, Bruno went to Rome, where he wished to defend himself before the procurator of his order. Here, he learned that the works of Jerome and John Chrysostom with the commentary by Erasmus had been found in his possession—a book that had been condemned by the Catholic Church in 1559. Circumstances that are not fully clear—it is likely that he was accused of a crime that had been committed by a confrere—led to his decision to flee from Rome (cf. Proc. 144, 157, 170–71, 190–92; Doc. 39). After turning his back on the order at the age of twenty-eight, Bruno began a *peregrinatio* through Italy and the whole of Europe that was to last for fifteen years.

Dissatisfied with the Aristotelian natural philosophy, Bruno initially embraced a radical materialism, drawing on the atomistic theory of Democritus and the Epicureans as well as the teachings of Avicebron (matter as "divine nature"), the Stoics, and other philosophers who held that the Forms are to be regarded as only "some accidental dispositions of matter" (BDI 262). Bruno believed that he had overcome such positions by adopting a different concept of (animate) matter; all things considered, however, the divergence from Aristotle did not amount to a detachment from Averroism. His rapprochement with Platonism and with a poetic world that found its point of reference in Platonism played a fundamental role in opening up Bruno's own philosophical path. He took the Platonic tradition back to its Pre-Socratic sources, thereby allowing a physical conception of "the Being and the One" to emerge. A number of autobiographical passages indicate that Bruno went through a process of intellectual maturation from 1578 onward. This seems to have had materialistic, animistic, and Neoplatonic phases, and it involved personal tribulations (BDI 262, 1100f., 1168). From this time on, Bruno—who had asserted that "every land is a native land for the true philosopher," and who was later given the name "chevalier errant" of philosophy by a more shrewd *réfugié*, Pierre Bayle— interpreted exile as his fate.

In the winter of 1578, Bruno crossed the Alps. The two preceding years, in which he wandered through Italy, were a time of unrest and of increasing difficulties. In order to earn his living, he taught Latin and gave elementary courses in astronomy, which he based (as was customary at the time) on the *Sphaera* of John Holywood (Sacrobosco). In 1578, during a lengthy stay in Venice, Bruno had a short book printed with the title *De' segni de' tempi* (On the Signs of the Times). This book, which seems to be no longer extant, was most probably an adaptation or even a translation. In the difficult years between 1576 and 1578, he probably felt attracted to mathematical-cabbalistic magic. This was probably a period in which he studied the work of Agrippa of Nettesheim and other scholars.

In the spring of 1579, Bruno went to Geneva, where the Italian Protestant parish had been founded in 1552 by the Neapolitan Galeazzo Caracciolo. Although his stay in Geneva was brief, it was decisively important for the attitude he adopted to the Reformation in its concrete embodiment: for although he always fought against the main theological points of the Reformation (election by grace and redemption by faith alone) on the theoretical level, and regarded the Catholic doctrine about "good works" as one of the few principles of Christianity that were worth retaining, he would henceforth deeply abhor the nexus between religion and politics in civil society, resulting in an ever stricter social and cultural control. On May 20, 1579, he matriculated at the University of Geneva as *sacrae theologiae professor*. Although a formal profession of faith was no longer required in such cases, he converted to Calvinism in order to be fully integrated into the Italian parish, with the intention of "remaining there, in order to live in freedom and to be safe" (Proc. 160). Soon, however, he clashed with the authorities because of his demand for genuine philosophical freedom and his rejection of every kind of *auctoritas*. Bruno—doubtless unaware of the consequences that were to be expected—criticized one of the professors of philosophy at the university. He printed a pamphlet that pointed out twenty philosophical errors in one of Antoine de la Faye's lectures, and this led immediately to Bruno's trial before the consistory on charges of defamation. The outcome of these events was Bruno's excommunication. He was absolved from the interdict only after he had apologized (Doc. 33–36).

After a quick departure from Switzerland, Bruno decided, probably not by chance, to go to Toulouse, a stronghold of Catholic orthodoxy, where he worked as lector in philosophy at the public university and gave lectures "for two years in succession on the text *De anima* of Aristotle and other lectures in philosophy" (Proc. 161). It was probably in these years that he wrote the first draft of a work on the *ars lulliana* which was connected with this teaching; Bruno later cites it under the title *Clavis magna,* but it is now lost. Bruno holds that there is a distinction and a link between the art of invention and the art of memory *(ars memoriae),* and he introduced the combinational element into mnemotechnics, which he calls "a discursive architecture and skill of the rational soul, which develops from the vital principle of the world to become the vital principle of all things and of individuals" (BOL II, 1 56).

The danger of civil wars between Catholics and Huguenots led Bruno to leave Toulouse, and he went to Paris, where he stayed until March 1583. In order to make himself known in the intellectual circles of the French capital, Bruno, as an external teacher of the university, offered a cycle of thirty lectures that were devoted primarily to the analysis of thirty divine attributes. His starting point was the first treatise of the first part of the

Summa theologiae of Thomas Aquinas, *De Deo uno* (Proc. 161). These lectures took up the traditional nomenclature of the Aristotelian-Thomistic metaphysics—as did a lecture held in Zurich about ten years later, which appeared posthumously under the title *Summa terminorum metaphysicorum*, with an appendix on the *Applicatio entis*—and offered Bruno the opportunity to tackle the problem of being: the *substantia* and the *praedicamenta*. Thanks above all to his Lullian-mnemotechnical teaching, which he also gave in private, he became a member of a group of *lecteurs royaux* who were active outside the Sorbonne and usually met in the Collège de Cambrai. This brought him into contact with circles at court who sought to maintain an equal distance vis-à-vis Catholic and Protestant rigorism.

In 1582 Bruno dedicated to Henry III his first surviving book, the *De umbris idearum (On the Shadows of Ideas)*, to which an *Ars memoriae (Art of Memory)* was appended. In the same year, he published the *Cantus Circaeus* (which included a shorter *Ars memoriae*), the comedy *Candelaio*, and *De compendiosa architectura et complemento artis Lulli*. These writings offer an initial systematization of his thinking. The Lullian text is a compendium—exposition and commentary—of Lull's *Ars magna (The Great Art)*. In 1587 Bruno published a new commentary on this work by Lull, with greater detail and a clearer structure, under the title *De lampade combinatoria Lulliana*. This was not yet a presentation of his own personal *ars inventiva*, the "art of invention," on which he was continually working; that would bear fruit toward the end of his life in the *Lampas triginta statuarum*, a book that had to wait until the end of the nineteenth century for its posthumous publication. This text develops approaches contained in the *Ars memoriae* and presents an original and complex theory of symbolism in general. In this context, we should also mention Bruno's *De imaginum compositione (On the Composition of Images)*, published in Frankfurt in 1591; this sets out a general "art of invention" on the basis of a new mnemotechnics. Bruno's intention in the two commentaries is to show the basis of combinatorics, which suggests the convergence of Being and thinking and the unity of the elements of the real and individual universe. Bruno is attracted by the possibility of an *ars generalis*—the art of arts, the science of sciences—which makes noetic and cosmological principles synonymous, embraces both real and ideal Being, and is both an ontology and an epistemology. The methodology of this *ars* requires a progression from the elementary epistemological concepts to their combination, which takes account of the antitheses and is open for an infinite number of variations. In speculative terms, *De umbris idearum* is certainly the most important of the works published in 1582. Here, we already find Nicholas of Cusa's idea of the "convergence of opposites" *(coincidentia oppositorum)*, which is linked to Anaxagoras's principle of "everything in everything" *(omnia in omnibus)*. The "ideas" of which *De umbris* speaks are not logical universals, and the substance is not a logical abstraction, but a concrete unity which is allness. The analogy between metaphysics, physics, and logic—"i.e., between the prenatural, natural, and rational things" (BOL II,1 38)—which introduces the theory of the three worlds *(metaphysicus/archetypus, physicus/naturalis,* and *rationalis/umbratilis)* is extremely important. This is a Platonic and Neoplatonic motif, also found in Aristotle from a different perspective, which Bruno develops at great length in his writings, and many other authors take a position close to his, for example, Ficino, Giovanni Pico, and Giulio Camillo.

With regard to the Neoplatonism of the *De umbris,* which pays particular attention to Plotinus, we must emphasize that although Bruno always sees this language as metaphorical, this does not mean that he regards the metaphysical, archetypal world of the ideas and the rational world of the shadows as unreal. The problem is that we do not know the former world as it is in itself, and hence can speak of it only in a metaphorical manner; and the latter is in fact a world of symbols, of signs that point to the *phantasmata:* "For what presents itself to the senses is not the objects that genuinely exist, although the objects which we perceive can be called signs, since they are a mirror and enigma of the objects" (BOL II, 2 212; cf. BOL II, 1 22–23). Bruno explores the problem of an original and constant structure of the ideas, which remains eternally and also manifests itself as a general and continuous change on the level of individual beings. As far as the world of phenomena is concerned, there is a "very rapid flowing of the natural objects," but from the ontological perspective there exists "only one body of universal Being, one structure, one governance, one principle, one goal." Bruno writes: "In general, we see in those things that change, that the movement ends in rest, and the rest ends in movement" (BOL II, 1 24 and 75). This means that the world of Ideas does not overlap with the natural world; nor is it separated from the natural world. Rather, it is the real world itself, which presents itself as the constant structure of that which is subject to change.

Bruno takes great care to set out and to study in greater depth the metaphysical basis necessary for the *Ars memoriae* (above all following Plotinus, and the commentaries by Ficino and Nicholas of Cusa). At the same time, his goal is to explore the practical consequences of a mnemotechnical-combinatory system (and not only on the level of epistemological theory): the *ars* "is so powerful that it seems to act beyond nature, above nature, and even against nature when the business in hand requires it" (BOL II, 2 62). Human knowledge, which occurs at least initially on the basis of the perception of images that are transmitted and transformed by the activity of the *phantasia/ratio*, is a structurally symbolic, "shadowy" dynamic that interacts with nature on various levels. Bruno appeals several times to the Aristotelian assumption in the *De anima* that "our understanding [i.e., the operation of our understanding] either is imagination, or else does not exist without imagination" (BOL II, 3 91).

In his play *Candelaio*, Bruno indicates the philosophical implications of comedy when he declares that it "can help explain certain *shadows of the Ideas*." In the dedicatory epistle of the comedy "To Madam Morgana B.," which is open to various interpretations, Bruno offers some elements that can clarify this strange assertion. The salient point is the problem of the relationship between time and substance as is implied in the biblical verse: "There is nothing new under the sun," which Bruno attributes both to Solomon and to Pythagoras. He writes: "Time takes everything and gives everything; everything changes, nothing is destroyed; there is only One thing that cannot change, only One thing is eternal and can endure in eternity as One and the same" (Cand. 13–15). Bruno states very clearly that this identical One, which remains the same, is embodied as matter (cf., e.g., BDI 156). The problem of time also entails the problem of the soul. In *Sigillus sigillorum*, a short work that appeared in 1583, he writes that the *Simonidis tempus*, "the time of Simonides of Ceos," prevails in *De umbris*. This is the time which makes it possible to see and to find everything. But the *Candelaio* is based on the *tempus Pythagoricum indocilissimum omnium atque stultissimum*, "the time of Pythagoras, which is the most disobedient and foolish of all." Thanks to this time, everything is forgotten (BOL II, 2 162–63). What Bruno means here is that the "cold waters" from the spring of Mnemosyne, the mother of the Muses, and the swirling waters of the river Lethe refer to one and the same source. The experiences of the various characters in the comedy, the constant changes of roles and the disguises, are a metaphor for the transmigration of the soul and the change that is our fate. While the philosophy to which the text explicitly refers, and which the author acknowledges as his own, is that of Democritus/ Epicurus and Heraclitus, the characters in the comedy are in reality an embodiment of the concept of "shadow" that comes from Plotinus. Bruno echoes the third *Ennead*, which he had already employed in *De umbris*, in his depiction of the activity of the soul with its ups and downs in the great world-theater, in which there are many bad actors and it is rare to find one who is conscious of the role he is playing.

In his Parisian writings, Bruno arrived at a number of theoretical insights that were decisively important for the further development of his thought. Although he had written explicitly of the relationship between nature and *ars* in the *Ars memoriae* and the *Candelaio,* and had given a precise account of the unity between the physical world and the human spirit, it was necessary to develop such reflections in the context of one specific epistemology. Besides this, he still lacked some fundamental building bricks for his real aim, namely, a new and complete natural philosophy on the basis of the Platonic and Plotinian metaphysics, which in turn was oriented to a "cosmology" derived from the Pythagoreans, from Heraclitus, Democritus, and other Pre-Socratics. Bruno took an important, strongly monistic step, above all on the gnoseological level, in the *Sigillus sigillorum,* where we find a conception of the faculties of the soul (mind, imagination, reason, and understanding) as degrees of one and the same reality. He parts company with Plotinus by locating this reality against a completely immanentist background. The real problem, however, lay on the level of a physics/cosmology that ought to be able to offer a valid alternative to the Aristotelian physics, from which Bruno had distanced himself through his rapprochement with atomism. He saw the task of making a comparison with contemporary science, and especially with the Copernican theory, as essential and unpostponable, but—and this is the turning point—the concept of the infinite was to enter into natural philosophy and lay bare the de facto structure of the universe. As Bruno himself emphasizes, it was only this that made him "entirely certain" of the Copernican position. This radical shift occurred in 1583–1584 with the programmatic elaboration of the "Nolan philosophy," which must be understood in the sense of a new natural philosophy with the conception of a phenomenology of the *anima mundi* ("world-soul"). Bruno remained basically faithful to this philosophy until the final phase of his intellectual production, which found expression in the Latin poetic trilogy that was published several years later in Frankfurt. This is an additional reason to sketch the stages of his European *peregrinatio* in the years that followed, before we look at some of the most relevant theses of his thought.

As a result of the increasingly restrictive political-religious climate (Proc. 162), Bruno left Paris in April 1583, and decided to go to London, where a letter of recommendation from Henry III opened to him the doors of the house of the French ambassador, Michel de Castelnau. After he published in London a volume which included an *Ars reminiscendi*, he was able to begin a series of lectures in Oxford that summer. These dealt with natural philosophy, the problem of the world-soul, the heliostatic theory (linking Nicholas of Cusa, Ficino, and Copernicus), as well as the theory of Being and of knowledge that had been sketched in the *Sigillus sigillorum*. This text was included in the London volume, together with the *Explicatio triginta sigillorum*, which is preceded in some copies by a letter to the vice-chancellor of the University of Oxford. Here, Bruno presents himself as one who "is nowhere a foreigner" and "awakens slumbering minds." He affirms that he is not puffed up with pride at his own knowledge, but is driven by the wish to demonstrate the *imbecillitas vulgatae philosophiae* ("the weakness of common philosophy"; BOL II, 2 76–78). The opposition of a number of professors compelled him to break off his lectures and return to London, where he had contacts with the court and with intellectual circles in the capital who were open to a debate with contemporary science and provided a contrast to the Aristotelian and humanistic orientation of the university.

In the space of only two years, rather in the manner of an explosion, six important works appeared, composed in the form of dialogues: in 1584, *La cena de la Ceneri; De la causa, principio et uno; De l'infinito, universo et mondi;* and *Spaccio de la bestia trionfante;* in 1585, *Cabala del cavallo pegaseo. Con l'aggiunta dell'Asino cillenico;* and *De gl'heroici furori.* His use of the philosophical dialogue as a literary form and his choice to write in the Italian language were motivated by his opposition to academic life. The first three texts break with the prevalent Aristotelianism by developing an infinitistic cosmology based on a strictly monistic ontology. The foundation of this ontology was the idea of the unity of the principle which in all eternity gives life to the entire universe in the multiplicity and mutability of particular objects. The other three works set out the consequences of this cosmology on the anthropological level. He argues the necessity of a reform of social ethics and of life in society (which logically entails the reemergence of the concept of a civil religion). We also need an epistemology and an individual ethics that will center on the idea of a metamorphosis and a transcendence of the human person into the metaphysical horizon of the "heroic."

In the fall of 1585, Bruno accompanied the French ambassador back to Paris. In the following year, he published the *Figuratio Aristotelici Physici auditus* and four short dialogues about the work of the mathematician Fabrizio Mordente, who had invented a new kind of compass. Bruno's *Centum et viginti articuli de natura et mundo adversus Peripateticos* was published in the spring of 1586; this presents the theses he had put forward in a disputation held on May 28 in the Collège de Cambrai. Bruno left Paris "because of tumults" (Proc. 162) and went to Germany. He arrived in Marburg in July 1586, where he matriculated at the university as "Theologiae Doctor Romanensis" (Canone 1992, cited as "Pereg."; Pereg. 111) and immediately announced his intention of holding public lectures in philosophy.

After conflicts with the rector forced him to leave this city in Hessen, he moved to Wittenberg, where he matriculated at the university on August 20 as "Iordanus Brunus Nolanus doct. Italus" (Pereg. 113). He continued to teach the *ars memoriae* and the *ars inventiva,* but also began a two-year course of academic lectures as an assistant professor. These offered a reading of some works of Aristotle, especially the *Organon* and texts on natural philosophy, with a commentary, and they formed the basis for some of his own writings. In 1587 Bruno published *De lampade combinatoria Lulliana.* The *De progressu et lampade venatoria logicorum,* which appeared in the same year, treated Aristotelian logic, although with a mnemonic-Lullian methodology. The *Artificium perorandi,* which takes the pseudo-Aristotelian *Rhetorica ad Alexandrum* as its point of reference, was also written in 1587; it was published by Johann Heinrich Alsted in 1612.

The *Libri physicorum Aristotelis,* which were published only at the end of the nineteenth century, refer very specifically to Bruno's lectures on Aristotle's *Physics.*

In 1588 he published the *Camoeracensis acrotismus* (Collège de Cambrai Lecture) in Wittenberg. This reproduces the *Articuli* against the Peripetatics in the Parisian disputation two years earlier, with a commentary. It is thought that the *Lampas triginta statuarum* was also written in his Wittenberg period. After his decision to leave the town, Bruno bade farewell to the academic senate with an *Oratio valedictoria* on March 8, 1588. He then spent about six months in Prague, where he published the *De lampade combinatoria* with the brief *De specierum scrutinio* (a text that refers to Lull's *Ars magna*) as an appendix, and the *Articuli centum et sexaginta adversus . . . mathematicos,* which he dedicated to Rudolf II. After a brief stay in Tübingen in mid-November (Pereg. 127–29), Bruno went to Helmstedt, where he matriculated on January 13, 1589, at the Academia Julia, which had been founded by Duke Julius of Brunswick. The duke died in May 1589, and Bruno delivered an *Oratio consolatoria* at the university in his memory on July 1; this was published in the same year (Proc. 162–63). Despite the favorable attitude of the new duke Heinrich Julius, Bruno's stay in Helmstedt was not without its troubles: he was publicly excommunicated by the superintendent of the local Lutheran Church. He remained there until April 1590, and wrote a number of works devoted to the investigation of various questions of epistemology and physics: *De magia; Theses de magia; De rerum principiis et elementis et causis;* together with the important *De vinculis in genere; Medicina Lulliana;* and *De magia mathematica.* The intention of this last text was to investigate some themes of mathematical-cabbalistic magic; it includes inter alia a collection of excerpts from Agrippa's *De occulta philosophia.*

In June 1590 Bruno left Helmstedt for Frankfurt, where his main goal was to have a number of his works printed; but it appears that he continued his private teaching and that he was known, in the words of an acquaintance who would testify at his trial, as "a man of universal learning, but completely without religion" (Proc. 152–53; Pereg. 134–37). On July 2 he requested the senate of the city for permission to live in the printer's house, but this was rejected on the same day. After this, he found a room in the Carmelite monastery, which had been exempted by an imperial privilege from secular jurisdiction. Probably as a result of an expulsion order, Bruno moved to Zurich at the end of January or the beginning of February 1591, where he was able to hold the course of lectures mentioned above, *Summa terminorum metaphysicorum,* on the terminological-conceptual nomenclature of metaphysics and the triad *mens, intellectus,* and *anima mundi.* In the course of this year, his three Latin philosophical poems with a prose commentary appeared: *De triplici minimo et mensura; De monade, numero et figura;* and *De innumerabilibus, immenso et infigurabili.*

Bruno argues that the Aristotelian-Ptolemaic cosmos collapses wretchedly in the light of a "schooled perception by the senses" and of "weighty reasons," just like many castles in the air that are the fruit of fear, error, and deceit. Bruno first defends the heliostatic theory, and then overcomes this by a position that resolutely vindicates the *physical reality* of the Copernican system. In this way, he totally rejects the fictional interpretation maintained by Andreas Osiander and others, who regarded the Copernican theory simply as a computational hypothesis in an astronomical-mathematical perspective. At the same time, he resolutely defends the infinity of the universe, by denying the existence of a sphere of fixed stars: "infinite effect of the infinite cause, the true and living trace of the infinite power" (BDI 34). The universe is completely uniform, without any center, and is homogeneous in its material and spatial constitution: "one looks in vain for the center or the boundary of the universal world"; "we can affirm that the universe as a whole is a center" (BDI 12, 321). The universe is filled with a plurality of worlds and innumerable planetary systems. The work *Cena de le Ceneri,* with the necessary epistemological presuppositions of *Sigillus sigillorum,* appears as the prelude and manifesto of a new worldview that recognizes the significance and the implications of the merger between a conception of Being (as one, infinite, immovable) and of becoming (the variability of bodies and of the things in the universe) which belongs to the "old, true" pre-Platonic philosophy, with the achievements of contemporary science: in the homogeneous universe, there exist neither "natural places" of the elements nor a quintessence out of which the heavenly bodies are made. There is no "otherness" of the essence which would find expression in the difference in natural movement (linear or circular), nor any difference between the earthly and the heavenly worlds. The Earth, with its rotational movement on its own axis and its orbit around the Sun, has the same ontological reality as the other heavenly bodies: "As far as substance and matter and the kind of location are concerned, [the terrestrial body] cannot be shown to be different from any other heavenly body" (BDI 162).

The rapprochement with the atomistic theory takes full effect here. We read in one of the *Articuli* of the disputation which Bruno held in 1586 at the Collège de Cambrai: "It is thus against nature that all the parts of the earth tend towards the center point, without sometimes wandering off to the perimeter of the globe. What we say about the earth, we apply also to the sun and the other stars, in which, because of the same principles, the same composition can be observed" (BOL I, 1 186). Like the Earth, accordingly, the other heavenly bodies, too, are composite bodies that are subject to the phenomena of change. In the *Cena de le Ceneri* and *De l'infinito, universo et mondi,* Bruno harks back to Plato's *Timaeus* when he affirms that the heavenly bodies are dissoluble, although they "will not dissolve": "For the celestial bodies are dissoluble; but it is possible that they will remain eternally the same, thanks either to an internal or to an external power, since atoms flow into them to the same extent that atoms flow out of them" (BDI 155, 477); Bruno returns several times to this delicate point. Atomistic presuppositions also lead him to reject decisively the Aristotelian concept of coming into being and passing out of existence. Bruno adopts the Pythagorean-Ovidian hypothesis that "everything changes, nothing ceases to exist," and declares that one should speak of change rather than cessation. In *De la causa, principio et uno,* the problem appears in a completely different light, in the perspective of the one, eternal, infinite substance:

Every production ... is alteration, whereby the substance always remains one and the same; for there is only one substance, one divine essence.... Accordingly, everything that constitutes the diversity of genera and species, differences and properties; everything that consists of coming into being and passing out of existence, in change and in transition, is not an existent, nor Being itself. Rather, it is a condition and a circumstance of what is and of Being. (BDI 324 and 327)

The activity of the formal principle finds expression in the varied composition of matter. The general physical efficient cause is the universal intellect, "which is the first and primary faculty of the world-soul" (BDI 231), the inner creator who is one, just as the matter upon which, or within which, it exercises his creative activity is one. The question of the accidental forms, which occupied a central position in Bruno's reflections from his youth onward, is thus solved by means of the concept of the unique substantial form, the *anima mundi* (world-soul), the single source of all forms. The unity of form and the unity of matter do not lead to a substantial dualism, since the principle of the coincidence of opposites—the principle of the absolute unity as the identity of being and the ability to be, a unity that is manifested as infinite actuality—allows us to see an overarching unity, namely, the unity of the divine substance in the infinite All: "One, I say, is the absolute possibility; one the act; one the form or soul; one the matter or body; one the object; one the being; one that which is greatest and best" (BDI 318). In *De l'infinito,* Bruno discusses the fundamental assumptions of the new cosmology (which is outlined in the *Cena* and elaborated in its definitive form in *De immenso*): the movement of the Earth, the infinite, homogeneous space, infinite worlds, and the question of the emptiness and of the atomic structure of matter. Employing the form of an academic treatise, Bruno also demonstrates the inappropriateness of the Scholastic distinction between God's *potentia absoluta* and *ordinata* ("absolute" and "applied power"). He affirms succinctly: "One who denies the infinite effect, denies the infinite power" (BDI 385); the fruit of the splendid wedding between Christian theology and Aristotelianism is both foolish and blasphemous.

Bruno does not arrive at the thesis of the infinity of the universe on the basis of any strong theological argument; he has recourse to the theological argument only in order to denounce the absurdity and godlessness of the positions that are regarded as the bulwark of the "science" of faith. In general, no decisive importance should be attributed to theological themes in the development of Bruno's thought. He refers to theological themes in many of his works in order to strengthen his own position, but theology is certainly not the field in which he made his "discoveries."

When we bear in mind the cosmological principles and deductions in the dialogues *Cena de le Ceneri* and *De l'infinito,* it is impossible to overlook the ontological-physical discourse in *De la causa, principio et uno* with its definitive acceptance of the fundamental concept of the substance-principle/infinite efficient cause, which also implied a dispute with Averroes's theory of matter as indeterminate dimensions and with Albert the Great's doctrine of the *inchoatio formae.* It is not by chance that philosophers such as Jacobi, Schelling, and even Hegel, Schopenhauer, Feuerbach, Spaventa, and many others have regarded Bruno's *De la causa* as his chef

d'oeuvre, since it elaborates a coherent and strongly articulated philosophy of oneness in the perspective of a "physical universe." In the context
of his natural philosophy, that is, the "Nolan philosophy," *De la causa* is
the true *clavis magna* ("great key"), an omnipresent text that stands in the
background of all his other writings.

Bruno regards every idea of "another place" than the infinite universe
as a product of the imagination. The *De umbris idearum* (harking back to
Plotinus and Proclus) uses the term *superessentiale, unitas supersubstantialis*
for the principle of every essence and subsistence and for the absolute and
infinite form of Being; and this does not point in any way to a "place." The
unknowability and ineffability of the One goes back, on the one hand, to
the tradition of negative theology and to one particular understanding of
"pure nothing," which pointed back to the Plotinian *Enneads* via Proclus,
Pseudo-Dionysius, and Master Eckhart. On the other hand, it is crucial
that *De la causa* reaches the notion of indifference of the one infinite substance (the All-One) vis-à-vis the two substances (soul/thinking and mat-
ter/extension) that communicate themselves, or which we are permitted
to know (so to speak). What we are offered in the myths and concepts of
the ancient theogonies and cosmogonies—namely, the conceivability, the
unknowability, and the "infigurability" of something that lies beyond every differentiation—needs to be contemplated. This is the topic of Bruno's
Lampas triginta statuarum (Lantern of Thirty Statues), which contrasts the
triad *chaos* ("which is the first of all things . . . incommunicable and greedy
for everything"), *orcus seu abyssus* (the underworld or abyss, the passive and
receptive power, *privatio*), and *nox* (the night, primal matter) with the triad
mens, intellectus, and *spiritus seu amor* (i.e., *anima mundi,* the world-soul).

The last of these is an ever-recurrent motif in his work, a theme that
merges with that of the three worlds; Bruno dedicates a separate treatise to
it in the *Summa terminorum metaphysicorum.* He insists that the true home
of the soul is nature, understood as the image of the divine essence—the
spatial-temporal infinite All—and as the theater of culture, *domus sapientiae.* In the "Nolan philosophy," the intellectual substance is no less permanent than the material; indeed, "the understanding, the spirit, the soul,
the life that permeates everything, is in everything and moves the whole
of matter . . . since the intellectual substance cannot be outstripped by the
material substance, but rather contains it" (BDI 243–44). As was already

the case in Plotinus and Ficino, the doctrine of the *anima mundi* with the idea of the chain of Being and the extension of the general efficient cause, the *spiritus* forms the basis of magical activity, thanks to the continuity between every soul (and every body linked to the soul) and the world-soul. The concept of creation is decisively rejected: in the context of the All-One, the universe "cannot be brought into being," "does not pass away," and is "immovable." The heavenly bodies, the worlds—that is, the stars and the innumerable solar systems that are analogous to our own—are "brought into being," but not the universe, which is the infinite substance (BOL I, 1 173ff., 179–80, 183).

This shows us the inappropriateness of the traditional description of the "Nolan philosophy" as pantheistic; we must bear in mind the fundamental "difference between the All and the things in the All" (BDI 322), which Bruno strongly emphasizes: "For this unity is unique and constant and abiding; this One is eternal; every face, every countenance, every other thing is vanity, is as nothing" (BDI 324). While the "causes and initial motivations" are in fact immanent (BDI 937), there is a radical disproportion between infinite and finite, between Being and "modes of Being," "accidents of Being": "You do not come any closer to the proportion, similarity, unity, and identity of the infinite as a human being than as an ant, nor any closer as a star than as a human being"; "since the substance and Being are distinct and detached from quantity . . . we must necessarily say that substance is essentially without number and without measure" (BDI 320, 334).

It is clear that there is no place in such a philosophy for the Hebrew-Christian concept of a personal God and creator. The anti-Christian polemic reaches its high point already in the *Spaccio de la bestia trionfante,* with its reflections on the concept of natural religion and on religion as law, and in the *Cabala del cavallo pegaseo,* and Bruno returns several times in the poetic trilogy of 1591 to this critique and to the relationship between reason and faith, philosophy and religion.

In the Frankfurt trilogy *De minimo, De monade,* and *De immenso,* Bruno takes up some central themes of the "Nolan philosophy" in an emphatically atomistic perspective. Whereas, however, the concept of the atom, as the absolute physical "minimum" and substratum of all bodies, underlines the homogeneity of the infinite All on the material level (and denies the dualism between matter and form), the distinction between atom, mini-

mum, and monad relates to the theory of the three worlds that is elaborated in these three poems, which appeared in 1591, but had partly been put
into written form at an earlier date after lengthy reflection.

Not long after his return to Frankfurt, where he oversaw the printing of
De monade/De immenso and *De imaginum compositione,* the Venetian patri-
cian Giovanni Mocenigo invited Bruno to Venice, so that he might "teach
him the art of memory and invention" (Proc. 155). Bruno's hope of obtaining
a position at the University of Padua probably played a decisive role here; at
the end of August, he went to Padua, where he taught "some German pupils" (Proc. 153). He settled definitively in Venice around December of that
year, and resided in Mocenigo's house from March 1592. Mocenigo had already contacted the Venetian inquisitor, and he submitted a complaint on
May 23, in which he accused Bruno of heresy. Bruno was arrested that same
evening and was brought to the prison of San Domenico di Castello (Proc.
143–45 and 148). The Venetian phase of his trial lasted only a few months.
Even before the last interrogation of Bruno on July 30, 1592 (Proc. 195ff.),
that is, before the legal proceedings were over, the highest ranks of the central Court of the Inquisition insisted that the prisoner be handed over to
Rome (Proc. 200–201; Pereg. 181). On February 27 Bruno was brought to
the Roman prison of the Holy Office. After a long and dramatic trial, which
lasted for seven years, the verdict was read to the accused on February 8,
1600, in the presence of the assembled congregation of the cardinals of the
Inquisition and other witnesses. Bruno was convicted as an "impenitent,
obstinate, and stubborn heretic" (Proc. 339ff.). The personal intervention of
Pope Clement VIII played the decisive role in sealing Bruno's fate. On the
morning of February 17, he was led to the Campo de Fiori, where "he was
stripped naked and tied to a stake, and burnt alive" (Proc. 348). The verdict also ordered that all the books and manuscripts of the philosopher that
were in the possession of the Holy Office "were to be publicly destroyed
and burnt before the steps on Saint Peter's Square" (Proc. 343).

Note: For further reading see Bruno and Singer in the References. See also the following documents: Spampanato [Doc.]; Canone 1992 [Pereg.]; Firpo 1993 [Proc.]. For secondary sources see Bönker-Vallon; *Bruniana & Campanelliana;* Canone; Ciliberto; Ciliberto and N. Mann; Couliano; De Léon-Jones; Gatti; *Giordano Bruno;* Heipcke, Neuser,
and Wicke; Ordine; Saiber; Salvestrini; Sturlese 1987; and Yates. A helpful Internet site
is *La biblioteca ideale di Giordano Bruno* (Italian and Latin works with source references):
http://giordanobruno.signum.sns.it/bibliotecaideale/.

19

FRANCISCO SUÁREZ

(1548–1617)

Scholasticism after Humanism

Emmanuel J. Bauer

Sixteenth-century Spain was a land of stark antitheses, where cosmopolitan attitudes and a sense of new beginnings, on the one hand, clashed with the state Inquisition and a rigid, narrow-minded distrust of all that was new, on the other hand. After the completion of the Reconquista, a nonchalant spirit of conquest became widespread in economic and political affairs as well as in the intellectual-cultural and religious spheres. The Iberian peninsula remained largely untouched by the upheavals of the Reformation, and became the "native land" of the Catholic renewal after the Council of Trent. In keeping with the humanist maxim *ad fontes* ("back to the sources"), scholars looked afresh at the great currents of medieval Scholasticism and attempted to tackle the new questions of their age with the methods and metaphysical approaches of that Scholasticism. In the course of a general return to Aristotle, the classical directions taken by the medieval schools experienced a renaissance in the Scholasticism of the modern period.

This Scholasticism, which originally had strong confessional ties,[1] began in the Dominican school founded in Salamanca by Francisco de Vitoria (1483/93–1546), which became a center of consistent Thomism. Here for the first time, after centuries of tradition, the *Liber Sententiarum* of Peter Lombard was replaced as the basis of philosophical-theological instruction by the *Summa theologiae* of Aquinas. Names such as Domingo de Soto, Melchior Cano, Domingo Báñez, and Didacus Masius evoke the tremendous intellectual power of the so-called men of Salamanca *(Salmanticenses);* and they were joined in their work by the Discalced Carmelites of Alcalá *(Complutum)* under John of St. Thomas and the Benedictines under Josef Saënz d'Aguirre. In addition to a revitalization of Scholastic approaches that had not been so important up to that time (Giles of Rome, John Baconthorp, and Henry of Ghent), this new élan of the Thomists led almost necessarily—in keeping with the ancient rivalry—to a revival of Scotist thought on the part of members of the Franciscan order, although the most important representatives of Scotism in Baroque Scholasticism worked in Italy, not in Spain.

In parallel to these restorative tendencies, the so-called Jesuit philosophy emerged in the newly founded Society of Jesus. This current of Scholastic teaching did indeed take up the medieval inheritance, but was less indebted to authorities; its scholars worked independently and critically, sometimes even eclectically, and developed a system in which nominalist and Scotist elements coalesced with a fundamentally Thomistic realism to form a new entity that took heed of the humanist demands. The universities in Evora and Coimbra (which had belonged to Spain since the annexation of Portugal by Philip II) were the centers of Jesuit formation and teaching, and their importance was due above all to the two defining authorities of the Jesuit school, Pedro da Fonseca (1528–1599), the "Portuguese Aristotle," who taught in Coimbra until 1573, and Francisco de Suárez, who was a professor at the same university from 1597.

1. Cf. Specht 1976, xxxix; Honnefelder 205; Grabmann 550. Most recently, R. Darge has investigated the Scotist and Thomistic roots of Suárez's metaphysics and presented a differentiated evaluation of his thinking (cf. Darge 387–405). He writes: "Suárez' project takes on its own specific philosophical profile by developing Thomas' program of the inner transcendental exposition of being, on the basis of the new concept of being which was influenced by Scotism. . . . On the basis of its partial aspects, therefore . . ., Suárez' transcendental exposition of Being can be seen as belonging equally to the history of the influence of the Scotist *scientia transcendens* and to the history of the influence of Thomas' transcendental science" (ibid. 405).

Suárez could be called the personification of the intellectual vigor that was generated in the so-called golden century of Spanish history. He illustrates the monopoly of the Jesuits in the sector of ecclesiastical education, and symbolizes the great influence exercised by the newly founded order in the Europe of the sixteenth and seventeenth centuries. He was born to a noble family in Granada in 1548. After a basic humanistic education and the study of canon law in Salamanca, he entered the Society of Jesus at the age of sixteen. After his novitiate, his theological teachers at the university of Salamanca included Juan Mancio, a pupil of Francisco de Vitoria, O.P., and Henricus Henríquez, S.J. After his ordination to the priesthood in 1572, he was appointed to teach at a number of colleges of his order.

From 1571 to 1574, he taught philosophy in Segovia, and then lectured in theology in Avila, Segovia, and Valladolid until 1580. At an early age, Suárez attracted attention with his unusually free style of teaching, which revived the medieval method, and his own order instituted an investigation that led to an unexpected outcome: Suárez was appointed professor of theology at the Roman College (the later Pontifical Gregorian University), where he met with great success. Reasons of health led him to return to Spain in 1585; he was appointed to the chair of Gabriel Vázquez in Alcalá, and Vázquez replaced him in Rome. In order to avoid continuous rivalries and debates with Vázquez after the latter returned from Rome, Suárez withdrew to Salamanca in 1593 and devoted his energies to the elaboration of his metaphysics and the completion of his commentary on Aquinas's *Summa theologica;* he sometimes replaced a confrere as lecturer, and wrote some brief occasional treatises. In 1597, at the express wish of Philip II, he became professor of theology in Coimbra. Increasingly, Suárez became the theological master of his order, although he was never officially appointed or recommended for such a position. In Coimbra, he planned to write an independent systematic compendium of theology, which would take Thomas as its point of orientation; but he was distracted by the need to produce studies of canon law, writings related to the controversy about grace, and other treatises. His plans were also interrupted by a period of two years spent in Rome to defend his position in the discussion of the possibility of sacramental confession in writing. He now limited himself to the publication of his lectures, without expanding these. In 1617, in view of Suárez's competence in canon law, the pope sent him to Lisbon on a mission of mediation in the conflict between the authorities of state and church in Portugal. He died there on September 25.

The *Disputationes metaphysicae,* published in 1597, soon set the standard for philosophical and theological teaching not only at Catholic, but also at Protestant, universities for almost two centuries. Hugo Grotius (1583–1645), who found decisive input for his doctrine of natural and international law in his older contemporary Suárez, regarded him as "a theologian and philosopher of so great a subtlety that he scarcely has any equal."[2] Arthur Schopenhauer draws on the astonishing erudition of Suárez' *Metaphysics,* which he frequently quotes, praising it enthusiastically as a "genuine compendium of the entire wisdom of scholasticism" which is refreshingly different from the "loquacious prattling of dull German professors of philosophy—that quintessence of flatness and boredom."[3] Similarly, Franz Brentano praises Suárez's chef d'oeuvre as a treasure trove of the medieval Aristotelian theory. Suárez's reputation as one of the most important and preeminent scholars of the so-called Baroque Scholasticism, the late Scholasticism of the early modern period, is due not least to his *Disputationes metaphysicae,* in which the method of the systematic presentation of metaphysics made its definitive breakthrough in Scholastic philosophy, and to the *De legibus ac Deo legislatore,* his treatise on legal philosophy and the philosophical idea of the state. Matthias Joseph Scheeben, author of a monumental twentieth-century work on dogmatics, sees Suárez as "the most fruitful of all the more recent scholastics, a man distinguished in equal parts by clarity, level-headedness, depth, and prudence."[4] Even Martin Heidegger believes that the questions posed by Suárez display a greater acuteness and autonomy than Thomas himself. It was not for nothing that he was soon given the honorific title *doctor eximius.*

In the wake of the Council of Trent and the Thomistic renaissance in Spanish Scholasticism that it prompted, Suárez presents himself as an in-

2. Hugo Grotius, *Epistolae omnes,* Amsterdam, 1687: Epistula 154 Joanni Cordesio: "tantae subtilitatis theologus ac philosophus, ut vix quemquam habeat parem."

3. Cf. Arthur Schopenhauer, *Fragmente zur Geschichte der Philosophie,* in *Saemtliche Werke,* 6 vols., ed. Eduard Griesbach (Leipzig: Reclam, 1890–1891), vol. 4, 70.

4. Scheeben 451.

terpreter of Aquinas, but he diverges from him on essential points. In addition to numerous smaller Scholastic schools, there were the two great traditions of classical Thomism and Scotism; Suárez creates a third great tradition of Scholastic thinking that integrates Thomistic, Scotist, and nominalist positions and unites these to form a new synthesis. A historical view of Suárez, stripped of ideology, has dominated scholarship in recent decades. It has reached the surprising conclusion that he followed the Scotist rather than the Thomistic approach to metaphysics.

The "Suárezism" that bore his name became the definitive doctrine even outside the Jesuit order: only a few Catholic universities remained untouched by the Suárezist-Jesuit educational monopoly that had become a principal instrument in the Counter-Reformation renewal efforts. One notable exception was the Benedictine university of Salzburg (1617/22–1810), which maintained a very autonomous and nuanced relationship to Suárez until the onset of the Enlightenment in the mid-eighteenth century. Despite some influence from the Jesuit philosophy, Salzburg taught a strict and largely authentic Thomistic Thomism with a Dominican provenance.[5] The *Disputationes metaphysicae* were used as a manual for students even at many Protestant universities in the seventeenth and eighteenth centuries. This meant that Suárez became the universal philosophical authority in the course of the seventeenth century, and his work became the standard textbook. Suárez and his teachings continued to influence philosophy well into the modern period, via German Scholasticism and in particular via Christian Wolff, who brought to a formal conclusion the new concept of metaphysics that originated with Duns Scotus and the structure of metaphysics that was manifested in Suárez. The traces of Suárez's metaphysics can be seen in the philosophy of a Descartes (who studied at the Jesuit school in La Flèche), a Spinoza, or a Leibniz, as well as in the understanding of metaphysics by Kant or Charles S. Peirce. Suárez is not the only link between the understanding of metaphysics in the medieval and modern periods, but he more than any other scholar brought a decisive influence from the rational tradition of the Middle Ages to bear upon the enlightened rationality and metaphysics of the modern period.[6] Étienne

5. Cf. Bauer.

6. Cf. Honnefelder 209; on the contemporary discussion of Suárez's metaphysical approach, cf. Darge 4–138.

Gilson points out the historical importance of the *doctor eximius* for the rationalistic approaches of the modern period, when he writes: "The spirit of profundity, which Kant praises in German philosophy, goes back via Wolff to Suárez."[7] The history of his influence continues into the twentieth century, in the context of neo-Scholasticism, when various Jesuit houses of studies (the Gregorian University in Rome, Valkenburg, Innsbruck) became the centers of a philosophy that found its orientation in Suárez's metaphysics, although the neo-Scholastic interpretation of Suárez suffered greatly under the problem that the questions were approached and expounded too much from the perspective of the interpreter's own doctrine. In other words, Suárez was presented either as an authentic Thomist (or as one who pursued Thomas's thinking to its logical conclusion) or as a non-Thomist; but his own genuine positions were not brought to light. There is no doubt that Suárez himself offers the starting point for such interpretations: in order to legitimate himself vis-à-vis the authority of Aquinas, which was dominant in Spanish Baroque Scholasticism and which the Jesuit order proclaimed to be obligatory for theological studies, he frequently concealed the genuine intentions of the positions he took, and presented his teaching as more Thomistic than it really was.

SUÁREZ'S METAPHYSICS

The Innovative Element in Methodology and Structure

Suárez's influence on contemporary academic theology and on the philosophy of the modern period is due primarily to his *Disputationes metaphysicae,* which went through twenty editions in a very brief space of time. The intention of this work is to make a systematic presentation of philosophy against the background of Christian principles and to set out the metaphysical presuppositions and foundations of theology. Suárez is convinced that no one can develop into a good theologian unless he first establishes the sure foundations of metaphysics,[8] since metaphysics reflects on the natural, knowable matters without which theology is nothing more than the

7. Gilson 1962, 120.
8. *Quemadmodum fieri nequit ut quis Theologus perfectus evadat, nisi firma prius metaphysicae jecerit fundamenta:* Suárez, *Disputationes metaphysicae* [DM], *Ad lectorem.*

requirement of a naked faith. If theology is to be able to justify the claim of the Christian faith to be true, it cannot dispense with the metaphysical opening up of the most general and highest natural principles, which encompass all that exists and are the foundation and guarantee of all knowledge. Suárez understands himself primarily as a philosopher who attempts on the basis of natural knowledge—*ratione naturali*—to penetrate objectively the substance of the questions; but he is always conscious that philosophy is "the handmaiden of divine theology," and is always ready to interrupt the purely philosophical line of thought to point to the theological implications of the metaphysical principles, that is, to show in what sense one should draw on these "in order to confirm the theological truths."[9] This explains the double goal of his work, which was intended both as a propaedeutic text for students of theology and as a modern commentary on Aristotle's *Metaphysics*. This is already expressed in the subtitle,[10] which announces the elaboration of a natural theology antecedent to the divine revelation, and the systematic discussion of the basic questions in the twelve books of Aristotle's *Metaphysics*. This academic program, which emphasizes both the autonomy of the human person and the humanistically oriented return to the Aristotelian sources, shows that the spirit of the Renaissance also plays a decisive role in the *Disputationes*.

The epistemological foundations of theology had been called into question by the crisis of the divisions in faith within Christendom, and by the critique of the doctrinal structure of Scholasticism both by the humanists and by the reinvigorated, independent Aristotelianism of the sixteenth century; this is the constellation that generates the special conception and intention of Suárez's metaphysics. In order to offer theology a sure foundation for its truth, metaphysics had to free itself from the suspicion of arbitrariness that attached to it because of the many rival traditions. This liberation meant that metaphysics must avoid specifically theological questions; in order to clarify disputed questions, it must make possible the recourse to an indisputable first principle; and it must be able to guarantee the knowledge it gained by means of a clear and systematic methodology. Suárez takes up

9. Ibid.

10. The title of the original edition is as follows: *Metaphysicarum disputationum in quibus et universa naturalis theologia ordinate traditur, et quaestiones omnes ad duodecim Aristotelis libros pertinentes accurate disputantur.*

this challenge and attempts—unlike Descartes, who anchors the certainty of knowledge in the distinct and clear insight of the reason—to deduce the truth and rationality of the answer from the tradition and from the metaphysical structure of the matter under dispute.

In order to achieve this goal, he first undertakes a comprehensive reception of the tradition. On every question, he presents and discusses all the important positions that have been taken from Greek antiquity via the Middle Ages up to the Renaissance philosophers. He sets out the historical origins of the different positions, drawing in part on the inchoative science of textual criticism. He gives an account of the theses, presents a balanced investigation of their justification and an assessment of them, and then offers and justifies his own solution to the problem. It is not the weight of an authority that decides the truth of an opinion, but the convincing power of the arguments. What we have here, therefore, is no empty compilation of various historical approaches, nor the cheap eclecticism of which Suárez is sometimes accused, but an independent, constructive work marked by intellectual honesty and a capacity for differentiation, in which the problems are outlined and stripped back to their real core.

At the same time, Suárez very consciously orients the methodology and structure of his teaching to the inner logic of the problems themselves, thereby breaking with the traditional manner of presentation in the form of a commentary that was tightly bound to the formal structure of the Aristotelian *Metaphysics,* where each successive chapter was treated either "by way of commentary" (Thomas) or "by way of query" (Duns Scotus). He replaces this with the method of disputation, where the principal metaphysical problems are understood in their inherent interconnection as a structured whole, and are presented separately and systematically. In his revolutionary new method, Suárez unites a mode of presentation that is oriented to the questions themselves with an illumination of the truth that is based on the history of the problems; the latter is inspired by humanist scholarship. He thus moves on the border between the methodology of medieval Scholasticism and that of the philosophy of the modern period.

It is not only his innovative methodology, which is emancipated from the medieval canon, that makes Suárez a forerunner of the modern understanding of metaphysics, but also his definition, in the first disputation, of its subject matter and structure *(de natura primae philosophiae seu meta-*

physicae). Since this concerns the "first philosophy" in the Aristotelian sense, that is, the science that seeks to know that which is intelligible in the highest sense, that which is first (the first principles), and the causes of all that exists,[11] one might suppose that the precise subject matter of metaphysics would be the *ens abstractissime sumptum* (being as understood in the most abstract sense). But Suárez finds this specific link to the all inclusive and most abstract concept of the existent, to everything that can be known with the help of the reason, to be too imprecise, since it also includes the mere concepts of the reason that possess no reality of their own. This is why he explicitly affirms that the truly appropriate subject matter of metaphysics is only being either insofar as it is a real existent *(ens in quantum ens reale)*[12] or insofar as it can be abstracted from matter in terms of its being *(ens, in quantum ens seu in quantum a materia abstrahit secundum esse).* Suárez thus stands in the broader context of the Aristotelian-Thomistic tradition, but the decisive influence comes from Duns Scotus and his concept of reality.

For Aristotle, the center of metaphysical investigations is being qua being (linked directly or indirectly to *ousía* or essence); Thomas broadens the content of the concept of the *ens inquantum ens* to cover the existent as a whole *(ens commune),*[13] which also includes the "objective" Being *(esse objectivum),* namely, the object of cognition in the mind.[14] Suárez, however, emphasizes the formal object of the *ens reale,* which refers not to the thing that now exists *de facto,* but to everything that is really possible. The term *ens reale* is applicable to every being that has a true and real essence *(quod habet veram et realem essentiam).*[15] In other words, as a concept it is not a fiction or chimera, but possesses a true essence capable of real existence *(veram et aptam ad realiter existentum essentiam).*[16] The reality of the existent depends on the suitability of its essence for a real existence. Metaphysics must therefore begin by identifying the "transcendental" definition of the concrete being, which, as the first and most general definition, is common to all forms of being that are suitable for existence, and

11. Cf. Aristotle, *Met.* I (A), c. 2, 982a–982b 4.
12. Suárez, DM 1, 1, 26.
13. Cf. Thomas Aquinas, *In Met., Prooem.;* ibid., lb. 4, lc. 4; ibid., lb. 6, lc. 1.
14. Cf. idem, *STh.* I, q. 16, a. 3 ad 2; *De ver.,* q. 1, a. 1 ad 7.
15. Suárez, DM 2, 5, 8.
16. Ibid., 2, 4, 5. Cf. also ibid., 1, 1, 6.

which therefore "transcends" every distinction between substance and accident, material and immaterial, or finite and infinite. For Suárez (like Scotus), metaphysics as a whole is a transcendental science, "the most general science"[17] of the "universal transcendent concepts,"[18] and especially of the "most abstract meaning of being."[19] On the basis of the specific forms of the beings, the first principles and causes are to be investigated through the clarification of the real essence.

Against the background of this transcendental-philosophical concept of metaphysics, Suárez investigates in the first part of his *Disputationes* the properties *(proprietates)* and causes *(causae)* of being in general. In the second part, he investigates the various genera of existents, namely, the *ens absolutum,* the *ens finitum,* and finally, in the last *disputatio,* the *ens rationis,* although this is known in a merely mental sense *(objective),* and exists in the intellect only—and this means, in keeping with Suárez's position, that it ought in fact to be excluded from the precise subject matter of metaphysics.[20] Strictly speaking, as an immaterial substance, the doctrine of the soul would come under metaphysics, but Suárez follows the prevailing custom in excluding it from metaphysics.

Although Suárez explicitly rejects a division of metaphysics into a general science of Being and a special doctrine about God and the intelligences, as was proposed by his confrere Benedictus Perera (1535–1610),[21] in actual fact the structure of his *Disputationes* launches the development that led to the separation of metaphysics into a general ontology *(metaphysica generalis)* and a special doctrine of the immaterial substances *(metaphysica specialis).* This became the norm in German university philosophy, and found its classical form in the *Prima philosophia* of Christian Wolff. Its influence can be demonstrated even in the strict Thomism that we find in representatives of Spanish Scholasticism or the Salzburg school.[22] Following Duns Scotus, who discusses the doctrine of transcendentals and cat-

17. Cf. ibid., 1, 5, 14.
18. Cf. ibid., 1, 2, 27: "rationes universales transcendentales."
19. Cf. ibid., 1, 2, 23: "abstractissima ratio entis."
20. Cf. ibid., 1, 1, 6–7.
21. Cf. ibid., 1, 3, 10–12. On Pere(i)ra, see Paul Richard Blum, "Benedictus Pererius: Renaissance Culture at the Origins of Jesuit Science," *Science and Education* 15 (2006): 279–304.
22. Cf. Bauer 604–8.

egories under the heading of metaphysics, Suárez is primarily concerned with the transcendental knowledge of being as such, that is, with the investigation of the general, formal properties that belong to all existents. This does not prevent him from positing God, as the highest being, as the first theme of metaphysics, and from including the finite being in his investigation, in accordance with Aristotle's table of categories. In his transcendental understanding, therefore, Suárez unites the two great currents of interpretation of the Aristotelian concept of metaphysics: a deontologization of metaphysics by defining it primarily as the science of the highest being (which begins as early as Theophrastus), and an ontologization of metaphysics by understanding it as a general science of Being (which can be seen in Alexander of Aphrodisias). The *Disputationes metaphysicae* was the first comprehensive systematic presentation of metaphysics. Martin Grabmann describes this as "a monumental achievement of scholastic speculation, indeed of philosophical speculation as a whole—a work ample in its methodology, independent, and pioneering in many respects."[23]

The Basic Metaphysical Conception

The substance of the positions Suárez takes is another indicator of his tendency to create an independent system of his own. It was impossible for him to prescind from Thomas, who was the real authority in Baroque Scholasticism; but in many respects, the Scotist understanding of Being was another strong (though latent) influence on him. At the same time, he was not unreceptive to nominalist ideas. This tendency finds expression, very generally, in the broadening of the concept of the really existent to include that which is really possible, and in the focusing of metaphysical interest on the element of the existent that we can know, the concept of essence.[24] All this presages paradigms that were to become central to metaphysics in the modern period.

The Scotist and nominalist influences, with an additional contribution from the spirit of the Renaissance, take a very concrete form in Suárez's choice of a starting point. He begins with the concrete reality of the individual object, in order to deduce from this the conditions and principles of the real being that is capable of existence. His starting point is thus the be-

23. Grabmann 559.
24. Cf. Leinsle 1988, 58.

ing as expressed in the participle of the verb 'to be' *(ens ut participium)*, the really existing existent, in order to uncover the general metaphysical structure of the being as expressed in the noun *(ens ut nomen)*. For this purpose, he prescinds from the actual existence and considers the existent under the aspect of the real essence, that is, as a thing that has or can have Being.[25] He attempts to develop the concept of being as such in accordance with the abstraction which makes it the proper subject matter of metaphysics.[26] Since this perspective depends decisively on the way in which we know, an investigation of this kind must also take into account the *formal* concept of being, which encompasses both the subjective act of knowing and its intentional achievement, the image that represents the object that has been understood. In order for a unified experience of the world as a whole to be possible, one must assume that the formal concept of the existent possesses unity, simplicity, and transcendental commonality. To this, there necessarily corresponds one single and unified *objective* concept of being and the possibility of forming a completely homogeneous, completely detached, pure concept of being as such.[27]

When we bear in mind that the *conceptus obiectivus* is nothing other than the object itself, insofar as it is known or understood through the relevant formal concept, we must ask whether this kind of epistemological realism means that the requirement of the unity of the objective concept of being is in fact equivalent to the Scotist idea of the univocity of Being. Suárez, who agrees with Thomas in insisting on the *analogia entis*,[28] holds that this risk is not present, provided that the concept designates a form or essential nature that is inherently present in all the analogues.[29] The basis of the unified objective concept of the existent is a transcendental concept of being *(ratio entis)*, which in its general core designates neither substance nor accident, neither God nor creature, but all of these in a uniform manner, insofar as they agree *in essendo,* "in being existents."[30] This general formal element of the concept of being, in which all real existents concur, is the *actus essendi*. The real meaning of the "analogy of being" *(analo-*

25. Cf. Suárez, DM, 2, 4, 3ff.
26. Cf. ibid., 2, 1, 14: "propria et adaequata ratio entis."
27. Cf. ibid., 2, 2, 8–20: "conceptus obiectivus perfecte praecisus."
28. Cf. ibid., 28, 3, 10–17.   29. Cf. ibid., 28, 3, 10ff., and 32, 2, 1ff.
30. Cf. ibid., 2, 2, 8.

gia entis), and the reason for the transcendental character of the concept
of Being, is that all real existents share inherently in this Being or this entity—not that only an analogue participates inherently, while the others
participate in a merely external sense.

Suárez presupposes in the "Being" the unity of a concept that is common to the members of the relationship, and this undeniably means that
his teaching about analogy bears a certain resemblance to the Scotist thesis of the univocity of Being. However, he cannot follow Scotus in understanding the *ens* as a univocal predicate in the true sense of this term: Suárez does not assert that all beings express in only *one* way the fact that they
are beings. This affinity to the Scotist solution, and the presupposition of a
unified *conceptus obiectivus,* explain why Suárez takes the analogy of predication *(analogia attributionis),* rather than proportional analogy *(analogia
proportionalitatis),* to afford the exact description of the relationship of the
various forms of beings. The analogy of proportion denotes the similarity
of a relationship (e.g., between that of the finite being to its Being, and that
of the divine being to its Being), but the analogy of predication or attribution denotes a relationship where one is dependent on the other, a dependence that is the result of the specific participation of each member in a
common form. Since the creature is primarily something and not simply
nothing, before it can have a relationship to something, there can be nothing other than an *analogia attributionis* between God and the creature. In
this case, the members of the relationship inherently possess the relevant
ratio entis; at the same time, they are in a relationship of dependence.[31] In
the tension between a purely univocal and a purely equivocal concept of
Being (i.e., "being" means always the same thing, or it is the same word
for completely different things—both of which are rejected as imprecise),
there can be no doubt that Suárez is closer to univocity than to equivocity.

Against the background of the unified objective concept of Being, and
of the analogous understanding of Being, we can now identify other fundamental conditions of Being in addition to the *ratio entis;* these are to be
found in everything that has Being. Every existent, since it is an *ens reale,*
is an *unum, bonum,* and *verum* (one, good, true). Among these convertible
transcendental attributes of Being, it is the problem of unity that partic-

---

31. Cf. ibid., 28, 3, 10ff.; and 32, 2, 1ff.: "unius ad aliud."

ularly concerns Suárez. Unlike Aristotle and Thomas, he argues, in complete agreement with Duns Scotus and William of Ockham, for the primacy of the individual. It is not the universal (the *universale*, or the *ens ut commune omnibus*) that is the *primum cognitum* (the first formal object of the intellect to be grasped), but the concrete individual object. Thomas holds that the singular can be known only indirectly, through a *conversio ad phantasmata*, that is, by means of a reflection on the "sense appearances" of things and on the conditions that have led to the genesis of these images;[32] but Suárez affirms the immediate, direct knowability of the individual as individual.[33] Compared with this, the universal concept, which has no real existence in itself but is formed by means of abstraction, on the basis of similarities in the individual concepts, is a merely secondary figure. These different viewpoints are the result of the differing identification of the principle of individuation. Thomas anchors the *principium individuationis* in the matter that is predetermined with a view to individual quantity *(materia quantitate signata)*; accordingly, it is not possible for the intellect—which must abstract from matter in order to arrive at knowledge—to have direct knowledge of the individual being.[34] But for Suárez, inspired by the Scotist theory of "thisness" *(haecceitas)*, it is clear that the individual substance requires for its singularity no other principle of individuation than its own entity and the genuine principles of its essence, namely, matter, form, and their union.[35]

Since Being is absolutely the first, the most universal, and simple, its meaning can be further illuminated only through the articulation of the relationship of the fact that it is existent to its *modi*, that is, through the explication of the various modes of the real being. The first division of being is that into the *ens simpliciter infinitum* and the *ens finitum:* the unqualifiedly infinite and the finite being. This is antecedent to all further differentiations because it concerns being as being, the *essentia* itself, which constitutes the being as being.[36] Finitude and infinity are *modi* that determine the essence as such in view of its reality, and as such bring to expression a certain measure of "essential perfection."[37] In terms of the abstract on-

32. Cf. Thomas Aquinas, *STh* I, 84, 7. 33. Cf. Suárez, DM 6, 6, 1ff.
34. Cf. Thomas Aquinas, *STh* I, 86, 1. 35. Suárez, DM 5, 6, 1.
36. Cf. ibid., 4, 1, 8.
37. Cf. ibid., 4, 8, 10: "perfectio essentialis."

tological structure, this subdivision would in fact be the clearest division
of all—but this is not the case from the human perspective *(quoad nos)*.
This means that it must first be made accessible to our knowledge through
a series of further differentiations, which are the direct consequences of
the first division but lie closer to human experience. For example, we must
draw a distinction between an existent that has its existence from its own
self thanks to its own perfection, and an existent that has received its Being from others *(ens a se—ens ab alio)*; this means that we must also draw
a distinction between a being that exists necessarily and a being that can
also not exist *(ens necessarium—ens contingens)*; between a being whose essence includes its existence, and a being that possesses its Being thanks to
participation in the perfect Being of another *(ens per essentiam—ens per
participationem)*; and finally, between the uncreated being and the created
being *(ens increatum—ens creatum)*. That which necessarily exists through
itself, through its own perfect essence, is as a whole actually existing in reality. Every other being, as a real existent, is in principle a possible existent,
capable of existence; but it does not de facto exist always and as a whole at
any particular moment *(actus purus—ens potentiale)*.

This makes it clear that in this context, infinity refers to the "completely indivisible infinity of perfection"[38] which is real in itself; this is based on
the totality of the perfection of the essence.[39] Accordingly, God—as the
absolutely Infinite—is nothing other than the absolute existent, possess-
ing all the perfection in which a being can ever participate.[40] There can be
no doubt that the equation of reality and perfection influenced Spinoza in
his concept of reality; similarly, it is impossible to overlook in Suárez's definition of infinity the presage of Spinoza's concept of God and of substance
as the sum of all perfections. From the opposite angle, the finitude of being
denotes nothing other than the limitation of the inner intensity or of the
intensive quantity of its "existent-ness." Unlike the Thomists, Suárez did
not consider it helpful to explain finitude through the assumption that the
ens finitum is made up of an act of Being that is pure in itself and a potential
essence that limits this act.

This reflection already points to the ontological constitution of the created being. Suárez parts company with both the Thomists (who are com-

---

38. Ibid., 30, 2, 25.   39. Cf. ibid., 28, 2, 10.
40. Ibid., 39, 3, 19. Cf. ibid., 28, 1, 18.

pelled by the thesis of the limitation of the unlimited *esse* by the potential essence to regard the created being as a compound of real existence and essence as two genuinely distinct things) and the Scotists (who postulate a merely modal difference between existence and essence). He maintains the middle path of a mental distinction with a factual basis *(distinctio rationis cum fundamento in re)* between the actually existing essence and the actual existence.[41] In his view, everything that is needed for the Being and the genuine existence of a thing is already contained in its actual essence. The actual existence can contribute nothing new in terms of entity or actuality that would not already be present. The (real and actual) Being through which the essence of the creature is constituted formally in the actuality of the essence is the true Being of existence itself.[42] (Coming into existence is equivalent to being transferred from the merely objective possibility in God before the creation into the actual state.) Although there is no necessary connection between the being of the actual essence and the being of the actual existence *(esse essentiae actualis,* the *esse existentiae actualis),* as there is in the case of the uncreated necessary being (God), they do constitute a factual identity. This is why they can be separated only in the realm of the human understanding.

As contingent beings, finite things display one particular universal constellation of causes that are constitutive of their substantiality. Suárez distinguishes between two internal causes *(causa formalis* and *materialis)* and two external causes *(causa efficiens* and *finalis).* The first cause *(causa prima*—God) and the exemplary cause *(causa exemplaris)* of all is God. In keeping with the Jewish and Christian belief in creation, he presupposes the existence of God as a truth, but he also attempts to demonstrate this philosophically. He relies here both on Anselm's argument, convinced that what it affirms is real, and on the inference from creature to creator to prove God's existence. He changes the latter by rejecting the starting point in the Aristotelian principle of causality *(omne quod movetur ab alio movetur)* and replacing this by the metaphysical principle of coming into being *(omne quod fit ab alio fit).* This had a lasting influence on the philosophical discussion of the question of God's existence in the modern pe-

41. Cf. ibid., 31, 1, 13.
42. Cf. ibid., 31, 4, 4: *Illud esse, quo essentia creaturae formaliter constituitur in actualitate essentiae, est verum esse existentiae.*

riod, and especially on Spinoza's thinking. Suárez's approach appears truly modern in the following reasoning: The nonrepugnance of the essential definitions of things, as well as the ultimate common basis which is shared by absolutely all beings and establishes them existents, is the reality that is prior to the creation; therefore Suárez considers this reality to be so independent in relation to God that it cannot be abolished even by God's omnipotence.[43]

IMPLICATIONS FOR THEOLOGY
AND LEGAL PHILOSOPHY

Suárez became an important figure and won recognition not only through his metaphysics but also through his doctrine of congruence, which was his contribution to the clarification of the virulent controversy between the Jesuits, who followed Luis de Molina (1535–1600), and the strict Thomists, who were led by the Dominican Domingo Báñez (1528–1604), about the cooperation between God and the creature in the free action of the human person.

In the field of legal philosophy, Suárez's explications of natural law and international law had a profound influence on the development of Western intellectual history. His approach to a solution is based on an understanding of "person" that sees in personality the highest actuality of a substantial nature endowed with reason, in the traditional sense maintained by the metaphysics of substance; at the same time, however, he sees personality in the modern sense as the spirit's self-possession, thanks to which the human being is the free and autonomous subject of his actions and decisions.

On the question of congruence, therefore, Suárez chooses a standpoint oriented to action and to the subject, and concentrates accordingly on the moral-psychological aspect of the cooperation between the infallible working of grace and the freedom of the human will; the metaphysical definition of the relationship between the infallibility of the divine will and the freedom of the creaturely will moves into the background. In order to do justice both to the absolute authority of God and to the mod-

---

43. Cf. Idem, *De Sanct. Trin. Mysterio* 9, 6, 19f.; also Honnefelder 294.

ern human consciousness of freedom, Suárez maintains the Augustinian variant of congruism, with the basic idea that actual grace becomes effective by accommodating itself *(congruit)* to the metaphysical constitution of the human will and to its modes of conduct. The *gratia sufficiens* (supporting grace) becomes *gratia efficax* (effective) not through a new intervention by God (as the Thomists hold), but through the greater congruity with the free assent of the human being. God knows what is more suitable to human freedom in virtue of his *scientia media,* through which he foresees the free potential actions *(futuribilia)* of the human person, that is, the free decisions of the will that would be made under specific circumstances and conditions.

In this concept, the human person has the role of a free, living instrument of God.[44] In order to accomplish things that lie beyond his natural capacities, the human person must possess not only a passive capacity for obedience (like irrational creatures), but also an active one[45] that allows him to accomplish all possible supernatural achievements—not, however, by his own power (in the Pelagian sense), but only as God's instrument. Accordingly, this is not a capacity *(potentia)* for immediate active behavior, but rather an active instrumentality, a capability for being drawn by God, who is the "principal agent," into the supernatural activity. This capacity presupposes a basis in the creaturely endowment of the human person, which God activates so that it is capable of higher things. This, however, does not mean that the human person is forced into pure passivity. In his capacity for obedience, he is genuinely empowered to accept or to reject the divine power that raises him up to become God's instrument, or else to pervert this power into the opposite act. This preserves the freedom and the specific causality of the human person.

Suárez's concern for the dignity and freedom of the human person also finds expression in his legal philosophy, which is presented above all in his *Tractatus de legibus ac Deo legislatore* (1612). As the title announces (. . . on God as lawmaker), this is ultimately a theology of creation translated into juridical categories. Suárez explicitly takes account of the subjective dimension of the concept of law, by making a distinction between law *(ius)*

44. Cf. Leinsle 1995, 307–10.
45. Cf. Suárez, *De incarnatione* 31, 5–6 (*Opera omnia* 18, 103–52).

as the moral claim to a just matter, or entitlement or right in some matter, and law *(lex)* as the basis of equality and as a rule for honorable conduct.[46] The *lex* is the real meaning and purpose *(ratio)* of the law. As a moral ordering of conduct, or as a general, clear, reliable, and adequately promulgated just prescription, it is reserved exclusively to rational beings.[47] God turns out to be the highest legislator, who imparts the law to all persons, peoples, and nations. The creatures participate in his eternal *lex,* which is a true law, in the form of natural law *(ius naturale),* which is based neither on a verdict of the human will nor on an act of the divine will alone. Its real basis lies, on the one hand, in God's rational legislation and in the order he has imposed upon his creation, an order to which he obligated himself by creating subjects who were capable of good and evil; and, on the other hand, in the creation of the "right reason" *(recta ratio),* in which he has given the human person the formal principles for distinguishing between good and evil. This means ipso facto the promulgation of this universal and immutable law, which follows from the nature of things. In a very modern move, the human person is given here the responsible role of interpreting the worldly conditions and the divine claims in the creation.

This allows Suárez to formulate the democratic claim entailed by the thesis of the sovereignty of the people. The human person is naturally free, but in order to realize himself, he needs fellowship and societal structures, which are impossible without authority and without a certain limitation on personal freedom. Authority in the state belongs to the people, who therefore have the right to choose their form of government and, if necessary, to resist their ruler *(tota respublica superior est rege).* Positive law should be an application to concrete human situations and to societal constellations of the natural law which belongs to the essence of the human person.

Suárez's posthumous relevance and influence on the philosophy of law is due not least to his doctrine of the law of the nations. In the tradition of Roman law, the *ius gentium* is regarded as lying between natural law and civil law; but Suárez does not understand it as *ius intra gentes* in the strict sense, that is, not as the totality of the domestic laws of each people, but as *ius inter gentes* in the sense of law between the states. Since it is not promul-

---

46. Cf. Idem, *De legibus ac Deo legislatore* 2, 17, 2.
47. Cf. ibid., 1, 4, 2; 1, 12, 4.

gated by statute, and is derived not from nature but from modes of dealing with others that have emerged over time, the law of nations is a customary law based on the idea of contract, that is, a mutable, positive human law.[48] It is generated by the idea of a unity of humankind that is not only something specific to the species, but is also political and moral—a unity that regulates the mutual relationships of the peoples inter alia through an international law concerning trade and diplomacy, as well as a law regulating war and peace. Thanks to his influence on the Protestant teachers of natural law (above all H. Grotius), Suárez, with F. de Vitoria, laid the foundation stone for the further development of the traditional law of nations into international law as we understand this today.

48. Cf. ibid., 2, 19, 1–6.

Note: For further reading see Suárez and *Francisco Suárez, "Der ist der Mann,"* in the References. For secondary sources see Bauer; Courtine; Craig; Darge; Doyle; Fernandes; Gracia; Gilson 1962; Goudriaan; Grabmann; Honnefelder; Leinsle 1988 and 1995; Robinet; Scheeben; Specht; *Francisco Suárez, "Der ist der Mann";* Vollrath; and Werner. Online resources: Jacob Schmutz, *Scholasticon,* http://www.scholasticon.fr/Information/Suarez_fr.php, contains a bibliography and links to primary sources online; Sydney Penner, http://www.people.cornell.edu/pages/sfp26/suarez.html.

20

TOMMASO CAMPANELLA
(1568–1639)

*The Revolution of Knowledge
from the Prison*

Germana Ernst

Germana Ernst

THE REJECTION OF ARISTOTLE AND
THE ENCOUNTER WITH TELESIO

Campanella's first work, the *Philosophia sensibus demonstrata*, was published in Naples in 1591.[1] This large tome consists of eight *disputationes* in defense of the natural philosophy of Bernardino Telesio, in response to the attack by the lawyer Giacomo Antonio Marta, who had defended Aristotle. Campanella wrote this work at the age of twenty-one, in the Dominican convent in a little town in Calabria, his native region, which at that period belonged to the viceroyalty of Naples and was under Spanish rule.

---

1. The bibliography on Campanella is very ample. See Firpo 1940. To date, this is the only available work offering a comprehensive description of Campanella's works and of the events connected to them. An updating of the editions of the philosopher's works and of studies of him can be found in the journal *Bruniana and Campanelliana*, ed. Eugenio Canone and Germana Ernst (Pisa and Rome, 1995–). The most complete and comprehensive work on Campanella in English with an extensive bibliographical list is Headley 1997.

He was born on September 5, 1568, in the village of Stilo. His family was very poor; his father was a cobbler. He himself recalls at the beginning of his *Syntagma de libris propriis* that he decided at the age of fourteen to enter the Dominican Order because he was fascinated by the eloquence of a preacher and by the figures of Albert the Great and Thomas Aquinas— and especially because this seemed to him the most suitable way to satisfy his precocious and intense desire to dedicate himself to a life of study.

It is not by chance that the preface which opens the *Philosophia* begins with the word "truth," which is depicted in an allegory on the frontispiece as a sphere floating on the water, while the winds that blow from every quarter try to sink it and a young Dominican attempts to reach it by swimming. The author begins by affirming that the truth may for a time be hidden and persecuted, but at the end it emerges from the darkness and shines out once more. He does not hesitate to state that one must prefer the truth even to one's own life. In this preface, Campanella traces the fundamental outlines of his first years of study, confessing that the reading of the Aristotelian works that were used as textbooks in the Dominican convents had awakened in him more doubts than certainties: the masters did not know how to answer his questions, or they gave only embarrassed replies that did not satisfy the young student. In this way, he ended up in a disturbing state of fear *(timebam animo iuvenili)* and of loneliness, completely isolated within the entire philosophical tradition.

Finally, the intuition of a new philosophy is kindled within him— not a philosophy drawn from the books and the intellect of Aristotle, but from things themselves, via the senses and experience. Nothing can prevent this prospective from irrupting with force: *post haec incaluit veritas, et intus cogi minus poterat.* He is accused of maintaining doctrines similar to those of Telesio, but this verdict (which is meant as a condemnation) only awakens in him the joy at having finally discovered a companion and a guide. At Cosenza, he reads the first edition of the *De rerum natura iuxta propria principia,* and senses from the very first pages onward the novelty and the coherence of a doctrine which, in keeping with his own aspirations, "derives the truth from the things examined by the senses, not from the chimeras." His desire to meet Telesio in person was frustrated because the elderly philosopher died just at that time; Campanella felt compelled to deliver an emotional and reverent homage to the coffin, which was ex-

posed in the cathedral of the city, by pinning verses to the catafalque. This
intellectual encounter, in which the young Dominican has the impression
of receiving the spiritual inheritance of the new philosophy, remained imprinted indelibly on his mind. In a sonnet in the *Scelta di alcune poesie filosofiche,* he celebrates the man whose arrows pierced and slew the tyrant Aristotle who held sway over people's minds, restoring to the human person
that *libertas philosophandi* that is inseparable from the truth.

In the first pages of the *Syntagma,* Campanella seeks to explain why, after so many readings of Aristotle and of his Greek, Arab, and Latin commentators, but above all of Plato, the Neoplatonists, physicians such as
Hippocrates and Galen, natural scientists such as Pliny, atomists, and Stoics, his troubled search finally came to repose in the philosophy of Telesio *(sed Telesius me delectavit).* He underlines two closely linked aspects
of this philosophy: freedom of philosophizing and reliance upon things
themselves *(tum ob libertatem philosophandi, tum quia ex rerum natura,
non ex dictis hominum penderet).* Inspired by the disinterested love of the
truth, and remote from vain academic honors, the authentic philosophical
style is incarnated in the thought and in the life of Telesio. According to
Campanella, this style is so rare that in the entire history of thought, only
twenty-four true philosophers can be identified—and only four of these
belong to modern times. He does not reveal their names, but two are absolutely certain: Socrates in antiquity and Telesio in modern times. Besides
this, the philosophy of Telesio reestablishes those correct links between
objects and words that had worn thin and perished in the Aristotelian tradition. Convinced that the totality of truth was included once and for all
in the corpus of Aristotle's writings, his followers no longer noticed the necessity of verification by means of experience. On the contrary, this was
perceived as a disturbing threat. Campanella finds in Telesio the response
to the requirement that one emerge from a labyrinth of paper and words
(within which books generate other books, while reason, forgetful of its
relationship to experience, degenerates into sophisms and disputes about
words) in order to observe and study the divine book of nature *(Il mondo
è il libro dove il Senno Eterno / scrisse i propri concetti . . .,* as he writes in another famous sonnet). Human books must always be compared with *this*
book, since they are never more than imperfect copies of it. This comparison serves to complete them and to correct their errors.

NATURAL PHILOSOPHY

The central nucleus of this first work *Philosophia sensibus demonstrata* consists of a systematic critique of Aristotle's philosophy, on the physical, cosmological, and metaphysical levels, in the light of Telesio's principles which were combined with ideas deriving from the Platonic, Neoplatonic, and Hermetic traditions. The work by Campanella that presents the most organic treatment of the principles of the physical and natural world is the *Physiologia*, the first of the four parts of his *Philosophia realis*, published at Frankfurt in 1623; the other sections deal with *Ethica, Politica,* and *Oeconomica*. In the definitive edition, published at Paris in 1637, all four parts (but especially the first part, on natural philosophy) are accompanied by ample *Quaestiones* on specific problems in the light of the opinions of philosophers both ancient and modern. The *Physiologia* begins with the affirmation that when the most powerful, wisest, and best First Being decided to create the world—which is defined as the "statues and images" that represent his infinite boons—he spread out an "almost infinite" space in which to place such a *statua*. This happened at the beginning of that duration and flow of things that we call time; time is an image of the eternity from which it flows forth.

This space is defined as the "basis of existence, in which the world resides," and as "the first substance, or residence, or capacity that is immobile, incorporeal, and thus able to receive any corporeal thing." It is homogeneous in every one of its parts ("high" and "low," "inside" and "outside," "right" and "left" are human words referring to the physical objects that have been given their positions), and if the world did not exist, we would have to imagine the space as empty. In reality, however, it desires fullness and is endowed with an attractive force, since it "enjoys supporting entities" *(gaudet . . . substare entibus)* and hates to remain alone. The physical objects are completely in accord with this, since they in turn "enjoy mutual contact" *(mutuo gaudent contactu)* and hate the emptiness that separates them. God locates matter in space. In a clear contrast to the idea of Aristotle and Averroes, who define matter as privation and as a pure contrivance of reason *(ens rationis)*, Campanella regards matter as a physical entity, *informe, absque figura et expers actionis,* but capable of spreading, bending, dividing itself, uniting itself, and assuming every figure, just as the wax receives every seal. In terms of the imagination, matter is divisible at the point of infinity, but in reality, it is divisible into the most minute particles known as atoms. It is called "the second substance, basis of all forms, passive principle of composite things" *(secunda substantia, basis formarum, principium passivum compositionis rerum).*

God inserts warmth and coldness into this physical mass. These two active and self-diffusing principles are incorporeal, but can exist only in physical objects. Each of them wishes to take hold of and occupy the greatest possible quantity of matter, and it is in the contrast between these two that the two first bodies or elements in the world have their origin. These bodies or elements are the sky—formed of matter transformed by the heat, which therefore is extremely hot and clear, thin, and mobile—and the earth, consisting of matter that has been made immobile, dark, and dense by the cold. All the second existents have their origin from these first elements, which are the seats of the two first principal agents: for God utilizes the opposition of the first elements for the production of all beings, which in their infinite multiplicity and diversity realize the infinite degrees of the first Idea of God, "in whom resplend all modes of being and the activities of all things that emanate from him" *(in quo relucent modi omnes entitatis et operationes rerum ab ipso emanantium).* In this perspective, the sky is no longer subdivided into spheres but is one single unit; since it is hot, it moves in virtue of its own intrinsic operation, which conserves it and gives it life. There is no need to have recourse to extrinsic intelligent motive forces. The movements of the heavenly bodies and of the Sun, which are extremely varied and complex in terms of velocity, distance, and angles, transmit to the Earth all those degrees of heat and of light that provide essence to things. A variety differentiated in this way is necessary in order to bring about variety in this world. Campanella insists with great emphasis that God makes use of the elements as his unconscious craftsmen *(fabri)* and instruments in the production of all that exists. Here, their only tendency is to expand.

He also underlines that the world is a marvelous statue that represents the infinite *modi* of the first Idea, just as the book he is writing at the moment not only displays the material traces of the letters and the ink, but also represents the idea that he has in his own mind. In the light of these principles, Campanella explains the various aspects of the natural world, from the celestial and meteorological phenomena to the waters, from the minerals to the plants, and finally dwells with special attention on the more articulated and complex organisms of animals and human beings. Their origin lies in a particular degree of attenuation of the heavenly heat, namely, the *spiritus*. Thanks to its subtlety and its movement, the *spiritus* is able to detach itself from that portion of matter that is its wrapping. It is aware of the dangers that threaten it from outside, and is capable of organizing and molding the matter in which it is enclosed in such a way that it constructs the instruments that guarantee both preservation and life. Campanella was proud of his knowledge in the medical field; one of his works is a *Medicina* in seven books, published at Lyons in 1635. Here, as in other texts, he takes delight in underlining the wonderful organization of the human body and of its limbs, pointing out how the functions and the specific and particular purposes of the individual organs form a harmony in a marvelous total order that confirms the presence of the divine skill (*ars*) in every fiber of nature.

THE SENSE OF THINGS

Another text in which Campanella takes up topics dear to Telesio and develops them with greater amplitude and originality is the *De sensu rerum et magia* (Frankfurt, 1620; Paris, 1637). In the first chapter, the author declares the explanatory principle of the entire work: a being cannot share with others what it does not have in itself (*Ens nullum aliis dare posse quod ipsum in se non habet*). Since it is perfectly obvious that animals are endowed with sensitivity, and this cannot have its origin in nothing, we must affirm that "the elements, as their cause, and all things else have a sense." He then clarifies his own positions, repeating that everything that is born from the sky and the Earth receives from these two elements all that it possesses. He describes how the heat of the Sun acts, and replies to potential objections. In particular, he criticizes the positions of Lucretius and of the Atomists, who assert that sense is born of insentient things; for this would mean that human beings, who weep and laugh, have their origin in elements that do not weep and do not laugh. Campanella repeats his own positions, affirming that laughing and weeping preexist in the elements and bodies, however, not in the same way as in humans; and that everything is present in its own causes, but in a different way. He continues his polemic against the Atomists by denying that active and incorporeal forces such as heat, light, and cold can be generated by a casual encounter between inert particles that are passive and lack qualities. Taking up the Lucretian example, he affirms that even if one were to throw around the letters of the alphabet an endless number of times, they would never come together by chance to form the book that he is writing with conscious skill. We grant that a sword and a book are composed by conscious skill to fulfill a particular purpose; a fortiori, it is absurd to attribute to chance, rather than to the divine skill, the much more marvelous composition of the eye, of the heart, of a plant, or of the world as a whole.

When Campanella goes on to specify what is meant by "sense," he defines this first of all as *passio*. We sense when we undergo a change, which may be pleasant or unpleasant, depending on whether it is perceived as useful or harmful for the preservation of life. The one who senses does not receive in himself the entire form of the thing that is sensed (since that would imply a destruction of its own form); in the act of sensing, the spirit undergoes a partial change, thanks to which it is capable of appreciating the entirety of the nature of the object that is sensed. Aristotle is wrong to maintain that sense experience takes place via information: it takes place via transformation. Taking his analysis one stage deeper, Campanella writes that sense is not simply passion (for one can in fact suffer things one does not sense, e.g., when one is stung by an insect while one sleeps), but perception of passion and judgment concerning the object that inflicts the suffering. Thanks to sense, every being is endowed with the capacity to distinguish between that which benefits its existence and that which is harmful. And this means that every being is closely linked to the production and the very order of things: if the first elements and the beings that are derived from them did not sense, the entire world would be chaos, since they would be deprived of the ability to perceive the preservation or destruction of their own existence. The link between self-preservation and the sense sufficient to accomplish this task is both the bond and the explicative principle of the various levels of reality. Every being shares in life and in sense, according to various degrees and in specific forms: some, such as the heavenly bodies and light, are endowed with a sense that is much more acute and pure than that of animals, while others, such as minerals and metals, are endowed with a sense that is more obtuse and darker, because of the heaviness of matter.

In the animal organisms, the vital and cognitive functions are linked to the *spiritus,* which Campanella identifies with the organic and sentient soul. The spirit has its origin in the solar heat which, since it is enclosed within matter and cannot exhale as it would like, models and organizes physical bodies in the ways most suited to its needs. The spirit is physical, although it consists of matter that is extremely subtle, hot, mobile, and passible. Despite every distinction in terms of moods and abilities, the spirit is one, and has its seat in the brain, from which, running through the very slender channels of the nerves, it fulfills all its many functions. Through the organs of sense, it enters into contact with external reality, and all its passions and all its knowledge have their origin in the modifications that the spirit undergoes. Campanella refutes the Aristotelian definition of the soul as the act or form of the organic body: since it is physical, subtle, and mobile, the spirit is not fixed to the organ. Its relationship to the body is comparable to that of many persons in one house or city, who are capable of carrying out different tasks in a variety of ways. For Campanella, the memory, the imagination, discourse, and reason itself do not demand specific abilities or forms, since they are all functions of one and the same sentient soul, which is capable of conserving the modification and the impressions it has received and of reusing these when similar situations arise, or of examining them and extending them. The *discursus* is an act of sensing in that which is similar, an act of passing and of moving *(discurrere) a simili ad simile,* and there are as many discourses and syllogisms as there are types of similitude (of essence, of quality, of quantity, etc.). Even the Aristotelian "universal" is connected with the sentient spirit, since it is nothing other than a universal knowledge without particulars, for which knowing or understanding is sensing in a confused and distant way, while *sentire* is knowing closely and directly.

The dimension of sense knowledge makes it possible to draw a comparison between the level of the animals and the more specifically human level, in order to reveal both the affinities and the differences. Campanella likes to emphasize the extraordinary abilities of animals: they are equipped with sense organs that are sometimes superior to those of human beings, and they know how to carry out marvelous and skilled operations. They adopt forms of collective organization, and know how to employ medical and military skills; besides this, they are endowed with forms of reasoning, of language, of natural prophecy, and even—as in the case of elephants—with forms of religiosity.

But such analogies must not be permitted to obscure or to cast doubt upon the diversity and the specific character of the human level. To begin with, the human person is equipped with a *spiritus* that is much more refined and pure than the animal *spiritus,* capable of moving with agility between cerebral cells more spacious than those of animals. This allows the human person to draw up extremely complex chains of argumentation. But the authentic, radical difference in the human person consists in the fact that he is endowed not only with the *spiritus* that links him to all other natural beings, but also with a *mens* of divine origin that constitutes and establishes the dimension that is specifically his. The evidence pointing to the existence of this *mens,* and hence to the excellence and the divinity of the human person, is manifold, but it is basically linked to the principle enunciated at the beginning of Campanella's book: *effectum nullum supra propriam causam elevari posse.* The human being does not exhaust all his abilities within the natural world. He can *intelligere et desiderare et amare operarique effectus altissimos supra elementa.* Accordingly, his origin does not lie in the elements. He is dependent, not on the elements, but on a much more eminent cause, which we call "God." His ability to stretch out with his thought and his desire toward the infinite proves that he is the son, not of the Sun and the Earth, but of an infinite cause. This leap is not mere empty imagination, as Aristotle holds, but "this advancement from similar to similar without end is the power of those who participate in infinity" *(hunc progressum de simili in simile absque fine esse actum virtutis participantis infinitatem).* The human person's connection to a supernatural world is confirmed by his power to go beyond nature and the immediate limits of natural self-preservation: the philosopher and the monk can despise physical goods, honors, and pleasures in order to devote themselves to much higher goods and goals. This connection is further confirmed by the fact that the human being can attain superior forms of prophecy and ecstasy that are not reducible to natural facts explicable by means of physiological or medical theories; and it is confirmed by the freedom of the human will, which consists in the ability to resist external coercions, to evaluate and weigh up the objects of one's choice (which are usually a mixture of good and evil), and to choose the greater good even when this is not linked to an immediate advantage or usefulness.

The fourth book of the *De sensu* deals with natural magic. While staying in Naples as a young man (1590–1592), Campanella had made the acquaintance of Giambattista Della Porta (died 1615), one of the most famous exponents of this tradition, and had held discussions with him. After a first edition in four books in 1558, which had caused a certain commotion because of its revelation of the ingredients of the ointment used by witches, Della Porta had published a second, expanded edition of his *Magia naturalis* in 1589. This included recipes, counsels, and explanations in a great variety of fields, from household economy to cosmetics, from the art of distillation to optical phenomena, from magnetism to secret writings, with a predilection for the strangest and most unusual phenomena and remedies. Taking up images from Plotinus, which had been made popular by texts of Marsilio Ficino, Giovanni Pico della Mirandola, and Heinrich Cornelius Agrippa von Nettesheim, the Neapolitan magician declared that the role of the wise man consisted in wedding the things of Earth to the things of heaven, just as the farmer weds the elm to the vine, and in knowing how to extract from the generous womb of nature the secrets that it contains. Referring to an ample tradition, he listed the most curious hidden properties of minerals, plants, and animals. He asserts that it is impossible to offer a rational explanation of the relationships of sympathy and antipathy that exist among natural beings, and that we must be content to observe that "nature has taken delight in this great spectacle."

In the pages dealing with magic, Campanella endeavors to read anew and to reinterpret this tradition in the light of his doctrine of the sense of things. The magician is the one who knows the specific quality of the sense that is inherent in every thing, and is able to utilize it in an appropriate manner. He is also able to induce particular alterations and passions in the *spiritus*. He knows how to increase the vital values, suggesting the foods, drinks, climates, sounds, and herbal and animal remedies that benefit and intensify the vital energies. He knows the secrets of procreation and of illnesses, and he will be able to awaken passions that are suited to the pursuit of specific goals. He will also know how to explain unusual phenomena, such as premonitions (the causes that prepare certain events may already be present in the air, and may be perceived before the events themselves take place). He can explain how the true and real metamorphoses that occur in those who are bitten by a rabid dog, or in the country people in Apulia who are bitten by tarantulas, are due to the fact that the temperament of these unfortunate persons is altered by the spread in their organism of the spirit of the animal that has attacked them; this spirit gets the upper hand in the victims. If one has recourse to the doctrine of the sense, which can remain in beings and in the air in latent forms as if asleep, but can then reawaken on certain occasions, it becomes possible to explain facts such as the bleeding of a corpse in the presence of the assassin, or the possible efficacy of the weapon salve that heals a wound when applied to the weapon, or the reason why (according to a celebrated example which is recorded in every book about magic) an ancient fear causes a drum of sheepskin to break into pieces when a drum of wolf's skin resounds.

CAMPANELLA'S POLITICAL THOUGHT

Political reflection occupies a very prominent place in Campanella's philosophy, and constitutes a genuine leitmotiv that is present throughout his thinking from his early years until the last years of his exile in Paris, and which has dramatic repercussions on his own life, since it is at the origin of the failed "conspiracy" of Calabria in 1599 and the subsequent long years of imprisonment in the Neapolitan jails. From the outset, Campanella's political thought centers on one of its most constant nuclei: the relationship between religion and politics, in all the complexity of its articulations. During his stay in Padua in 1593, he wrote the *Monarchia Christianorum* (now lost) and the *De regimine Ecclesiae,* in order to redefine the relationships between the temporal and the ecclesiastical powers in the perspective of a universal monarchy and of the reunification of "the one flock under the one shepherd." Two years later, immediately after the abjuration to which he was condemned by the Inquisition because of "a strong suspicion of heresy," he wrote in Rome the *Dialogo politico contro Luterani, Calvinisti ed altri eretici,* deploring any laceration of Christian unity and underlining the pernicious consequences, on the political level, of the Reformed doctrines about grace. In 1598, at the age of thirty, he returned to Calabria after ten years' absence in which his restless itinerary had led him from Naples to Rome, then to Florence, and then to Padua, in contact with courtly milieus, with cultural academies, universities, and famous personages. Taking up once more the subject of the universal monarchy, he completed his *Monarchia di Spagna,* which has only recently been published in its original Italian version, stripped of all the interpolations that were inserted (without the author's knowledge) from Giovanni Botero's *Ragion di stato* and that fundamentally altered all the translations and printed editions of this treatise.

When he sets out the theoretical coordinates of the work, the author emphasizes that three orders of causes combine to form and maintain every political organism: God, prudence, and opportunity. This leads him to criticize the positions of Machiavelli, who limits himself to a consideration of the empirical causes alone, without integrating these into a more ample prophetical and providential framework. In the light of these considerations, the epochal and universal role of the Spanish sovereign is identified with that of the biblical Cyrus. The Spanish king is to liberate the church from the infidels and gather the peoples together under one single faith—a task that the Catholic king can accomplish only in complete agreement with the pope.

Campanella insists on drawing a distinction between prudence and shrewdness, which he identifies with the Machiavellian raison d'état. Whereas prudence is the instrument of organic unity, and aims to promote the prosperity of the societal body and to reinforce the bonds between the various members who make up this societal body, shrewdness seems to be a technique for the egotistic self-affirmation of the individual. As such, it is doomed to failure, as is demonstrated by the merely apparent and ephemeral successes of the tyrants and of the Machiavellian heroes.

The central chapters of the work take up questions about the sovereign, the laws, the arms, and the treasury, and there is a great deal of harsh criticism of the Spanish misgovernment with its ruinous political economy and the appalling administration of justice. The third and final part reviews the most important political powers of the day, in order to suggest the most suitable means of aggregating them to the universal monarchy. The most famous chapter is that on the Low Countries. Here, Campanella deplores the mistakes made by the Catholic king and suggests that the political and religious rebellion can be ended by means of a series of stratagems that are so subtle and unscrupulous that they justify the celebrated verdict of the learned Hermann Conring (1606–1681), who defined the Dominican as "the sternest critic of Machiavelli's teachings and, at the same time, their secret propagator" *(Machiavelli dogmatum . . . acerrimus pariter reprehensor et fucatus doctor).*

In the course of 1599, however, the pace of events quickened. His reading of prophetical and apocalyptic texts, the appearance of signs in the sky and of unusual natural phenomena such as eclipses, comets, earthquakes, torrential rains, and rivers overflowing their banks, but above all the conditions of wretchedness and injustice and the profound social and political disorder in his country, convinced the Dominican that with the end of the century, a period of great changes was drawing near. The organization of a vast movement now began, supported even by noblemen and churchmen, and contacts were made with the Turkish fleet. The intention was to transform the province into a republic, extricating it from the tyranny of the king of Spain; Campanella, whom some witnesses call "the first man of the world, legislator and Messiah," was to promulgate "the new law and restore everyone to the natural liberty." The insurrection failed when two accomplices denounced the plot to the Spanish authorities. A ferocious repression followed. Armed troops were sent in, and many persons were arrested and executed in a cruel manner. Campanella was singled out as the spiritual head of the conspiracy. He was tried for heresy and spent twenty-seven years in prison in Naples.

A few years after the events in Calabria, he wrote his most celebrated pamphlet, the *La Città del Sole,* "The City of the Sun," which is both the program of a failed insurrection and its philosophical idealization. When he published it in 1623 as an appendix to the *Politica,* Tobias Adami was so struck by its purity and luminosity that he defined it as a precious gem and claimed that this ideal republic was superior to the models proposed by Plato in antiquity and by Thomas More in recent times, because it was inspired by the great model of nature. And in fact, the simplest and most persuasive key to reading Campanella's utopia is the reference to nature, understood as the expression of the intrinsic divine skill, and the critique of contemporary society, which is unjust and unhappy precisely because it moves away from that model, or does not imitate it in the correct manner. The city's happiness will grow the more it becomes a body politic *(cor-*

po di repubblica). Protected and defended by its seven concentric circles of walls, situated in a place with an ideal climate that is beneficial to bodily health, and located on the slopes of a hill in order that the air may be lighter and purer, it will be all the more similar to a living organism, if the individual members, in their variety and the diversity of their functions, are all coordinated toward the common good. Campanella argues that the two most famous and controversial aspects of this pamphlet, the community of goods and the sharing of wives, are in conformity with the law of nature; he does not hesitate to affirm that private property and monogamous marriage have a wholly historical and cultural origin, so that they possess a basis and a value only within the context of particular civil laws. Other significant aspects, such as the organization of work and the conception of knowledge, show clearly the importance of the reference to nature.

On the question of work, Campanella once again takes up the cudgels against Aristotle, who had excluded craftsmen, farmers, and manual workers from the list of citizens with full rights. In the *Syntagma*, Campanella urges that one should go into the workshops and stores to consult the dyers, the smiths, the goldsmiths, and the farmers, because one finds in them "more real and true philosophy than in the schools of philosophers" *(plus philosophiae realis et verae . . . quam in scholis philosophorum)*. In the new republic, every member exercises a role equal in dignity, since all contribute to the unity and prosperity of the entire organism. For the inhabitants of the City of the Sun, no activity is mean or low, and no service is thought beneath their dignity. The only thing they despise is laziness; thereby, they emphasize the dignity of labor and overturn an absurd concept of nobility that is linked to inactivity and vice. As for knowledge, the walls are not only circles that enclose the city and protect it, but also the wings of an extraordinary theater and the pages of the encyclopedia of knowledge, since the walls of the arcaded loggias and the houses are painted with images of all the arts and sciences. Knowledge is not shut up in books which are kept in separate places such as libraries, but is displayed for all to see, in such a way that its depiction by means of images favors a more rapid and easier learning. From their earliest years, children run through this theater of knowledge under appropriate guidance and following correct rhythms and itineraries, and learn joyfully, as if playing a game, without hard work and struggle.

THE ENCYCLOPEDIA OF THE SCIENCES

During his long years in prison, Campanella dedicated himself inten-
sively to the grandiose work of reformation and refoundation of the entire
encyclopedia of knowledge which he had desired ever since his youth. Let
us recall here only a few examples from his very ample literary production.
The *Scelta di alcune poesie filosofiche,* an anthology of poetry in which the
most difficult philosophical concepts are expressed in very vigorous verse,
was published by Adami in Germany in 1622. His interests in linguistic
and literary problems find expression in the *Philosophia rationalis,* which
consists of five parts: *Poëtica, Dialectica, Grammatica, Rhetorica,* and *His-
toriographia.* He also wrote a *Theologia* in thirty books, in which the traditional theological questions are reexamined in new perspectives that take
account of the problems that have emerged in modern times; an *Astrologia*
in six books, in which he proposes to liberate this teaching from the superstition of the Arabs and to establish it on the basis of a natural and conjec-
tural learning; and the *Medicina,* which we have already mentioned.

One particularly important work is the *Ateismo trionfato* (Atheism
Conquered), which Campanella also referred to as *Antimachiavellismo.*
Repeating his criticism of Machiavelli and of the raison d'état, he seeks
to prove that religion is not—as the politicians declare—a completely human invention, a useful fiction thought up by the shrewdness of priests
and princes in order to attain power and to keep hold of it. Through a wide-
ranging rational investigation that reviews religious beliefs and philosophical doctrines, Campanella seeks to demonstrate that, on the contrary, religion is a natural virtue and power that is intrinsic to the human person
and to all of nature. After the natural quality of religion has been demonstrated, the next step is to show, on the basis of a comparison with the other religions, that the Christian religion, the expression of the rationality
of the divine Word, is in perfect harmony with the natural religion that is
brought to perfection (but not abolished) by the addition of the dogmas
and sacraments. It follows that the Christian religion, precisely because it
can be seen to have the greatest conformity with nature, is the most suited
to the position of a universal religion.

Another very interesting work is the *Apologia pro Galileo,* written in
1616, the year in which Copernicus was suspended *donec corrigatur* and the

first rumblings of the theological opposition to Galileo's discoveries were heard. Campanella had met Galileo in Padua in 1593, when they both were young men, and he displayed a constant esteem and friendship for the scientist, despite his disagreement with some of his teachings, especially the atomistic theses. The *Apologia* is an act of great courage and intellectual honesty on the part of its author, not only because Campanella speaks about this delicate question while he himself is in prison (as he was later to recall, his was the only voice raised in defense of Galileo), but also because he does not defend his own teachings. Campanella's image of a living and organic book of nature is very different from Galileo's image of a book written with mathematical characters. Besides this, Campanella has reservations about the Copernican doctrine, which was not easy to square with Telesio's physics, especially with regard to the motion of the Earth. What he defends is the *libertas philosophandi* of Galileo and of the Christian scientist in general, whose first right and duty is to read the book of nature. With great lucidity, Campanella grasps the nub of the problem, which he identifies in the marriage between Aristotelianism and theology. An undue dogmatic value has been conferred on the Aristotelian philosophy; but like every human doctrine, this too must be corrected on the basis of a comparison with the book of nature. If it no longer corresponds to experience, it must be abandoned, without fearing negative repercussions on theology.

The most monumental of these works, not simply because of its size, is the *Metaphysica*, which Campanella called with justified pride "the Bible of the philosophers." He began this work as a young man and rewrote it many times in the following years. It was finally published in Paris in 1638, less than a year before his death. It is structured in three parts and eighteen books, and takes up all the doctrines of the entire philosophical and theological tradition, adopting an attitude of complete liberty vis-à-vis the various schools. The Prooemium begins by underlining the idea that only God possesses the fullness of truthfulness (*veracitas*), while all human beings lie in certain respects, whether out of fear or ignorance or deliberate intention, whether in pursuit of goals thought to be good, or driven by passions. The only true master is God, both because he is free of passions and because, as creator, he is not ignorant even of the smallest things. This leads to the exhortation to study the book of nature, which God wrote by creating things *(dicere autem Dei ac scribere est ipsum facere realiter)* and to compare every human book with the book written by God's own hand. The doctrine of metaphysics is indispensable for identifying the connections between the individual sciences, since it treats of the first principles and the ends of things, and of the foundations of the sciences. Transcending physics and philosophy, metaphysics "is elevated to the first causes and to the highest cause, from where we gradually can contemplate causation and cognition of everything" *(ad primas causas erigitur et ad supremam, unde causationem et cognitionem omnium gradatim contuemur).*

When he replies to the fourteen "doubts" *(dubitationes)* with which the work begins, and which express all the possible doubts about human knowledge in general and the knowledge of the senses in particular, Campanella adopts a Socratic attitude and a position of "learned ignorance" *(docta ignorantia)*, where the consciousness of the limits, the uncertainties, and the inexhaustible infinity of knowledge are the starting point of every true investigation which intends to abstain both from presumptuous dogmatic certainties and from the sterile cognitive refusal of the skeptics. The overcoming of the skeptical doubt is guaranteed by the doctrine of self-knowledge, thanks to which Campanella can distinguish between two different cognitive modalities; here, he returns with greater emphasis to teachings already mentioned in other works. Appealing explicitly to passages in St. Augustine, he affirms that the knowledge the subject has of his own self is of a different nature from the mediated and reflected knowledge he has of external objects. This self-knowledge coincides with his own being, and is the knowledge that Augustine calls *praesentia perennis* and Thomas (referring to Augustine) calls *notitia praesentialitatis* (perennial presence—notion of presence). It is certain that we exist; it is therefore certain that we are able to exist—since even if I *am* mistaken, it is certain that I *can* both be mistaken and not be mistaken. This means that the *posse* ("I can") is just as certain as the *esse* ("I am"). It follows that the first most certain principle is that "we are, and can know, and will" *(nos esse et posse scire et velle).* The uncertainties and doubts begin when one turns one's attention to the specific objects, passing from the certainty of the notion of presence to the objective notion and to the process of alienation that is induced by external things. It is precisely the stream of this additional knowledge coming from the external world that can obscure the original inborn and hidden knowledge that the soul has of its own self, inducing in the soul a kind of self-forgetfulness. A self-knowledge of this kind, connected to one's own being, is the precondition of all other knowledge: "We can, know, and will other things because we are capable of, and know and will, ourselves" *(nos possumus, scimus et volumus alia quia possumus, scimus et volumus nos ipsos)*. Campanella writes that every being knows itself because it is just what it is. It then senses the other things "by sensing itself transformed into the others" *(dum sentit se immutatum in alia)*. In any case, it is indubitable that all knowledge is knowledge of oneself: *semper . . . scire est sui.*

The *Metaphysica* is full of inspiring ideas, but it remains largely unread. Here, we must mention the central doctrine of the "primalities" *(primalitates)*, which affirms that since the first infinite Being draws its essence from the infinite principles of power, wisdom, and love, every finite being, qua being, is constituted and structured by these same primal principles (for want of a better term), according to differentiated modalities and proportions. Qua beings, things are structured by the primalities; qua distinct and limited, things are composed of finite degrees of being and infinite degrees of nonbeing. This means that "nothing" does not exist, either in God or outside of him; but God makes use of "nothing" in order to constitute the finitude and the distinction of beings. In the light of the doctrine of the primalities and of the three great influences (necessity, fate, and harmony) which transmit the modes of the Idea in the world, Campanella reexamines fundamental questions that have been the object of controversy, for example, the relationship between necessity and contingency; the relationship between human liberty, fate, and providence; the immortality of the soul; and above all, the problems connected with evil, sin, and suffering.

Campanella was freed from his prison in Naples in 1626 and was moved to Rome, where he lived until 1634. The episode during his stay in Rome which caused the greatest commotion was linked to his astrological skills, and to the desire of Pope Urban VIII to make use of these skills to thwart the voices that proclaimed ever more insistently that he would soon die because of a threatening eclipse of the Sun. Summoned to the papal palace, Campanella carried out the practices of natural magic which he describes in the pamphlet *De siderali fato vitando,* where he takes up ideas of Marsilio Ficino and declares his intention of teaching how one can use appropriate remedies and take precautions in order to avoid the evils that are threatened by the stars. This work was printed at Lyons in 1629 as the seventh and last book in the *Astrologia,* and risked compromising the pope himself through accusations of engaging in superstitious practices. Campanella quickly wrote an *Apologeticus,* in order to demonstrate that the practices suggested in the *De fato* were not superstitious, but completely natural.

Following new threats from Spain, Campanella was obliged to go into exile in Paris in 1634. In addition to overseeing the printing of his works, he dedicated himself with great vigor to the interests that were nearest to his heart, namely, the political and prophetical ideas. In a series of writings, he lucidly defines the causes of the unrelenting decline of the Spanish power and the ascent of the French monarchy. On the occasion of the much longed-for birth of the Dauphin (later Louis XIV, the Sun King), he composed an *Ecloga* in Latin. Its verses express once again his confidence that an epoch of unity and peace is drawing near, when all ungodliness, treacheries, lies, and conflicts will be abolished. Work, which will be distributed among all persons, will no longer be toilsome labor, but will become play; the lambs will have no fear of the wolves, and the sovereigns will reign for the good of the peoples.

Campanella was disturbed by sad foretokens of an imminent solar eclipse, and attempted to thwart the threats, but he died at dawn on May 21, 1639.

Note: For further reading see Campanella and Symonds in the References. For secondary sources see Amabile; Badaloni 1965; Blanchet; Delumeau; *Encyclopedia Bruniana e Campanelliana;* Ernst; Firpo 1940, 1947, 1974, 1998; Headley; Lerner 1985, 1995; Mönnich; Walker.

Accademia. 1999–. *Revue de la Société Marsile Ficin.* Vols. I to IX.

Acta Cusana. Quellen zur Lebensgeschichte des Nikolaus von Kues. 1976–2000. Vol. 1. Edited by Erich Meuthen. Hamburg: Meiner.

Ægidius Romanus [Giles of Rome]. 1967. *De regimine principum.* Rome: Apud Bartholomaeum Zanettum 1607; reprint Aalen: Scientia.

Agrippa von Nettesheim, Heinrich Cornelius. 1569. *Of the Vanitie and vncertaintie of Artes and Sciences, Englished by Ja[mes] San[ford] Gent.* London. [Available online at Early English Books Online, EEBO]

———. 1967. *De occulta philosophia.* Edited by Karl Anton. Nowotny and Graz: Akademische Verlagsanstalt.

———. 1970. *Opera.* Basle, 1578; reprint edited by Richard H. Popkin; Hildesheim: Olms.

———. 1980. *Declamation on the Nobility and Preeminence of the Female Sex,* in Guillaume Alexis, Sir Thomas Elyot, and Heinrich Cornelius Agrippa von Nettesheim, *The Feminist Controversy of the Renaissance: Facsimile Reproductions.* Delmar, N.Y.: Scholars' Facsimiles and Reprints.

———. 1992. *De occulta philosophia libri tres.* Edited by V. Perrone Compagni. Leiden, New York, and Cologne: Brill.

———. 1996. *Declamation on the Nobility and Preeminence of the Female Sex.* Translated by Albert Rabil. Chicago: University of Chicago Press.

Aiken, J. A. 1980. "Leon Battista Alberti's System of Human Proportions." *Journal of the Warburg and Courtauld Institutes* 43: 68–96.

Alberti, Leon Battista. 1834–1849. *Opere volgari.* 5 vols. Edited by A. Bonucci. Florence: Tipografia Galileiana.

———. 1969. *The Family in Renaissance Florence.* Translated by Renée Neu Watkins. Columbia: University of South Carolina Press.

———. 1971. *The Albertis of Florence: Leon Battista Alberti's "Della Famiglia."* Translation, introduction, and notes by G. A. Guarino. Lewisburg, Pa.: Bucknell University Press.

———. 1972. *On Painting and On Sculpture. The Latin Texts of "De pictura" and "De statua."* Edited and translated by C. Grayson. London: Phaidon.

————. 1960–1973. *Opere volgari.* 3 vols. Edited by C. Grayson. Bari: Laterza.

————. 1987. *Dinner Pieces: A Translation of the Intercoenales.* Translated by D. Marsh. Binghamton, N.Y.: MRTS.

————. 1988. *On the Art of Building in Ten Books.* Translated by J. Rykwert, N. Leach, and R. Tavernor. Introduction by J. Rykwert. Cambridge, Mass.: MIT Press.

————. 2003. *Momus.* English translation by S. Knight, Latin text by V. Brown and S. Knight. Cambridge, Mass.: Harvard University Press.

Albertini, Tamara. 1997. *Marsilio Ficino. Das Problem der Vermittlung von Denken und Welt in einer Metaphysik der Einfachheit.* Munich: Fink.

————. 2001. "L'anima artista in Marsilio Ficino: Uno filosofia della bellezza del pensiero," in *La pluralità estetica: Lasciti e irradiazioni oltre il Novocento,* edited by G. Marchianò, 27–39. Arezzo and Turin: Trauben.

————. 2001. "Intellect and Will in Marsilio Ficino: Two Correlatives of a Renaissance Concept of the Mind," in *Marsilio Ficino: His Theology, His Philosophy, His Legacy,* edited by Michael J. B. Allen and Valery Rees, 203–25. Leiden: Brill.

Allen, Michael, J. B. 1981. *Marsilio Ficino and the Phaedran Charioteer.* Berkeley and Los Angeles: University of California Press. [Latin-English]

————. 1984. *The Platonism of Marsilio Ficino: A Study of His Phaedrus Commentary, Its Sources and Genesis.* Berkeley, Los Angeles, and London: University of California Press.

————. 1989. *Icastes: Marsilio Ficino's Interpretation of Plato's "Sophist."* Berkeley, Los Angeles, and Oxford: University of California Press. [Latin-English]

————. 1994. *Nuptial Arithmetic: Marsilio Ficino's Commentary on the Fatal Number in Book VIII of Plato's "Republic."* Berkeley, Los Angeles, and London: University of California Press. [Latin-English]

————. 1995. *Plato's Third Eye: Studies in Marsilio Ficino's Metaphysics and Its Sources.* Aldershot: Ashgate.

————. 1998. *Synoptic Art: Marsilio Ficino on the History of Platonic Interpretation.* Firenze: Olschki.

Allen, Michael J. B., Valery Rees, and Martin Davies, eds. 2002. *Marsilio Ficino: His Theology, His Philosophy, His Legacy.* Brill's Studies in Intellectual History 108. Leiden: Brill.

Amabile, Luigi. 1882. *Fra Tommaso Campanella, la sua congiura, i suoi processi e la sua pazzia.* 3 vols. Naples: Morano.

————. 1887. *Fra Tommaso Campanella ne' castelli di Napoli, in Roma e in Parigi.* 2 vols. Naples: Morano. [The five volumes by Amabile, with a sixth volume containing an index of names, have been reprinted with a preface by Nicola Badaloni and an introduction by Tonino Tornitore. Paris and Turin: Les belles lettres and Nino Aragno, 2006.]

Anastos, Milton V. 1948. "Pletho's Calendar and Liturgy." *Dumbarton Oaks Papers* 30, no. 4: 183–305.

Andersson, D. C. 2004. "'Th'Expense of Spirit in a Waste of Shame': Aristotelian Exposure in Montaigne," in *Exposure: Unveiling Bodies and Revealing Representations,* edited by K. Banks and J. Harris, 159–68. Oxford: Peter Lang.

André, João Maria, Gerhard Krieger, and Harald Schwaetzer, eds. 2006. *Intellectus und Imaginatio. Aspekte geistiger und sinnlicher Erkenntnis bei Nicolaus Cusanus*. Amsterdam and Philadelphia: Grüner.

Aristoteles latine interpretibus variis. 1995. Berlin, 1831; reprint Munich: Fink.

Athanassiadi, Polymnia. 2002. "Byzantine Commentators on the Chaldaean Oracles: Psellos and Plethon," in *Byzantine Philosophy and Its Ancient Sources*, edited by Katerina Ierodiakonou, 237–52. Oxford: Clarendon Press.

Backus, Irena, ed. 1997. *The Reception of the Church Fathers in the West: From the Carolingians to the Maurists*. Vol. 2. Leiden: Brill.

Badaloni, Nicola. 1965. *Tommaso Campanella*. Milan: Feltrinelli.

———. 1989. "Sulla Costruzione e sulla Conservazione della Vita in Bernardino Telesio," in *Bernardino Telesio nel 4° Centenario della Morte*, 11–49. Naples: Istituto nazionale di studi sul Rinascimento meridionale.

Bakker, Paul J. M. M. 2007. "Natural Philosophy, Metaphysics, or Something in Between? Agostino Nifo, Pietro Pomponazzi, and Marcantonio Genua on the Nature and Place of the Science of the Soul," in *Mind, Cognition, and Representation: The Tradition of Commentaries on "De anima,"* edited by Paul J. J. M. Bakker and Johannes M. M. H. Thijssen, 151–77. Aldershot: Ashgate.

Bauer, Emmanuel J. 1996. *Thomistische Metaphysik an der alten Benediktineruniversität Salzburg. Darstellung und Interpretation einer philosophischen Schule des 17./18. Jahrhunderts*. Salzburger Theologische Studien 1. Innsbruck and Vienna: Tyrolia.

Bausi, Francesco. 1985. *I "Discorsi" di Niccolò Macchiavelli. Genesi e strutture*. Florence: Sansoni.

———. 1998. *Filosofia o eloquenza?* Naples: Liguori. [Letters of Giovanni Pico and Ermolao Barbaro.]

Baxandall, M. 1971. "Alberti and the Humanists," in *Giotto and the Orators: Humanist Observers of Painting in Italy and the Discovery of Pictorial Composition, 1350–1450*, 121–39. Oxford: Clarendon Press.

Bejczy, I. 2003. "Historia praestat omnibus disciplinis: Juan Luis Vives on History and Historical Study." *Renaissance Studies* 17: 69–83.

Bellito, Christopher M., Thomas M. Izbicki, and Gerald Christianson, eds. 2004. *Introducing Nicholas of Cusa: A Guide to a Renaissance Man*. New York and Mahwah, N.J.: Paulist Press.

Bernardinello, S. 1968. "I testi bessarionei della metafisica di Aristotele." *Rivista di studi bizantini e neoellenici* 5: 127–45.

Bertelli, Sergio, and Piero Innocenti. 1979. *Bibliografia Machiavelliana*. Verona: Edizioni Valdonega.

Besomi, Ottavio, and Mariangela Regoliosi, eds. 1986. *Lorenzo Valla e l'umanesimo italiano. Atti del Convegno internazionale di studi umanistici*. Padua: Antenore.

Bessarion. *Oratio dogmatica de unione*. 1958. Edited by Emmanuel Candal. Rome: Pontificium Institutum Orientalium Studiorum.

———. 1961. *De Spiritus Sancti processione ad Alexium Lascarin Philanthropinum. Graece et Latine*. Edited by Emmanuel Candal. Rome: Pontificium Institutum Orientalium Studiorum.

Bianca, C. 1983. "La formazione della biblioteca latina del Bessarione," in *Scrit-*

tura, biblioteche e stampa a Roma nel Quattrocento, 103–65. Vatican City: Scuola vaticana di paleografia, diplomatica, e archivistica.

Bianchi, L. 2003. "Pomponazzi politicamente corretto? La disuguaglianza fra gli
uomini nel *Tractatus de immortalitate animae,*" in *Studi sull'aristotelismo del
Rinascimento,* 63–99. Padua: Il Poligrafo.

Biondi, Albano. 1997."La doppia inchiesta sulle Conclusiones e le traversie ro-
mane del Pico nel 1487," in *Giovanni Pico della Mirandola.* Edited by Gian
Carlo Garfagnini, 197–212. Studi pichiani. Florence: Olschki.

Black, Crofton. 2006. *Pico's Heptaplus and Biblical Hermeneutics.* Leiden: Brill.

Blackwell, Constance, and Sachiko Kusukawa, eds. 1999. *Philosophy in the Sixteenth and Seventeenth Centuries: Conversations with Aristotle.* Aldershot: Ashgate.

Blanchet, Léon. 1963. *Campanella.* Paris: Alcan, 1920; reprint New York: Franklin.

Blum, Paul Richard. 1998. *Philosophenphilosophie und Schulphilosophie. Typen des
Philosophierens in der Neuzeit.* Stuttgart: Steiner.

———, ed. 1999. *Marsilio Ficino in Mitteleuropa.* Verbum—Analecta Neolatina,
Vol. 1, No. 1. Budapest.

———, ed. 1999. *Sapientiam amemus, Humanismus und Aristotelismus in der Renaissance.* Munich: Fink.

———. 2000. "Francesco Patrizi in the 'Time Sack': History and Rhetorical Philosophy." *Journal of the History of Ideas* 61: 59–74.

———. 2002. "'Saper trar il contrario dopo aver trovato il punto de l'unione':
Bruno, Cusano e il platonismo," in *Letture Bruniane I–II,* edited by Eugenio
Canone, 33–47. Pisa and Rome: IEPI.

———. 2004. *Philosophieren in der Renaissance.* Stuttgart: Kohlhammer.

———. 2007. "The Immortality of the Soul," in *The Cambridge Companion to
Renaissance Philosophy,* edited by James Hankins, 211–33. Cambridge: Cambridge University Press.

Bolzoni, L. 1980. *L'universo dei poemi possibili. Studi su Francesco Patrizi da Cherso.*
Rome: Bulzoni.

Bönker-Vallon, A. 1995. *Metaphysik und Mathematik bei Giordano Bruno.* Berlin:
Akademie.

Bonner, Anthony. 2007. *The Art and Logic of Ramon Llull: A User's Guide.* Leiden:
Brill.

Bori, Pier Cesare. 2000. *Pluralità delle vie. Alle origini del Discorso sula dignità uma-
na di Pico della Mirandola.* Milan: Feltrinelli.

Borsi, F. 2006. *Leon Battista Alberti: The Complete Works.* Translated by Rudolf
G. Carpanini. New York: Electa/Rizzoli.

Borsi, F., and S. Borsi. 1941. *Leon Battista Alberti. Une biographie intellectuelle.* Paris: Hazan.

Brickman, B. *An Introduction to Francesco Patrizi's Nova de universis philosophia.*
Ph.D. dissertation, Columbia University, New York.

Brooke, John Hedley, and Ian Maclean, eds. 2005. *Heterodoxy in Early Modern Science and Religion.* Oxford: Oxford University Press.

Bruniana & Campanelliana. Ricerche filosofiche e materiali storico-testuali. 1995– [From 1998 also a series of "Supplementi."]

Bruno, Giordano. 1958. *Dialoghi italiani: Dialoghi metafisici e dialoghi morali.* Edited by G. Gentile; 3rd ed. edited by G. Aquilecchia, Florence: Sansoni. [Abbreviated as BDI.]

———. 1961–1962. *Opera latine conscripta, publicis sumptibus edita, recensebat F. Fiorentino.* 3 vols. in 8 fascicles. Edited by F. Tocco, G. Vitelli, V. Imbriani, and C. M. Tallarigo. Naples and Florence, 1879–1891; reprint Stuttgart–Bad Canstatt: Frommann. [Abbreviated as BOL.]

———. 1964. *The Expulsion of the Triumphant Beast.* Translated by Arthur D. Imerti. New Brunswick, N.J.: Rutgers University Press.

———. 1965. *The Heroic Frenzies.* Translated by Paul Eugene Memmo. Chapel Hill: University of North Carolina Press.

———. 1975. *The Ash Wednesday Supper.* Translated by Stanley L. Jaki. The Hague: Mouton.

———. 1991. *De umbris idearum.* Edited by R. Sturlese. Florence: Olschki.

———. 1991. *On the Composition of Images, Signs, and Ideas.* Edited by Dick Higgins, translated by Charles Doria. New York: Willis, Locker, & Owens.

———. 1993. *Candelaio.* Edited by G. Aquilecchia. Paris: Les belles lettres. [*Oeuvres complètes 1*; French-Italian; abbreviated as Cand.]

———. 993ff. *Oeuvres complètes.* Edited by G. Aquilecchia. Paris: Les belles lettres. [French-Italian]

———. 1995. *The Ash Wednesday Supper = La Cena de le Ceneri.* Translated by Lawrence S. Lerner and Edward A. Gosselin. Toronto: University of Toronto Press.

———. 1998. *Cause, Principle, and Unity and Essays on Magic.* Translated by Robert de Lucca and Richard J. Blackwell. Cambridge: Cambridge University Press.

———. 2000. *Opere magiche.* Edited by Michele Ciliberto et al. Milan: Adephi.

———. 2002. *The Cabala of Pegasus.* Translated by Sidney L. Sondergard and Madison U. Sowell. New Haven, Conn.: Yale University Press.

———. 2007. *Centoventi articoli sulla natura e sull'universo contro i Peripatetici/ Centum et viginti articull de natura et mundo advesus Peripateticos.* Edited by Eugenio Canone. Pisa and Rome: Serra.

Bruyère, N. 1984. *Méthode et dialectique dans l'oeuvre de La Ramée: Renaissance et âge Classique.* Paris: Vrin.

Buck, August. 1985. *Machiavelli.* Darmstadt: Wissenschaftliche Buchgesellschaft.

Burckhardt, Jacob. 1958. *The Civilization of the Renaissance in Italy.* New York: Harper. [1st ed. 1860.]

Busi, Giulio, et al. 2004. *The Great Parchment: Flavius Mithridates' Latin Translation, the Hebrew Text, and an English Version.* Turin: Aragno.

Campanella, Tommaso. 1637. *De sensu rerum et magia* (1620), in *Opera Latina 1.* Paris: L. Boullenger, 1636; I. Du Braye.

———. 1637. *Disputationum in quatuor partes suae philosophiae realis libri quatuor.* Paris: D. Houssaye.

———. 1925. *Del senso delle cose e della magia*. Edited by A. Bruers. Bari: Laterza.

———. 1927. *Lettere*. Edited by Vincenzo Spampanato. Bari: Laterza.

———. 1939. *Epilogo magno*. Edited by Carmelo Ottaviano. Rome: R. Accademia d'Italia.

———. 1954. *Tutte le opere di Tommaso Campanella, Vol. 1: Scritti letterari*. Edited by Luigi Firpo. Milan: Mondadori. [The only volume published.]

———. 1961. *Metaphysica*. Paris [: D. Langlois], 1638; anastatic reprint by Luigi Firpo, Turin: Bottega d'Erasmo.

———. 1975. *Opera latina Francofurti impressa annis 1617–1630*, anastatic reprint by Luigi Firpo, Turin: Bottega d'Erasmo. 2 vols. 1: *Prodromus philosophiae instaurandae, De sensu rerum et magia, Apologia pro Galileo;* 2: *Realis philosophiae epilogisticae partes IV, Astrologicorum libri VII*.

———. 1981. *La città del sole: Dialogo poetico = The City of the Sun: A Poetical Dialogue*. Biblioteca italiana. Translated by Daniel John Donno. Berkeley and Los Angeles: University of California Press.

———. 1992. *Philosophia sensibus demonstrata*. Edited by Luigi De Franco. Naples: Vivarium.

———. 1994. *Apologia pro Galileo/A Defense of Galileo*. Edited by Richard J. Blackwell. Notre Dame and London: University of Notre Dame Press.

———. 1997. *La città del Sole*. Edited by Luigi Firpo; new edition by Germana Ernst and Laura Salvetti Firpo, Rome and Bari: Laterza.

———. 1997. *Monarchie d'Espagne et Monarchie de France*. Edited by Germana Ernst; French translation by Serge Waldbaum and Nathalie Fabry. Paris: Presses universitaires de France.

———. 1998. *Le poesie*. Edited by Francesco Giancotti. Turin: Einaudi.

———. 2001. *Apologia pro Galileo/Apologie pour Galilée*. Edited by Michel-Pierre Lerner. Paris: Les belles lettres.

———. 2002. *Monarchie du Messie*. Edited by Paolo Ponzio, French translation by Véronique Bourdette. Paris: Presses universitaires de France.

———. 2003. *Opusculi astrologici. Come evitare il fato astrale, Apologetico, Disputa sulle Bolle*. Edited by Germana Ernst. Milan: Rizzoli.

———. 2004. *Ateismo trionfato*. Edited by Germana Ernst. Pisa: Edizioni della Normale.

———. 2004. *La Città del Sole/The City of the Sun*. Edited by Daniel J. Donno. Berkeley, Los Angeles, and London: Kessinger Publishing. [1st ed. 1981.]

———. 2007. *Syntagma de libris propriis et recta ratione studendi*. Edited with translation by Germana Ernst. Pisa and Rome: Febrizio Serra.

———. 2007. *Del senso delle cose e della magia*. Edited by Germana Ernst. Bari: Laterza.

Campanini, Saverio, and Giulio Busi, eds. 2005. *The Book of Bahir: Flavius Mithradites' Latin Translation, the Hebrew Text, and an English Version*. Turin: Aragno.

Camporeale, Salvatore I. 1973. *Lorenzo Valla: Umanesimo e teologia*. Florence: Istituto nazionale di studi sui Rinascimento.

———. 2002. *Lorenzo Valla: Umanesimo, Riforma e Controriforma*. Rome: Edizioni di storia e letteratura.

Canning, Joseph. 1996. *A History of Medieval Political Thought: 300–1450*. London: Routledge.

Canone, Eugenio, ed. 1992. *Giordano Bruno. Gli anni napoletani e la "peregrinatio" europea*. Cassino: Università degli studi. [Abbreviated as Pereg.]

———, ed. 1998. *Brunus redivivus. Momenti della fortuna di Giordano Bruno nel XIX secolo*. Pisa and Rome: IEPI.

———. 2003. *Il dorso e il grembo dell'eterno. Percorsi della filosofia di Giordano Bruno*. Pisa and Rome: IEPI.

Canone, Eugenio, and Leen Spruit. 2007. "Rhetoric and Philosophical Discourse in Giordano Bruno's Italian Dialogues." *Poetics Today* 28, no. 3: 363–91.

Capelli, A. 1998. *Cronologia, cronografia e calendario perpetuo dal principio dell'èra cristiana ai nostri giorni*. 6th rev. ed. Milan: Hoepli.

Caroti, S. 1999. "Pomponazzi e la 'reactio': Note sulla fortuna del pensiero oxoniense e parigino nella filosofia italiana del Rinascimento," in *Filosofia e scienza classica, arabo-latina medievale e l'età moderna*, Ciclo di seminari internazionali, . . . 1996, edited by G. Federici Vescovini, 255–88. Louvain-la-Neuve: Fédération internationale des instituts d'études médievales.

Casarella, Peter J., ed. 2006. *Cusanus: The Legacy of Learned Ignorance*. Washington, D.C.: The Catholic University of America Press.

Casini, Lorenzo. 2006. *Cognitive and Moral Psychology in Renaissance Philosophy: A Study of Juan Luis Vives' "De anima et vita."* Ph.D. dissertation, Uppsala University Universitetstryckeriet, Uppsala.

———. 2006. "Juan Luis Vives' Conception of the Freedom of the Will and Its Scholastic Background." *Vivarium* 44: 396–417.

———. 2007. "The Renaissance Debate on the Immortality of the Soul: Pietro Pompanazzi and the Plurality of Substantial Forms," in *Mind, Cognition, and Representation: The Tradition of Commentaries on Aristotle's "De anima,"* edited by P. J. J. M. Bakker and Johannes M. H. Thijssen, 127–50. Aldershot: Ashgate.

Cassirer, Ernst. 1995. *Das Erkenntnisproblem in der Philosophie und Wissenschaft der neueren Zeit*. Vol. 1. Darmstadt: Wissenschafliche Buchgesellschaft. [Reprint of the 3rd ed. 1922.]

———. 2000. *The Individual and the Cosmos in Renaissance Philosophy*. New York: Harper & Row, 1964; reprint Mineola, N.Y.: Dover Publications. [1st ed. 1927.]

Cassirer, Ernst, Paul Oskar Kristeller, and John Herman Randall, eds. 1948. *The Renaissance Philosophy of Man: Selections in Translation*. Chicago: University of Chicago Press.

Cassuto, U. 1918. *Gli Ebrei a Firenze nell'età del Rinascimento*. Florence: Galletti e Cocci.

Céard, J. 1981. "Matérialisme et théorie de l'âme dans la pensée padouane: Le 'Traité de l'immortalité de l'âme de Pomponazzi.'" *Revue philosophique* 106: 25–48.

Celenza, Christopher S. 2004. *The Lost Italian Renaissance: Humanists, Historians, and Latin's Legacy*. Baltimore: Johns Hopkins University Press.

Chastel, André. 1975. *Marsile Ficin et l'art*. Geneva: Droz.

Chomarat, J. 1997. "Faut-il donner un sens philosophique au mot humanisme?" *Renaissance and Reformation* 21: 51–54.

Ciliberto, M. 1996. *Introduzione a Bruno*. Rome and Bari: Laterza.

Ciliberto, M., and N. Mann, eds. 1997. *Giordano Bruno, 1583–1585: The English Experience/L'esperienza inglese*. Florence: Olschki.

Constant, Eric A. 2002. "A Reinterpretation of the Fifth Lateran Concil Decree 'Apostolici regiminis' (1513)." *Sixteenth Century Journal* 33: 353–79.

Copenhaver, Brian P. 1999. "Number, Shape, and Meaning in Pico's Christian Cabala: The Upright Tsade, the Closed Mem, and the Gaping Jaws of Azazel," in *Natural Particulars: Nature and the Disciplines in Renaissance Europe,* edited by Anthony Grafton and Nancy Sirasi, 25–76. Cambridge, Mass.: MIT Press.

———. 2002. "The Secret of Pico's Oration: Cabala and Renaissance Philosophy," in *Renaissance and Early Modern Philosophy,* Midwest Studies in Philosophy 26, edited by Peter A. French, Howard K. Wettstein, and Bruce S. Silver, 56–81. Malden, Mass.: Blackwell.

Copenhaver, Brian P., and Charles B. Schmitt. 1992. *Renaissance Philosophy.* Oxford: Oxford University Press.

Couliano, Ioan P. [Ioan P. Culianu]. 1987. *Eros and Magic in the Renaissance*. Chicago: University of Chicago Press.

Courtine, Jean-François. "Le principe d'individuation chez Suárez et chez Leibniz." 1983. *Studia Leibnitiana,* Suppl. 23: 174–90.

———. *Suárez et le système de la métaphysique*. 1990. Paris: Presses universaires de France.

Craig, William Lane. 1988. *The Problem of Divine Foreknowledge and Future Contingents from Aristotle to Suárez*. Leiden, New York, and Copenhagen: Brill.

Craven, William G. 1981. *Giovanni Pico della Mirandola: Symbol of His Age.* Geneva: Droz.

Cruselles Gómez, José María, ed. 1993. *Un Valenciano universal: Joan Lluis Vives.* Valencia: Ajuntament de València.

Cusanus, Nicolaus. 1962. *Opera.* 3 vols. Edited by Jacques Lefèvre d'Étaples. Paris: Typ. Ascensianis, 1514; reprint Frankfurt: Minerva.

———. 1967. *Opera.* Strasbourg, 1488; reprint, 2 vols., edited by Paul Wilpert, Berlin: de Gruyter.

———. 1991. *The Catholic Concordance.* Translated by Paul E. Sigmund. Cambridge: Cambridge University Press.

———. 1993. *Toward a New Council of Florence: "On the Piece of Faith" and Other Works.* Translated by William F. Wertz. Washington, D.C.: Schiller Institute.

———. 1997. *Selected Spiritual Writings.* Translated by H. Lawrence Bond. New York: Paulist Press.

———. 2001. *Complete Philosophical and Theological Treatises of Nicholas of Cusa.* 2 vols. Translated by Jasper Hopkins. Minneapolis: Banning Press. [Available online at http://cla.umn.edu/sites/jhopkins.]

———. 1932–2007. *Nicolai de Cusa Opera omnia. Iussu et auctoritate Academiae Litterarum Heidelbergensis ad codicum fidem edita.* 20 vols. Leipzig and Hamburg: Meiner.

Cuttini, E. 2005. *Unità e pluralità nella tradizione europea della filosofia: Girolamo*

Savonarola, Pietro Pomponazzi e Filippo Melantone. Soveria Mannelli: Rubbettino.

Darge, Rolf. 2004. *Suárez' transzendentale Seinsauslegung und die Metaphysiktradition*. Studien und Texte zur Geistesgeschichte des Mittelalters 80. Leiden and Boston: Brill.

De Franco, Luigi. 1989. *Bernardino Telesio: La vita e l'opera*. Cosenza: Edizioni Periferia.

De Grazia, Sebastian. 1994. *Machiavelli in Hell*. New York and London: Harvester Wheatsheaf.

De Léon-Jones, K. S. 1997. *Giordano Bruno and the Kabbalah: Prophets, Magicians, and Rabbis*. New Haven, Conn., and London: Yale University Press.

Delumeau, Jean. 2008. *Le mystère Campanella*. Paris: Fayard.

De Pace, Anna. 2002. *La scepsi, il sapere, l'anima. Dissonanze nella cerchia laurenziana*. Milan: LED.

Di Liscia, Daniel A., Eckhard Kessler, and Charlotte Methuen, eds. 1997. *Method and Order in Renaissance Philosophy of Nature: The Aristotle Commentary Tradition*. Aldershot: Ashgate.

Di Napoli, Giovanni. 1963. *L'immortalità dell'anima nel Rinascimento*. Turin: SEI.

———. 1970. "Libertà e fato in Pietro Pomponazzi." In *Studi in onore di Antonio Corsano*, 175–220. Manduria: Lacaita.

———. 1971. *Lorenzo Valla: Filosofia e religione nell'umanesimo italiano*. Rome: Edizioni di storia e litteratura.

Domínguez Reboiras, Fernando, Pere Villalba i Varneda, and Peter Walter. 2002. *Arbor scientiae, der Baum des Wissens von Ramon Lull: Akten des Internationalen Kongresses aus Anlass des 40-jährigen Jubiläums des Raimundus-Lullus-Instituts der Universität Freiburg i. Br.* Turnhout: Brepols.

Doni, M. 1975. "Il *De incantationibus* di Pietro Pomponazzi e l'edizione di Guglielmo Grataroli." *Rinascimento*, 2nd ser., 15: 183–230.

Dorez, L., and L. Thuasne. 1967. *P. de la Mirandole en France (1485–1488)*. Paris: Leroux, 1897; reprint Geneva: Droz.

Dougherty, M. V., ed. 2008. *Pico della Mirandola: New Essays*. Cambridge: Cambridge University Press.

Douglas, A. H. 1910. *The Philosophy and Psychology of Pietro Pomponazzi*. Cambridge: Cambridge University Press.

Doyle, John. 2004. "Francisco Suárez on The Law of Nations," in *Religion and International Law*, edited by Mark W. Janis, 103–20. Leiden: Nijhoff.

Ebbersmeyer, Sabrina, and others, eds. 2003. *Sol et homo: Mensch und Natur in der Renaissance*. Paderborn: Fink.

Eberl, J. T. 2005. "Pomponazzi and Aquinas on the Intellective Soul." *The Modern Schoolman* 83: 65–77.

Edelheit, Amos. 2008. *Ficino, Pico, and Savonarola: The Evolution of Humanist Theology, 1461/2–1498*. Leiden and Boston: Brill.

Edwards, William. 1960. *The Logic of Iacopo Zabarella (1533–1589)*. Ph.D. dissertation, Columbia University, New York.

Enciclopedia Bruniana & Campanelliana. 2006. Edited by Eugenio Canone and Germana Ernst. Pisa and Rome: Istituti Editoriali e Poligrafici Internazionali. [A collection of articles on the major philosophical concepts of Giordano Bruno (sixteen articles) and Tommaso Campanella (sixteen articles).]

Ernst, Germana. 1991. *Religione, ragione e natura. Ricerche su Tommaso Campanella e il tardo Rinascimento.* Milan: Franco Angeli.

———. 2002. *Il carcere, il politico, il profeta. Saggi su Tommaso Campanella.* Pisa and Rome: Istituti Editoriali e Poligrafici Internazionali.

———. 2002. *Tommaso Campanella. Il libro e il corpo della natura.* Bari and Rome: Laterza. [This monograph reconstructs the principal stages of Campanella's intellectual history. English edition: Dordrecht, 2009.]

———. "Campanella," in *Stanford Encyclopedia of Philosophy,* available online at http://plato.stanford.edu/entries/campanella.

Fachard, Denis. 1996. "Implicazioni politiche nell'Arte della guerra," in *Niccolò Machiavelli. Politico storico letterato. Atti del Convegno di Losanna 27–30 settembre 1995,* edited by Jean-Jacques Marchand, 149–73. Rome: Salerno.

Farmer, S. A. 1998. *Syncretism in the West: Pico's 900 Theses (1486): The Evolution of Traditional Religious and Philosophical Systems: With Text, Translation, and Commentary.* Tempe: MRTS.

Farndell, Arthur. 2006. *Gardens of Philosophy: Ficino on Plato.* London: Shepheard-Walwyn.

Feingold, M. 2001. "English Ramism: A Reinterpretation," in *The Influence of Petrus Ramus: Studies in Sixteenth and Seventeenth Century Philosophy and Science,* edited by M. Feingold, J. S. Freedman, and W. Rother, 127–76. Basel: Schwabe.

Feingold, M., J. S. Freedman, and W. Rother, eds. 2001. *The Influence of Petrus Ramus: Studies in Sixteenth and Seventeenth Century Philosophy and Science.* Basel: Schwabe.

Fernandes, João Manuel Azevedo Alexandrino. 2005. *Die Theorie der Interpretation des Gesetzes bei Francisco Suárez.* Rechtshistorische Reihe 303. Frankfurt: Peter Lang.

Fernandez-Santamaria, J. A. 1990. *Juan Luis Vives: Escepticismo e prudentia en el rinascimento.* Salamanca: Ediciones Universidad de Salamanca.

Ferri, L. 1876. *La psicologia di Pietro Pomponazzi secondo un manoscritto inedito dell'Angelica di Roma.* Rome: Salviucci.

Fetz, R. L. 1995. "Montaigne: Selbsterfahrung und Identität," in *Das 16. Jahrhundert. Europäische Renaissance,* edited by H. Kuester, 53–75. Regensburg: Pustet.

———. 1998. "Das Tun des Eigenen. Lebenskunst und Selbstidentität bei Michel de Montaigne," in *Die Renaissance und die Entdeckung des Individuums in der Kunst,* Die Renaissance als erste Aufklärung II, edited by E. Rudolph, 167–212. Tübingen: Mohr Siebeck.

Ficino, Marsilio. 1964, 1965, 1970. *Théologie platonicienne de l'immortalité des âmes.* 3 vols. Edited and translated by R. Marcel. Paris: Les belles lettres. [Latin-French; abbreviated as *Platonic Theology.*]

———. 1975. *The Philebus Commentary.* Edited by Michael J. B. Allen. Berkeley and Los Angeles: University of California Press. [Latin-English.]

———. 1975– *The Letters of Marsilio Ficino.* 7 vols. so far. Translated by members of the Language Department of the School of Economic Science, London. London: Shepheard-Walwyn.

———. 1983. *Opera omnia.* Basle, 1576; reprint Turin: Bottega d'Erasmo (also Paris: Phénix, 2000). [Abbreviated as Op.]

———. 1985. *Commentary on Plato's "Symposium on Love."* Edited by Sears Reynolds Jayne. Dallas: Spring Publications.

———. 1988. *Lettere.* Vol. 1. Edited by S. Gentile. Florence.

———. 1989. *Three Books on Life.* Edited and translated by C. Kaske and J. R. Clark. Binghamton: MRTS.

———. 2001–2006. *Platonic Theology.* 6 vols. Edited by James Hankins et al. Cambridge, Mass.: Harvard University Press.

Firpo, Luigi. 1940. *Bibliografia degli scritti di Tommaso Campanella.* Turin: V. Bona.

———. 1947. *Ricerche campanelliane.* Florence: Sansoni.

———. 1974. "Campanella, Tommaso," in *Dizionario biografico degli Italiani,* 17:372–400. Rome: Istituto dell'Enciclopedia italiana.

———. 1993. *Il processo di Giordano Bruno.* Edited by D. Quaglioni. Rome: Salerno. [Abbreviated as Proc.]

———. 1998. *I processi di Tommaso Campanella.* Edited by Eugenio Canone. Rome: Salerno.

Fois, Mario. 1969. *Il pensiero cristiano di Lorenzo Valla nel quadro storico-culturale del suo ambiente.* Rome: Liberia editrice dell'Università Gregoriani.

Fornaciari, Paolo Edoardo. 1992. *Parafrasi della "Repubblica" nella traduzione latina di Elia del Medigo.* Florence: Olschki.

Frame, D. M. 1965. *Montaigne: A Biography.* New York: Harcourt, Brace, & World.

Francisco Suárez, "Der ist der Mann." 2004. Apéndice Francisco Suárez *De generatione et corruptione.* Homenaje al Prof. Salvador Castellote (Facultad de Teología San Vicente Ferrer/Series valentina 50), Valencia: Facultad de Teología San Vicente Ferrer. Cf. http://www.salvadorcastellote.com/investigacion.htm [text of *De generatione*].

Frank, Günter. 1995. *Die theologische Philosophie Philipp Melanchthons (1497–1560).* Leipzig: Benno.

Freedman, J. S. 1993. "The Diffusion of the Writings of Petrus Ramus in Central Europe c. 1570–c. 1630." *Renaissance Quarterly* 46, no. 1: 98–152.

Freigius, Johannes. 1583. *Mosaicus, continens historiam ecclesiasticam* .... Basel: Henricpetri.

French, Peter A., Howard K. Wettstein, and Bruce S. Silver, eds. 2002. *Renaissance and Early Modern Philosophy.* Midwest Studies in Philosophy 26. Malden, Mass.: Blackwell.

Friedrich, H. 1967. *Montaigne.* 2nd rev. ed. Berne: Francke. [1st ed. 1949.]

Gadol, J. B. 1969. *Leon Battista Alberti: Universal Man in the Early Renaissance.* Chicago: University of Chicago Press.

Galimberti, A. 1983. "Intelletto e libertà nell'ultimo Pomponazzi (alle radici del naturalismo rinascimentale)," in *Aristotelismo veneto e scienza moderna,* 2 vols., edited by L. Olivieri, 2.685–94. Padua: Antenore.

Gandillac, Maurice de. 1942. *La philosophie de Nicolas de Cues.* Paris: Aubier.

Ganoczy, A. 1966. *Le jeune Calvin*. Wiesbaden: Steiner.

Garfagnini, Gian Carlo, ed. 1984. *Marsilio Ficino e il ritorno di Platone. Studi e documenti*. 2 vols. Florence: Olschki.

————, ed. 1997. *Giovanni Pico della Mirandola: Convegno internazionale di studi nel cinquecentesimo anniversario della morte (1494–1994): Mirandola, 4–8 ottobre 1994*. Studi pichiani. Florence: Olschki.

Garin, Eugenio. 1937. *Giovanni Pico della Mirandola. Vita e dottrina*. Florence: Sansoni.

————, ed. 1952. *Prosatori latini del Quattrocento*. Milan and Naples: Ricciardi.

————. 1955. "Ricerche sulle Traduzioni di Platone nella prima metà del sec. XV." *Medioevo e Rinascimento* 1 (Florence): 339–74.

————. 1961. *La cultura filosofica del Rinascimento italiano*. Florence: Sansoni.

————. 1963. *Giovanni Pico della Mirandola*. Parma: Comitato per le celebrazioni centenarie in onore di Giovanni Pico.

————. 1964–1967. *Geschichte und Dokumente der abendländischen Pädagogik*. 3 vols. Reinbek: Rowohlt. [Texts in Latin and German.]

————. 1973. "Il Platonismo come ideologia della sovversione europea. La polemica antiplatonica di Giorgio Trapezunzio," in *Studia Humanitatis* (Festschrift für Ernesto Grassi zum 70. Geburtstag), edited by Eginhard Hora and Eckhard Kessler, 113–20. Munich: Fink.

————. 1975. *Italian Humanism: Philosophy and Civic Life in the Renaissance*. Translated by Peter Munz. Westport, Conn.: Greenwood Press.

————. 1975. "Studi su Leon Battista Alberti," in *Rinascite e rivoluzioni*. Rome and Bari.

————, ed. 1997. *Renaissance Characters*. Translated by Lydia G. Cochrane. Chicago: University of Chicago Press.

————. 2008. *History of Italian Philosophy*. 2 vols. Translated by Giorgio A. Pinton. Amsterdam: Rodopi. [1st ed. 1945.]

Gatti, Hilary. 1999. *Giordano Bruno and Renaissance Science*. Ithaca, N.Y.: Cornell University Press.

————, ed. 2002. *Giordano Bruno: Philosopher of the Renaissance*. Aldershot: Ashgate.

Gayà, J. 1979. *La teoría luliana de los correlativos*. Palma de Mallorca: L. C. San Buenaventura.

Geffen, David. 1973–1974. "Insights into the Life and Thought of Elijah Medigo Based on His Published and Unpublished Works." *Proceedings of the American Academy for Jewish Research* 41: 69–86.

Gentile, Sebastiano, Sandra Niccoli, and Paolo Viti, eds. 1984. *Marsilio Ficino e il ritorno di Platone: Mostra di manoscritti stampe e documenti 17 maggio–16 giugno 1984: Catalogo*. Florence: Le Lettere.

Gentile, Sebastiano, and Stéphane Toussaint, eds. 2006. *Marsilio Ficino: Fonti, testi, fortuna: Atti del convegno internazionale (Firenze, 1–3 ottobre 1999)*. Rome: Edizioni di storia e letteratura.

Georgius Trapezuntius. 1965. *Comparationes philosophorum Aristotelis et Platonis*. Venice, 1523; reprint Frankfurt: Minerva.

Giachetti Assenza, V. 1980. "Bernardino Telesio: Il Migliore dei Moderni. I Riferimenti a Telesio negli Scritti di Bacone." *Rivista Critica di Storia della Filosofia* 35: 41–78.

Giacon, C. 1960. "L'aristotelismo avicennistico di Gasparo Contarini," in *Atti del XII Congresso Internazionale di Filosofia, Vol. 9: Aristotelismo padovano e filosofia aristotelica*, 109–19. Florence: Sansoni.

Gilson, Étienne. 1961. "Autour de Pomponazzi: Problématique de l'immortalité de l'âme en Italie au début du XVIᵉ siècle." *Archives d'histoire doctrinale et littéraire du moyen âge* 28: 163–79.

———. 1962. *Being and Some Philosophers*. 2nd ed. Toronto: Pontifical Institute of Medieval Studies.

Giordano Bruno: 1548–1600: Mostra storico documentaria. Florence: Olschki.

Giovio, Paolo. 1972. *Gli elogi degli uomini illustri (letterati, artisti, uomini d'arme)*. Edited by R. Meregazzi. Rome: Istituto poligrafico dello Stato, Libreria dello Stato.

Gonzalez, Enrique. 1987. *Joan Lluis Vives*. Valencia: Generalitat Valenciana.

Goudriaan, Aza. 1999. *Philosophische Gotteserkenntnis bei Suárez und Descartes im Zusammenhang mit der niederländischen reformierten Theologie und Philosophie des 17. Jahrhunderts*. Brill's Studies in Intellectual History 98. Leiden and Boston: Brill.

Grabmann, Martin. 1926. "Die Disputationes metaphysicae des Franz Suárez in ihrer methodischen Eigenart und Fortwirkung." *Mittelalterliches Geistesleben. Abhandlungen zur Geschichte der Scholastik und Mystik* 1 (Munich): 525–60.

Gracia, Jorge. 1998. "Suárez (and Later Scholasticism)," in *Routledge History of Philosophy, Vol. 3: Medieval Philosophy*, edited by John Marenbon, 452–74. London and New York: Routledge.

Grafton, A. 2000. *Leon Battista Alberti: Master Builder of the Italian Renaissance*. Cambridge, Mass.: Harvard University Press.

Graiff, F. 1976. "I prodigi e l'astrologia nei commenti di Pietro Pomponazzi al *De caelo*, alla *Meteora*, e al *De generatione*." *Medioevo* 2: 331–61.

———. 1979. "Aspetti del pensiero di Pietro Pomponazzi nelle opere e nei corsi del periodo bolognese," *Annali dell'Istituto di Filosofia* [Università di Firenze] 1: 69–130.

Granada, Miguel A. 1988. *Cosmología, religión y política en el Renacimiento: Ficino, Savonarola, Pomponazzi, Maquiavelo*. Barcelona: Anthropos Editorial del Hombre.

Gray, Hanna H. 1965. "Valla's Encomium of St. Thomas Aquinas and the Humanist Conception of Christian Antiquity," in *Essays in History and Literature, Presented by Fellows of The Newberry Library to Stanley Pargellis*, edited by Heinz Bluhm, 37–51. Chicago: Newbury Library.

Gregory, Tullio. 1953. "L'Apologia ad censuram di Francesco Patrizi." *Rinascimento* 4: 89–104.

Guerlac, Rita. 1979. *Against the Pseudodialecticians: A Humanist Attack on Medieval Logic*. Dordrecht and Boston: Reidel.

Hadot, Pierre. 1995. *Philosophy as a Way of Life: Spiritual Exercises from Socrates to Foucault*. Malden, Mass.: Blackwell.

Hankins, James. 1990. "Cosimo de' Medici and the 'Platonic Academy.'" *Journal of the Warburg and Courtauld Institutes* 53: 144–62.

———. 1991. "The Myth of the Platonic Academy of Florence." *Renaissance Quarterly* 44: 429–75.

———. 1991. *Plato in the Italian Renaissance.* 2 vols. Leiden: Brill.

———. 1994. *Plato in the Italian Renaissance.* 3rd ed. Leiden: Brill.

———. 2003–2004. *Humanism and Platonism in the Italian Renaissance.* 2 vols. Rome: Edizioni di storia e letteratura.

———, ed. 2007. *The Cambridge Companion to Renaissance Philosophy.* Cambridge: Cambridge University Press.

———. 2007. "The Platonic Academy of Florence and Renaissance Historiography," in *Forme del neoplatonismo. Dall'eredità ficiniana ai platonici di Cambridge,* edited by Luisa Simonuti. Florence: Olschki.

Hartfelder, Karl. 1889. *Philipp Melanchthon als Praeceptor Germaniae.* Berlin.

Headley, John M. 1997. *Tommaso Campanella and the Transformation of the World.* Princeton, N.J.: Princeton University Press.

Heipcke, K., W. Neuser, and E. Wicke, eds. 1991. *Die Frankfurter Schriften Giordano Brunos und ihre Voraussetzungen.* Weinheim: VCH and Acta Humaniora.

Henry, P. 1979. "F. Patrizi da Cherso's Concept of Space and Its Later Influence." *Annals of Science* 36: 549–75.

Hillgarth, J. N. 1971. *Ramon Lull and Lullism in Fourteenth-Century France.* Oxford: Clarendon Press.

Höltgen, K. J. 1965. "Synoptische Tabellen in der Medizinischen Literatur und Die Logik Agricolas und Ramus." *Suddhofs Archiv* 49: 371–90.

Honnefelder, Ludger. 1990. *Scientia transcendens. Die formale Bestimmung der Seiendheit und Realität in der Metaphysik des Mittelalters und der Neuzeit (Duns Scotus—Suárez—Wolff—Kant—Pierce).* Hamburg: Meiner.

Hooykas, R. 1958. *Humanisme, Science et Réforme. Pierre De La Ramée (1515–72).* Leiden: Brill.

Hoppe, Gerhard. 1901. *Die Psychologie des J. L. Vives.* Berlin: Mayer und Müller.

Huarte, Juan. 1594. *Examen de ingenios. The examination of mens wits. In which, by discouering the varietie of natures, is shewed for what profesion each one is apt, and how far he shall profit therein. Translated out of the Spanish tongue by M. Camillo Camilli. Englished out of his Italian by R. C. Esquire.* London: C. Hunt.

Idel, Moshe. 1992. "The Magical and Neoplatonic Interpretations of the Kabbalah in the Renaissance," in *Essential Papers on Jewish Culture in Renaissance and Baroque Italy,* edited by D. B. Rudermann, 107–69. New York: Columbia University Press.

———. 2000. "'Book of God' and 'Book of Law' in Late XVth Century Florence." *Accademia* 2: 5–17.

Innocenti, C. 1995–1996. "Una fonte neoplatonica nel *De incantationibus* di Pietro Pomponazzi: Marsilio Ficino." *Interpres* 15: 439–71.

———. 1997. "Il fondamento astrologico della realtà nel *De incantationibus* e nel *De fato* di Pietro Pomponazzi." *Nouvelles de la République des Lettres,* 49–77.

Iorio, D. A. 1991. *The Aristotelians of Renaissance Italy: A Philosophical Exposition.* Lewiston: Mellen.

Jadin, I. 1986–1987. "Pomponace mythique: La sincerité religieuse de Pietro Pomponazzi dans le miroir de sa réputation française." *Tijdschrift voor de studie van de verlichting en van het vrije denken* 14–15: 7–101.

Jardine, Nicholas. "Keeping Order in the School of Padua," in *Method and Order in Renaissance Philosophy of Nature: The Aristotelian Commentary Tradition,* edited by E. Kessler, D. di Liscia, and C. Methuen, 183–209. Aldershot: Ashgate.

Jardine, Nicholas, and A. Segonds. 2001. "A Challenge to the Reader: Ramus on *Astrologia* without Hypothesis." In *The Influence of Petrus Ramus: Studies in Sixteenth and Seventeenth Century Philosophy and Science,* edited by M. Feingold, J. S. Freedman, and W. Rother, 248–66. Basel: Schwabe.

Jarzombek, Mark. 1989. *On Leon Battista Alberti: His Literary and Aesthetic Theories.* Cambridge, Mass., and London: MIT Press.

Kahn, Victoria. 1985. *Rhetoric, Prudence and Skepticism in the Renaissance.* Ithaca, N.Y.: Cornell University Press

Kallendorf, Craig W., ed. 2002. *Humanist Educational Treatises.* Cambridge: Cambridge University Press.

Karamanolis, George. 2002. "Plethon and Scholarios on Aristotle," in *Byzantine Philosophy and Its Ancient Sources,* edited by Katerina Ierodiakonou, 253–82. Oxford: Clarendon Press.

Keefer, Michael H. 1988. "Agrippa's Dilemma: Hermetic 'Rebirth' and the Ambivalences of *De vanitate* and *De occulta philosophia.*" *Renaissance Quarterly* 41: 614–53.

Kessler, Eckhard. 1988. "The Intellective Soul." In *The Cambridge History of Renaissance Philosophy,* edited by C. B. Schmitt et al., 485–534. Cambridge: Cambridge University Press.

———. 1987. "Von der Psychologie zur Methodenlehre. Die Entwicklung des methodischen Wahrheitsbegriffes in der Renaissancepsychologie." *Zeitschrift für philosophische Forschung* 41: 548–70.

———. 1992. "Selbstorganisation in der Naturphilosophie der Renaissance." *Selbstorganisation. Jahrbuch für Komplexität in den Natur, Sozial- und Geisteswissenschaften* 3: 15–29.

———. 1993. "Pietro Pomponazzi: Zur Einheit seines philosophischen Lebenswerkes," in *Verum et Factum: Beiträge zur Geistesgeschichte und Philosophie der Renaissance zum 60. Geburtstag von Stephan Otto,* edited by T. Albertini, 397–419. Frankfurt and New York: Peter Lang.

———. 2008. "Von Alexanders Seelenlehre zur neuen Naturphilosophie: Pietro Pomponazzi," in Alexander of Aphrodisias, *Enarratio de anima ex Arostotelis institutione,* introduction by Eckhard Kessler, lxii–lxxi. Stuttgart–Bad Cannstatt: Frommann-Holzboog.

Kessler, Eckhard, and Ian Maclean, eds. 2002. *Res et Verba in der Renaissance.* Wiesbaden: Harrassowitz.

Kingdon, R. M. 1967. *Geneva and the Consolidation of the French Movement, 1564–1572.* Geneva: Droz.

Kircher, Timothy. 2006. *The Poet's Wisdom: The Humanists, the Church, and the Formation of Philosophy in the Early Renaissance.* Leiden: Brill.

Klibansky, R. 1943. "Plato's Parmenides in the Middle Ages and the Renaissance." London: Warburg Institute.

Kraye, Jill, ed. 1996. *The Cambridge Companion to Renaissance Humanism*. Cambridge Companions to Literature. Cambridge: Cambridge University Press.

——, ed. 1997. *Cambridge Translations of Renaissance Philosophical Texts*. 2 vols. Vol. 1. *Moral Philosophy*; Vol. 2, *Political Philosophy*. Cambridge: Cambridge University Press.

——. 2000. "The Immortality of the Soul in the Renaissance: Between Natural Philosophy and Theology." *Signatures* 30: 51–68.

——. 2002. *Classical Traditions in Renaissance Philosophy*. Aldershot: Ashgate.

Kraye, Jill, and M. W. F. Stone, eds. 2000. *Humanism and Early Modern Philosophy*. London: Routledge.

Kremer, Klaus, and Klaus Reinhard, eds. 2005. *Die Sermones des Nikolaus von Kues. Merkmale und ihre Stellung innerhalb der mittelalterlichen Predigtkultur. Akten des Symposions in Trier vom 21. bis 23. Oktober 2004*, edited by Paulinus Trier (MFCG 30).

Kretzmann, Norman, et al., eds. 1982. *The Cambridge History of Later Medieval Philosophy: From the Rediscovery of Aristotle to the Disintegration of Scholasticism, 1100–1600*. Cambridge: Cambridge University Press.

Kristeller, Paul Oskar. 1955. "Two Unpublished Questions on the Soul of Pietro Pomponazzi." *Medievalia et Humanistica* 8: 76–101.

——. 1956. "Ficino and Pomponazzi on the Place of Man in the Universe," in his *Studies in Renaissance Thought and Letters*, 1.279–86. Rome.

——. 1963. "Giovanni Pico della Mirandola and His Sources." In *L'Opera e il Pensiero di Giovanni Pico della Mirandola nella storia dell'umanesimo*, 1.85–107. Florence: Istituto nazionale di studi sul Rinascimento.

——. 1964. *Eight Philosophers of the Italian Renaissance*. Stanford, Calif.: Stanford University Press.

——. 1964. *The Philosophy of Marsilio Ficino*. Gloucester, Mass: Peter Smith.

——. 1967. *Le thomisme et la pensée italienne de la Renaissance*. Montreal and Paris: Institute d'Études Médiévales and Vrin.

——. 1968. "The Myth of Renaissance Atheism and the French Tradition of Free Thought." *Journal of the History of Philosophy* 6: 233–43.

——. 1970. "Francesco Patrizi da Cherso: Emendatio in libros suos novae philosophiae." *Rinascimento* 10: 215–18.

——. 1972. "Byzantine and Western Platonism in the Fifteenth Century," in his *Renaissance Concepts of Man and Other Essays*, 86–109. New York: Harper & Row.

——. 1973. *Supplementum Ficinianum*. 2 vols. Florence, 1937; reprint Florence: Olschki.

——. 1974. *Medieval Aspects of Renaissance Learning: Three Essays*. Durham, N.C.: Duke University Press.

——. 1979. *Renaissance Thought and Its Sources*. New York: Columbia University Press.

——. 1983. "Aristotelismo e sincretismo nel pensiero di Pietro Pomponazzi," in

Aristotelismo veneto e scienza moderna, 2 vols., edited by L. Olivieri, 2.1077–99. Padua: Antenore.

———. 1956–1996. *Studies in Renaissance Thought and Letters.* 4 vols. Rome: Edizioni di storia e letteratura.

Kusukawa, Sachiko. 1995. *The Transformation of Natural Philosophy: The Case of Philipp Melanchthon.* Cambridge: Cambridge University Press.

Kusukawa, Sachiko, and Ian Maclean, eds. 2006. *Transmitting Knowledge: Words, Images, and Instruments in Early Modern Europe.* Oxford: Oxford University Press.

Labowsky, L. 1961. "'Aristoteles *De Plantis* and B. Bessarion stud. 2.'" *Mediaeval and Renaissance Studies* 5: 132–54.

———. 1968. "An Unknown Treatise of Teodoro Gaza." *Mediaeval and Renaissance Studies* 6: 173–93.

———. 1979. *Bessarion's Library and the Biblioteca Marciana.* Rome: Edizioni di storia e litteratura.

Laffranchi, Marco. 1992. "Il rinnovamento della filosofia nella Dialectica di Lorenzo Valla." *Rivista di filosofia neo-scholastica* 84: 13–60.

Lagarde, Bernadette. 1973. "Le *De differentiis* de Pléthon d'apres l'autographe de la Marcienne." *Byzantion* 43: 312–43.

Langer, Ullrich, ed. 2005. *The Cambridge Companion to Montaigne.* Cambridge: Cambridge University Press.

Lehrich, Christopher I. 2003. *The Language of Demons and Angels: Cornelius Agrippa's Occult Philosophy.* Leiden: Brill.

Leinkauf, T. 1990. *Il neoplatonismo di Francesco Patrizi come presupposto della sua critica ad Aristotele.* Florence: La Nuova Italia.

———. 1991. "Geometrisches Paradigma und geozentrisches Interesse." *Berichte zur Wissenschaftsgeschichte* 14: 217–29.

Leinsle, Ulrich Gottfried. 1985. *Das Ding und die Methode. Methodische Konstitution und Gegenstand der frühen protestantischen Metaphysik.* Augsburg: Maroverlag.

———. 1988. "Die Scholastik der Neuzeit bis zur Aufklärung," in *Christliche Philosophie im katholischen Denken des 19. und 20. Jahrhunderts, Vol. 2: Rückgriff auf scholastisches Erbe,* edited by Emerich Coreth, Walter M. Neidl, and Georg Pfligersorffer, 54–69. Graz: Styria.

———. 1995. *Einführung in die scholastische Theologie* (Uni-Taschenbücher 1865). Paderborn.

Lelli, Fabrizio. 1994. "Pico tra filosofia ebraica e 'qabbala,'" in *Pico. Poliziano e l'Umanesimo di fine Quattrocentro,* edited by P. Viti, 193–223. Florence: Olschki.

Lemay, R. 1976. "The Fly against the Elephant: Flandinus against Pomponazzi on Fate," in *Philosophy and Humanism: Renaissance Essays in Honor of Paul Oskar Kristeller,* edited by E. Mahoney, 70–99. Leiden: Brill.

Lerner, Michel-Pierre. 1985. *Pansensisme et Interprétation de la Nature chez Tommaso Campanella.* Ph.D. dissertation, Sorbonne, Paris.

———. 1992. "Le Parménidisme de Telesio," in *Bernardino Telesio e la Cultura Napoletana,* edited by R. Sirri and M. Torrini, 79–105. Naples: Guida.

———. 1995. *Tommaso Campanella en France au XVIIe siècle*. Naples: Bibliopolis.

Levi, Anthony. 2002. *Renaissance and Reformation: The Intellectual Genesis*. New Haven, Conn.: Yale University Press.

Llull, Ramón. 1906–1950. *Obres de Ramon Lull*. 21 vols. Palma de Mallorca: Comissió editora Lulliana. [Abbreviated as ORL.]

———. 1965. *Opera*. 8 vols. Edited by I. Salzinger. Mainz, 1721–1742; reprint Frankfurt: Minerva. [Abbreviated as MOG.]

———. 1975–. *Opera Latina*. Vols. 1–4, Palma de Mallorca: Maioricensis Schola Lullistica, 1959–1967; Vols. 6 ff., Turnhout: Brepols. [Abbreviated as ROL.]

———. 1985. *Die neue Logik*. Edited by C. H. Lohr, German translation by V. Hösle and W. Büchel. Hamburg: Meiner. [Latin-German.]

———. 1985. *Selected Works of Ramón Llull (1232–1316)*. 2 vols. Translated by Anthony Bonner. Princeton, N.J.: Princeton University Press.

———. 1993. *Doctor Illuminatus: A Ramón Llull Reader*. Translated by Anthony Bonner. Princeton, N.J.: Princeton University Press.

———. 1994. *Ramon Llull's New Rhetoric: Text and Translation of Llull's "Rethorica Nova."* Edited by Mark D. Johnston. Davis, Calif.: Hermagoras Press.

———. 1995. *The Book of the Lover and the Beloved*. Translated by Mark D. Johnston. Warminster: Aris & Phillips.

———. 1996. *Opera*. 2 vols. Reprint of the 1651 Strasbourg edition, with an introduction by Anthony Bonner. Stuttgart–Bad Cannstatt: Frommann.

———. 2002. *The Art of Contemplation*. Translated by E. Allison Peers. 1925; reprint San Francisco: Ignatius Press.

Lohr, Charles H. 1988. *Latin Aristotle Commentaries, Vol. 2: Renaissance Authors*. Florence: Olschki.

———. 1988. "The Sixteenth-Century Transformation of the Aristotelian Natural Philosophy," in *Aristotelismus und Renaissance: In Memoriam Charles B. Schmitt*, edited by E. Kessler, C. H. Lohr, and W. Sparn, 89–99. Wiesbaden: Harrassowitz.

Lorenzo Valla: A Symposium. 1996. *Journal of the History of Ideas* 57, no. 1.

Lotti, B. 1994. "Cultura filosofica di Bessarione," in *Bessarione e l'Umanesimo*, edited by Istituto Italiano per gli studi filosofici, 79–103. Naples: Vivarium.

Machetta, Jorge M., and Claudia d'Amico, eds. 2005. *El problema del conocimento en Nicolas de Cusa. Genealogía y projección*. Buenos Aires: Biblos. Presencás Medievales, Estudios.

Machiavelli, Niccolò. 1961. *Arte della guerra e scritti politici minori*. A cura di Sergio Bertelli (= Niccolò Macchiavelli: *Opera* 2). Milan: Feltrinelli.

———. 1977. *The Prince: A New Translation, Backgrounds, Interpretations, Peripherica*. Edited by Robert Martin Adams. New York: Norton.

———. 1979. *The Portable Machiavelli*. [The Private Letters—The Prince—The Discourses—A Fable: Belfagor, the Devil Who Took a Wife—The Mandrake Root—From The Art of War—The Life of Castruccio Castracani of Lucca—From The History of Florence.] Translated by Peter E. Bondanella and Mark Musa. Hammondsworth: Penguin Books.

———. 1981. *Il Principe e altre opere politiche . . .* Introduction by Delio Cantimori, edited by Stefano Andretta. Milan: Garzanti.

———. 1994. *De principatibus*. Testo critico a cura di Giorgio Inglese. Rome: Nella sede dell'Istituto.

———. 1997. *Discourses on Livy*. Translated by Julia Conaway Bondanella and Peter E. Bondanella. New York: Oxford University Press.

———. 2001a. *Discorsi sopra la prima deca di Tito Livio*. 2 vols., continuous pagination. A cura di Francesco Bausi. Rome: Salerno.

———. 2001b. *L'arte della guerra, Scritti politici minori*. A cura di Jean-Jacques Marchand, Denis Fachard e Giorgio Masi. Rome: Salerno.

———. 2006. *Il principe*. A cura di Mario Martelli. Corredo filologico a cura di Nicoletta Marcelli. Rome: Salerno.

———. 2008. *The Prince*. Translated by Peter Constantine. New York: Modern Library.

Mack, Peter. 1993. *Renaissance Argument: Valla and Agricola in the Traditions of Rhetoric and Dialectic*. Leiden and New York: Brill.

Maclean, I. 1990. "Philosophical Books in European Markets, 1570–1630: The Case of Ramus." In M. Feingold, J. S. Freedman, and W. Rother, eds., *New Perspectives on Renaissance Thought: Essays in the History of Science, Education and Philosophy: In Memory of Charles B. Schmitt,* edited by John Henry and Sarah Hutton, 253–63. London: Duckworth.

———. 2001. "Logical Division and Visual Dichotomies: Ramus in the Context of Legal and Medical Writing." In *The Influence of Petrus Ramus: Studies in Sixteenth and Seventeenth Century Philosophy and Science,* 228–47. Basel: Schwabe.

Mahoney, Edward P. 1982. "Neoplatonism, the Greek Commentators and Renaissance Aristotelianism," in *Neoplatonism and Christian Thought,* edited by Dominic J. O'Meara, 169–77, 264–83. Norfolk: International Society for Neoplatonic Studies.

———. 1968. "Nicoletto Vernia and Agostino Nifo on Alexander of Aphrodisias: An Unnoticed Dispute." *Rivista Critica di Storia della Filosofia* 32: 270–271. [Also in Mahoney, Edward P. *Two Aristotelians of the Italian Renaissance: Nicoletto Vernia and Agostino Nifo*. Aldershot: Ashgate/Variorum, 2000.]

Marcel, Raymond. 1958. *Marsile Ficin (1433–1499)*. Paris: Les belles lettres.

Marino, John A. 1994. "The Italian States in the 'Long Sixteenth Century,'" in *Handbook of European History 1400–1600: Late Middle Ages, Renaissance and Reformation, Vol. 1: Structures and Assertions,* edited by Thomas A. Brady, Heiko A. Oberman, and James D. Tracey, 331–67. Leiden: Brill.

Masai, F. 1956. *Pléthon et le Platonisme de Mistra*. Paris: Les belles lettres.

Matton, S. 1986. "De Face À Face: Charpentier–La Ramee." *Revue des sciences philosophiques et théologiques* 70: 67–86.

Maurer, A. 1956. "Between Reason and Faith: Siger of Brabant and Pomponazzi on the Magic Arts." *Mediaeval Studies* 18: 1–18.

Meerhoff, K. 1991. "Logic and Eloquence: A Ramusian Revolution?" *Argumentation* 5: 357–74.

———. 2001. "Beauty and the Beast: Nature, Logic and Literature in Ramus," in *The Influence of Petrus Ramus,* edited by M. Feingold, J. S. Freedman, and W. Rother, 200–214. Basel: Schwabe.

Meerhoff, K., and J.-C. Moisan, eds. 1997. *Autour de Ramus. Texte, Théorie, Commentaire*. Quebec: Nuit blanche.

Meier-Oeser, Stephan. 1989. *Die Präsenz des Vergessenen. Zur Rezeption der Philosophie des Nikolaus Cusanus vom 15. bis zum 18. Jahrhundert*. Münster: Aschendorff.

Melanchthon, Philipp. 1834–1860. *Philippi Melanthonis Opera quae supersunt omnia*. Edited by Karl Gottlieb Bretschneider and Heinrich Ernst Bindseil. *Corpus Reformatorum*, 28 vols. Halle: Schwetschke. [Abbreviated as CR.]

———. 1977. *Melanchthons Briefwechsel: Krit. u. kommentierte Gesamtausg*. Edited by Heinz Scheible et al. Stuttgart–Bad Cannstatt: Frommann-Holzboog.

———. 1997. *Melanchthon deutsch*. 2 vols. Edited by Michael Beyer, Stephan Rhein, and Günther Wartenberg. Leipzig: Evangelische Verlagsanstalt.

———. 1999. *Orations on Philosophy and Education*. Edited by Sachiko Kusukawa. Cambridge: Cambridge University Press.

Mesnard, Pierre. 1955. "Une application curieuse de l'humanisme critique à la théologie: L'Éloge de saint Thomas par Laurent Valla." *Revue thomiste* (Toulouse) 55: 159–76.

Meuthen, Erich. 1992. *Nikolaus von Kues 1401–1464. Skizze einer Biographie*. 1964; 7th ed., Münster: Aschendorff.

Mikkeli, Heikki. 1992. *An Aristotelian Reponse to Renaissance Humanism: Jacopo Zabarella on the Nature of Arts and Sciences*. Helsinki: Finnish Historical Society.

Mioni, E. 1960. "Contributo del card. Bessarion all'interpretazione della metafisica aristoteliana." In *Atti del XII Congresso Internazionale di Filosofia, Vol. 9: Aristotelismo padovano e filosofia aristotelica*, 173–82. Florence.

Mitrović, B. 2005. *Serene Greed of the Eye: Leon Battista Alberti and the Philosophical Foundations of Renaissance Architectural Theory*. Munich: Deutscher Kunstverlag.

Mohler, Ludwig. 1923–1942. *Kardinal Bessarion als Theologe, Humanist und Staatsmann*. 3 vols. Quellen und Forschungen aus dem Gebiet der Geschichte 20.22.24. Paderborn (Reprint Aalen: Scientia, 1967): Vol. 1, *Darstellung* (1923); Vol. 2, *Bessarionis In Calumniatorem Platonis libri IV* (1927); Vol. 3, *Aus Bessarions Gelehrtenkreis* (1942).

Mojsisch, B. 1990. "Einleitung," to his German translation of Pietro Pomponazzi, *Abhandlung über die Unsterblichkeit der Seele*, vii–xxxv. Hamburg: Meiner.

Monfasani, John. 1976. *George of Trebizond. A Biography and a Study of His Rhetoric and Logic*. Leiden: Brill.

———. 1984. *Collectanea Trapezuntiana: Texts, Documents, and Bibliographies of George of Trebizond*. Binghamton, N.Y.: MRTS.

———. 1989. "Was Lorenzo Valla an Ordinary Language Philosopher?" *Journal of the History of Ideas* 50: 309–23.

———. 1995. *Byzantine Scholars in Renaissance Italy: Cardinal Bessarion and Other Emigrés: Selected Essays*. Aldershot: Ashgate.

———. 2004. *Greeks and Latins in Renaissance Italy: Studies on Humanism and Philosophy in the 15th Century*. Aldershot: Ashgate.

————. 2005. *Nicolaus Scutellius, O.S.A., as Pseudo-Pletho: The Sixteenth-Century Treatise "Pletho in Aristotelem" and the Scribe Michael Martinus Stella*. Florence: Olschki.

————. 2005. "Pletho's Date of Death and the Burning of His *Laws*." *Byzantinische Zeitschrift* 98: 459–63.

Mönnich, Michael W. 1990. *Tommaso Campanella. Sein Beitrag zur Medizin und Pharmazie der Renaissance*. Stuttgart: Wissenschaftliche Verlagsgesellschaft.

Monsegú, Bernardo. 1961. *Filosofía del humanismo de Juan Luis Vives*. Madrid: Consejo Superior de Investigaciones Científicas, Instituto "Luis Vives" de Filosofía.

Montaigne, Michel de. 1962. *Oeuvres completes*. Edited by A. Thibaudet and M. Rat. Paris: Bibliothèque de la Pléiade.

————. 1991. *The Complete Essays*. Translated by M. A. Screech. London: Penguin Classics.

————. 2007. *Les Essais*. Edited by Jean Balsalmo, Michel Magnien, and Cathérine Magnien-Simonin. Paris: Gallimard.

Muccillo, M. 1981. "La vita e le opere di Aristotele nelle 'Discussiones peripateticae' di Francesco Patrizi da Cherso." *Rinascimento* 21: 53–119.

————. 1986. "Marsilio Ficino e Francesco Patrizi da Cherso," in *Marsilio Ficino e il ritorno di Platone. Studi e documenti*, edited by G. C. Garfagnini, 2.615–79. Florence: Olschki.

————. 1993. "La biblioteca greca di Francesco Patrizi," in *Bibliothecae selectae da Cusano a Leopardi*, edited by E. Canone, 73–118. Florence: Olschki.

Müller-Jahncke, Wolf-Dieter. 1973. *Magie als Wissenschaft im frühen 16. Jahrhundert. Die Beziehung zwischen Magie, Medizin und Pharmazie im Werk des Agrippa von Nettesheim*. Ph.D dissertation, University of Marburg.

————. 1975. "The Attitude of Agrippe von Nettesheim (1486–1535) towards Alchemy." *Ambix* 22, no. 2: 134–50.

————. 1985. *Astrologisch-magische Theorie und Praxis in der Heilkunde der frühen Neuzeit*. Sudhoffs Archiv 25. Stuttgart: Verlag.

Mulsow, Martin. 1998. *Frühneuzeitliche Selbsterhaltung. Telesio und die Naturphilosophie der Renaissance*. Tübingen: Niemeyer.

Nakam, G. 1982. *Montaigne et son temps: Les événements et les Essais*. Paris: Nizet.

————. 1984. *Les Essais de Montaigne: Miroir et procès de leur temps*. Paris: Nizet.

Nardi, B. 1958. *Saggi sull'aristotelismo padovano dal secolo XIV al XVI*. Rome.

————. 1965. *Studi su Pietro Pomponazzi*. Florence: Sansoni.

Nauert, Charles A., Jr. 1965. *Agrippa and the Crisis of Renaissance Thought*. Urbana: University of Illinois Press.

Nauta, Lodi. 2003. "Lorenzo Valla's Critique of Aristotelian Psychology." *Vivarium* 41: 120–43.

————. 2003. "William of Occam and Lorenzo Valla: False Friends, Semantics and Ontological Reduction." *Renaissance Quarterly* 56: 613–51.

Neuhausen, K. A., and E. Trapp. 1979. "Lateinische Humanistenbriefe zu Bessarions Schrift In calumniatorem Platonis." *Jahrbuch der Österreichischen Byzantinistik* 28: 141–65.

Noreña, Carlos G. 1970. *Juan Luis Vives.* The Hague: Nijhoff.

———. 1990. *A Vives Bibliography.* Lewiston: Mellen Press.

Oliva, C. 1926. "Note sull'insegnamento di Pietro Pomponazzi." *Giornale critico della filosofia italiana* 7: 83–103, 179–90, 254–75.

Olivieri, L. 1983. *Certezza e gerarchia del sapere: Crisi dell'idea di scientificità nell'aristotelismo del secolo XVI. Con un apprendice di testi inediti di Pomponazzi, Pendasio e Cremonini.* Padua: Antenore.

———. 1983. "La scientificità della teoria dell'anima nell'insegnamento padovano di Pietro Pomponazzi," in *Scienza e filosofia all'Università di Padova nel Quattrocento,* edited by A. Poppi, 203–22. Padua: LINT.

———. 1990. "Filosofia e teologia in Pietro Pomponazzi tra Padova e Bologna," in *Sapere e/è potere: Discipline, dispute e professioni nell'università medievale e moderna. Il caso bolognese a confronto, Vol. 2: Verso un nuovo sistema del sapere,* edited by A. Cristiani, 65–84. Bologna: Comune di Bologna, and Istituto per la storia di Bologna.

O'Malley, John W. 1974. "Some Renaissance Panegyrics of Aquinas." *Renaissance Quarterly* 27: 174–192.

———. 1993. *Religious Culture in the Sixteenth Century: Preaching, Rhetoric, Spirituality, and Reform.* Brookfield, Vt., and Aldershot: Varorium.

Ong, W. J. 1958. *Ramus, Method, and the Decay of Dialogue.* Cambridge, Mass: Harvard University Press. (New ed. Chicago: University of Chicago Press, 2004)

———. *Ramus and Talon Inventory: A Short-Title Inventory of the Published Works of Peter Ramus, 1515–1572 and of Omer Talon, ca. 1510–1562 in Their Original and in Their Variously Altered Forms.* Cambridge, Mass: Harvard University Press.

Oracles Chaldaïques. Recension de Georges Gemiste Pléthon. 1995. Edited by Brigitte Tambrun-Krasker. Athens and Paris: Academy of Athens and Vrin.

Ordine, Nuccio. 1996. *Giordano Bruno and the Philosophy of the Ass.* New Haven, Conn.: Yale University Press.

Otto, Stephan. 1992. *Das Wissen des Ähnlichen: Michel Foucault und die Renaissance.* Frankfurt: Peter Lang.

Pagnoni Sturlese, M. R. 1977. "I corsi universitari di Pietro Pomponazzi e il MS. Neap. VIII. D. 81." *Annali della Scuola normale superiore di Pisa,* cl. di lettere e filosofia, ser. 3, 7: 801–42.

Park, Katherine, and Eckhard Kessler. 1988. "The Concept of Psychology," in *The Cambridge History of Renaissance Philosophy,* edited by Charles B. Schmitt and others, 455–63. Cambridge: Cambridge University Press.

Patrizi, Francesco. 1553. *La città felice. Dialogo dell'honore, il Barignano. Dialogo della diversità de' furori poetici.* Venice: G. Griffio. [Abbreviated as CF]

———. 1581. *Discussionum peripateticarum tomi primi libri XIII.* Venice: D. de Franciscis, 1571; Basle. [Abbreviated as DP.]

———. 1587. *Della nuova geometria quindeci libri XV.* Ferrara: Baldini. [Abbreviated as G.]

———. 1583. *La militia romana di Polibio, di Tito Livio e di Dionigi di Alicarnasso di Francesco Patricii dichiarata.* Ferrara: D. Mammarellus.

———. 1591. *Nova de universis philosophia, in qua aristotelica methodo ad primam causam ascenditur, deinde nova ac peculiari modo platonica rerum universitas a conditore Deo deducitur.* Ferrara: B. Mammarellus. [Abbreviated as NP.]

———. 1593–1595. *Paralleli militari di Francesco Patrizi nei quali si fa paragone delle Milizie antiche in tutte le parti con le moderne.* Rome: L. Zannetti and G. Facciotto.

———. 1963. *L'amorosa filosofia* (1577). Edited by J. C. Nelson. Florence: Le Monnier. [Abbreviated as A.]

———. 1970. *Emendatio in libros suos novae philosophiae.* Edited by P. O. Kristeller. *Rinascimento* 10: 215–18. [Abbreviated as E.]

———. 1971. *Della historia dieci dialoghi di M. Francesco Patriti, ne' quali si ragiona di tutte le cose appartenenti all' historia.* Venice: A. Arrivabene, 1560; reprint E. Kessler, ed., *Theoretiker humanistischer Geschichtsschreibung.* Munich: Fink. [Abbreviated as H.]

———. 1969–1971. *Della Poetica.* 3 vols. Edited by D. Aguzzi Barbagli. Florence: Istituto nazionale di studi sul rinascimento. [Abbreviated as P.]

———. 1975. *Lettere ed opuscoli inediti.* Edited by D. Aguzzi Barbagli. Florence: Istituto nazionale di studi sul rinascimento. [Abbreviated as LO.]

———. 1994. *Della retorica, dieci dialoghi di M. Francesco Patritito.* Venice: F. Senese, 1562; reprint, ed. A. L. Puliafito Bleuel, Lecce: Conte. [Abbreviated as R.]

Pelacani da Parma, Biagio. 1974. *Le Quaestiones de anima.* Edited by G. Federici Vescovini. Florence: Olschki.

Perez-Garcia, P. 1993. "Joan Lluis Vives y su tiempo," in *Joan Lluis Vives, un valenciano universal,* edited by Cruselles Gómez, 23–24. Valencia: Ajuntament de Valencia.

Perfetti, Stefano. 1998. "'An anima nostra sit mortalis': Una 'quaestio' inedita discussa da Pietro Pomponazzi nel 1521." *Rinascimento,* 2nd ser., 38: 205–26.

———. 1999. "Docebo vos dubitare: Il commento inedito di Pietro Pomponazzi al *De partibus animalium* (Bologna 1521–1524)." *Documenti e studi sulla tradizione filosofica medievale* 10: 439–66.

———. 1999. "Three Different Ways of Interpreting Aristotle's *De partibus animalium:* Pietro Pomponazzi, Niccolò Leonico Tomeo, and Agostino Nifo," in *Aristotle's Animals in the Middle Ages and Renaissance,* edited by C. Steel et al., 289–308. Leuven: Leuven University Press.

———. 2000. *Aristotle's Zoology and Its Renaissance Commentators (1521–1601),* 33–63. Leuven: Leuven University Press.

———. 2004. "Pietro Pomponazzi," in *Stanford Encyclopedia of Philosophy,* edited by E. N. Zalta, available at http://plato.stanford.edu/archives/win2004/entries/pomponazzi/.

Perrone Compagni, V. 1999. "Introduzione," to her Italian translation of Pietro Pomponazzi, *Trattato sull'immortalità dell'anima,* v–xcvi. Florence: Olschki.

———. 2004. "Critica e riforma del Cristianesimo nel *De fato* di Pomponazzi," in her Italian translation of Pietro Pomponazzi, *Il fato, il libero arbitrio e la predestinazione,* 2 vols., edited by R. Lemay, 2.*ix–clviii.* Turin: Aragno.

Piaia, Gregorio, ed. 2002. *La presenza dell'aristotelismo padovano nella filosofia del-la prima modernità.* Padova and Rome: Antenore.

Pico della Mirandola, Gianfrancesco. 1994. *Ioannis Pici Mirandulae viri omni dis-ciplinarum genere consumatissimi vita.* Edited by B. Andreolli. Modena: Aedes muratoriana.

Pico della Mirandola, Giovanni. 1942. *De Hominis Dignitate, Heptaplus e scritti vari.* Edited by E. Garin. Florence: Vallecchi.

———. 1943. *Of Being and Unity (De ente et uno).* Translated by Victor M. Hamm. Milwaukee: Marquette University Press.

———. 1946–1952. *Disputationes adversus astrologiam divinatricem.* 2 vols. Edited by E. Garin. Florence: Vallecchi.

———. 1965. *On the Dignity of Man.* Translated by Charles Glenn Wallis. *On Being and the One.* Translated by Paul J. W. Miller. *Heptaplus.* Translated by Doug-las Carmichael. Indianapolis: Bobbs-Merrill

———. 1972. *Opera.* 2 vols. Basle, 1572; reprint Turin: Bottega d'Erasmo.

———. 1977. *Heptaplus: or, Discourse on the Seven Days of Creation.* Translated by Jessie Brewer McGaw. New York: Philosophical Library.

———. 1984. *Commentary on a Canzone of Benivieni.* Translated by Sears Jayne. New York: Peter Lang.

———. 1985. *Oratio de Hominis Dignitate.* Edited by E. Garin. Pisa: Scuola Nor-male Superiore.

———. 1986. *Commentary on a Poem of Platonic Love.* Translated by Douglas Car-michael. Washington, D.C.: The Catholic University Press of America.

———. 1993. *Oeuvres philosophiques.* Edited by G. Tognon and O. Boulnois. Par-is: PUF.

———. 1994. *Commento sopra una canzone d'amore.* Edited by Paolo De Angelis. Palermo: Novecento.

———. 1994. *Sonetti.* Edited by G. Dilemmi. Turin: Einaudi.

———. 1995. *Conclusiones nongentae: Le novecento tesi dell'anno 1486.* Edited by Albano Biondi. Florence: Olschki.

———. 1995. *De Ente et Uno, Responsiones à Antonio Cittadini,* in S. Toussaint, *L'Esprit du Quattrocento.* Paris: Champion.

———. 1997. *Expositiones in Psalmos.* Edited by Antonio Raspanti. Florence: Olschki.

———. 2003. *Discorso sulla dignità dell'uomo.* Edited by Francesco Bausi. Parma: Fondazione Pietro Bembo.

Pierre de la Ramèe. Revue des sciences philosophiques et théologiques. 1986. 70: 2–100.

Pine, M. 1986. *Pietro Pomponazzi: Radical Philosopher of the Renaissance.* Padua: Antenore.

———. 1998. "Pomponazzi, Pietro," in *Routledge Encyclopedia of Philosophy,* 10 vols., edited by E. Craig, 7.529–33. London: Routledge.

———. 1999. "Pietro Pomponazzi's Attack on Religion and the Problem of *De fato,*" in *Atheismus im Mittelalter und in der Renaissance,* edited by F. Niewöh-ner and O. Pluta, 145–72. Wiesbaden: Harrassowitz.

Plastina, S. 1992. *Gli alunni di Crono. Mito linguaggio e storia in Francesco Patrizi da Cherso (1529–1597)*. Soveria Mannelli: Rubbettino.

Platzeck, E. W. 1962–1964. *Raimund Lull. Sein Leben, seine Werke, die Grundlagen seines Denkens*. 2 vols. Düsseldorf: Schwann.

Plethon, Georgius Gemistus. 1866. *Patrologiae Cursus completus. Series Graeca*. Vol. 160. Edited by J.-P. Migne. Paris: Migne. [Contains various works in Greek and Latin.]

———. 1966. *Traité des lois*. Edited by C. Alexandre, translated by A. Pellissier. Paris, 1858; reprint Amsterdam: Hakkert.

———. 1987. *Georgiou Gemistou Plethonos Periareton / Georges Gemiste Pléthon: Traité des vertus*. Edited and translated by Brigitte Tambrun-Krasker. Athens, Leiden, and New York: Akadēmia Athēnōn and Brill.

———. 1988. *Georgii Gemisti Plethonis Contra scholarii pro Aristotele obiectiones*. Edited by E. V. Maltese. Leipzig: Teubner.

———. 1989. *Contre les objections de Scholarios en faveur d'Aristote*. Edited by Bernardette Lagarde. *Byzantion. Revue internationale des études byzantines* 59: 354–507.

Pluta, O. 1986. "Pietro Pomponazzi und die Schule von Padua," in Pluta, *Kritiker der Unsterblichkeit in Mittelalter und Renaissance*, 55–60. Amsterdam: Grüner.

———. 2001. "The Transformation of Alexander of Aphrodisias' Interpretation of Aristotle's Theory of the Soul," in *Renaissance Readings of the "Corpus Aristotelicum,"* Proceedings of the Conference held in Copenhagen . . . 1998, edited by M. Pade, 147–65. Copenhagen: Museum Tusculanum.

Pomponazzi, Pietro. 1514. *Tractatus utilissimus in quo disputatur penes quid intensio et remissio formarum attendatur nec minus parvitas et magnitudo*. Bologna: De Benedictis.

———. 1518. *Apologia*. Bologna: Ruberia.

———. 1519. *Defensorium sive Responsiones ad ea quae Augustinus Niphus adversus ipsum scripsit de immortalitate animae*, including C. Javelli, *Solutiones rationum animi mortalitatem probantium quae in Defensorio . . . a Pomponatio formantur*. Bologna: Ruberia.

———. 1521. *Tractatus de nutritione et auctione*. Bologna: De Benedictis.

———. 1556. *De naturalium effectuum causis, sive De incantationibus*. Edited by G. Gratarolo. Basel: Henricus Petri.

———. 1563. *Dubitationes in quartum Meteorologicorum Aristotelis librum*. Venice: Franciscus de Franciscis.

———. 1954. *Tractatus de immortalitate animae*. Edited by G. Morra. Bologna: Nanni & Fiammenghi. [English translation, *On the Immortality of the Soul*, in *The Renaissance Philosophy of Man*, edited by E. Cassirer et al., 280–381. Chicago and London, 1948.]

———. 1957. *Libri quinque de fato, de libero arbitrio et de praedestinatione*. Edited by R. Lemay. Lugano: Thesauri Mundi.

———. 1966–1970. *Corsi inediti dell'insegnamento padovano*. Vol. 1: *Super libello De substantia orbis expositio et quaestiones quattuor (1507)*; Vol. 2: *Quaestiones physicae et animisticae decem (1499–1500; 1503–1504)*. Edited by A. Poppi. Padua: Antenore.

———. 1970. *Opera. De naturalium effectuum causis, seu De incantationibus liber; De fato, libero arbitrio, praedestinatione, providentia Dei libri V.* Basel: Henricus Petri, 1567; reprint of *De incantationibus,* Darmstadt: Hildesheim and New York: Olms.

———. 1989. "Utrum anima sit mortalis vel immortalis." Edited by W. van Dooren. *Nouvelles de la République des Lettres,* 71–135.

———. 1995. *Tractatus acutissimi, utillimi et mere peripatetici.* Venice: Scotus, 1525; reprint Casarano: Eurocart.

———. 2004. *Expositio super primo et secundo De partibus animalium.* Edited by S. Perfetti. Florence: Olschki.

Popkin, Richard H. 2003. *The History of Scepticism from Savonarola to Bayle.* Oxford: Oxford University Press.

Poppi, Antonino. 1970. *Saggi sul pensiero inedito di Pietro Pomponazzi.* Padua: Antenore.

———. 1972. *La dottrina della scienza in Giacomo Zabarella.* Padua: Antenore.

———. 1988. "Fate, Fortune, Providence, and Human Freedom," in *The Cambridge History of Renaissance Philosophy,* edited by C. B. Schmitt et al., 641–67. Cambridge: Cambridge University Press.

Pring-Mill, R. 1961. *Microcosmos lullià.* Palma de Mallorca: Dolphin Book Company.

Proclus. 1583. *Procli Lycii Diadochi Platonici Philosophi Eminentissimi Elementa Theologica et Physica. Opus omni admiratione prosequendum quae Franciscus Patricius de Graecis fecit Latina.* Ferrara: Mammarellus.

Puliafito, A. L. 1987. "Per uno studio della Nova de universis philosophia di Francesco Patrizi da Cherso. Note alla Panaugia," in *Atti e memorie dell'Accademia Toscana di scienze e lettere. La Colombaria,* new ser. 38, 7: 160–99.

———. 1988. "'Principio primo' e 'principi principiati' nella De nova universis philosophia di Francesco Patrizi." *Giornale critico della filosofia italiana* 67: 154–201.

Purnell, F. 1976. "F. Patrizi and the Critics of Hermes Trismegistus." *Journal of Medieval and Renaissance Studies* 6: 155–78.

Raimondi, F. P. 2000. "Pomponazzi's Criticism of Swineshead and the Decline of the Calculatory Tradition in Italy." *Physis* 37: 311–58.

Rainolds, John. 1986. *John Rainolds's Oxford Lectures on Aristotle's "Rhetoric."* Edited by Lawrence D. Green. Newark: University of Delaware Press.

Ramberti, R. 1997. "Stoicismo e tradizione peripatetica nel *De fato* di Pietro Pomponazzi." *Dianoia* 2: 51–84.

Ramus, Petrus. 1964. *Dialectique (1555).* Edited by M. Dassonville. Geneva: Droz.

———. 1964. *Dialecticae Institutiones, Aristotelicae Animadversiones (1543).* Edited by W. Risse. Facsimile ed. Stuttgart–Bad Cannstatt: Frommann.

———. 1965. *Scholae in Tres Primas Liberales Artes (1581).* Facsimile ed. Frankfurt.

———. 1967. *Scholarum Physicarum Libri Octo, in Totidem Acroamaricos Libros Aristotelis (1583).* Facsimile ed. Frankfurt.

———. 1969. *Collectaneae, Praefationes, Epistolae, Orationes (1599).* Edited by W. Ong. Facsimile ed. Hildesheim: Olms.

———. 1969. *De Religione Christiana Libri IV.* Facsimile ed. Frankfurt.

———. 1969. *The Logike of the Moste Excellent Philosopher P. Ramus, Martyr (1574)*. Facsimile ed. Amsterdam: Theatrum Orbis Terrarum.

———. 1971. *Oeuvres Diverses (1577)*. Facsimile ed. Geneva.

———. 1971. *Rudiments of Latin Grammar, 1585*. Facsimile ed. Menston: Scolar Press.

———. 1974. *Scholarum Metaphysicarum Libri Quatuordecim in Totidem Metaphysicos Libros Aristotelis (1583)*. Facsimile ed. Frankfurt: Minerva.

———. 1976. *Pro Aristotele Adversus Iac. Schecium (1571)*. Facsimile ed. Frankfurt: Minerva.

———. 1986. *Arguments in Rhetoric against Quintilian (Rhetoricae distinctiones in Quintilianum)*. Translated by C. E. Newlands. Dekalb, Ill.: Northern Illinois University Press.

———. 1992. *Peter Ramus's Attack on Cicero: Text and Translation of Ramus's "Brutinae Quaestiones."* Edited with an introduction by James J. Murphy, translated by C. Newlands. Davis, Calif.: Hermagoras.

———. 1996. *Dialectique 1555: Un Manifeste de la Pléiade*. Edited by N. Bruyère. Paris: Vrin.

———. 2005. *Pro Philosophica Parisiensis Academiae Disciplina Oratio Ad Carolum Lotharingum (1551)*. Facsimile ed. Frankfurt.

———. 2005. *Scholarum Mathematicarum Libri Unus et Triginta (1569)*. Introduction by F. Daly. Facsimile ed. Hildesheim: Olms.

Randall, John Herman. 1948. "Introduction" to Pomponazzi, "On the Immortality of the Soul," in *The Renaissance Philosophy of Man*, edited by E. Cassirer et al., 257–79. Chicago and London: University of Chicago Press.

———. 1961. *The School of Padua and the Emergence of Modern Science*. Padua: Antenore.

Regoliosi, Mariangela. 1993. *Nel cantiere del Valla, Elaborazione e montaggiodelle "Elegantie"* (with critical edition: *Il primo proemio delle "Elegantie"*). Humanistica 3. Rome: Bulzoni.

Renaudet, A. 1953. *Préreforme et humanisme à Paris pendant les premières guerres d'Italie (1497–1517)*. Paris: Libairie d'Argences.

Risse, Wilhelm. 1964. *Die Logik der Neuzeit, Vol. 1: 1500–1640*. Stuttgart–Bad Cannstatt: Frommann.

———. 1983. "Zabarellas Methodenlehre," in *Aristotelismo veneto e scienza moderna*, edited by L. Olivieri, 1.155–72. Padua: Antenore.

Robinet, A. 1981. "Suárez im Werk von Leibnitz." *Studia Leibnitiana* 13: 76–96.

Rossi, Paolo. 1983. "Aristotelici e moderni: Le ipotesi e la natura," in *Aristotelismo veneto e scienza moderna*, edited by L. Olivieri, 1.123–54. Padua: Antenore.

Rowland, Ingrid D. *Giordano Bruno: Philosopher/Heretic*. New York: Farrer, Straus and Giroux.

Rummel, Erika. 1995. *The Humanist Scholastic Debate in the Renaissance and Reformation*. Cambridge, Mass.: Harvard University Press.

Ruocco, Ilario, ed. 2003. *Il Platone latino. Il Parmenide: Giorgio di Trebisonda e il cardinale Cusano*. Florence: Olschki.

Rykwert, J., and A. Engel, eds. 1994. *Leon Battista Alberti*. Mantua: Palazzo del Te and Milan: Electra.

Saiber, Arielle. 2005. *Giordano Bruno and the Geometry of Language*. Literary and Scientific Cultures of Early Modernity. Aldershot: Ashgate.

Salatowsky, S. 2006. *De anima: Die Rezeption der aristotelischen Psychologie im 16. und 17. Jahrhundert*. Amsterdam and Philadelphia: Grüner.

Salvestrini, V. 1958. *Bibliografia di Giordano Bruno (1582–1950)*. 2nd ed. Edited by L. Firpo. Florence: Sansoni.

Scheeben, Matthias J. 1959. *Handbuch der katholischen Dogmatik*. Vol. 1. 3rd ed. Introduction by M. Grabmann (*Gesammelte Schriften*, ed. J. Höfer, Vol. 3). Freiburg i.Br.: Herder.

Scheible, Heinz. 1992. "Melanchthon." *Theologische Realenzyklopädie* 22: 371–410.

———. 1997. *Melanchthon. Eine Biografie*. Munich: Beck.

Schepper, Marcus de. 2000. "April in Paris (1514): J. L. Vives Editing B. Guarinus," in *Myricae: Essays in Neo-Latin Literature in Memory of Josef Ijsewijn*, edited by Dirk Sacré and Gilbert Tournoy, 195–200. Leuven: Leuven University Press.

Schmidt-Biggemann, Wilhelm. 1983. *Topica universalis. Eine Modellgeschichte humanistischer und barocker Wissenschaft*. Hamburg: Meiner.

———. 2004. *Philosophia perennis: Historical Outlines of Western Spirituality in Ancient, Medieval, and Early Modern Thought*. Dordrecht: Springer.

Schmitt, Charles B. 1983. *Aristotle and the Renaissance*. Cambridge, Mass., and London.

———. 1985. "Aristotle among the Physicians," in *The Medical Renaissance of the Sixteenth Century*, edited by A. Wear, R. K. French, and I. M. Lonie, 1–15. Cambridge: Cambridge University Press.

Schmitt, Charles B., and others, eds. 1988. *The Cambridge History of Renaissance Philosophy*. Cambridge: Cambridge University Press.

Schuhmann, K. 1986. "Thomas Hobbes and Francesco Patrizi." *Archiv für Geschichte der Philosophie* 68: 253–79.

———. 1988. "Hobbes and Telesio." *Hobbes Studies* 1: 109–33.

———. 1988. "Zur Entstehung des neuzeitlichen Zeitbegriffs: Telesio, Patrizi, Gassendi." *Philosophia Naturalis* 25: 37–64.

———. 1990. "Telesio's Concept of Matter," in *Atti del Convegno Internazionale di Studi su Bernardino Telesio*, 115–34. Cosenza: Accademia Cosentina.

———. 1992. "Le Concept de l'Espace chez Telesio," in *Bernardino Telesio e la Cultura Napoletana*, edited by R. Sirri and M. Torrini, 141–67. Naples: Guida.

Scribano, M. E. 1981. "Il problema de libero arbitrio nel *De fato* di Pietro Pomponazzi." *Annali dell' Istituto di Filosofia* [Università di Firenze] 3: 23–69.

Sellberg, E. 2001. "The Usefulness of Ramism." In *The Influence of Petrus Ramus: Studies in Sixteenth and Seventeenth Century Philosophy and Science*, edited by M. Feingold, J. S. Freedman, and W. Rother, 107–26. Basel: Schwabe.

Senger, Hans Gerhard. 2002. *Ludus sapientiae. Studien zum Werk und zur Wirkungsgeschichte des Nikolaus von Kues*. Leiden: Brill.

Serjeantson, R. W. 2001. "The Passions and Animal Language: 1540–1700." *Journal of the History of Ideas*, 425–44.

Setz, Wolfram. 1975. *Lorenzo Vallas Schrift gegen die Konstantinische Schenkung De falso credita et ementita Constantini donatione. Zur Interpretation und Wirkungs-*

geschichte. Bibliothek des Deutschen Historischen Instituts in Rom 44. Tübingen: Niemeyer. [Text in appendix.]

Sharratt, P. 1975. "Nicolaus Nancelius *Petri Rami Vita,* edited with an English Translation." *Humanistica Lovaniensia* 24: 161–277.

Shaw, Prudence. 1978. "La versione ficiniana della 'Monarchia.'" *Studi Danteschi* 51: 289–408. [Translation of Dante's *De monarchia.*]

Simonsohn, S. 1996. "G. P. della Mirandola on Jews and Judaism." In *From Witness to Witchcraft: Jews and Judaism in Medieval Christian Thought,* 403–17. Wiesbaden: Harrassowitz.

Singer, Dorothea Waley. 1950. *Giordano Bruno, His Life and Thought.* New York: Schuman. [Includes English translation of *On the Infinite Universe.*]

Soder, Josef. 1973. *Franz Suárez und das Völkerrecht. Grundgedanken zu Staat, Recht und internationalen Beziehungen.* Frankfurt: Metzner.

Spampanato, V. 1933. *Documenti della vita di Giordano Bruno.* Florence: Olschki. [Abbreviated as Doc.]

Specht, Rainer. 1976. "Introduction" to F. Suárez, *Über die Individualität und das Individuationsprinzip (Fünfte metaphysische Disputation),* edited, translated, and with introduction by R. Specht, xv–xl. *Text und Übersetzung.* Philosophische Bibliothek 294a. Hamburg: Meiner.

Spruit, Leen. 1992. "Elementi Aristotelici e Polemica Anti-Peripatetica nella Dottrina dell'Anima Divina di Telesio." *Verifiche* 21: 351–70.

———. 1995. *Species intelligibilis: From Perception to Knowledge.* Vol. 2. Leiden: Brill.

Starobinski, J. 1982. *Montaigne en mouvement.* Paris: Gallimard.

Stausberg, Michael. 1998. *Faszination Zarathushtra. Zoroaster und die Europäische Religionsgeschichte der Frühen Neuzeit.* Berlin and New York: de Gruyter.

Stormon, E. J. 1981. "Bessarion before the Council of Florence: A Survey of His Early Writings (1423–1437)." *Byzantine Australiensia* 1: 128–56.

Stupperich, Robert, ed. 1951. *Melanchthons Werke in Auswahl.* Gütersloh: Bertelsmann. [Abbreviated as MSA.]

Sturlese, R. 1987. *Bibliografia, censimento e storia delle antiche stampe di Giordano Bruno.* Florence: Olschki.

Suárez, Francisco. 1866. *De incarnatione,* 2 vols. In *Opera omnia,* vols. 17–18, edited by C. Berton. Paris: L. Vivès.

———. 1856–1878. *Opera omnia. Editio nova, a D. M. Andre et Carolo Berton juxta editionem Venetianam XXIII Tomos in f° continentem, accurate recognita.* 27 vols. Paris: Vives.

———. 1944. *Selections from Three Works of Francisco Suárez, S.J.: De Legibus, Ac Deo Legislatore, 1612; Defensio Fidei Catholicae, Et Apostolicae Adversus Anglicanae Sectae Errores, 1613; De Triplici Virtute Theologica, Fide, Spe, Et Charitate, 1621.* 2 vols. Translated by Gwladys L. Williams and Henry Davis. Oxford: Clarendon Press.

———. 1947. *On the Various Kinds of Distinctions (Disputationes Metaphysicae, Disputatio VII, De Variis Distinctionum Generibus).* Translated by Cyril O. Vollert. Milwaukee, Wis.: Marquette University Press.

————. 1950. *Extracts: Politics and Government from Defense of the Faith, Laws and God the Lawgiver, Tract on Faith, [and] Tract on Charity.* Translated by George Albert Moore. Chevy Chase, Md.: Country Dollar Press.

————. 1954. *The Dignity and Virginity of the Mother of God. Disputations I, V, VI from The Mysteries of the Life of Christ.* Translated by Richard J. O'Brien. West Baden Springs, Ind.: West Baden College.

————. 1964. *On Formal and Universal Unity; De Unitate Formali Et Universali.* Translated by James F. Ross. Milwaukee, Wis.: Marquette University Press.

————. 1965. *Disputationes metaphysicae,* 2 vols. In *Opera omnia,* vols. 25–26, edited by C. Berton. Paris: L. Vivès, 1866; reprint Hildesheim: Olms. [*Editio princeps:* Salamanca 1597; Latin/Spanish, edited by Rábade Romeo et al., 7 vols., Madrid 1960–1967.] Electronic version available at http://homepage.ruhr-uni -bochum.de/Michael.Renemann/suarez/index.html.

————. 1971–1976. *Tractatus de legibus ac Deo legislatore, in decem libros distributus.* 2 vols., in *Opera omnia,* edited by C. Berton, 5–6, Paris: L. Vivès, 1856. [*Editio princeps:* Coimbra, 1612; Latin/Spanish, with critical text by L. Pereña et al., 6 vols., Madrid, 1971–1976.]

————. 1982. *Suárez on Individuation: Metaphysical Disputation V, Individual Unity and Its Principle.* Translated by Jorge J. E. Gracia. Milwaukee, Wis.: Marquette University Press.

————. 1983. *On the Essence of Finite Being As Such, on the Existence of That Essence and Their Distinction De Essentia Entis Finiti Ut Tale Est, Et De Illius Esse, Eorumque Distinctione.* Translated by Norman J. Wells. Milwaukee, Wis.: Marquette University Press.

————. 1989. *The Metaphysics of Good and Evil According to Suárez: Metaphysical Disputations X and XI and Selected Passages from Disputation XXIII and Other Works.* Translated by Jorge J. E. Gracia and Douglas Davis. Munich: Philosophia.

————. 1994. *On Efficient Causality: Metaphysical Disputations 17, 18, and 19.* Translated by Alfred J. Freddoso. New Haven, Conn.: Yale University Press.

————. 1995. *On Beings of Reason = De Entibus Rationis: Metaphysical Disputation LIV.* Mediaeval Philosophical Texts in Translation 33. Translated by John P. Doyle. Milwaukee, Wis: Marquette University Press.

————. 2000. *On the Formal Cause of Substance: Metaphysical Disputation XV.* Translated by John Kronen. Milwaukee, Wis.: Marquette University Press.

————. 2002. *On Creation, Conservation, and Concurrence: Metaphysical Disputations 20, 21, and 22.* Translated by Alfred J. Freddoso. South Bend, Ind.: St. Augustine's Press.

————. 2004. *A Commentary on Aristotle's Metaphysics (Index locupletissimus in Metaphysicam Aristotelis).* Translated by John P. Doyle. Milwaukee, Wis.: Marquette University Press.

————. 2004. *The Metaphysical Demonstration of the Existence of God: Metaphysical Disputations 28–29.* Translated by John P. Doyle. South Bend, Ind.: St. Augustine's Press.

————. 2006. *On Real Relation = (Disputatio Metaphysica XLVII).* Translated by John P. Doyle. Milwaukee, Wis.: Marquette University Press.

Suarez-Nani, T. 1995. "Dignità e finitezza dell'uomo: Alcune riflessioni sul *De immortalitate animae* di Pietro Pomponazzi." *Rivista di storia della filosofia* 50: 7–30.

Symonds, John Addington, ed. 1878. *The Sonnets of Michael Angelo Buonarroti and Tommaso Campanella.* London: Smith, Elder, & Co.

Tambrun, Brigitte. 1999. "Marsile Ficin et le Commentaire de Pléthon sur les Oracles chaldaïques." *Accademia. Revue de la Société Marsile Ficin* 1: 9–48.

———. 2006. *Pléthon: Le retour de Platon.* Paris: Vrin.

Tavernor, R. 1998. *On Alberti and The Art of Building.* New Haven and London: Yale University Press.

Tavuzzi, M. 1995. "Silvestro da Prierio and the Pomponazzi Affair." *Renaissance and Reformation,* n.s., 19: 47–61.

Telesio, Bernardino. 1971. *Varii de Naturalibus rebus libelli.* Edited by Cesare Vasoli. Venice, 1590; New York and Hildesheim: Olms.

———. 1965–1976. *De Rerum Natura iuxta Propria Principia,* 3 vols., edited by Luigi De Franco. Cosenza and Florence: Casa del Libro and La nuova Italia.

———. 1981. *Varii de naturalibus rebus libelli.* Edited by Luigi De Franco. Florence: La nuova Italia.

Tommaso de Vio. 1938–1939. *Scripta philosophica: Commentaria in "De anima" Aristotelis.* 2 vols. Edited by P. I. Coquelle. Rome: Apud Institutum "Angelicum."

Tournay, G. 1994. "Juan Luis Vives and the World of Printing." *Gutenberg Jahrbuch* 69: 128–48.

Toussaint, Stéphane. 1995. *L'Esprit du Quattrocento.* Paris: Champion. [Contains Pico's *De ente et uno*]

———, ed. 2002. *Marsile Ficin ou les mystères platoniciens: Actes du XLIIe Colloque international d'études humanistes, Centre d'études supérieures de la renaissance, Tours, 7–10 juillet 1999.* Les cahiers de l'humanisme 2. Paris: Les belles lettres.

Treloar, John L. 1990. "Pomponazzi's Critique of Aquinas's Arguments for the Immortality of the Soul." *The Thomist* 54: 453–70.

———. "Pomponazzi: Moral Virtue in a Deterministic Universe," in *Renaissance and Early Modern Philosophy,* Midwest Studies in Philosophy 26, edited by Peter A. French, Howard K. Wettstein, and Bruce S. Silver, 44–55. Malden, Mass.: Blackwell.

Trinkaus, Charles. 1995. *In Our Image and Likeness: Humanity and Divinity in Italian Humanist Thought.* 2 vols. Chicago: University of Chicago Press, 1970; reprint Notre Dame: University of Notre Dame Press.

———. 1996. "Lorenzo Valla on the Problem of Speaking about the Trinity." *Journal of the History of Ideas* 57: 27–53.

Valcke, L. 1992. "Jean Pic de la Mirandole et le retour au 'le style de Paris': Portée d'une critique littéraire." *Rinascimento* 32: 253–73.

Valla, Lorenzo. 1934. *De libero arbitrio.* Edited by Maria Anfossi. Florence: Olschki.

———. 1948. *Dialogue on Free Will,* translated by Charles Trinkaus, in *The Renaissance Philosophy of Man,* edited by Ernst Cassirer, Paul Oskar Kristeller, and John Herman Randall, 145–82. Chicago: University of Chicago Press.

————. 1962. *Opera omnia.* Basle, 1540; reprint edited by Eugenio Garin, Turin: Bottega d'Erasmo. [In Vol. 2, reprint of texts which are not included in the 1540 edition.]

————. 1970. *Collatio Novi Testamenti.* Edited by Alessandro Perosa. Florence: Sansoni.

————. 1970. *De vero falsoque bono.* Edited by Maristella De Panizza Lorch. Bari: Adriatica.

————. 1973. *Laurentii Valle Gesta Ferdinandi Regis Aragonum.* Edited by Ottavio Besomi. Padua: Antenore.

————. 1977. *On pleasure—De voluptate.* Edited by A. Kent Hieatt and Maristella Lorch. New York: Abaris Books; reprint of the 1970 edition with translation. [Latin/English.]

————. 1978. *Antidotum primum, La prima apologia contro Poggio Bracciolini.* Res publica literaria Neerlandica 4. Edited by Ari Wesseling. Assen: Van Gorcum.

————. 1981. *Laurentii Valle Antidotum in Facium.* Edited by Mariangela Regoliosi. Padua: Antenore.

————. 1982. *Laurentii Valle Repastinatio dialectice et philosophice,* 2 vols., Vol. 1: *Retractatio totius dialecticae cum fundamentis universe philosophie* (2nd and 3rd versions); Vol. 2: *Repastinatio dialectice et philosphie* (1st version); continuous pagination. Edited by Gianni Zippel. Padua: Antenore.

————. 1984. *Epistole.* Edited by Ottavio Besomi and Mariangela Regoliosi. Padua: Antenore.

————. 1986. *De falso credita et ementita Constantini donatione.* Monumenta Germaniae historica 10. Edited by Wolfram Setz. Weimar: Böhlau, 1976; reprint.

————. 1986. *De professione religiosorum.* Edited by Mariarosa Cortesi. Padua: Antenore.

————. 1990. *L'arte della Grammatica.* Edited by Paola Casciano. Milan: Fondazione Lorenzo Valla and A. Mondadori.

————. 1993. *The Treatise of Lorenzo Valla on the Donation of Constantine: Text and Translation into English.* Edited by Christopher B. Coleman. New Haven: Yale University Press, 1922; reprint Toronto: Toronto University Press.

————. 1994. *Orazione per l'inaugurazione dell'anno accademico 1455–1456.* Edited by Silvia Rizzo. Rome: Roma nel Rinascimento.

————. 1994. *The Profession of the Religious and the Principal Arguments from the Falsely-Believed and Forged Donation of Constantine.* Edited and translated by Olga Zorzi. Pugliese and Toronto: Centre for Reformation and Renaissance Studies.

————. 1996. *Le postille all' "Institutio oratoria" di Quintiliano.* Edited by Lucia Cesarini Martellini and Alessandro Perosa. Padua: Antenore.

————. 1998. *De reciprocatione "sui" et "suus."* Edited by Elisabet Sandström. Göteborg: Acta Universitatis Gothoburgensis.

————. 2007. *On the Donation of Constantine.* Edited and translated by G. W. Bowersock. Cambridge, Mass.: Harvard University Press.

Van der Poel, Marc. 1997. *Cornelius Agrippa: The Humanist Theologian and His Declamations.* Leiden and New York: Brill.

Vansteenberghe, Edmond. 1974. *Le cardinal Nicholas de Cusa (1401–1464). L'action —la pensée.* Paris: Champion, 1920; reprints Frankfurt: Minerva, 1963, Geneva: Slatkine.

Vasoli, Cesare. 1989. *Francesco Patrizi da Cherso.* Rome: Bulzoni.

v1995. "L'individuo in Pomponazzi," in *L'individu dans la pensée moderne (XVIe– XVIIIe siècles),* edited by G. M. Cazzaniga and Y. C. Zarka, 95–113. Pisa: ETS.

————. 1999. *Quasi sit deus. Studi su Marsilio Ficino.* Lecce: Conte.

————. 2006. *Ficino, Savonarola, Machiavelli: Studi di storia della cultura.* Turin: N. Aragno.

Verbeek, T. 2001. "Notes on Ramism in the Netherlands," in *The Influence of Petrus Ramus: Studies in Sixteenth and Seventeenth Century Philosophy and Science,* edited by M. Feingold, J. S. Freedman, and W. Rother, 38–53. Basel: Schwabe.

Verdon, Timothy, and John Henderson, eds. 1990. *Christianity and the Renaissance: Image and Religious Imagination in the Quattrocento.* Syracuse, N.Y.: Syracuse University Press.

Vernia, Nicoletto. 1516. *Contra perversam Averrois opinionem de unitate intellectus et de anime felicitate,* in Albert of Saxony, *Acutissime questiones super libros De physica auscultatione.* Venice.

Villey, P. 1976. *Les sources et l'évolution de Montaigne.* 2 vols. Paris: Hachette, 1933; reprint Osnabrück: Zeller.

Viti, Paolo, ed. 1994. *Pico, Poliziano e l'Umanesimo di fine '400.* Florence: Olschki.

Vives, Juan Luis. 1964. *Opera omnia, distributa et ordinata in argumentorum classes praecipuas.* 8 vols. Edited by Gregorio Mayans y Siscar. Valencia, 1782; reprint London: Gregg Press. [Abbreviated as M.]

————. 1987–. *Selected Works of J. L. Vives.* 8 vols. Edited by Constantinus Matheeussen, Charles Fantazzi, and E. George. Leiden: Brill.

————. 1990. *The Passions of the Soul: The Third Book of "De Anima et Vita."* Edited by Carlos G. Noreña. Lewiston: Mellen Press.

Vollrath, Ernst. 1962. "Die Gliederung der Metaphysik in eine Metaphysica generalis und eine Metaphysica specialis." *Zeitschrift für philosophische Forschung* 16: 258–84.

Walker, D. P. 1990. *Spiritual and Demonic Magic from Ficino to Campanella.* London: Warburg Institute, 1958; reprinted with an Introduction by Brian P. Copenhaver, University Park: Pennsylvania State University Press.

Wallace, William. 1992. *Galileo's Logic of Discovery and Proof.* Dordrecht and Boston: Kluwer.

Webb, Ruth. 1989. "The 'Nomoi' of Gemistos Plethon in the Light of Plato's 'Laws.'" *Journal of the Warburg and Courtauld Insitutes* 52: 214–19.

Werner, Karl. 1962. *Franz Suarez und die Scholastik der letzten Jahrzehnte.* 2 vols. New York: B. Franklin. [1st ed. 1861.]

Wilmott, M. J. 1985. "'Aristoteles exotericus, acroamaticus, mysticus': Two interpretations of the Typological Classification of the 'Corpus Aristotelicum' by Francesco Patrizi da Cherso." *Nouvelles de la république des lettres* 1: 67–96.

Wilson, C. 1953. "Pomponazzi's Criticism of the Calculator." *Isis* 44: 355–62.

Wind, Edgar. 1958. *Pagan Mysteries in the Renaissance*. Oxford: Oxford University Press.

Wirszubski, Chaim. 1989. *Pico della Mirandola's Encounter with Jewish Mysticism*. Cambridge, Mass.: Harvard University Press.

Witt, Ronald G. 2003. *In the Footsteps of the Ancients: The Origins of Humanism from Lovato to Bruni*. Leiden: Brill.

Wonde, J. 1994. *Subjekt und Unsterblichkeit bei Pietro Pomponazzi*. Stuttgart and Leipzig: Teubner.

Woodhouse, C. M. 1986. *Gemistos Plethon: The Last of the Hellenes*. Oxford: Clarendon Press.

Yamaki, Kazuhiko, ed. 2002. *Nicholas of Cusa: A Medieval Thinker for the Modern Age*. Richmond, Surrey, U.K.: Curzon Press.

Yates, Frances A. 1964. *Giordano Bruno and the Hermetic Tradition*. London: Routledge & Kegan Paul.

———. 1966. *The Art of Memory*. Chicago: University of Chicago Press.

Zabarella, Jacopo. 1590. *De rebus naturalibus libri XXX*. Cologne: Ciotti.

———. 1966. *De rebus naturalibus libri xxx*. In *Aristotelis libros De Anima*, Frankfurt, 1606–1607; reprint Frankfurt: Minerva.

———. 1966. *Opera logica*. Cologne, 1597; reprint Hildesheim: Olms. [Abbreviated as OL.]

———. 1985. *De methodis, Liber de regressu*. Introduction by Cesare Vasoli. Bologna.

Zambelli, Paola. 1976. "Magic and Radical Reformation in Agrippa von Nettesheim." *Journal of the Warburg and Courtauld Institutes* 39: 69–103.

———. 1994. "Pomponazzi, i greci e Ferrara," in M. Bertozzi, *Alla corte degli estensi: Filosofia, arte e cultura a Ferrara nei secoli XV e XVI. Atti del convegno internazionale di studi, Ferrara, 5–7 marzo 1992*, 41–64. Ferrara: Università degli Studi.

———. 1997. "Pomponazzi sull'alchimia: Da Ermete a Paracelso?" In *Studi filologici e letterari in memoria di Danilo Aguzzi-Barbagli*, edited by D. Boccassini, 100–22. Stony Brook, N.Y.: Forum Italicum.

———. 2001. "Pietro Pomponazzi's *De immortalitate* and His Clandestine *De incantationibus*: Aristotelianism, Eclecticism, or Libertinism?" *Bochumer Philosophisches Jahrbuch für Antike und Mittelalter* 6: 87–115.

Zanier, G. 1975. *Ricerche sulla diffusione e fortuna del "De incantationibus" di Pomponazzi*. Florence: La nuova Italia.

———. 1992. "La biologia teoretica nell'ultima fase del pensiero pomponazziano," in *Filosofia, filologia, biologia: Itinerari dell'aristotelismo cinquecentesco*, edited by D. Facca and G. Zanier, 105–30. Rome: Ateneo.

Zippel, Gianni. 1970. "L'autodifesa di Lorenzo Valla per il processo dell' inquisizione napoletana (1444)." *Italia medioevale e umanistica* 13: 59–94.

CONTRIBUTORS

TAMARA ALBERTINI is associate professor of philosophy at the University of Hawai'i at Manoa, specializing in Renaissance and Islamic thought. Her research in Renaissance philosophy focuses on Nicholas of Cusa, Marsilio Ficino and Charles de Bovelles. She is also interested in mathematical figures and other visual means as "philosophical language" in Renaissance works. She is the president and a founding member of the International Charles de Bovelles Society.

D. C. ANDERSSON is research fellow at the Max-Planck-Institut für Wissenschaftsgeschichte Berlin. He is the author of *Lord Henry Howard and the Intellectual Culture of Elizabethan England* (Boydell and Brewer, 2009), and is co-editor of works by Francis Bacon.

EMMANUEL J. BAUER is professor of philosophy in the Theological Faculty of Salzburg University. His writings include a book on Thomism at the Benedictine University of Salzburg during the seventeenth and eighteenth centuries (published 1996) and a book on the philosophy of freedom in neuroscience and psychotherapy (2007).

PAUL RICHARD BLUM is T. J. Higgins, S.J., Chair of Philosophy at Loyola University, Maryland. In addition to Renaissance studies, he has published on modern Schoolphilosophy (1998). His most recent book is *Philosophy of Religion in the Renaissance* (Aldershot, 2010).

MICHAELA BOENKE teaches Renaissance philosophy at the Ludwig Maximilian University, Munich. She has published studies on Alberti, Ficino, Fracastoro, Telesio, Descartes, Newton, Schelling, and others. Her latest books are on Renaissance psychology, *Körper, Spiritus, Geist. Psychologie vor Descartes* (2005); and a Latin-German edition of Fracastoro's *Turrius sive de intellectione* (2006).

EUGENIO CANONE is director of research at the Consiglio Nazionale delle Ricerche at the institute Lessico Intellettuale Europeo e Storia delle Idee (ILIESI) in Rome. He has edited a number of works by Giordano Bruno and has published, among other studies, *Il dorso e il grembo dell'eterno. Percorsi della filosofia di Giordano Bruno* (2003) and *Magia dei contrari. Cinque studi su Giordano Bruno* (2005). He is co-editor of *Bruniana & Campanelliana* and editor of several related book series.

GERMANA ERNST is professor of Renaissance philosophy at the University Roma Tre. She has edited numerous works by Thomas Campanella and is co-editor of *Bruniana & Campanelliana.* Her most recent book is *Tommaso Campanella. The Book and the Body of Nature* (Springer, 2009).

RETO LUZIUS FETZ is emeritus chair of philosophy at the Catholic University of Eichstätt-Ingolstadt. His published works range from Aquinas to Montaigne to Whitehead, Piaget, and Cassirer.

GÜNTER FRANK is director of the Melanchthonhaus and the Europäische Melanchthon-Akademie in Bretten. In addition to his many publications regarding Philipp Melanchthon, he has published widely on medieval and early modern philosophy and theology, including a book on the philosophy of religion from the Renaissance to the Enlightenment (Stuttgart, 2003).

JILL KRAYE is professor of the history of Renaissance philosophy and librarian at the Warburg Institute, University of London. A collection of her articles, *Classical Traditions in Renaissance Philosophy,* was published in 2002. Her current research focus is the revival of Stoicism in the Renaissance and early modern periods.

HEINRICH C. KUHN teaches at the Institute for Renaissance Intellectual History and Renaissance Philosophy, Ludwig-Maximilians-University, Munich. He founded and is the chief administrator of Web4Ren Forum (W4RF), which provides many sorts of information of potential relevance to those interested in Renaissance intellectual history (http://www.phil-hum-ren.uni-muenchen.de/W4RF/YaBB.pl).

SACHIKO KUSUKAWA is a fellow in the history and philosophy of science at Trinity College, Cambridge. Her most recent interest is in scientific illustration in the early modern period; she is editor, with I. Maclean, of *Transmitting Knowledge: Words, Images and Instruments in Early Modern Europe* (Oxford University Press, 2006).

CEES LEIJENHORST is associate professor of the history of modern philosophy in the Philosophy Department of Radboud University, Nijmegen. His research interests are Renaissance philosophy, the philosophy of Thomas Hobbes, and the history of philosophy of the mind. His publications include *The Mechanisation of Aristotelianism: The Late Aristotelian Setting of Thomas Hobbes' Natural Philosophy* (2002).

THOMAS LEINKAUF is professor of philosophy and director of the Leibniz Research Center at the University of Münster. He has published on German Idealism, Platonism, and many Renaissance thinkers. He is also general editor of the German edition of the collected works of Giordano Bruno (Hamburg, 2007–).

CHARLES LOHR is professor emeritus of theology at the University of Freiburg at the Raimudus-Lullus-Institute, and now lives at Fordham University. He is editor of *Traditio; Commentaria Aristotelica Graeca: Versiones Latinae;* and *Raimundi Lulli Opera.* His numerous publications address the reception of Aristotle in the Latin West and Lullism.

HEIKKI MIKKELI is university lecturer in European area and cultural studies at the Renvall Institute at the University of Helsinki. His publications include *Europe as an Idea and an Identity* (1998) and *Hygiene in the Early Modern Medical Tradition* (1999), as well as a textbook on interdisciplinarity (2007).

WOLF-DIETER MÜLLER-JAHNCKE is a pharmacist and teaches the history of pharmacology at the University of Heidelberg. He is director of the Hermann-Schelenz-Institut für Pharmazie- und Kulturgeschichte in Heidelberg and past president of the Académie Internationale d'Histoire de la Pharmacie. He publishes regularly on the history of astrology and magic.

PETER SCHULZ is professor of communication theory at the School of Communication Sciences and director of the Institute of Communication and Health at the University of Lugano. His publications include books and articles on Edith Stein, as well as on friendship and self-love in Plato and Aristotle (2000).

DETLEF THIEL is an independent scholar. He has held lectureships in philosophy at Trier University. He is co-editor of the collected works of Salomo Friedlaender/Mynona (9 vols. to date) and has written books on Jacques Derrida (1990), and Platonism (1993). His other publications include works on Plato, Aquinas, Cusanus, Ficino, Francis Bacon; for example, "Die Predigten des Nikolaus von Kues in Flandern und den Niederlanden. Zur Psychökonomie des Ablasses," *Journal de la Renaissance* 6 (2008).

STÉPHANE TOUSSAINT is chargé de recherche of the Centre d'Études Supérieures de la Renaissance (CNRS—Université de Tours) and president of the Société Marsile Ficin; he is editor of the journal *Accademia* and of several reprints of rare Renaissance texts. His most recent book is *Humanismes/Antihumanismes de Ficin à Heidegger* (Paris, 2008).

INDEX

Philosophers of the Renaissance was designed and typeset in
Arno Pro by Kachergis Book Design of Pittsboro, North Carolina.
It was printed on 60-pound House Natural Smooth and bound
by Sheridan Books of Ann Arbor, Michigan.